Dennis Smelt

9 March 2017

THE IMPOSSIBLE MACHINE: A GENEALOGY OF SOUTH AFRICA'S TRUTH AND RECONCILIATION COMMISSION

Adam Sitze meticulously traces the origins of South Africa's Truth and Reconciliation Commission back to two well-established instruments of colonial and imperial governance: the jurisprudence of indemnity and the Commission of Inquiry. This genealogy provides a fresh, though counterintuitive, understanding of the TRC's legal, political, and cultural importance. The TRC's genius, Sitze contends, is not the substitution of "forgiving" restorative justice for "strict" legal justice but, rather, the innovative adaptation of colonial law, sovereignty, and government. However, this approach also contains a potential liability: if the TRC's origins are forgotten, the very enterprise intended to overturn the jurisprudence of colonial rule may perpetuate it. In sum, Sitze proposes a provocative new means by which South Africa's Truth and Reconciliation Commission should be understood and evaluated.

Adam Sitze is Assistant Professor of Law, Jurisprudence, and Social Thought at Amherst College, where he teaches courses on colonial law, psychoanalysis, and philosophy of law.

The Impossible Machine

A Genealogy of South Africa's
Truth and Reconciliation Commission

ADAM SITZE

The University of Michigan Press
Ann Arbor

Published in the United States of America by
The University of Michigan Press
Manufactured in the United States of America
⊗ Printed on acid-free paper

2016   2015   2014   2013   4   3   2   1

A CIP catalog record for this book is available from the British Library.

Library of Congress Cataloging-in-Publication Data
    Sitze, Adam.
        The impossible machine : a genealogy of South Africa's Truth and Reconciliation
    Commission / Adam Sitze.
            pages   cm
        Includes bibliographical references and index.
        ISBN 978-0-472-11875-5 (cloth : alk. paper) — ISBN 978-0-472-02910-5 (e-book)
            1. South Africa. Truth and Reconciliation Commission.   2. Justice, Administration
    of—South Africa—History.   3. Rule of law—South Africa—History.   4. Judges—South
    Africa—History.   5. Apartheid—South Africa.   I. Title.
        KTL470.S58   2013
        968.06—dc23

                                                                        2013006630

For my parents

Contents

Acknowledgments

Denken ist danken; no attempt at thinking is complete unless it includes some attempt at thanking. This is particularly true for a book such as this, whose thinking came into being through an especially long and circuitous path. This book originated in a dissertation written under the direction of John Mowitt in the Department of Cultural Studies and Comparative Literature at the University of Minnesota, Twin Cities. Even though the present text bears little resemblance to that dissertation, the hand of my dissertation committee nevertheless remains impressed upon its every page. In addition to John, whose astonishing and capacious mind is matched only by his generous spirit, I thank Cesare Casarino, Lisa Disch, Qadri Ismail, and Thomas Pepper for their teaching and friendship. In the MacArthur Program at the University of Minnesota, I had the privilege to encounter unusually concrete and detailed discussions over matters South African. For creating and maintaining that rare intellectual space, I thank Bud Duvall, Allen Isaacman, Jim Johnson, and Karen Brown Thompson.

The dissertation began to pass into a book manuscript under the guidance of two editors at the University of Michigan Press, Jim Reische and Melody Herr. I thank Jim and Melody for their counsel as well as for their superhuman patience. My outside reviewers exposed important weaknesses in the manuscript. I thank André du Toit, Daniel Herwitz, Fiona Ross, and several anonymous reviewers for their thoughtful, probing, and in many cases unanswerable criticisms. Along the way, claims were tested and honed in dialogue with many interlocutors. For their correspondence and conversation about this book, I thank Zackie Achmat, Rita Barnard, Louise Bethlehem, Claudia Braude, Timothy Campbell, Tasneem Carrim, Johnny de Lange, Christopher Dole, Antje du Bois-Pedain, Tony and Hillary Hamburger, Brent Harris, Verne Harris, Helen Kinsella, Mark Kende, Ahmed

Kathrada, Stephanie Marlin-Curiel, Monika Mehta, Fazela Mohamed, Saliem Patel, Surren Pillay, Sayres Rudy, Joseph Schneider, Charlie Sugnet, Jody Swilky, and Amanda Swarr.

For enabling, encouraging, and, when all else failed, finally demanding the completion of this book, I thank my dear colleagues in Amherst College's Department of Law, Jurisprudence and Social Thought (LJST). Founded in 1992, LJST is a department that to this day retains all the vitality, inventiveness, and excitement of an ongoing event. I couldn't wish for better intellectual companions than David Delaney, Lawrence Douglas, Megan Estes, Nasser Hussain, Austin Sarat, and Martha Umphrey. Along with Tom Dumm and Andy Poe, my intrepid comrades in "theory corridor," my LJST colleagues have provided steadfast friendship during trying times, unsparing criticism and exacting standards, and above all good humor and ready laughter. Special thanks are due to Austin, who threw his shoulder behind this book at critical moments early and late in its development; and to Nasser, whose writings, co-teaching, and (memorable) commentary have been hugely influential both for this book's content and for its form.

If Part 1 of this book is a footnote to Nasser's research on the jurisprudence of emergency, Part 2 is a footnote to Premesh Lalu's studies of the postcolonial episteme. It is no hyperbole to thank Premesh not only for his thought but also for spurring my interest in South Africa in the first place. This book is in many ways just the latest chapter in an ongoing discussion that began with this irrepressible teacher, insatiable intellect, and dear friend almost twenty years ago on Minneapolis's Franklin Avenue. It was therefore both fitting and a great privilege to be able to host Premesh at Amherst College as a Copeland Fellow during the 2011–12 academic year, when further conversations with him allowed me to put the finishing touches on this book.

Amherst College is also a place where skilled undergraduates play an uncommonly direct part in faculty research, and this book is no exception. It was written with the research assistance of six phenomenally talented students: Charles Bourjaily, Jessie Oh, Harshit Rathi, Adam Shniderman, Meghna Sridhar, and Nicole Starrett. Nicole's work on the manuscript was especially astute: I thank her for her detailed edits, perceptive critiques, and key recommendations. For the opportunity to hire and work with these gifted students, as well as for his unwavering and indispensable support over the years, I thank Amherst College's Dean of Faculty Gregory Call.

This is a book that has been written in libraries, both in South Africa and the United States. My ability to travel to these libraries was enabled by an ACLS/SSRC/NEH International and Area Studies Fellowship and by a grant from the Amherst College Faculty Research Award Program, as funded by the H. Axel Schupf '57 Fund for Intellectual Life. I thank these programs for supporting research in the humanities at a moment when the very future of the humanities seems to be in question. I also thank the librarians, archivists, and curators responsible for the libraries where I worked: the Library of Congress, in Washington, DC (the Main Reading Room, African and Middle Eastern Reading Room, and Law Library in particular); the Folger Shakespeare Library in Washington, DC (where Georgianna Ziegler, David Schalkwyk, and Gail Kern Paster were especially accommodating); the Mayibuye Archives at the University of the Western Cape, in Cape Town; the Western Cape Records and Archives Service, also in Cape Town; the National Archives of South Africa in Pretoria; the Department of Historical Papers in the William Cullen Library, at the University of Witswatersrand in Johannesburg (alongside the learned Michele Pickover and Zofia Sulej); and Archive Services at the University of South Africa, in Pretoria (especially Marié Coetzee). Special mention must be made of the masterful librarians at Amherst College's Robert Frost Library, under the direction of Bryn Geffert, where this book was completed. Douglas Black, Steven Heim, Michael Kelly, and Winnifred Manning never failed to procure even the most obscure materials. Predawn conversations with Paul Trumble on the steps of Frost got the day off on the right foot. Gretchen Gano provided bibliographic assistance at a clutch moment, while Judith Lively and Susan Sheridan helped me navigate the stacks and juggle my many materials. Margaret Groesbeck and Michael Kasper continue to provide enduring examples of the life of the mind. In an age where telecommunications devices promise to turn one and all into "prosthetic gods," and where information retrieval seems as effortless as drinking a mouthful of water, it is easy, though hardly wise, to take for granted the irreplaceable daily labors that make our libraries what they are today, and what they will not cease to be in the future: the very spine of intellectual life.

No one in my family would disagree with the proposition that this book has been as a pox upon our home. I thank my beloved Mary for treating its many symptoms with the wit, poise, and understanding of a true writer. I thank dear Daniel and Julia for being impossible in just the right way, in a way that has everything to do with the best impossibilities named in this book.

For permission to use their respective texts, I thank Dr. Jack and Greig Coetzee. For her exquisitely scrupulous copyediting, I thank Jill Butler Wilson. For creating such an exhaustive and precise index, I thank Cher Paul. All errors in this book are the sole responsibility of G. W. F. Hegel, who asked whether "fear of error is not just the error itself," argued that "only out of error does truth arise," and invited his reader to see in the "fear of error" a "fear of truth itself." He should have known better. All failures to thank, by contrast, are my responsibility alone.

INTRODUCTION

I.

Whatever else it has accomplished, South Africa's Truth and Reconciliation Commission (TRC) has succeeded in eluding the scholarship that has attempted to take it as an object of knowledge. Perhaps because of its unusual mix of public testimony, psychotherapy, political theology, and juridical procedure, which for some endowed it with an intrinsically elusive "hybrid" quality—or perhaps, as this book shall argue, for another set of reasons altogether—the TRC has baffled description to the same degree that it has invited fascination. "We are still groping for the language to adequately assess the significance of the TRC," acknowledged Wilhelm Verwoerd in 2000.[1] Wendy Orr, one of eighteen commissioners to serve on the TRC, noted a related phenomenon: "TRC members developed their own discourse and language."[2] Search for a language, invention of a language— signs, each, of a subtle dynamic that has not yet emerged as a central concern for scholarship on the TRC but that is nevertheless indispensable for our understanding of the thing itself.

In 1998, the thrust and shape of this dynamic were captured perfectly by a political cartoon that appeared in the South African weekly the *Mail & Guardian*.[3] Construing the TRC as a Rube Goldberg monstrosity, an ornate apparatus that somehow manages to inhale demons and exhale angels, the image also referred to something else: the difficulty of referring to the TRC itself. By coupling a busy cadre of pixies, goblins, elves, and genies who operate this transitional mechanism with a sign that confidently designates it (using an arrow for added emphasis) a "Truth Commission Thingummy," Dr. Jack's image condensed with brilliant concision the double disconnect that confronted scholars who found themselves intrigued by the TRC at that time. Encountering, on the one hand, a device whose inner mechanisms remained inscrutable, and, on the other, a name that did not exactly fit the thing it proposed to designate, early scholarship on the TRC tended to pose and answer questions of two general sorts: How on earth does this thing work? And what in the world should we call this thing?

Since the first studies of the TRC began to appear over a decade ago, a single scholarly field has come to dominate the global debate over these questions. Transitional justice, a field that was born in the early 1990s, seeks to produce theories and practices that will help to restore the rule of law, to do justice to victims of state violence, and to bring to an end "cultures of impunity" in countries where young democracies are striving to emerge after years of rule by authoritarian regimes. For some readers, this field's monopoly on the study of the TRC today will be self-evident, even unquestionable. It is perfectly obvious, these readers will want to assume, that anyone who now desires to study the TRC will want not only first to immerse him- or herself in existing transitional justice scholarship, but also thereafter to rely upon this field's lexicon and basic concepts, its historical self-understanding and paradigmatic antitheses, its existing institutions and prevailing methodologies. Other readers perhaps will be less afflicted by certainty on this point. These readers will have noticed a sense of creeping doubt within transitional justice about the sufficiency and consistency of the field's empirical and historical descriptions, on the one hand, and its ethical and therapeutic prescriptions, on the other.[4] For these readers, there still may be something about the TRC that eludes transitional justice, and part of the reason to continue studying the TRC will be to enhance the field's existing terms and concepts, to refine its histories and paradigms, and to circulate these improvements within its many institutions. Still other readers, meanwhile, will have even more serious misgivings about the field. These readers may have been persuaded by scholars who criticize transitional justice from the exterior—without subscribing to its discourse or entering into its horizon of self-understanding—in order to call the very premises of the field into question. For these scholars, the dominance of transitional justice— this "reconciliation industry" composed of "transitional justice entrepreneurs"[5]—is worse than insufficient for understanding the TRC; it is downright obstructive. For these scholars, the language of transitional justice not only functions to stifle the emancipatory politics that the TRC was designed to serve; worse, it's also a new name for the old colonial theory and practice

Dr. Jack, "Truth Commission Thingummy," *Mail & Guardian,* 1998.

of "trusteeship," of Western humanitarian experts presuming to speak for and thus to save otherwise helpless, powerless, and voiceless non-Western victims.[6]

The Impossible Machine provides a fourth perspective on the TRC. This is a view that will not be easily reconciled either with most existing studies of the TRC within transitional justice, or with the theories, lexicons, methods, and debates that many today have come to associate with the study of the TRC. Stated in negative terms, our claim will be that the two inaugural questions of TRC scholarship—How does this thing work? And what should we call this thing?—can and should be answered outside of the hermeneutic horizon specific to the field of transitional justice. Stated in positive terms, our claim will be that the TRC's concrete operation, as well as its novelty and audacity as event, are most illuminatingly named with reference to the TRC's counterintuitive precedents in colonial sovereignty and governmentality.

We will pursue this claim through two general inquiries, each of which will take up and reconsider one of the claims made within the field of transitional justice about the TRC's unprecedented status. The first such inquiry takes place in chapters 1–4. The purpose of chapter 1, "Indemnity and Amnesty," is to question the consensus that has developed within transitional justice about the TRC's origins. According to this consensus, the TRC is unprecedented among mechanisms of transitional justice because of the individual and conditional, rather than general, scope of the amnesty it offers: this unique twist on amnesty not only gave the TRC a middle way between the retributive justice of Nuremberg and the blanket amnesties of Chile and Argentina; it also allowed the TRC to exchange amnesty for truth. Chapter 1 argues that it is time to ask a different question: whether the TRC is unprecedented with regard to the theory and practice of indemnification that preceded the TRC in South Africa itself.

It is well known that the legislation that established the TRC—Promotion of National Unity and Reconciliation Act 34 of 1995 (hereinafter PNR Act)—emerged in and through a debate over South Africa's 1990 and (especially) 1992 indemnity acts.[7] But, as Florian Kutz, Antje Du Bois-Pedain, and Louise Mallinder recently have shown, these indemnities are only the most recent in a series—indeed, a pattern—in South Africa that dates back to 1914.[8] This book both builds on the indispensable work of these scholars and takes that work in a new direction. Well before indemnity came into prominence during the period of formal apartheid, it had a systematic place and function during earlier periods of South African colonialism and segregation. Alfred Venn Dicey, the leading theorist of South Africa's dreaded system of parliamentary sovereignty, went so far as to call indemnity the "highest exertion and crowning proof of sovereign power."[9] Given indemnity's theoretical and practical significance within South African legal order, and given its status as the most direct and concrete precedent in South African law for the TRC's practice of individualized, conditional amnesty, it is reasonable to wonder what new or different understanding of the TRC we might acquire if we evaluate its amnesties from the perspective of indemnity jurisprudence. In particular, what might we learn about the TRC if, instead of viewing it as a variation on transitional mechanisms in Germany and Latin America, we were to view it instead as a variation on the theory and practice of indemnity in South African law?

Chapter 2, "Indemnity and Sovereignty," begins this task by outlining the place and function of indemnity within Dicey's jurisprudence. By tracing indemnity to its origins in seventeenth-century England, we can see that it has its innermost source in an antinomy created in and by the English Revolution, between the *sovereignty of law* (the revolutionary principle that nobody is above the law) and the *law of sovereignty* (in Hobbes's words, "the law over them that have sovereign power," namely, that "the safety of the people is the supreme law,"[10] or again, in the Ciceronian terms on which Hobbes draws, *salus populi suprema lex esto*). Given this origin, this book argues, we can also specify the precise place and function of indemnity within Dicey's jurisprudence. It is the claim of chapter 2 that Dicey's specific contribution as jurist was to have offered up the convention of indemnity as a way to reconcile this antinomy. The indemnity convention, as Dicey theorized it, allowed for the sovereignty of law because it established the norm of individual legal responsibility and stipulated that even if one accused of illegal action was acting on good faith in the name of public safety and security in that action, the illegality of one's acts first must be clearly stated. Only afterward, when Parliament legalized this illegality, would one be absolved of legal liability. At the same time, indemnity allowed for any person (and not just a police officer) to commit a crime on two conditions: first, that it was committed in good faith service to the public good; and second, that it was necessary for the preservation of public safety. It was because the indemnification convention allowed for the reconciliation of the legal sovereignty of Parliament and the rule of law with the political sovereignty of the people—because it reconciled sovereign power with itself in the wake of the revolution that tore it asunder—that Dicey could call indemnity the "highest exertion and crowning proof of sovereign power." Indemnity was not then simply one among many topics within Diceyan jurisprudence. It was the very keystone of that jurisprudence. Exactly like a keystone held together an arch, the indemnity convention holds together the two pillars of sovereign power, the sovereignty of law (there is no one higher than the law) and the law of sovereignty (*salus publica suprema lex esto*). In its absence, these two arches would collapse.

It may come as a surprise to some readers that a book on South Africa's TRC should begin by returning to obscure debates in nineteenth-century English jurisprudence (rather than to a supposedly more obvious choice— say, debates over retroactive justice and international law in Germany after World War II). But as Dipesh Chakrabarty has argued, it is difficult to speak intelligibly about the theories and practices of colonial politics without connecting them to their origins in the traditions of European politics and even theology.[11] The mark of Eurocentrism, to be clear, is not that a discourse should happen to look at or speak of Europe; colonial anthropology, Euro-centric to a fault, trained its voice and gaze almost entirely upon populations outside of Europe. It is that a discourse should, whether explicitly or im-plicitly, reify the experiences and events of European politics into coherent and self-evidently desirable philosophical norms, in relation to which the often violent experiences and events of colonial politics then figure merely as empirical deviations, pathologies, perversions, or imitations.[12] Against this sort of reification, Chakrabarty proposes a research itinerary that traces the peculiar shape and structure of colonial politics to the ambivalences, contra-dictions, and ironies that were already latent in European political theory and practice to begin with, the unselfconscious manifestation of which ex-plains why the basic concepts of modern political philosophy, which now are undoubtedly global and even inescapable, are today inadequate and even un-usable on their own terms.[13] Although Chakrabarty describes this research as "history," this book will pursue a version of that research that is closer to the sort of work that Michel Foucault, writing in 1971, called "genealogy."[14] Whereas history speaks of the origins of the present in a morally consoling way, reassuring us that the norms that govern our conduct today have devel-oped in a manner both necessary and rational, genealogy traces those same norms to an origin that disquiets and disturbs us, an unexpectedly divided origin that neutralizes our sense of piety by revealing our morals to entail presuppositions that we find repugnant and immoral. If history discovers forgotten pasts that explain why the present is the way it is, genealogy re-veals select precursors of the present that not only have been left in oblivion but that needed to have been left there in order for the present to achieve its own self-presence and self-identity, its own goodwill and clean conscience. History treats archival evidence as the basis for the production of a record that aspires to be both dispassionate and neutral, both exhaustive and com-plete. For genealogy, by contrast, the archive is an occasion for a very differ-ent sort of writing: polemic, eristic dialectic, or, as Nietzsche once wrote, in an oft-forgotten subtitle, *Streitschrift*.

The Impossible Machine offers a genealogy of precisely this sort. It is a genealogy that attends, in particular, to what Foucault once called "juridical forms"—schemas and figures that originate in specific theories and practices of law, but that then become dislocated and abstracted from their origin, mi-grating and drifting into other legal fields (or even fields other than law, such as philosophy and literature) where they then continue to produce juridical effects, only now under nonjuridical names.[15] Understood in this sense, the point of tracing the TRC's unique amnesty power to indemnity in the theory and practice of Diceyan jurisprudence, and then tracing Diceyan jurisprudence to the conflicts of seventeenth-century England, is not then to seek in the resolution of those conflicts a universal norm by which to evaluate or measure the TRC's successes or failures. It is to clarify the sense in which Dicey's jurisprudence is the counterintuitive point of reference that allows us to think anew not only about the limits of the TRC, but also of the academic discipline that monopolizes commentary on the TRC. Diceyan jurisprudence has this status not because of its timeless coherence, but because from the very beginning it hosted kernels of incipient incoherence—kernels that manifested themselves in concrete situations of juridical and political crisis that, in turn, enabled and even demanded the remarkable conceptual inventions we witness in the TRC.

One such kernel, to which we shall pay special attention, is the fact that the innermost inside of parliamentary sovereignty as Dicey defines it—indemnity, or the power to "legalize illegality"—was practiced only in the colonies. When Dicey delivered his lectures in 1884, indemnity had not been used in England since 1766. In the decades before Dicey gave his lectures, indemnity had been used only in the Cape Colony (in 1836, 1847, and 1853), Ceylon (Sri Lanka) (in 1848), Antigua (in 1867), Mauritius (in 1867), and New Zealand (in 1868 and 1882). It was not, then, an accident that the examples of indemnity that were most prominent in Dicey's jurisprudence—the Irish indemnity of 1798 and the Jamaican indemnity of 1867—should derive from the colonies as well.[16] In the years after Dicey's lectures, indemnity would be used only once in England, in 1920. In Diceyan jurisprudence, indemnity is thus more than just a keystone. It is an *ivory* keystone, the material or substance of which was derived from the colony and imported into the metropole. In concrete terms, the relation between legality and illegality in Dicey's theory of indemnity was therefore also a relation between metropole and colony, between Europe's inside and its outside. The illegality that indemnity legalized was, since 1766, illegality committed in the name of the Crown to maintain order in colonial territories. Indemnity was not then simply a way to reconcile the sovereignty of law and the law of sovereignty. It was also a technique for reconciling imperial violence in the colony with liberal legality in the metropole.[17]

From Dicey, then, we learn that the *innermost inside* of the English Constitution acquired its coherence from a juridical paradigm (the indemnification convention) that, for more than a century, derived almost exclusively from and was applied almost exclusively to the colonies. Although this may initially seem to be a paradox, it is in fact simply a sign of the rigor and passion of Dicey's commitment to imperialism.[18] Nasser Hussain has argued that colonial rule must be read as the "limit case" of the modern attempt to formulate a coherent relation between the rule of law and political sovereignty.[19] Anthony Anghie, meanwhile, has argued that it was only in the nonsovereign colonies that unfettered sovereign power was theorized and practiced, thus making it a mistake to think that modern concepts of sovereignty were invented in Europe and then exported to the colonies.[20] Interpreted on its own terms, with reference to the case law it generalizes into its theory of sovereignty and law, Diceyan jurisprudence confirms these insights. On the terms of Dicey's insistence on imperial unity, the fact that indemnity, the very center of the English Constitution, only existed *in concreto* outside of England itself is not at all a paradox. To the contrary, it is proof positive that Dicey's English Constitution could achieve unity with itself only to the degree that the metropole remained united with its colonial possessions. For this same reason, however, we see how Dicey's emphasis on indemnity also left his jurisprudence as a whole vulnerable to considerable perplexities.

The third chapter of this book shows how the latent incoherence of Dicey's theory of indemnity became manifest in the practice of indemnity in twentieth-century South Africa. The claim of chapter 3 is that the exigencies of colonial rule—of governing populations who were not citizens, who were barely even subjects, and who were always potential enemies—precipitated the actualization of a theoretical confusion that was dormant, from the beginning, in the internal logic and order of Dicey's text, above all in its emphasis on indemnity. In apartheid South Africa, indemnity jurisprudence became prospective instead of retrospective (legalizing illegality before, rather than after, the event), ceased to be limited by the test of "political necessity" (leaving "good intentions" as the only measure of whether an illegality should be legalized), and settled into a permanent, normal state of affairs (instead of remaining occasional, temporary, and exceptional). In general, indemnity for the apartheid state was less a juridical convention that limited illegal state activity (as it was for Dicey) than a widespread, unstated assumption that illegal activity inevitably would be legalized by the state so long as it was not committed in demonstrably bad faith (a qualification that, however permissive, was nevertheless still individual in scope). Under apartheid, in other words, indemnity reversed itself: instead of legalizing illegality, it illegalized legality itself, reconciling the rule of law with precisely the sort of arbitrary exercises of violence that the rule of law was designed to restrain and oppose. Under apartheid, indemnity thus no longer served, as it did for Dicey, as the keystone of parliamentary sovereignty. It morphed into the juridical form with reference to which the apartheid state granted its security forces informal but definite carte blanche to use whatever means necessary to win their "total war" against individuals and populations opposed to apartheid. It became a redoubled version of what it always already was in the first place: a technique for suppressing anticolonial rebellions.

As such, chapter 4 argues, the indemnification convention is important for the TRC in not one but two ways. On the one hand, the crisis of this convention—its radicalization of the mere expectation of indemnity into the inevitability or even guarantee of indemnity; its facilitation of a culture of impunity among the state's security and police forces; its conversion of an exceptional measure, the "highest exertion and crowning proof of sovereign power," into a normal mode of governance—was one of the concrete conditions for the state criminality and human rights abuses that rendered the invention of an institution like the TRC necessary. On the other hand, the individualized characters of the TRC's amnesties and the two conditions that governed their conferral—full disclosure and political objective—reiterated key elements in the indemnity jurisprudence of the apartheid state. Just as the notoriously slippery "full disclosure" requirement of the Amnesty Committee reiterated the bona fide condition of indemnity jurisprudence (which required nothing more than "honest" intentions to grant indemnity), so the "political objective" principle of the TRC reiterated the "necessity" clause of indemnity jurisprudence. Indemnity jurisprudence was not merely the most concrete and direct precedent for the PNR Act in South African law; it also ended up guiding, to a surprising degree, the actual practices of the TRC's Amnesty Committee. In the terms of H. L. A. Hart, indemnity jurisprudence provided the "secondary rules" with implicit reference to which the Amnesty Committee recognized and enacted the "primary rules" explicitly set forth in the PNR Act.[21] There is, in short, a very subtle but concrete sense in which the Amnesty Committee allowed "indemnity" to survive in and as "amnesty."

If this is important, it is because it provides us with a new and different criteria for evaluating the success or failure of the Amnesty Committee. From a genealogical perspective, the genius of the Amnesty Committee was its attempt to inventively mitigate the theoretical impasses and crises it inherited from the indemnification convention that preceded it. But this was also the locus of the Amnesty Committee's most constitutive risk. By limiting itself to an implicit mitigation of those impasses rather than an explicit resolution or dissolution of their terms and, at worst, by employing with little substantive modification the same conditions and principles that defined indemnity jurisprudence under apartheid (only now under a new name, "amnesty"), the Amnesty Committee risked leaving in place the conventions of the same indemnity jurisprudence that the TRC, in its *Truth and Reconciliation in South Africa Report* (hereinafter *TRC Report*), emphatically recommended bringing to an end.[22] From a genealogical perspective, the genius of the TRC and its most dangerous risk are both one and the same thing, two sides of one and the same basic audacity: "amnesty" in the TRC is really a name for its attempt to create *an indemnity to end all indemnities.* At best, we might say, the Amnesty Committee will have succeeded in this endeavor: in its attempt to turn the indemnification convention against itself, it will have effectively rendered indemnity permanently unusable, inoperable, or (in the terms of Hart) "defeasible."[23] On this read, the truly daring function of the TRC as a "mechanism" will have been its attempt to render a prior machine inoperative: not only will the TRC have explicitly condemned the apartheid state's radicalization of the indemnification convention (which it did by criticizing the "culture of impunity" that emerged within the apartheid state), but it also will have used the indemnification convention against itself, displacing it with a new discourse on the desirability of extending forgiveness in the name of *ubuntu*. At worst, however, the Amnesty Committee will have accomplished none of this. It only will have interpreted and applied the amnesty provisions set forth explicitly in the PNR Act (what Hart would call "primary rules") with implicit reference to the very same conventions (in Hart's terms, "secondary rules") that governed indemnity jurisprudence in Diceyan thought. From this perspective, it is both significant and troubling that, in 2006, the Mbeki administration amended the prosecution policy of the National Director of Public Prosecutions, conferring on it the power, in effect, to replicate the work of the TRC's Amnesty Committee—to offer exemptions from prosecution in exchange for information about past crimes—but now behind closed doors. Although this policy was characterized in public debate as a second amnesty, the policy itself was grounded in apartheid-era indemnity jurisprudence, and bore more than a passing resemblance to the Indemnity Act of 1990.[24] Advocates of the TRC criticized this policy for undermining the delicate relation of "carrots and sticks" that the TRC adopted toward those it called "perpetrators" (in which the promise of "amnesty for truth" was supplemented by the silent threat of future prosecutions). From a genealogical perspective, however, this policy had a more disquieting significance still. It suggests that rather than succeeding in its attempt to use indemnity "one last time," the TRC's Amnesty Committee instead functioned as a means for the survival, in postapartheid South Africa, of one of the worst juridical conventions of the apartheid state, if not colonial jurisprudence more generally.[25] From this perspective, indemnity jurisprudence is a key part of the puzzle for understanding what seems to many observers to be the renewal of authoritarianism within the postapartheid state.[26]

II.

"Individualized" and "conditional" amnesty was only one of the unprecedented juridical forms that transitional justice claims to have found in the TRC. A second was the unprecedented way in which the TRC represented the voices of the ordinary victims of apartheid, which was supposed to have facilitated a sort of national catharsis or healing. As Tom Lodge put it, the idea behind the TRC was that its mandate "would extend beyond the issue of indemnity to harness 'the cleansing power of truth.'"[27] According to this claim, no prior commission of its type had placed ordinary people so fully and completely at its center as did the TRC.

Chapters 5 and 6 of this book question this claim. On genealogical grounds, there are at least two very different origins of the TRC's emphasis on what it called "victim testimony." The first may be found in the British tradition of the Commission of Inquiry. André du Toit has noted that "the underlying and invisible bureaucratic procedures" that "were at the core of the TRC process . . . have hardly figured in public debate and discussion."[28] Chapter 5 addresses this gap. It traces the bureaucratic procedures of the Commission of Inquiry to its origins in prerevolutionary England, when medieval political order was giving way to the new juridical theories and practice that soon would become the inner norms of the modern administrative state. From this perspective, the commission was an important part of what the French philosopher Michel Foucault once called the "governmentalization of the state," in which the strength and stability of a given political order was measured no longer primarily by the territory it defended but, rather, by the felicity of its management of the natural and social life entrusted to its care.[29] The Commission of Inquiry was a device for the sovereign to pose for itself the question of why and how its biopolitical strategies had failed or were failing, in a recurrent attempt to calibrate and fine-tune those strategies, to adjust the relation between government and population in an incessant effort to achieve a fit between the two, to understand the norms internal to a population by studying their pathologies and anomalies—in a ceaseless attempt, that is to say, to administer the population's health, wealth, welfare, and safety in the most optimal way possible.

Much the same aim governed the Commissions of Inquiry established in the nineteenth and twentieth centuries to investigate the conduct of police and military forces in their often brutal attempts to suppress colonial riots and rebellion. Because of the loss of life that frequently was involved in these sorts of events, one might expect that the colonial state's response to them would assume a juridical form more consistent with the general emphasis within imperial jurisprudence on the rule of law (e.g., the prosecution of state officials who killed and tortured in the course of their duties). But to expect this would be to misunderstand both the premises of colonial governance and the regime of truth that structured Commissions of Inquiry. Because colonial governance understood the colonial subject not as a potential bearer of rights but (as Arendt put it) as a potential source of labor (or "biopower," in Foucault's terms),[30] and because the Commission of Inquiry originated as a biopolitical technique for the management and administration of natural and social resources, colonial Commissions of Inquiry treated native riots more or less on the same model as they did the pollution of water, the inefficient distribution of grain, the wasteful expenditure of the public purse, or the spread of an epidemic. Because of the tacit schemas with reference to which Commissions of Inquiry framed the problems they pose for themselves, they were bound to understand these riots and rebellions not as the expression of latent political desire and intellect, but merely as the mark of a disequilibrium within the health, welfare, and safety of populations, a disequilibrium that could and should be understood historically and etiologically, and that could and should be prevented in the future by knowledge-based adjustments to existing governmental policy—by a government, in other words, that presumed itself better informed about the populations whose lives (or biopower) it was entrusted with administering. In these terms, riots were not expressions, however inchoate, of a will for self-governance (or other emancipatory possibilities);[31] they were problems to be solved within the existing dispensation of the colonial state, only now with new and improved techniques of management. As they were deployed under colonial conditions, Commissions of Inquiry therefore functioned as substitutes for political self-representation: they took on the task of representing the health, safety, and well-being of natives who, as the paternalist principle of colonial rule would have it, "cannot represent themselves."

This applied even and especially when Commissions of Inquiry take unusual and strenuous steps to archive "native voices." To illuminate this dynamic, chapter 5 turns to an analysis of the Jamaica Royal Commission (JRC), a Commission of Inquiry that was created in 1866 to conduct an "impartial" investigation of the brutal suppression of the Morant Bay Rebellion in 1865 by British colonial administrators. An exemplary attempt on the part of nineteenth-century British imperialists to reconcile the extreme violence of colonial rule, on the one hand, with liberal claims about the civilizing mission and the rule of law, on the other, the JRC was extraordinarily open to the voices of the victims of colonial violence. In the sixty hearings it held, the JRC listened to the testimony of over seven hundred of those involved in the uprising and its suppression, recording that testimony in a publication that ended up exceeding one thousand pages in length.[32] Yet even and especially in this rigorously inclusive commission, the biopolitical frame of intelligibility that defined the colonial Commission of Inquiry continued to operate. Not only did this frame determine the ways in which native voices were registered, collected, and interpreted; it also created the epistemic conditions for the neutralization of British courts as a site where colonial violence could be litigated and redressed.

Of particular interest in this case is liberal philosopher J. S. Mill's attempt in 1866 to use the JRC's final report as the premise to argue for the prosecution of Governor Edward John Eyre, the colonial administrator responsible for ordering the summary executions and unlawful detentions that were committed by English forces in the course of the suppression of the Morant Bay Rebellion. Because the Commission of Inquiry's regime of truth oriented its findings powerfully toward a default position of "equilibrium," balancing out its criticisms of the excesses of martial law with praise and sympathy for Eyre, Mill's strenuous attempts to pursue civil and criminal prosecutions of Eyre and others were neutralized and even undermined in advance by the very epistemic field in which he grounded his claims. After showing how the JRC's report painstakingly counterbalanced the possibility of a critique like Mill's by allowing for a latticework of other opposed readings, chapter 5 explores the curious regularity with which Commissions of Inquiry narrated their findings with reference to the terms and tropes associated with "tragedy," understood, above all, as a genre which could explain a strange sort of violence, for which everyone and no one was to blame. In the discourse of the Commission of Inquiry, tragedy was both a juridical logic (a way of speaking about ambiguous and chaotic situations in which normal tests of civil and criminal liability and guilt are difficult or impossible to apply) and a juridical rhetoric (a discourse on the status of illegal state killing as not only lamentable, regrettable, and unfortunate but also unavoidable and, indeed, "necessary"). The tragic narratives set forth in the reports of various Commissions of Inquiry provided colonial governance with a chance, on the one hand, *to encounter and recognize its own limits:* in these reports, one sees colonial administrators recognize that they are condoning murder and torture, acts that violate the same rule of law that confers on colonialism its sense of purpose and mission as a project. But these same narratives also, at the same time, allowed colonial administrators *to disavow those same limits*, for the notion of the "tragic" allowed them to argue that as regrettable and lamentable as the violent actions of colonial authorities may be, those actions were nonetheless "necessary," "inevitable," and "could not be otherwise." In this, as in other respects, the JRC was paradigmatic: it was the "model" Commission of Inquiry.

Chapter 6 traces the development of this administrative apparatus and narrative strategy as it manifests itself in twentieth-century South Africa. Foucault has argued that *government precedes the state*, that the abstract entity known as "the state" can only come into being under conditions that have first been constituted as a problem for governmentality. To this, chapter 6 adds that *the Commission of Inquiry precedes government*. The knowledge acquired by Commissions of Inquiry prepared the conditions under which governance based on knowledge—a government of instrumental reason, of manipulating things and populations to the end of the *salus populi*—could then come into being in an enduring way. This had particular application under conditions of colonial rule, where the mechanisms of metropolitan, liberal governmentality were militarized in constant anticipation of native rebellion on the part of insecure settlers. In the twentieth century, the Union of South Africa and then the Republic of South Africa would create more than a dozen commissions to acquire information, in particular, about the causes and circumstances of a given riot, disturbance, or commotion of the multitude. These commissions together comprise a loose but internally consistent genre that chapter 6 calls the "Tumult Commission."

Like the "Native Question" Commissions with which they were concurrent, South Africa's Tumult Commissions were tasked with not only understanding but also articulating the terms under which it would become possible to manage "race relations," in particular the relationships of hostility that colonial domination created between South Africa's various populations. The more the apartheid state deployed Tumult Commissions as a means to this end, however, the more these commissions radicalized the incoherence that was latent in their colonial predecessors. The colonial Tumult Commission, as exemplified by the JRC, was designed to convert incipient hostility into relative equilibrium: in its investigations of colonial massacres, its conclusions almost invariably balanced out criticisms of excessive force by police with criticisms of unruly natives. The apartheid state's Tumult Commissions, by contrast, pushed this scheme to its limit, pursuing the norm of equilibrium to such an extreme that the Tumult Commission turned into its opposite: a mechanism of disequilibrium. Since at least the JRC, which was accused by English radicals of being a "whitewash,"[33] the Tumult Commission's pursuit of equilibrium functioned not only to reveal but also to conceal the brutality of colonial massacre. Reiterated now in a world context defined not by colonialism but by decolonization, not by Victorian racism but by universal human rights, not by trusteeships and mandates but by the increasingly postcolonial character of international law,[34] the illegitimacy of this pursuit became visible: not only was injustice done, but now it was seen to be done. Deployed under conditions where world opinion no longer openly affirmed colonization as a norm of global governance, the apartheid state's colonial Tumult Commissions were seen to be openly pathological: they were publicly understood to conceal more than they revealed, to increase more than decrease hostility, to produce more than reduce instability.

No longer an effective mechanism of governance, the Tumult Commission was now little more than an empty ritual, a legal husk devoid of any trace of truth or justice. It became what, latently, it always already was: an administrative means to the end of maintaining a colonial rule founded in the last instance on military force.

From the genealogy of the Tumult Commission, we are left with at least one puzzling question. In his uncompromising 2009 book *The Deaths of Hintsa*, Premesh Lalu treated the event of the death of King Hintsa in 1835 not only as an occasion to question the troubling continuities between the disciplinary apparatus of colonial history and that of postapartheid history but also as a symptom capable of throwing into relief the regime of truth that governed the TRC's inquiry into the conflicts of the past.[35] The strong implication of Lalu's argument is that the TRC is an heir to and perhaps even unwittingly deploys the same disciplinary apparatus that governed and enabled the writing of colonial history. Lalu's insight is confirmed in the present book's genealogy of the Tumult Commission. Already in the Tumult Commission, one finds the operation of many of the same devices that contemporary scholars of transitional justice attribute to the TRC (e.g., its mandate to be evenhanded in its distribution of blame between "perpetrators" and "victims"; its use of a mode of historical narration that focuses on the "tragic" quality of political conflict in South Africa; a focus on the feelings of the "victims"; its solicitation of the "voices" and "testimony" of the "victims" of state violence; its inquiry into the truth that itself begins to function as a form of justice, that is, the dissolution, at once therapeutic and political, of the sort of "bitter feelings" that are the raw material for civil war; and its attempt to compensate the victims of state violence). What then does it mean that we can find so many of the defining attributes of the TRC operating under conditions defined not by democratic transition but by colonial and even apartheid domination? Did the TRC simply repeat this colonial legacy? Was the TRC's inquiry into the past governed by an administrative apparatus (the Commission of Inquiry) and the narrative strategy coupled to it (the tragic impasse), the coherence of which derives from a past (the genealogy of the Tumult Commission) that the TRC failed to investigate?

Chapter 7 takes up these questions. It begins by considering the strongest argument that the TRC did in fact break the epistemic field it inherited from the Tumult Commission: that Kader Asmal's earliest calls for a Truth Commission redeployed the apparatus of the Tumult Commission now within a horizon defined by "catharsis," in the revolutionary sense given to that term by the Italian Marxist thinker Antonio Gramsci. By setting forth a vision of a commission that would produce "historical catharsis," Asmal and his coauthors did not "reconcile" Gramsci's discourse on revolutionary catharsis with the apparatus of Tumult Commission; nor did they simply pour the political "contents" of "historical catharsis" into the Tumult Commission's otherwise neutral administrative "container." Rather, they reiterated the innermost poetics of the Tumult Commission under new conditions, in a way that made "the tragic" signify the very opposite of what it signified for the Tumult Commission. Whereas the apparatus of the Tumult Commission mobilized the discourse of the tragic to explain the "necessary evil" or "lamentable necessity" of state repression, the TRC redeployed a different dimension in that same discourse to signify emancipation from a repressive state—to produce a "historical catharsis" in which the unethical basis of the apartheid state itself would become self-evident to one and all. After rereading Asmal alongside Gramsci, chapter 7 traces the uncomfortable way that Gramscian catharsis (with its emphasis on general criminality) coexists and coincides with the Tumult Commission (with its emphasis on particular crimes) in the TRC's final report. From a genealogical perspective, this chapter argues, the *TRC Report* is best read as a disjunctive synthesis of incomplete repetitions and insufficient differences, as an unstable composite of incommensurable epistemic demands, where competing juridical forms coincide without synthesis. To underline this reading, chapter 7 concludes by tracing the way this disjunctive synthesis plays itself out in two literary texts published in 1998, Antjie Krog's well-known *Country of My Skull* and Greig Coetzee's comparatively unknown play *Past Imperfect*.

Chapter 8 takes account of a different way in which the apparatus of the Tumult Commission persists in contemporary discourse on the TRC. The aim of that chapter is to outline the conditions for a translation of *ubuntu* that would be able to remain alert and alive to the more general sense in which the TRC reiterated modes of colonial sovereignty and governmentality. The claim of chapter 8 is that the specifically critical question we need to pose of this jurisprudence has very little to do with the ethnophilosophical terms that so often, even today, govern and inform its framing. It is whether—or, rather, to what degree—the *ubuntu* jurisprudence exemplified in and by the TRC succeeded in putting "out of commission" the colonial jurisprudence that was its most uncannily proximate predecessor. The specifically critical thrust of the *ubuntu* jurisprudence that is the avowed conceptual core of the TRC consists, in particular, in the way it displaces the central justification of martial law in South Africa since at least 1900, namely, the Ciceronian maxim *salus populi suprema lex esto*.[36] Antjie Krog has argued that the authors of South Africa's constitution turned to the concept of *ubuntu* because they could not find in Latin phrases and Roman Dutch concepts a word to describe a vision for a postapartheid society.[37] Our genealogy gives rise to a different claim: the most felicitous translations of *ubuntu* will have recourse not to its "pure" African meaning but, rather, to its impurity, that is, its conflictual metonymy with the very worst maxim of apartheid jurisprudence. *Ubuntu*, on this read, is a name for the political and juridical order that will have emerged once the logic—and not merely the Latin—of *salus publica* has not only entered into crisis and incoherence but is now definitely abrogated by disuse, where its existence as a political rationality has been rendered irreversibly inoperable or defeasible. At its best, *ubuntu* jurisprudence will have rendered inoperative the logical relation between part and whole that was the driving force of Cicero's maxim. At its worst, however, *ubuntu* jurisprudence will not *dis*place Ciceronian republican reason at all, but only will *re*place it, occupying the same place and fulfilling the same function in postapartheid jurisprudence as Cicero's maxim did for apartheid jurisprudence. From this perspective, the question we ought to ask of the TRC is not, whether its exchange of justice for truth was an effective way to build postconflict societies. It is rather the extent to which the TRC's own jurisprudence and own exercises of administrative power managed to reiterate— not merely to repeat, but also to alter and to dissolve—the worst juridical forms of the apartheid state. The task of critique coming out of the TRC, this book concludes, is to keep one's finger on the pulse of this difference, or, put differently, to make sure that, in the reiteration of *salus* in and through *ubuntu*, the work of difference outlasts the inertia of repetition.

III.

Let's return now to the point of departure in this introduction. With its slapstick tangle of gears, belts, and pulleys, Dr. Jack's 1998 "Truth Commission Thingummy" poses the two questions that silently but surely have governed research on the TRC: How in the world will this thing work? And what on earth should we call this thing? Underlying both questions is the assumption, soundly rooted in South African law and jurisprudence, that the TRC is a "mechanism."[38] But what exactly is a "mechanism"? It is not recalled often enough, in this highly technological epoch, that the English term *machine* derives from the Greek word *mēkhanē*, which denoted a theatrical apparatus, an elaborate crane devised of pulleys and weights to lift actors, specifically those impersonating gods, into the air, so that they could appear to their audience suddenly to float or fly.[39] Understood in this sense, a "machine" is not a thing made of steel and glass or plastic and silicon, a thing of gasoline or electricity. Nor is it, as the term is sometimes used in the social sciences, a mere system or process, a technique for producing certain sorts of patterns of conduct in individuals and populations. In its etymological sense, at least, a "machine" is a device or contrivance that is used to produce miraculous "stage effects" and that works only to the extent it remains invisible and offstage.

There's little doubt that the TRC created highly dramatic spaces in which miraculous events seem to have occurred. The TRC sometimes seemed as though it would operate as a sort of "pardon machine"[40] that attempted to make the impossible—the pardoning of the unpardonable—possible. In the TRC's victim hearings, for instance, one could witness freedom fighters experiencing changes of heart and mind, torture victims directly addressing their humiliated torturers, securocrats formerly immune from any oversight or scrutiny being questioned and criticized in public, and so on. All of this amounted, without question, to a specific form of theater.[41] The juridical problem, however, is how to understand these dramatic miracles in relation to the legal and administrative "machinery" that allowed them to come into being in the first place. If the TRC was an "*impossible* machine," this was because the TRC aspired to make "impossibles" just as surely as "war machines" aspire to make war. The TRC was, on this read, a miracle-making machine, a machine designed "to miraculate"—to create effects and events that should not be possible according to the known and probable laws of the world. Yet, to the precise extent that the TRC presented itself as an "*impossible* machine," it also invited (as all claims to make miracles must) disbelief and skepticism. Adjust your inflection just a tiny bit, in fact, and you'll notice how easy it is to speak of this "*impossible* machine" now as nothing more than an "impossible *machine*"—a complicated apparatus with an inner operation that was not only inscrutable but also ineffective, a transitional mechanism with aims that were never very realistic in the first place, a device that not only didn't work as advertised but, in failing to miraculate, failed to work at all. The TRC was, in this declension, a machine whose mandate was either too good to be true, too broad to be practical, or too constrained to be transformative—one that, in any case, did not deliver and arguably could not have delivered on its great potential.[42] On this view, we should not be enchanted with the TRC; we should be positively disenchanted with it. Or, at the very least, we should want to "tinker" with the TRC paradigm in order to make sure that future Truth Commissions—Truth Commissions that model themselves after the TRC, only now in new and different contexts—do in fact produce the "impossibles" the TRC wanted to but did not make possible.

In this book we shall seek to break out of this bipolar oscillation. The point of construing the TRC as an "impossible machine" is to accept, as a point of departure for the analysis of the TRC, the falsity of the antithesis between miracle and fraud, between enchantment with the TRC and disenchantment with it. It's a way to mark the dialectical sense in which those who deify the TRC as an "*impossible* machine" speak in unwitting agreement with those who denigrate the TRC for being an "impossible *machine*," and vice versa. It is to pose a question at once critical and dialectical: if this debate is therefore not a debate at all—if this disagreement amounts to two different sides of the same coin—what then? What would happen, what understanding of the TRC would we receive, were we to bracket both ways of thinking of this "impossible machine"? Perhaps we would not ask how the TRC managed, against all odds, to make the impossible possible or why it failed to live up to this promise. Perhaps we would clear a space where we could begin to pose a prior question: how did this "impossible machine" come into being in the first place? Were we able to pursue this question with rigor and probity, we also might become able to recall that, before we either became amazed by this miraculous washing machine that scrubbed devils into angels or became chagrined by this incoherent device that seems simply to have whitewashed apartheid, failing to produce either truth or reconciliation, the thingummy we wanted to think about was first *itself* an unthinkable and unprecedented impossibility. And with this, we will have gone a long way toward retrieving and comprehending the volatile kernel of eventness that transitional justice misrecognizes when it reifies the TRC into a "paradigm."

Part 1

Chapter 1

INDEMNITY AND AMNESTY

1.1 One of the main concerns of transitional justice has been the question of why and how South Africa's TRC is unprecedented. The consensus within transitional justice is that the TRC is unprecedented because its amnesties were not issued en masse but were individualized and conditional upon public, full disclosure of crimes.[1] This consensus is reached by way of a narrative, international in scope, which contrasts the TRC with the Latin American Truth Commissions, on the one hand, and the Nuremberg Trials, on the other. According to this narrative, the TRC is distinct both from the retributive justice dispensed at the Nuremberg Trials and from the blanket amnesties passed in Latin America during the 1970s and 1980s, because its power to offer amnesty was, on the one hand, individualized (not general) and, on the other, not exclusive of punishment (because there was the chance that, absent full disclosure, an amnesty application could fail). On this view, the TRC was unprecedented for the way it offered a sort of "third way" or "golden mean" between blanket amnesty and individualized punishment.[2] Indeed, the TRC's "individualized, accountable amnesty process,"[3] its focus on the "concrete particular,"[4] was one of the main reasons it was able to lay claim to a paradigmatic status within the field of transitional justice. It is as though South Africa's practice of individualized amnesty were the last and best chapter in an international learning curve, the apex and the exemplar of transitional justice, the best illustration of how to conduct a transition from authoritarian rule to liberalism, the most compelling reason why the TRC should be studied as a "model" around the world.[5]

Although this narrative quickly took hold within studies of the TRC, it rests on a set of premises that are far from unquestionable. To begin, there is good reason to doubt the narrative of the Nuremberg Trials as a simple paradigm of retributive justice. As only one small but significant part of a complicated juridical response to Nazism that cannot be understood apart from later extraditions, trials, and reparations, the executions that resulted from the Nuremberg Trials especially cannot be evaluated apart from Chancellor Konrad Adenauer's amnesties of 1949 and 1954, which together exempted from punishment close to one million former Nazis whose crimes could be said to have been committed on a "political basis."[6] Similar combinations of execution and amnesty emerged in postwar France (where 791 collaborationists were executed for treason and close to 30,000 were exempted from severe punishments by amnesty laws passed in 1947 and 1951) and Italy (where fifty fascists were executed and many thousands more were covered by a 1946 amnesty law).[7] In their punishment of Nazi, fascist, and collaborationist leaders and their exemption from punishment of those leaders' followers, the amnesty laws of postwar Europe remained re-markably loyal to the shape and structure of the ancient Athenian amnesty of 403 BC. That law excluded from its protections the Thirty Tyrants and other leaders of the oligarchic overthrow of democracy, exposing most to trial and execution, while permitting the great mass of their followers to go unpunished.[8] Given the commensurability of postwar, European "retribu-tive justice" with this "paradigmatic" origin of amnesty as such,[9] it becomes difficult to maintain that the Nuremberg Trials are somehow the *opposite* of amnesty, as some scholars of transitional justice are wont to argue. To the contrary, if by "amnesty" we mean a reconciliation of the divided city in which capital punishment of a leading few is coordinated with a forgetting of the crimes of the complicit many, we are obliged to conclude that the "re-tributive justice" of postwar Europe was in fact perfectly consistent with the theory and practice of amnesty.[10] There is even a persuasive argument to be made that the trials of Nazis functioned as a sort of mass public education about the meaning and basis of complicity in political evil (and arguably even "collective catharsis").[11] Understood in this way, it becomes even more difficult to say that the trials of Nazis were incommensurable with the TRC, for the latter, not unlike the former, aspired to the status of a cathartic ritual that sought to educate the public and to establish the moral and intellectual foundations for a new rule of law and that used amnesty as a means to that end.[12] In short, as Stéphane Leman-Langlois has argued in his indispensable essay on the topic, transitional justice's attempt to problematize the crime of apartheid with reference to Nuremberg is less significant for its juridical or historical substance than for its formidable rhetorical function, which is to say, its capacity to stifle the difficult questions involved with the possibility of putting apartheid officials on trial and its ability to legitimate the unusual administrative apparatus the postapartheid government established instead.[13]

We also have grounds for doubting the assertion that the TRC's individualized amnesties are distinct from the blanket amnesties that were passed during many of the political transitions that took place in Latin America in the 1980s and 1990s.[14] One of the main reasons why it was not necessary for the TRC's Amnesty Committee to offer a blanket amnesty of a Latin American type is that the loyalty of the South African Defence Force (SADF) was already all but guaranteed by the categorical indemnities that preceded the 1995 legislation that created the TRC. In 1976 and again in 1980, the South African Parliament passed amendments to the 1957 Defence Act that augmented the already very powerful indemnity provisions established by Section 103 of that act. The effect of these amendments, as we shall see in section 3.2, was that SADF members were already indemnified in advance for any illegal acts they might commit in honest and good faith service to the public good. In 1961 and 1977, meanwhile, the South African Parliament passed extremely wide indemnity acts that protected not only South African police officers but also a large numbers of state officials from prosecution for the civil and criminal wrongs they inflicted in the course of the Sharpeville Massacre of 1960 and the suppression of the Soweto Uprising of 1976. Both of these events fell within the TRC's juridical and investigative mandate, but there are many signs that the indemnity provisions of the Defence Act, in combination with the specific indemnity acts passed in 1961 and 1977, decreased or even nullified the power of the TRC's "carrots and sticks" approach: it is unclear why any state official, member of the SADF, or officer of the South African Police would feel obliged to run the risk of trading truth for amnesty when he or she was already expressly protected from prosecution by prior indemnity legislation.

These protections from prosecution were widened even more by the indemnity acts passed by the South African Parliament in 1990 and 1992, especially those passed in 1992. In 1990, following negotiations between the African National Congress (ANC) and the National Party (NP), the South African Parliament passed the Indemnity Act of 1990. Its purpose was, "for the sake of reconciliation and for the finding of peaceful solutions" to conflict in South Africa, to establish official regulations for the conferral of temporary immunity or permanent indemnity on members of ANC, PAC, and other liberation movements for illegal acts committed with a political objective.[15] To this end, the act conferred on President de Klerk an extremely broad set of powers to protect persons against civil and criminal proceedings in the name of reconciliation and peaceful constitution transformation (as set forth in the Groote Schuur Minute of May 4, 1990).[16] On top of allowing the president the use of his existing powers of pardon and parole,[17] the act authorized him to grant not only indemnity (unconditionally or on conditions "he may deem fit") but also an otherwise unspecified power of immunity (again, unconditionally or on conditions "he may deem fit").[18] In his use of these powers, which amounted to what Du Bois-Pedain rightly has called a "blanket competence,"[19] President de Klerk was advised by an extraordinarily confidential set of indemnity committees, whose members were chosen by the president and sworn to secrecy.[20] All indemnity acts, as we shall see in section 2.3, function to legalize illegality, and in this, the Indemnity Act of 1990 was no different. It gave de Klerk the blanket authority to protect not only members of the liberation movement but also the agents and officials of the apartheid state from criminal and civil liability for certain illegal acts they may have committed in the prior decade.

Apparently, however, even these already broad and secret powers of indemnity were not broad or secret enough for President de Klerk. So he used his President's Council to supplement the Indemnity Act of 1990 with the Indemnity Act of 1992 and, most controversially, the Further Indemnity Act of 1992. The latter, in particular, cannot be described except as an act of extreme executive arbitrariness. Whereas the Indemnity Act of 1990 applied to all parties of the South African conflict, the sole purpose of the Further Indemnity Act of 1992 was to indemnify officials and persons who committed civil and criminal wrongs in support of the apartheid regime. Whereas the Indemnity Act of 1990 was the result of conciliatory negotiations between the ANC and the NP, de Klerk's turn to the President's Council was a stunningly unilateral decision: the Further Indemnity Act of 1992, in fact, marked this council's first, last, and sole use since it was created in and by the failed Constitution of 1983 for the express purposes of circumventing parliamentary debate and expanding executive authority.[21] Although the Further Indemnity Act cannot technically be said to be completely bereft of procedure—it did create a National Council of Indemnity to process applications for indemnity[22]—the council was, like the indemnity committees established by the Indemnity Act of 1990, completely secret, and so the extent and quality of the exercise of its powers remains unclear even today. In addition to de Klerk's considerable existing executive powers for pardoning, remitting punishment, commuting sentences, and granting early releases, the Indemnity Act of 1990 and, even more so, the Further Indemnity Act of 1992 conferred on the South African executive a breathtakingly chaotic capacity to create the ad hoc equivalent of a blanket amnesty for apartheid's loyalists. There is every indication that de Klerk used these powers to precisely this effect. The scholars who have devoted the most scrutiny to the indemnifications that took place in the years between 1990 and 1994 have estimated that at least thirteen thousand and up to twenty-one thousand persons were protected from prosecution in the course of this anarchic process (an estimate that does not include those already protected from prosecution by South Africa's indemnity jurisprudence of 1957, 1961, and 1977).[23] This is, even on the lowest estimate, about twice as many people as the 7,094 individuals—the majority of whom were, in concrete terms, drawn from the ranks of the liberation movements—who applied for amnesty for the TRC.

The 1995 PNR Act repealed the Indemnity Act of 1990 and the Further Indemnity Act of 1992, both of which stood very little chance of surviving constitutional review.[24] It also, however, stipulated that the protections these acts established "shall remain in force notwithstanding the repeal of those Acts."[25] This means that the concrete legal protections created by these indemnity acts stayed in effect, even and especially as the acts themselves were negated and subsumed by the much more palatable PNR Act.[26] Aside from the genealogical significance of this persistence of indemnity within the TRC, which I shall describe in more detail later in this chapter, the concrete legal protections these laws established relates directly to one of the self-described failings of the TRC, namely, its inability to induce SADF members to apply for amnesty.[27] Although the secrecy of the Indemnity Acts of 1990 and 1992 precludes any scholarly certainty on this point, there is a persuasive argument to be made that the sweeping protections established by these two acts obviated any need for SADF members to apply for amnesty from the TRC.[28] But if this is true, we also need to doubt the origin story according to which the TRC is unprecedented for its rejection of blanket amnesties of a Latin American sort. Despite the many differences between the "indemnification process" in South Africa between 1990 and 1994—which was, by turn, carefully negotiated, capriciously authoritarian, chaotically piecemeal, and rigorously confidential—and, for example, the single, blanket self-amnesty passed by military forces in Guatemala in 1986, the former has more than just a passing resemblance to the latter: both include secretive attempts by repressive states undertaken just prior to their departure from power to exempt significant portions of their military forces from being prosecuted for any crimes they may have committed. Here, however, is the really crucial point: we can argue that the TRC's individualized amnesties somehow differ in kind from blanket amnesties of the Latin American genre only to the extent that we artificially isolate the TRC from the indemnification process that is, according to the PNR Act itself, the TRC's own explicitly acknowledged precedent. Indeed, one of the reasons that the TRC "itself" did not have to engage in a blanket amnesty is that a blanket indemnity was already in effect prior to the inaugural hearing of the TRC's Amnesty Committee. It is perhaps even the case, in fact, that this categorical indemnity is one of the conditions that enabled the TRC itself to come into being in the first place: it is doubtful that, in the absence of a blanket indemnity, the SADF would have consented to any sort of political transition at all.[29]

In this sense, the critical question is not whether and why the TRC engaged in individualized and conditional amnesties rather than blanket amnesties. It is how to understand the relationships between the *individualized amnesties* for which the TRC is well known and the lesser-known *categorical indemnities* that not only preceded those amnesties and coexisted alongside them in silent antagonism to them (limiting their scope and effect as an incentive to elicit submissions to the Amnesty Committee) but arguably even enabled the existence of the TRC itself. To pose this question is not, of course, to forget that the TRC itself did indeed resist the temptation to issue blanket amnesties. From the "Explanatory Memorandum" appended to the "Amnesty Bill" unveiled by Dullah Omar, minister of justice, at a conference held by the Institute for a Democratic Alternative in South Africa (IDASA) in Cape Town on July 29–31, 1994,[30] it is clear that group indemnities were explicitly on the table as a legislative option during the earliest stages of TRC planning.[31] What's more, in November 1997, the TRC's Amnesty Committee, working independently from the rest of the TRC, granted thirty-seven ANC members a blanket amnesty that was publicly opposed by Desmond Tutu and others and that was eventually struck down in the courts.[32] But while the TRC was quite consistent in its refusal of this practice, the TRC itself was, as architects like Omar knew only too well, only the last and best of a series of indemnity acts;[33] and even in the event that its principled position on blanket amnesty was not enabled by the unprincipled positions of its immediate precedents, its amnesty still cannot be interpreted intelligibly without reference to those precedents. It follows from this that the problem of blanket amnesty cannot, then, be coherently posed in the terms assumed by transitional justice, where the TRC's individualized and conditional amnesties gain their meaning and value in opposition to the blanket amnesties of Latin America. Indeed, not only did blanket amnesty remain a simmering juridical question in post-TRC South Africa, but many blanket amnesties have been repealed in Latin America. Peru, for example, was ordered by the Inter-American Court of Human Rights to repeal two of its amnesty laws in 2001, and Argentina repealed two of its amnesty laws in 2003.[34] In Chile, meanwhile, the transnational prosecution of General Pinochet has created the political will to repeal that country's 1978 blanket amnesty.[35] If the point of comparing the TRC to various Latin American Truth Commissions was to argue that the former's individualized amnesties successfully avoided the pitfalls of the latter's blanket amnesties, it is far from clear, a decade later, whether the premise for this argument still holds. If recent events are any indication, in fact, the very opposite would seem to be true.

1.2 There is a third reason why the consensus that the TRC is unprecedented is built on a hollow foundation, and it happens to be the main reason, too. Transitional justice can only claim that the TRC's individualized and conditional amnesty process is "unprecedented" to the degree that it fails to pose a basic jurisprudential question: not whether the TRC's individualized amnesty process is unprecedented with regard to Latin America or the Nuremberg Trials, but whether it is unprecedented with regard to the theory and practice of indemnification that preceded the TRC in South Africa itself.

Let us clarify the question by outlining its premise. There can be no doubt that the TRC came into being in relation to—or, better, in opposition to—prior indemnity acts. It is well documented, both in transitional justice scholarship and in the *TRC Report* itself, that the authors of the PNR Act frequently defined it against the Further Indemnity Act of 1992. By almost any criterion, de Klerk's attempt to supplement the Indemnity Act of 1990 with the Further Indemnity Act of 1992 dissolved the last shreds of legitimacy that indemnity jurisprudence might have retained up until that point.

This was a law that was forced through Parliament by de Klerk alone, that was secretive in its implementation, and whose legal protections were created by and at the discretion of the same executive branch whose agents and employees were implicated in the very crimes the act legalized.[36] In response, the ANC promised to nullify any general amnesty passed by de Klerk in the waning days of the apartheid regime,[37] and the Further Indemnity Act turned out to be the occasion within civil society for a debate about the basis, essence, and limits of amnesty and political forgiveness for state crimes not only in South Africa but also in Zimbabwe (where indemnity jurisprudence was equally dominant).[38] The 1995 PNR Act, by contrast, was created with painstaking consultation with individuals and organizations in South African and international civil society. Its authors emphasized their desire for as much openness, transparency, and as much procedural fairness as possible. The result would be a commission whose membership would be determined not by the president alone, as was stipulated in the Indemnity Acts of 1990 and 1992, but by a council appointed by the president through consultation with Parliament. These differences, which, by any measure, are expressive of an extraordinary commitment to participatory democratic politics, are well acknowledged and well documented both by the TRC itself and by existing transitional justice scholarship. Here, in fact, the TRC's claim to be "unique" among Truth Commissions seems convincing.[39]

Given this emphasis, however, it's quite curious that so few scholars have analyzed in any depth an important conceptual displacement that took place precisely in the midst of this long moment of democratic consultation: gradually, painfully, and incompletely, the concept of "indemnity" began to disappear from public discourse, its place and function increasingly becoming occupied by the potentially very different concept of "amnesty." The necessity and significance of making an inquiry into this displacement is supported by public documents that were critical for the debate over the formation of the PNR and the TRC but that almost never figure into transitional justice scholarship, despite its frequent praise of this very same public process.[40] On June 7, 1994, Minister of Justice Dullah Omar issued a statement on what he called "amnesty/indemnity," accompanied by a memo inviting individuals, organizations, religious bodies, and members of the public to submit comments and proposals on the topic by June 30, 1994.[41] After asking for comments concerning all aspects of the proposed commission (its composition, procedures, framework for "reparation/compensation," time frame, mode of reporting to the nation, and so on), the minister's memo then turned to the matter of the legislation's "provision for amnesty/indemnity."[42] Sometimes using "amnesty/indemnity" as a single concept and sometimes using "amnesty" as an independent concept, Omar put forward five proposals to define this provision. Four of these proposals had direct and clear precedents in the Indemnity Act of 1990. Like the "indemnity" defined in this act, Omar's "amnesty/indemnity" commission would be administered by a specialized structure to deal with all applications and make recommendations; the offenses for which it would offer indemnity would need to have been committed before a clear cutoff date; the recommendations of the commission would be referred to the president, whose decision would be final; and there would be a fixed cutoff date for applications for amnesty/indemnity.[43] All of these provisions are essentially identical to equivalent provisions in the Indemnity Act of 1990.

The only provision that was not directly derived from indemnity jurisprudence was a reference to the 1993 Interim Constitution's famous postscript on national unity and reconciliation, which introduced the almost unprecedented concept of "amnesty" into South African jurisprudence.[44] But this was not just any provision. It was the proposal's most fundamental and overarching provision of all, for under South Africa's new dispensation, the Interim Constitution as interpreted by the Constitutional Court would function as the ultimate horizon and last appeal for any and all potential legislation, up to and including indemnity jurisprudence.[45] Understood in this way, the fused category "amnesty/indemnity" was not merely the symptom of conceptual confusion (although, as we shall see in a moment, it certainly is that). It was also, perhaps more important, a name for the unusual conceptual displacement that the Ministry of Justice had no choice but to try to theorize at that critical juncture in South Africa's negotiated settlement. On the one hand, the most fitting precedent in South African law that the ministry had at its disposal for crafting the sort of transitional legislation it had been called upon to draft—legislation that made indemnity conditional upon disclosure of illegal acts that were politically motivated—was the politically conciliatory Indemnity Act of 1990, the legitimacy of which had since been fatally compromised by the Further Indemnity Act of 1992. On the other hand, it was clear that an indemnity act of this sort, grounded as it was in the considerable executive powers specific to parliamentary sovereignty, would not pass muster under an Interim Constitution and constitutional review that were designed, in part, precisely to render the unchecked executive powers of parliamentary sovereignty defunct.[46] If the category "amnesty/indemnity" was a mark not simply of fusion but also of confusion, this is certainly not because the late Minister of Justice was a confused jurist. It's because he crafted a juridical category the internally divided character of which reflected, with great precision, a juridical situation that was *itself* internally divided to the precise degree it was revolutionary.[47] "Indemnity/amnesty" was a name for the disjunctive synthesis that became unavoidable once one system of law and sovereign power (the parliamentary sovereignty of the apartheid state, in which indemnity was, in Dicey's terms, the "highest exertion and crowning proof of sovereign power") passed into another (the *Rechtsstaat* of the postapartheid state, whose Constitution required amnesty in its extraordinary postscript). In the strange category "indemnity/amnesty," we thus find a set of mutually exclusive juridical concepts whose coexistence was as necessary as it was impossible. *Necessary* because the assumption of legal continuity that governed the South African transition required that the postscript's use of the word "amnesty" be interpreted with reference to its precedents in indemnity jurisprudence. *Impossible* because indemnity and amnesty weren't just mutually exclusive on their own terms, but were the most exemplary powers of two mutually exclusive constitutional orders: just as the new *Rechtsstaat* was founded on amnesty, so too was indemnity the "highest exertion and crowning proof" of the old Sovereign Parliament.

In its June 30 response to the minister of justice's statement, the Johannesburg branch of the Legal Resources Centre seized immediately on the memo's strange confusion of indemnity and amnesty, placing it first in their list of criticisms.

> Prior to dealing with the specific issues raised in the statement, clarity is required with regard to the concepts of amnesty and indemnity. The statement uses the terms amnesty and indemnity freely and interchangeably. However, indemnity, pardon, immunity, amnesty, and remission of sentence are five distinct and separate concepts, each with its own contents, implications and regulatory measures. It is therefore important to establish exactly whether the Commission will deal with indemnity and/or amnesty.[48]

As if to underline the need to clarify the problem of indemnity, the Legal Resources Centre would raise it again in the conclusion of their document.

In conclusion, a few thoughts on indemnity. It is improper and probably un-constitutional to deny a victim access to the courts because of his/her choice to testify before the Commission. Similarly there will result a miscarriage of justice if victims are barred from launching civil claims against their perpe-trators who have been granted indemnity against criminal prosecution. For South Africa to survive, it needs honest, fair play, and the enforcement of fundamental rights now.[49]

In the "Amnesty Bill" that the minister of justice unveiled at the IDASA conference of July 29–31, 1994, these criticisms would be taken to heart. In the "Explanatory Memorandum" that prefaced the bill, the minister of jus-tice introduced his draft legislation by first recalling the terms of the In-demnity Acts of 1990 and 1992 and then noting that the new Constitution obliged Parliament to pass some sort of Amnesty Act.[50] He then proceeded to define the difference between "indemnity" and "amnesty."

A distinction ought to be drawn between indemnity, amnesty, parole and the exercise of the prerogative of mercy. Indemnity is to be given to persons who have not yet been tried for any offence committed with a political ob-ject.

Amnesty is granted to persons who have been convicted of an offense and who are serving or have served a period of imprisonment.

Parole is given to individuals who have served a portion of their sentence and who in the opinion of the Parole Board may be released conditionally and are subject to supervision. Parole is granted and supervised by a Parole Board in terms of the Prisons Act.

The prerogative of mercy is reserved to the Head of State to commute a sentence of death to a term of imprisonment, usually for life.

The proposed Bill deals only with amnesty and indemnity.

It is necessary to keep these distinctions in mind in the quest for the solu-tion to the problems the country is facing. In the case of amnesty, the courts have heard evidence, delivered judgment and have passed a sentence. Often appeals have been heard and dismissed. Except in rare cases, the trial has been open to the public and those called upon to make the decision to grant relief to the prisoners, have easy access to the record from which the gravity of the offence, the motivation and whether or not the sentence was appro-priate may be considered.

Applications for indemnity made before a trial has been held may also be granted to a group or class of persons who were part of a movement or organisation whose declared policy was to commit offences in order to bring about political change. A prerequisite for such blanket indemnity would be an acknowledgement by both the organisation and the individuals that the offences were committed to bring about political change. The offences committed by the members of the liberation movements were acknowledged, numerous trials were conducted in which the motivation for the commission of the offences was established.[51]

Following this introduction we find a draft bill that is as intriguing for what it contains as for what it does not contain. Although the minister's "Statement on Amnesty/Indemnity" of June 7, 1994, emphasized the necessity for the "victims" of human rights violations to speak for themselves,[52] there is no mention in the July 1994 "Amnesty Bill" of the dramatic "victim hearings" for which the TRC would become perhaps best known across the world. But in its legislative scope, as in its legislative language, the July 1994 "Amnesty Bill" is also intriguing for what it *does* contain. This earliest draft of the bill, meanwhile, declared that its purpose was "[t]o provide for the granting of amnesty and indemnity from civil and criminal liability for acts committed with a political object; to provide for the compensation of persons prejudiced by the granting of such indemnity or amnesty; and to provide for matters connected therewith."[53] In accordance with the postscript of the Constitution of the Republic of South Africa, which requires the enactment of an act of Parliament for the granting of amnesty, the bill then proceeded to establish what it calls an "Amnesty Commission."[54] The powers of this commission, the bill proposed, should be two: amnesty and indemnity. The three main features of these two powers, as the bill defines them, were identical. Both amnesty and indemnity could be granted unconditionally or conditionally as the commission deems fit with respect to bona fide political offenses committed during the mandated period.[55] Both amnesty and indemnity forbade criminal and civil proceedings from being instituted or continued in a court of law against a person who has received amnesty or indemnity.[56] Finally, the bill stipulated that notice would be given to recipients of amnesty and indemnity in the *Government Gazette*. Despite these contiguities, amnesty and indemnity were nevertheless not in the end completely synonymous in this bill. The bill outlined three classes of persons to whom indemnity could

apply: those who have committed political crimes and were liable to prosecution, those who were awaiting trial or undergoing trial, and those who
already had stood trial but were awaiting sentence.[57] Amnesty, meanwhile,
applied to two classes of persons: those who had committed political crimes
and who were convicted of a political crime or who have served a period of
imprisonment and those who were convicted of an offense and who had
received a noncustodial form of punishment.[58] In addition, the bill proposed
that "any prisoner who has been or is purported to have been released under
any law during the period 8 October 1990 up to and including the date or
commencement of this Act, shall be deemed to have been granted amnesty
under the provisions of this Act" and that "any person who has been convicted and sentenced for an offence in respect of which amnesty would have
been granted had this Act been in force, may apply for such conviction and
sentence to be removed from the record."[59]

Even as amnesty in this bill shared an identical juridical root with indemnity, in other words, it also differed markedly from indemnity: it was
defined not only as a power to exempt from punishment *after* sentencing has
taken place (in contrast to indemnity, which the bill construed as a power
to exempt from punishment *before* sentencing has taken place), but it also
was given a retroactive power that indemnity lacked: in this bill, amnesty
was the power to change the legal record and legal status of the past. Given
these intricacies, it perhaps will come as no surprise that, Omar's emphatic
insistence to the contrary notwithstanding, the participants of the IDASA
conference would proceed to use the concepts of indemnity and amnesty
interchangeably anyway.[60]

This same substitutability, in fact, would reappear in the July 1994 draft
of the same Bill. Here, as in the earlier IDASA conference, the contiguity
between amnesty and identity showed signs of turning into something different: a systematic fusion between the two powers. Here amnesty and indemnity were conjoined either by a slash (e.g., Chapter IV of the bill called
for the establishment of an "Indemnity/Amnesty Committee," set forth the
"Eligibility for Indemnity/Amnesty," and outlined the procedures for "Applications for Indemnity/Amnesty") or by the ever-ambiguous "and" and "or"
(indeed the power at issue in this later draft is described neither as amnesty
nor as indemnity but rather, in an almost mechanical way, as "amnesty and
indemnity" and sometimes as "amnesty or indemnity," even if the draft bill
did refer more often to indemnity alone than to amnesty alone).[61] Even so,

the main differences between amnesty and indemnity remained in place. Although the remarkable retroactive powers that earlier drafts had ascribed to amnesty were absent from this draft, here, as in the first draft of the bill, amnesty was defined as a power to exempt from punishment after sentencing has taken place, and indemnity was defined as a power to exempt from punishment before sentencing has taken place.[62] In the winter of 1994, it would seem, amnesty had not yet fully displaced indemnity; it was not only indemnity's metonym but also its synonym, even as in constitutional terms it remained, unambiguously, its antonym.

We find a still different relation between indemnity and amnesty in a third document written during the period of the negotiated settlement. This text too, like the two we've just reviewed, is almost always absent from transitional justice scholarship. Authored in March 1995 by longtime state law adviser R. P. Rossouw at the request of Johnny de Lange, an ANC parliamentarian and the chair of the Justice Portfolio Committee (which was responsible for generating the PNR Act),[63] this text is revealing for the degree to which it derived its analysis of the meaning of the PNR Act's concept of "amnesty" from the indemnity jurisprudence that preceded it. The question put to Rossouw by de Lange pertained to "the meaning and legal effect of the amnesty" set forth in the postscript of the Interim Constitution: "What is the extent of amnesty? Does it relate to criminal liability only or does it relate also to civil liability? Does it relate to any other liability or disqualification?"[64] Rossouw's reply is remarkable for, among other things, its candor about the extreme difficulty involved in trying to understand the meaning of the concept of amnesty as it is set forth in the postscript to the South African Constitution. "The Constitution is silent on the matter," Rossouw writes. He continues, "The meaning of the word amnesty, by itself, does not assist. That meaning does not relate to any kind of liability whether it be civil, criminal, or any other kind of liability."[65] After reviewing dictionaries on the topic from several different countries, Rossouw then concluded that, in the absence of any enduring agreement on the meaning of the word *amnesty*, its limits and basis have been generated with reference to the legal traditions of a given country. What's more, even within these traditions, the meaning of *amnesty* had shifted over time.

[T]he meaning ascribed to the word in such dictionaries is based upon legal and constitutional practice obtaining in particular states or countries especially of the state where the dictionary has been published. . . . It would appear that the association of the word "amnesty" with the "forgetting" of a *criminal deed or liability* is made not by referring to the ordinary meaning of the word but on the strength of the fact that the word has often been used in the practice of a particular State or states generally in connection with such deed or liability. It is pointed out that practice of various States, and of the same State at different stages of history, has, however, not always been the same with regard to the subject-matter of amnesty.[66]

Faced with this absence of authority or consensus on the topic, Rossouw then began answering a slightly different question. Given the difficulty or even impossibility of defining *amnesty* not only on its own terms but also even comparatively, what, then, might the use of *amnesty* in South African law have to teach about its implications for criminal and (especially) civil liability? To answer this question, Rossouw operated on an important and revealing premise: that the most relevant precedents for the postscript's amnesty would be found in South Africa's indemnity jurisprudence.

> Where the word "amnesty" is used in South African Statute, and the meaning of that word has not been defined in that statute, it will serve no purpose to attempt to ascertain the meaning of the word, as used in such statute, by referring to a dictionary or to the constitutional or legal practice obtaining in another State or even that of South Africa at any particular point in time.
>
> In the Republic of South Africa the word "amnesty" has never been used in Acts of Parliament in respect of the extinguishing of delictual liability. "Indemnity" is the word that has up to now been employed in statutes, and the extent of the indemnity has always been indicated in express terms in every enactment providing for the granting of indemnity[.][67]

After clarifying his point with examples from the 1957 Defence Act, the 1990 Indemnity Act, and the 1992 Further Indemnity Act, Rossouw then generated a reading of the postscript's use of the word "amnesty" based on its differences from the indemnity jurisprudence that preceded it. This reading treated the postscript's "*amnesty*," in effect, as nothing more than an ordinary indemnity act whose key terms were extraordinarily implicit. On this basis alone was Rossouw able to carve out an answer to de Lange's question about liability: only by interpreting "amnesty" as an exceptional indemnity act was

Rossouw able to interpret it as a nullification of not only criminal liability but also civil liability.

> The post-script does not expressly refer to any liability but the requirement that amnesty shall be granted in respect of any act, omission or offence, can only mean that amnesty shall be granted in respect of the *liability* arising from the commission of the act, omission or offence. The use of the word "amnesty" in *connection with civil liability* is unusual and without precedent in South African law. A delict is not committed against the State (except where the State is in the position of a private person), and the commission of a delict which affects the rights of a private individual cannot be "forgiven" or overlooked by the State (in the absence of a statute empowering or obliging it to do so). The requirement that that provision shall be made for the granting of amnesty in respect of an act or omission which is not an offence must however be interpreted as a provision requiring the extension of civil liability arising from the commission of an act or omission.
>
> The legislature did not attempt to indicate the exact extent of the amnesty contemplated by it. It is pointed out that the granting of amnesty in respect of any *offence* goes further than the mere prohibition of the institution of actions to enforce criminal liability [i.e., an indemnity]. It affects the existence of that liability, and extinguishes it[.] If the effect of amnesty upon civil liability is to be proportionate with the effect of amnesty upon criminal liability, civil liability will be extinguished by amnesty. It is submitted that it was the intention of the legislature that a person who performed or committed an act, omission or offence referred to in the post-script should be freed from all liability arising from such performance or commission, such liability being extinguishing by the granting of amnesty.[68]

There are at least two reasons why this reading of the postscript is significant. First of all, to this as to every interpretation there is a politics. In parliamentary debate over the passage of the PNR Act in the winter of 1995, the National Party would argue that the postscript's amnesty was little more than the completion of the prior indemnification process that began with the Indemnity Acts of 1990 and 1992.[69] This approach, which construed amnesty as nothing more than an indemnity act of unusual size, had implications for understanding the juridical and political status of the antiapartheid struggle. Whereas the traditional function of amnesty within international law was to put an end to war, the traditional function of an indemnity in Diceyan juris-prudence was to retroactively legalize an illegality committed in the name of public safety. Whereas indemnity implies the existence of a legitimate state and an intact rule of law, amnesty in international law implies a war between legitimate belligerents.[70] To interpret the postscript as nothing more than an indemnity thus would have been to imply that violent acts committed by the ANC and Pan-African Congress (PAC) were nothing more than crimes, vi-olations of an otherwise legitimate law, and not acts committed in the course of a just war against an essentially and thoroughly criminal and illegitimate "occupation."[71] The ANC and PAC, not surprisingly, would therefore argue that the PNR Act was not simply an indemnity but, to the contrary, an un-usually forgiving amnesty, a generous act of mercy bestowed by the part of the victors of a military struggle on their defeated opponent—who, by rights, ought to have been punished for their crimes against humanity.[72] On this read, as Johnny de Lange would later put it, the amnesty of the postscript has nothing to do with crime: it is, to the contrary, a "peace pact."[73]

Rossouw's interpretation of the postscript threaded the needle of these two readings. Even though Rossouw does rest his reading on amnesty's prec-edents in indemnity jurisprudence, it cannot be said that this alone commit-ed him to the National Party's characterization of amnesty as nothing more than an indemnity of unusual size. Rather, Rossouw simply applied to the interpretation of amnesty the same principle that governed South Africa's transition in general: the fact of legal continuity between the apartheid state and the postapartheid state as his point of departure for the interpretation of amnesty. Johnny de Lange has described this principle well.

> Since our transition entailed a gradual, though marked shift from one legal order to another, it necessitated the acceptance of legal continuity. In consti-tutional, legal and practical terms this meant that the apartheid legal order remain the law of the land, even if unconstitutional, until amended by the democratic parliament, or declared unconstitutional by the Constitutional Court.[74]

Understood in this way, Rossouw's connection of amnesty to its precedents in indemnity jurisprudence was not some sort of subtle interpretive conces-sion to the National Party. It was, to the contrary, the necessary condition for understanding the sense in which the ANC's proposal of amnesty was, in fact, truly unprecedented. As articulated in 1995 by Kader Asmal, the notion of an exchange of amnesty for truth came into being under conditions where the Government of National Unity inherited from the apartheid state the chaotic and arbitrary indemnity and release procedures de Klerk already had set into motion.[75] "The indemnity process as a whole is by this stage in such disrepute," Asmal continued, "that only open amnesty and human rights hearings can achieve credibility for this endeavor."[76] To argue that amnesty must be understood with reference to its precedents in South African indemnity jurisprudence is not, then, to accept the NP's narrative of South Africa's transition. It is, in fact, the only possible horizon that allows us to fully pose the question of whether or not the power of amnesty itself marked a legal discontinuity with apartheid jurisprudence.[77]

Once we turn to the PNR Act itself, we see that it bears the marks of the relations of transposition and negation, condensation and displacement, reversal and opposition, substitution and supplementation that exist between the concepts of "indemnity" and "amnesty." On the one hand, as we have seen, the PNR Act repealed the Indemnity Acts of 1990 and 1992. On the other hand, it not only allowed existing indemnities to remain in force but also instructed members of the TRC's Amnesty Committee to "take account" of the criteria of the Indemnity Acts of 1990 and 1992 in their conferrals of amnesty.[78] On a simple reading of the PNR Act alone, there is already, therefore, a prima facie basis to argue that the amnesty was a *negation* of indemnity in a strictly Hegelian sense of the word: it destroyed *the husk* of the indemnification convention (through the repeal of the Indemnity Acts of 1990 and 1992), only to allow *the kernel* of that convention (its "criteria") to survive in a higher form (i.e., in the legitimate and highly praised TRC, rather than in the roundly condemned indemnity acts passed in the 1960s and 1970s). This, indeed, is how we should understand the fact that the verb form of the noun *amnesty* not only in Omar's 1994 "Amnesty Bill" but also in the *TRC Report* itself was not "to amnesty" (despite the fact that the use of *amnesty* as a verb is accepted in ordinary language) but "to indemnify."[79] What amnesty does when it produces its own concrete legal effect, it would seem, is not *amnesty* (or even *obliterate*) but *indemnify*.

This, in fact, is the key for understanding the strange way in which indemnity was foreclosed upon in the Constitutional Court ruling that would ultimately sanction the constitutionality of that same amnesty. In 1996, the amnesty agreement gave rise to *AZAPO et al. v. President of the Republic of*

South Africa et al., which John Dugard called the "most important case" to come before the Constitutional Court between its inception on February 15, 1995, and the adoption of the final Constitution on October 11, 1996.[80] One of the central questions before the Court was the same problem de Lange had asked Rossouw to clarify. As Justice Ismail Mahomed reported in his decision on the case, the counsel for the plaintiffs submitted that Chapter 3 of the Constitution, more particularly Section 22,

> conferred on every person the right to pursue, in the ordinary courts of the land or before independent tribunals, any claim which such person might have in civil law for the recovery of damages sustained by such a person in consequence of the unlawful delicts perpetrated by a wrongdoer. He contended that the Constitution did not authorise Parliament to make any law which would have the result of indemnifying (or otherwise rendering immune from liability) the perpetrator of any such delict against any claims made for damages suffered by the victim of such a delict. In support of that argument he suggested that the concept of "amnesty," referred to in the epilogue to the Constitution, was, at worst for the applicants, inherently limited to immunity from criminal prosecutions. He contended that even if a wrongdoer who has received amnesty could plead such amnesty as a defence to a criminal prosecution, such amnesty could not be used as a shield to protect him or her from claims for delictual damages suffered by any person in consequence of the act or omission of the wrongdoer.[81]

As Justice Didcott acknowledged in his concurring opinion, amnesty's exemption from all civil actions was a violation of the Interim Constitution's Section 22, which established the right to have access to courts.[82] Mahomed also acknowledged this point: in many, if not even most, contexts, "amnesty" was limited to criminal liability.

Mahomed then proceeded to engage in argumentation at once remarkably similar to and markedly different from Rossouw's. Blocked on constitutional grounds from interpreting amnesty with reference to indemnity jurisprudence,[83] Mahomed's path through international law was equally perilous. There was, after all, a decisive antinomy implicit in its attempt to define the word *amnesty*. On the one hand, the Court had no choice but to ground its interpretation of this word in international law. Without grounding the Interim Constitution's epilogue in a definition of amnesty that extended amnesty's powers beyond the prerogative of pardon, the TRC would have been able to grant only criminal immunity and not also civil immunity.[84] But in the event that the commission could not grant civil immunity, amnesty could not function as an incentive for perpetrators to confess the truth,[85] and the main legal support of the commission, perhaps even the political transition as a whole, would collapse. Since no other body of law allows the possibility to distinguish the limited power of pardon from amnesty broadly and generously defined, the Court had no choice but to use citations of international law to ground its interpretation of amnesty in the epilogue.

Yet this same interpretive gesture, which was absolutely necessary for the rescue of the concept of amnesty and everything founded on it, also placed the concept of amnesty in danger. As both Court citations indicate, customary international law is the only body of law that offers a coherent concept of a broadly defined amnesty.[86] In a sense, this inextricability of amnesty from international law provided unexpected support for the Constitutional Court's ruling against those critics who charged that its ruling violated international law. Contrary to *AZAPO et al.*'s attempt to find in international law grounds to counter amnesty, Article 6 (5) of Protocol II, in particular, establishes precisely the permissibility of amnesty under international law.[87] But the same inextricability also points like a bright red flashing arrow to the ground on which amnesty becomes impermissible. For even as Article 6 (5) permits amnesty following wars, the body of international law of which it is a part prohibits states from granting not only self-amnesties[88] (which broad amnesty would entail) but also amnesties for crimes against humanity, up to and including apartheid itself.[89]

This presented the Court with an antimony in the strict sense of the word. Amnesty is not only a limit concept of public law; it is also a limit concept of international law. It is situated at the very limit where public law and international law become indistinguishable: amnesties traditionally are given not only at the end of wars between states but also by states to the warring factions inside them. If the Court had defined the word *amnesty* with reference merely to the royal prerogative of pardon, amnesty would have remained too narrow, providing only for criminal immunity. The Court was thus forced to search for the meaning of *amnesty* outside the domain of public law. But if it had defined *amnesty* with reference to international law, where it has meaning as part of the peace treaty that puts an end to interstate war, *amnesty* certainly would have received a suitably broad definition, permitting both civil and criminal immunity; but it also would have risked becoming impermissible, since it would have amounted to a self-amnesty to one of the warring parties, the apartheid state. Since the struggle against apartheid was not merely one armed conflict among others but an armed conflict against the agents of a crime against humanity, for which international law prohibits amnesties, the international legal concept of "amnesty" would not work either. If the meaning of the word *amnesty* had been determined either wholly and purely by public law or wholly and purely by international law, amnesty would have become unworkable, and the compromise at the heart of the new Constitution would have collapsed.[90]

For the Court to ground the epilogue of the Interim Constitution in an ordinary and literal meaning of *amnesty*, it was thus necessary for it to turn to the definition found in international law, while at the same time finding both Protocol I of the Geneva Convention and the 1973 Convention for the Suppression of the Crime of Apartheid inapplicable to South Africa, even though both instruments were designed specifically to apply to South Africa. The Court justified the constitutionality of amnesty, in other words, by withdrawing from the touch of the very body of international law it could not do without. At the same time the Court *defined* amnesty by *applying* international law, it also *applied* amnesty to apartheid by *not applying* international law. Amnesty—and, by extension, the 1996 Constitution as well—acquired its validity when the Court withdrew from its *application* of amnesty the very body of law it applied to its *definition* of amnesty. Like Rossouw, then, Mahomed did not find much substance or guidance for the problem of civil liability in the word *amnesty* itself.

> I cannot, however, agree that the concept of amnesty is inherently to be limited to the absolution from criminal liability alone, regardless of the context and regardless of the circumstances. The word has no inherently fixed technical meaning. Its origin is to be found from the Greek concept of "*amnestia*" and it indicates what is described by Webster's Dictionary as "an act of oblivion." The degree of oblivion or obliteration must depend on the circumstances. It can, in certain circumstances, be confined to immunity from criminal prosecutions and in other circumstances be extended also to civil liability.[91]

Unlike Rossouw, however, Mahomed decided the question of amnesty without reference to the indemnity jurisprudence that preceded it—even as he remained loyal to the language of the PNR Act itself, which uses the word *indemnify* to describe amnesty's precise legal action or effect.[92] Whereas Rossouw's analysis of *amnesty* eschewed dictionaries and turned instead to the dissonance between the postscript and the indemnity jurisprudence that preceded it, Mahomed's analysis relied on lay and legal dictionaries alike— not, to be sure, because of any presumption about their intrinsic reliability, but, on the contrary, because of an inability to apply existing jurispruden- tial lexicons to the case before him. The silences in Mahomed's ruling were symptomatic of the double bind in which Mahomed found himself: consti- tutionally obliged to provide a definition to *amnesty*, he was nevertheless also constitutionally obliged not to apply either of the traditions of jurisprudence that otherwise would best apply (indemnity jurisprudence under apartheid, on the one hand, and the jurisprudence of amnesty in international law, on the other). Whence the second reason why Rossouw's memo is significant: it throws Mahomed's symptomatic silence into relief. Mahomed's silence on the relation between amnesty and indemnity jurisprudence was, we might say, a *pronounced* silence. At best, it was a manifestly juridical act—an ex- plicit attempt, as it were, to abrogate indemnity jurisprudence by disuse, to render it inoperative, to cast it once and for all into desuetude. At worst, by not calling into attention the conflict and difference between amnesty and indemnity, it implicitly prepared the ground for the silent persistence of the logic of indemnity jurisprudence in the TRC's theories and practices of "amnesty."

Precisely this often seems to take place in the scholarship of transitional justice. With some significant exceptions, most scholars of the TRC seem to remain entirely indifferent to the distinction between indemnity and am- nesty, using them interchangeably.[93] This condensation of two very different powers that, in jurisprudence as in public debate, even assumed the status of opposites obliges us to interpret many theoretical discussions of "amnesty" within transitional justice as symptoms of a very specific type. The juridi- cal repeal of indemnity and its replacement with "qualified amnesty" must, in short, be interpreted in light of a second dynamic: the survival of the convention of indemnification, or, more to the point, the way in which the imprint of a manifestly and indeed exclusively colonial indemnity jurispru- dence silently governs, from within, the theory and practice of the TRC. The hypothesis we shall entertain in this book is that this forgetting is neither accidental nor politically neutral. It is what Sigmund Freud, writing in 1901, called "motivated forgetting."[94] It is the inability to remember something unpleasant, threatening, or even painful. In particular, it is the forgetting of a jurisprudence that transitional scholars cannot possibly want to remember, much less inherit or assume, and the truth of which they indeed cannot possibly acknowledge being a constitutive part of their analyses of so humanitarian an institution as the TRC. Quite in contrast to Rossouw and Mahomed, who declare the word *amnesty* to be without content, more than a few scholars of transitional justice are quite interested in this word and its etymology, its possibilities for homonymy, and its most distant origins in ancient Greece.[95] Other scholars blur the concept in a different direction, assimilating amnesty in South Africa to Roman and Christian lexicons of pardon, clemency, and forgiveness. The desire at work in this "classical turn" in TRC commentary, this strange attempt to endow the TRC with a provenance in Athenian democracy, Roman Law, or Christian theology, results, however, in little more than willful blindness. The consoling myth or illusion, the reassuring misrecognition that the TRC reaffirms the ancient wisdom of the West, is ultimately little more than a baffle or screen, a device that allows transitional justice scholars to avoid confronting a much more proximate origin for "amnesty" in South Africa. It is motivated by a desire to forget the degree to which what transitional justice scholars call "amnesty" is an empty vessel that contains, among other things, the criteria and principles specific to the juridical power that apartheid jurists once called "indemnity." From this perspective, the attempt to make sense of the South African "amnesty" with primary reference to the paradigms of ancient Greece, Rome, or Jerusalem is afflicted with a fundamental and fatal irony: it resolves the differences between indemnity and amnesty through the very amnesia and forgetting against which the field of transitional justice so often moralizes.

1.3 Once we turn our gaze to the place and function of indemnity within South African legal history, we can see why it is very desirable for transitional justice scholars to invent a history of the TRC that allows for silence on any and all questions about the relation of amnesty to indemnity. Already in 1960, Herman Robert Hahlo and Ellison Kahn were able to observe that, in South Africa, "the Statute Book is studded with Indemnity Acts."[96] They did not attempt to provide support for their observation, apparently presuming it self-evident, but even the briefest glance at South African law prior to 1960 confirms their claim. The governors of the Cape Colony passed indemnity acts in 1836, 1847, 1853, and 1878 after declaring martial law in 1835, 1846, 1853, and 1877, respectively, in connection with the "Kafir Wars."[97] The Legislative Assembly of the Colony of Natal promulgated an indemnity act in 1874, after declaring martial law in 1873 during the repression of the "Amahlubi" Rebellion.[98] The Transkeian Territories Penal Code Act 24 of 1886, following the paradigm of "native law" proposed by the 1883 Commission on Native Law and Customs,[99] normalized this exceptional power, granting indemnity in advance to anyone who suppressed a riot on the orders of a magistrate or justice of the peace.[100] Between 1899 and 1902, during the South African war, English provincial authorities issued at least eight indemnity acts following the use of martial law.[101] This pattern did not cease with the Peace of Vereeniging established on May 31, 1902: between 1902 and 1910, the period that Martin Chanock has called fundamental to the modern legal system in South Africa,[102] at least four indemnity laws were promulgated.[103] Nor did it cease in the decade following the founding of the Union of South Africa in 1910: in 1914, 1915, 1919, and 1922, Parliament indemnified military and police officers for their violent suppression of the Rand Riots;[104] on December 31, 1920, an indemnity law was passed after South Africa took over the occupation and administration of "South-West Africa" (Namibia);[105] and in 1923, an indemnity law was proposed for the South African government's violent suppression of the "Bondelzwart" Rebellion.[106] With the onset of formal apartheid in 1948, the South African government's recourse to exceptional powers was normalized by the Public Safety Act of 1953 (which included emergency powers so extensive that martial law became almost unnecessary), the Defence Act of 1957 (which automatically conferred indemnity on any state employee, police officer, or private citizen who committed a crime in good faith to preserve public order), and Proclamation 400 of November 29, 1960 (Section 16 of which indemnified not only state employees, police officers, or other bureaucrats but also any chief or headman of *any* act committed by them or any person ordered to act by them).[107] Even with these powers written into law, the South African Parliament continued to pass additional and ever-wider indemnity acts. Between 1961 and 1994, the sovereign bodies of the apartheid state—whether the South African Parliament, the South African executive, or the state councils of the "independent Bantustans"—issued at least a dozen additional indemnity laws.[108] The protections these laws established would cover many of the very same police excesses that the *TRC Report* eventually would take as the object of its amnesty process (e.g., the Sharpeville Massacre of 1960; the Soweto Uprising of 1976; the states of emergency of July 1985, March and June of 1986, and June 1987; and the Bisho Massacre of 1992).[109]

In 1960, Hahlo and Kahn would argue that South Africa has the dubious honor of having the "best-developed case law" on martial law in the British Commonwealth.[110] But martial law *entails* indemnity: as James Rose Innes stated in 1900, "[T]he proclamation of martial law in a British colony absolutely necessarily implied that an Act of Indemnity should follow."[111] As colonial secretary Lewis Harcourt would put it in parliamentary debate over a South African indemnity in 1914, martial law is "a contradiction in terms, because it is a negation of all law, and action under it is illegal until it has been indemnified by the law-making power."[112] If South Africa has the best-developed case law on martial law in the British Commonwealth, it would seem to follow that its indemnity jurisprudence would be exceptionally developed as well.[113]

Indemnity's persistence within South African legal history begins to make more sense once we consider its place and function within South African legal theory. Scholars of South African law frequently have noted the influence of the British jurist Alfred Venn Dicey on South African jurisprudence. As Martin Chanock has put it, Dicey's 1885 text *Introduction to the Study of the Constitution* "dominated South African public law."[114] It hardly can come as a surprise, then, that Dicey and his student E. C. S. Wade would be quoted as authoritative sources in South African parliamentary debates over the meaning and limits of indemnity. But the circulation of Dicey's name in these debates is not accidental. Dicey is understood to have generated the concepts of parliamentary sovereignty and the rule of law that were so often at issue under apartheid.[115] According to Dicey, indemnity acts are, precisely, "the supreme instance of parliamentary sovereignty" and "the highest exertion and crowning proof of sovereign power."[116] If, as Hegel argues, the essence of a thing can only be understood with reference to its limit, we may say that, for Dicey, the essence of parliamentary sovereignty can only be understood with reference to indemnity.[117] If, moreover, Dicey did indeed dominate South African jurisprudence, then we may also say that the persistence of indemnity acts within South African legal history will have a coherent jurisprudential ground: for Dicey, indemnity is nothing less than the *exemplary act* of sovereign power under the conditions of parliamentary supremacy that prevailed in South Africa from 1910 to 1994.

1.4 *That* the TRC emerged in and through some sort of reiteration of the history and theory of indemnity in South Africa should not be in question. To the contrary, this should be as explicit and noncontroversial a theme in transitional justice literature as it was for Dullah Omar in his July 1994 unveiling of the "Amnesty Bill" at the IDASA Conference in Cape Town, for R. P. Rossouw in his March 1995 memo to Johnny de Lange, and for Kader Asmal in his speech to the House on May 17, 1995. Some readers might be tempted to object to this point: don't scholars of the TRC regularly make precisely this claim when they mention the precedents of the TRC in the Indemnity Acts of 1990 and 1992 or even the Indemnity Act of 1961? To this objection, there is a properly dialectical response: the differences in the *degree* to which we trace the TRC back to its precedents in indemnity jurisprudence correspond to a difference in *kind* in the sort of jurisprudential question we ask of the TRC. The farther back we go in our search for the precedents of the TRC's power of amnesty, the more we realize that we are dealing with a genre of jurisprudence that is qualitatively different from transitional justice. Just as the Indemnity Act of 1990 and the Further Indemnity Act of 1992 have their precedents in the Indemnity Act of 1961, the latter was explicitly based on the Indemnity Acts of 1914 and 1922,[118] which in turn were explicitly modeled on the Indemnity Act of 1900,[119] which itself was formed with reference to the indemnity acts that put an end to the martial law declared during the "Kafir Wars."[120] The more closely and rigorously we follow the indemnity jurisprudence that is the most direct source for the TRC's concept of "amnesty," in other words, the more apparent it becomes that this concept originates in a jurisprudence that transitional justice both *must* understand (if it is to retain any claim to understand its own exemplary case, the TRC, without itself enacting the very forgetting against which it moralizes) and *cannot* understand (to the extent it remains bound to its Eurocentric narratives and focused on moralistic normative and therapeutic claims). This is the jurisprudence of emergency—precisely the same jurisprudence that authorized the executive branch to suspend the rule of law and whose suspensions of the rule of law enabled, if not also authorized, the very "culture of impunity" that the TRC itself investigated and condemned.[121] That the

TRC itself is a product, however salutary, of the very legal culture it also censures is the troubling truth that the field of transitional justice cannot but misrecognize in its study of the TRC. If transitional justice were to consistently apply its normative *prescriptions for* the TRC ("amnesty, not amnesia," "forgive, don't forget," etc.) to its own *descriptions of* the TRC, then debate over the TRC would no longer take place on transitional justice's reified binary terms (truth vs. justice, vengeance vs. forgiveness, etc.). It would raise the juridical question of precisely *how*—through what exact combination of repetition and difference—the TRC's amnesty reiterated the indemnity jurisprudence that preceded it, and it would raise the political question of what it means for the TRC's attempt to transform the apartheid state that one of the TRC's central concepts originated in one of the most repressive branches of colonial jurisprudence. Before we can adequately pose these questions, however, we first will need to acquire an ability to recognize the theory and practice of indemnity on its own terms. And to accomplish this, we will need to take a detour through the writings of A. V. Dicey.

Chapter 2

INDEMNITY AND SOVEREIGNTY

2.1 Dicey often is said to be the main theoretical source of South African jurisprudence in the twentieth century. However, precisely what this means is by no means clear, for Dicey's main text, his 1885 *Introduction to the Law of the Constitution*, has been the object of wildly divergent readings in the last century.[1] The reading of Dicey in South Africa is no exception. On the one hand, Dicey's arguments that judges could interpret but not repeal statutes[2] and that bad law is still law that should be obeyed in court[3] enabled National Party jurists to find in Dicey a main theoretical source, perhaps even their main theoretical source, for the theory of parliamentary sovereignty that enabled the NP to argue against the judicial review of racist legislation.[4] On the other hand, Dicey's insistence that parliamentary sovereignty is inseparable from the second of his two "first principles" of the English Constitution, the rule of law, enabled liberal jurists to criticize the excesses of NP laws and policies—without, however, denying that their cruel and unjust character disqualifies apartheid laws from being considered law, and without endorsing the call of the then-illegal ANC for a revolutionary overthrow of apartheid.[5] In 1898, Dicey argued that Benthamite thought had splintered into two, confronting itself in two mutually exclusive guises: liberal individualism and socialist collectivism.[6] Less than a century later, the same could be said of Diceyan tradition itself: in 1994, with the end of formal apartheid, Diceyan thought confronted itself not only as the justification for the apartheid security state but also as the justification for the new form of legal liberalism that proposed to replace that state.

Albie Sachs, John Dugard, and Martin Chanock, among others, are thus surely right to argue that the criticism of apartheid on Diceyan grounds—as a violation of the rule of law—is, at best, insufficient.[7] If anything, their argument needs to be taken a step further. If it is the case, as Martin Chanock has observed, that the genesis and basis of the apartheid state were always more British than Roman-Dutch in the first place,[8] and if the rule of law was therefore always a constitutive part of apartheid governance, then we may cast doubt on the notion that the Diceyan criticism of the apartheid state ever constituted a substantive antidote or alternative to its cruelty and injustice. It would be more precise to say that Diceyan jurisprudence functioned as an important cog in the normal operation of the machine of the apartheid state: it was the latter's preferred form of self-correction and self-criticism.[9] But if this is so, then the need to reread and rethink Dicey today is all the more pronounced. For even as South Africa's new constitution dissolved Dicey's principle of parliamentary sovereignty by replacing it with the principle of constitutional supremacy, the framers of the new constitution also made a point of reiterating the discourse of the rule of law as one of the central motivations for that process of dissolution, repetition, and difference.[10] Unless we have a precise understanding of the way in which Dicey's emphasis on the rule of law was constitutive of apartheid jurisprudence in the first place, we cannot hope to understand the way this principle has been reiterated—that is, not only recited, but also, arguably, altered—in postapartheid South Africa.

2.2 As soon as we turn to Dicey's text, however, we encounter an unexpected source of difficulty: it is, in part, precisely the *simplicity* of Dicey's text (or, at least, its apparent simplicity) that engenders so much confusion about Dicey's claims. The easiest reading of Dicey's 1885 text, of course, is that it does nothing more than stipulate two juridical principles, the rule of law and parliamentary sovereignty, which it then binds together through an analysis of those vague but substantial juridical norms Dicey calls "conventions."[11] The trouble with this reading, however, is that it doesn't isolate with sufficient clarity what in this mix is singularly Diceyan. After all, Dicey was by no means the first British jurist to articulate the principle of parliamentary sovereignty. The more proximate sources of this principle in the English tradition are, of course, John Locke, Edward Coke, and William Blackstone. The same may be said for the principle of the rule of law. Setting aside the classical sources for this principle,[12] Dicey's account of the rule of law may be traced to the Australian colonial jurist W. E. Hearn, whose 1867 book *The Government of England* Dicey both cited with approval and freely adopted into his lectures.[13] Dicey's emphasis on "conventions of the constitution," finally, is not original to him either. To the contrary, analyses of this sort were quite standard in late nineteenth-century jurisprudence.[14]

To understand Dicey's specific contribution to jurisprudence, it is of course first necessary to understand what Dicey has to say about parliamentary sovereignty. In its simplest sense, parliamentary sovereignty as it is referred to in Dicey's lectures means nothing more than that Parliament has "the right to make or unmake any law whatever" and that "no person or body is recognized by the law of England as having a right to override or set aside the legislation of Parliament."[15] Here too, however, we would err were we to attribute this postulate to Dicey himself, for Dicey's paraphrase on this point is not substantively distinct from the key sentence of what Dicey himself refers to as the "classical passage on the subject" in Blackstone's *Commentaries on the Laws of England:* "What the Parliament doth, no power can undo."[16] For Dicey, as for John Austin before him, the task of understanding the English Constitution was a matter of understanding the place and function of sovereign power within it.[17] To gain analytic clarity about the English Constitution, Dicey thus regarded as essential the need to understand the totality of "rules which directly or indirectly affect the distribution or the exercise of the sovereign power in the state."[18] Not all of these rules, however, are written. Many of them exist in the mode of unwritten habits, understandings, or customs that implicitly or silently govern the conduct of all those individuals who discharge the sovereign power (e.g., ministers) without also being laws in any proper sense (i.e., without also being enforced by the courts).[19] As such, the only way to name them at all is to infer their existence from a historical analysis of ordered patterns in governmental conduct (whether that conduct be royal, parliamentary, or ministerial). Dicey's account of parliamentary sovereignty, like his approach to the English Constitution more generally, was, in short, as much historical as theoretical. To grasp its character as a juridical form, we too must return to the historical crisis from whence it springs: the Second English Civil War.

For Dicey (as for Bagehot, Hearn, and Todd before him), the theory of parliamentary sovereignty was intelligible only on historical grounds, as the product of the compromise that brought a close to the Second English Civil War.[20] At stake in this conflict, according to Dicey, was not the essence of sovereign power: the debate in the seventeenth century was not, in other words, over whether or not sovereign power as such could or should be divided. The dispute centered instead on the question of where, or in what seat of the English government, the undivided sovereign power should be located.[21] As part of the compromise that put an end to this dispute, the sovereign power that once inhered in the Crown now inhered instead in the statutes passed by Parliament, with the result that Parliament now exercised the undivided and omnicompetent lawmaking power that once belonged only to the king.[22]

Of the privileges that passed from the king to Parliament in this revolutionary transition, none was more important than that conferred by the maxim "The king can do no wrong." According to Dicey, this maxim is one of the conventions that comprise the law of the constitution,[23] and according to Wade, it is specific to the history of English law.[24] In his 1880 book *Parliamentary Government in the British Colonies*, Alpheus Todd (who Dicey called "a very judicious writer"),[25] explained the maxim's substance prior to the Second English Civil War.

> Rightly understood, this precept means that the personal actions of the sovereign, not being acts of government, are not under the cognizance of the law, and that as an individual he is not amenable to any earthly power or jurisdiction. He is, nevertheless, in subjection to God and to the law. For the law controls the king, and it is, in fact, 'the only rule and measure of the power of the Crown, and of the obedience of the people.' And while the sovereign is personally irresponsible for all acts of government, yet the functions of royalty which appertain to him in his political capacity are regulated by law, or by constitutional precept, and must be discharged him solely for the public good, and not to gratify personal inclinations.[26]

After the civil war, this maxim continued to be reiterated within English law, such that the monarch remained immune from ordinary civil and criminal prosecution.[27] But, particularly after the case of Lord Danby (1679), it also acquired a new political significance.[28] Whereas "The king can do no wrong" used to mean that the sovereign was only answerable to Parliament for "high crimes and misdemeanors, and for acts of mal-administration which were directly attributable to themselves," it now meant simply that "no mismanagement is imputable to the sovereign personally."[29] Crucially, this immunity did not extend to the king's ministers or servants.[30] In the book that Dicey claimed to have taught him "more than any other single work of the way in which the labors of lawyers established in early times the elementary principles which form the basis of the Constitution," W. E. Hearn clarified that the maxim "The king can do no wrong" did not preclude legal consequences for illegal acts committed by ministers or servants in the king's name.[31]

> Since no unlawful act is the act of the Crown, no command to do any such act can be a command of the Crown. No person, therefore, doing any unlawful act under colour of the Royal authority can shelter himself from the penal or other consequences of his act under the protection of that pretended command. No such command is a command of that nature which the law recognizes as binding upon the subject. The person to whom it is given consequently acts at his own peril.[32]

Hearn explained, in short, "Although the person of the King is at all times inviolate, the law shows in matters of right no delicacy or respect towards his servants. Every office is criminally responsible for his conduct in the execution of his office. . . . The law admits of no excuse for the commission of any wrongful Act."[33]

In this, its reiterated form, the maxim "The king can do no wrong" took on a new and radical meaning: it now simply meant that the king's ministers and later administrators of the government could not attribute their wrong actions to the king but instead must themselves accept individual responsibility for those actions.[34] As Dicey put it, that "no one can plead the orders of the Crown or indeed of any superior officer in defence of any act not otherwise justifiable by law" meant, in short, that "some person is legally responsible for every act done by the Crown."[35] The survival of absolute sovereign immunity after the seventeenth century therefore paradoxically entailed, as a logical consequence and counterpart of its continued existence, the emergence of an equally absolute ministerial liability.[36] In this way, one of the basic laws of the modern English Constitution—indeed, one of the core principles that Dicey would come to call the rule of law, namely, the precept that no one is above the law and that any minister or public servant who violates the law will be held individually liable for those violations before ordinary tribunals—emerged from a reiteration of one of the most absolutist maxims of seventeenth-century royalism.

But while this reiteration may have shifted the location of sovereign power—and, in shifting it, separated it from the immunity that had hitherto served as one of its definitive attributes under conditions of monarchy—it did not remove the existence or, indeed, necessity of the discretionary power that until then had been the exclusive provenance of the king. Under conditions of parliamentary sovereignty, as under conditions of monarchy, it was still occasionally imperative in times of tumult for the government to take sudden, extreme, and sometimes illegal measures to maintain the public's safety and security. But whereas, under royalism, the English monarch could accomplish this on the basis of prerogative alone (and, because of sovereign immunity, without exposure to subsequent liability or punishment), the precise opposite was true for Parliament. Parliament's minimization of the principle of sovereign immunity (or, more precisely, its localization and limitation of this principle to the person of the monarch alone) meant that any and all ministers or public servants who violated the law, even if in bona fide service to the public safety and security, would nevertheless remain individually liable for their actions in both civil and criminal courts after a tumult's end. As such, Parliament exposed itself much more than any monarch to a basic paradox of sovereign power. In times of tumult, Parliament's loyalty to the supremacy of law could come into conflict with its loyalty to the Ciceronian maxim that Emmerich de Vattel and John Locke, no less than Jean Bodin and Thomas Hobbes, characterized as the highest and last duty of all sovereign power, whether monarchical or parliamentary: *salus rei publicae suprema lex esto*, "The safety and security of the people is the supreme law." As a direct result of the way in which Parliament reiterated the maxim "The king can do no wrong," in other words, Parliament therefore exposed the Crown's ministers and servants to an antinomy between the *sovereignty of law* (the principle that nobody is above the law) and the *law of sovereignty* (or, in Hobbes's words, "the law over them that have sovereign power," i.e., that "the safety of the people is the supreme law").[37]

2.3 As Dicey construes it, the main significance of an indemnity act is that it resolves the conflict between *sovereignty of law* and *law of sovereignty*. We can understand how by considering Dicey's treatment of another of the juridical inheritances of the long seventeenth century, the writ of habeas corpus (which, of course, is another element of the rule of law that came into being through a reiteration of a monarchical prerogative).[38] Dicey argues that the Habeas Corpus Act of 1679 constitutes an element of the rule of law that, in its justiciability, is much more important for the accomplishment of political liberty than are the abstract sentiments expressed in the French Declaration of the Rights of Man or the American Bill of Rights.[39] The significance of the writ, in Dicey's view, hardly can be understated: because the writ of habeas corpus confers on the judiciary the authority to prevent or veto any action taken by the Crown that is in opposition to the rule of law, it constitutes the pivot point of judicial review under conditions of parliamentary sovereignty. The writ, Dicey therefore says, determines "the *whole* relation" of the judiciary to the executive.[40] It enables judges to supervise "the *whole* administrative action of government," including, above all, the executive's discretionary police power to preserve public safety by preventive means.[41] As such, the writ of habeas corpus is a—perhaps even *the*—bulwark that prevents the English Constitution from being corrupted by the kind of administrative impunity that pervades French *droit administratif,* where immunity from prosecution protects any and all ministers and public servants.[42] Because of the writ, England, unlike France, can punish crimes committed by its government.

Dicey acknowledges, however, that during periods of political unrest, the courts' capacity to issue a writ of habeas corpus does not so much preserve as endanger the integrity and order of the English Constitution. Under such conditions, the writ constitutes "an inconvenient or dangerous limitation on the authority of the executive government."[43] Together with the judicial oversight it enables, it restricts the government's power to maintain order and peace and thus compromises its ability to obey the "supreme law" (the "safety of the people"). It becomes necessary, then, for Parliament to pass a habeas corpus suspension act, authorizing the secretary of state to defer indefinitely the trials of those imprisoned under charges of treason.[44] Dicey insists that these acts are poorly named: pertaining only to those who are detained in custody under suspicion of treason, they in no way constitute a repeal of the habeas corpus acts or a suspension of those acts for the citizenry as a whole.[45] The English suspension act cannot be likened to the French *état de siège* (for, as Clinton Rossiter would later clarify in his commentary on Dicey, English martial law does not exempt the administration, as does crisis government in France, from the checks of the ordinary courts[46]) or to the Coercion Acts that, in 1881, conferred on the Irish executive an "absolute power of arbitrary and preventive arrest," as well as complete immunity from civil trial and prosecution for unlawful arrest.[47] Although these measures certainly may resemble the suspension act (for, as Dicey concedes, all of them increase the arbitrary powers of the government in general and of the executive in particular), they are, at root, distinct from it, because unlike these other measures of crisis government, the suspension act is fundamentally limited in scope and application. And the best proof of this, Dicey argues, may be found in the unwritten rule (the "convention") that "before a *Habeas Corpus* Suspension Act runs out," it is "almost invariably supplemented by legislation of a totally different character, namely, an Act of Indemnity."[48]

The analytic significance that Dicey's lectures accord to indemnity acts hardly could be more emphatic. Acts of indemnity, he says, are "the supreme instance of parliamentary sovereignty";[49] they constitute "the highest exertion and crowning proof of sovereign power";[50] they are "the last and supreme exercise of Parliamentary sovereignty."[51] To understand how and why Dicey is able to make such emphatic claims, we once again will need to call to mind the specifically systematic character of Dicey's account of the English Constitution. In the indemnity act, each of the three primary principles Dicey distills from that Constitution (parliamentary sovereignty, the rule of law, and constitutional conventions), his most important theoretical contribution to analytic jurisprudence (his critique of John Austin), and his deepest political commitments (his opposition to Irish home rule and his defense of imperial unity) all converge into a single example.

What precisely is an indemnity act? Dicey defines it as a retrospective statute with the object "to make legal transactions which when they took place were illegal, or to free individuals to whom the statute applies from liability for having broken the law."[52] For Dicey, the indemnity act is quite plainly a "legalization of illegality."[53] Under conditions of parliamentary sovereignty, parliament is the supreme power: it has the capacity to "legally change every law" and "the right to make or unmake any law whatever, without any body having a right to override or repeal its legislation."[54] It's not difficult to see how and why Dicey can call the indemnity act the "supreme instance" of Parliament's supremacy. By passing legislation that legalizes illegality, Parliament removes the capacity of the courts to find against indemnified individuals. In instances where the illegality in question is a violation of the writ of habeas corpus and where the illegal act therefore has been committed by the government itself, Parliament's legalization of this illegality has a general and fundamental significance. It removes the court's capacity to enforce the single most important law in English political and legal history pertaining to judicial oversight. The indemnity act, more than any other legislative act, therefore enables Parliament to express its sovereignty relative to the courts.[55]

For this very reason, in fact, we must also underline the fact that, for Dicey, indemnity acts are not, cannot, and ought not be automatic. Indemnity acts, that is to say, cannot and ought not afford the sort of sovereign immunity that was attached to the prerevolutionary Crown by the maxim "The king can do no wrong," and they cannot and ought not bear any resemblance to the legal immunity that protects civil servants in France. This is why it is of the utmost importance that the *convention* of retrospectively indemnifying certain classes of officials and ministers who break the law in the name of the public good never assume the written form of a general *statute*. Were indemnity to be explicitly and generally legislated—or, more to the point, were indemnity to be understood, as Frederick Pollock proposed, as an implicit and automatic part of any declaration of martial law, such that a separate indemnity act would be redundant and superfluous—the indemnification convention not only would cease to become retrospective but also would reintroduce into the English Constitution precisely the sort of sovereign immunity that was supposed to have been superseded in 1688. Indemnification of illegal ministerial or official acts legislated *in advance* of those acts would permit the return of exactly the sort of unchecked discretionary power that was exercised under monarchical conditions and that was all but extinguished under conditions of parliamentary sovereignty.[56] As long as it remained a convention—expected and anticipated, but never guaranteed—the retrospective indemnification of officials and ministers would permit discretionary power to be exercised under conditions of parliamentary sovereignty, in a way that would not also contradict or threaten the principle of the rule of law. Where indemnification remains a convention, Parliament could, for instance, choose to withhold indemnification from certain ministers or officials whose illegal or excessive actions were found to be performed not in bona fide service to public safety but for private gain, or those whose illegal or excessive actions were not warranted by the necessities of a case but were (in some important yet undefined way) malicious, cruel, or unscrupulous. Were the convention of indemnification to become a law, Parliament would be in the absurd position of having to violate the law in order to prosecute ministers who violate the law. Where the indemnification of officials remains a mere convention and not a law, so too then the rule of law would remain the norm, and Parliament would retain the last word over the conditions under which discretionary power may be exercised. As a convention, but *only* as a convention, the indemnity act could perform an exceptionally important function within the English Constitution: it could permit the old maxim "The king can do no wrong" to be reiterated under conditions now defined by the principles of parliamentary sovereignty and the rule of law.[57]

Even so, there is another sense in which the convention of indemnification is no different from any other convention of the English Constitution. Conventions of the constitution, according to Dicey, consist of "customs, practices, maxims, or precepts which are not enforced or recognized by the Courts," and they "make up a body not of laws, but of constitutional or political ethics."[58] As such, conventions have a very definite place within the English Constitution more generally. Their function is to determine the mode in which the discretionary powers of the Crown ought to be exercised, where discretionary power is defined as "every kind of action which can legally be taken by the Crown, or by its servants, without the necessity for applying to Parliament for new statutory authority."[59] Dicey emphasizes that these powers are essentially historical—or, better, residual—in character: the discretionary powers regulated by the conventions of the constitution are simply what remain of the old monarchical powers once they are subsumed in and by Parliament. But while conventions are not laws in the strict sense, the fact that they govern the exercise of sovereign power means that they nevertheless possess, despite their unwritten status, an essential and precise place and function in the English Constitution.[60] As such, the practice of indemnifying officials and ministers who break the law in the name of public safety can and must exist only and exclusively in the mode of what Dicey calls an "assurance" or "expectation" on the part of officials and ministers.

A Suspension Act would, in fact, fail of its main object, unless officials felt assured that, as long as they *bona fide*, and uninfluenced by malice or by corrupt motives, carried out the policy of which the Act was the visible sign, they would be protected from penalties for conduct which, though it might be technically a breach of law, was nothing more than the free exertion for the public good of that discretionary power which the suspension of the *Habeas Corpus* Act was intended to confer upon the executive. This assurance is derived from the expectation that, before the Suspension Act ceases to be in force, Parliament will pass an Act of Indemnity, protecting all persons who have acted, or have intended to act, under the powers given to the government by the statute. This expectation has not been disappointed. An Act suspending the *Habeas Corpus* Act, which has been continued for any length of time, has constantly been followed by an Act of Indemnity.[61]

How, then, does the convention of indemnification reconcile the *sovereignty of law* with the *law of sovereignty?* It is not recalled nearly often enough that the phrase of Dicey's that is most often taken to summarize his 1885 position on parliamentary sovereignty as a whole (i.e., his definition of parliament as "a body which can make or unmake every law; and which, therefore, cannot be bound by any law")[62] comes from the point in his lectures where he confronts the difficulties that emerge in his attempt to apply Austinian jurisprudence to the study of the English Constitution. According to Dicey, John Austin confused the *legal* definition of sovereign power with its *political* definition. Whereas Austin was correct to say that under the English Constitution, the electorate actually constitutes the sovereign power (for it is their political will that is expressed in and by the Parliament they elect), Austin was nevertheless incorrect to imply that this political sense of the word "sovereignty" possesses any legal validity; to the contrary, no judge would ever call into question the validity of a statute on the basis of supposed knowledge about how the will of the people may or may not be expressed in that statute.[63] The trouble with this confusion, Dicey argues, is that it causes us to misunderstand the essence and basis of the limits of parliamentary sovereignty[64] and, as such, precludes us from understanding the important and fundamental purpose of the many unwritten rules or conventions that govern the exercise of the sovereign power under conditions of parliamentary supremacy. Whereas the central place and function of constitutional conventions is the constraint of discretionary powers, their underlying purpose within the English Constitution, conceived analytically as a systematic and logically interconnected whole, is the reconciliation of the *legal sovereign* (Parliament) with the *political sovereign* (which Dicey alternately refers to, in an ambiguity that would prove fatal for the indemnification convention in South Africa, as the will of the electoral body, the electorate, the majority of electors, public opinion, or the will of the nation).[65] As Dicey puts it, conventions "have all one ultimate object. Their end is to secure that Parliament, or the Cabinet which is indirectly appointed by Parliament, shall in the long run give effect to the will of that power which in modern England is the true political sovereign of the State—the majority of the electors or (to use popular though not quite accurate language) the nation."[66]

This is why there is no way to understand Dicey's argument about parliamentary sovereignty apart from his criticism of and departure from Austin. Only by remaining analytically alert to the distinction between political and legal sovereignty—Dicey's main break with Austin—can we grasp Dicey's teaching regarding the ultimate purpose of constitutional conventions (which, in the estimation of at least one of Dicey's contemporaries, was also his "most magnificent contribution" to the study of English law).[67] Because Austin is not alert to this distinction, Dicey argues, Austin not only misunderstands conventions but also misunderstands sovereign power itself, for conventions are the only true and proper limit to parliamentary sovereignty. Because the electorate is "a body which does not, and from its nature hardly can, itself legislate, and which, owing to chiefly historical causes, has left in existence a theoretically supreme legislature," it follows that "the legislature, which (*ex hypothesi*) cannot be governed by laws, should be regulated by understandings [i.e., conventions] of which the object is to secure the conformity of Parliament to the will of the nation."[68] Dicey continues,

> And this is what has actually occurred. The conventions of the constitution now consists of customs which (whatever their historical origin) are at the present day maintained for the sake of ensuring the supremacy of the House of Commons, and ultimately, through the elective House of Commons, of the nation. Our modern code of constitutional morality secures, though in a roundabout way, what is called abroad the "sovereignty of the people."[69]

The purpose of the conventions is thus clear: to remove potential or real conflict between political and legal sovereignty, or, in Dicey's words, "to secure harmony between the action of the legislative sovereign and the wishes of the political sovereign."[70]

2.4 How in particular did the convention of indemnification accomplish this? The main features of the indemnification convention, as Dicey understood it, crystallized with the Indemnity Acts that were passed every year between 1795 and 1801.[71] Issued under conditions that J. S. Mill called "the most tyrannical period of modern Irish history,"[72] these acts followed the cruel and forbidding precedent established by the Indemnity Act of 1688:

they all required unsuccessful plaintiffs to pay double the costs. They also formalized the language of "necessity" that had already appeared in 1688 and that would become so important for twentieth-century indemnity jurisprudence. These acts "discharged" and "made void" all lawsuits over various acts "not justifiable by law, but which were yet so much for the public service, and so necessary for the suppressing of such insurrections, and for the preservation of the public peace, that the persons by whom they were transacted, ought to be indemnified."[73] Until 1799, however, indemnity acts did not include the distinction that would become decisive in twentieth-century indemnity jurisprudence, between acts committed in good faith in service to the public good and acts committed out of private malice and ill will.

This distinction originated in *Wright v. Fitzgerald*, the case that, more than any other in English legal history, established the rules that together would govern the judicial review of indemnity acts passed first by the English Parliament and later by the South African Parliament[74] and that indeed helped generate the jurisprudence of indemnity that would inform (without dominating) Dicey's lectures.[75] *Wright v. Fitzgerald* was a suit filed against the high sheriff of Tipperary County, Judkins Fitzgerald, by Mr. Wright, a man Fitzgerald had detained and tortured in May 1798, during the Irish Rebellion and under conditions of martial law. Catching Wright (a well-known professor of French) with a note written in French (which Fitzgerald was unable to read), Fitzgerald suspected Wright to be conspiring with the French to overthrow the English government of Ireland. Fitzgerald used the note as a justification first to imprison Wright (who, he had been informed, was one of the secret leaders of the rebellion) and then to beat him viciously and in public, all while Wright pleaded for a trial.[76] When a nearby officer present at the beating inquired into the reason for the punishment, Fitzgerald produced the note, the innocuous contents of which the officer then translated into English for Fitzgerald.[77] Despite the results of the translation, Fitzgerald proceeded to order one hundred more lashes (which were so severe that Wright's bowels were exposed and "could be perceived to be convulsed and working through his wounds"), commanded his men to form a firing squad to execute Wright (they refused), sought a rope to hang Wright (he could not find one), and then shut him in a "dark small room" for "six or seven days without medical assistance."[78]

In 1798, the English Parliament passed an indemnity act retroactively protecting from vexatious lawsuits any person who had participated in the suppression of the Irish Rebellion.[79] The protections of this law notwith-standing, Wright filed suit against Fitzgerald in March 1799 for assault and battery, on the grounds that "the indemnity only applied to cases in which the magistrates had acted on clear, or at least serious, evidence of treason, had taken all possible means of ascertaining the guilt of the persons they punished, and had exercised their power with common humanity."[80] In his charge to the jury, Justice Chamberlain set forth the principles that soon would become paradigmatic for the jurisprudence of indemnity.

> His lordship said, that the jury were not to imagine, that the legislature, by enabling magistrates to justify under the Indemnity Bill, had released them from the feelings of humanity, or permitted them wantonly to exercise pow-er, even though it were put down rebellion. No; it expected that in all cases there should be a grave and serious examination into the conduct of the sup-posed criminal; and every act should show a mind intent to discover guilt, not to inflict torture. By examination or trial, he did not mean that sort of examination and trial which they were then engaged in, but such examina-tion and trial, the best nature of the case, and the circumstances would allow of. That this must have been the intention of the legislature, was manifest from the expression—"magistrates and all other persons," which proved that as every man, whether magistrate or not, was authorized to suppress rebellion, and was to be justified by that law for his acts, it is required, that he should not exceed the necessity which gave him the power; and that he should show in his justification, that he had used every possible means to ascertain the guilt which he had punished; and above all, no deviation from the common principles of humanity should appear in his conduct.[81]

So directed, the jury found in favor of Wright, awarding him five hundred pounds in damages.[82] Following this verdict, however, Fitzgerald took the unusual step of petitioning Parliament directly, asking for a special indem-nity act (in addition to the general indemnity act Parliament already passed) to set aside the jury's decision in *Wright* and to protect him from the many other lawsuits pending against him.[83] In his appeal to Parliament, Fitzgerald falsely claimed that the jury had found against him because the judges in the case had demanded that he reveal the secret information he had received establishing Wright's collusion with the Irish rebels, a demand he claimed to have refused on the grounds that doing so would endanger his informants.[84]

After a vigorous debate lasting more than two weeks, Parliament did not end up granting him his special indemnity. Rather, they created another indemnity act,

> which was so drawn as to make such prosecutions as that of Fitzgerald almost impossible. It provided that in all cases in which sheriffs or other officers or persons were brought to trial for acts done in suppressing the rebellion, a verdict for the plaintiff should be null and void unless the jury distinctly found that the act had been done maliciously and not with an intent of suppressing rebellion, preserving public peace, or promoting the safety of the State; and that even where the juries did find that the act was "malicious," the judge or judges who tried the case should have the power of setting such verdicts aside.[85]

Opponents of this measure decried it as a "monster in our law" and a "monstrous novelty,"[86] arguing that it conferred on judges an extraordinary power and that the threshold it set for the proof of malice was impossible to satisfy. Moreover, as one lawyer for a man illegally detained by Fitzgerald put it, the bill was so widely drawn that it allowed reasonable cause for suspicion as a justifiable basis for murder.[87] This same lawyer criticized the bill for excluding from indemnification only crimes committed on the basis of "private malice" alone: "I think it impossible to enumerate all the outrages of man against man, or the crimes which might be committed without the perpetrator's being actuated by private malice."[88] Another lawyer for a different man illegally detained by Fitzgerald made the same point, sarcastically ventriloquizing the impossibly high threshold of proof that the bill demanded of plaintiffs.

> True, Mr. Fitzgerald flogged you, Mr. Wright, and wantonly imprisoned you, Mr. Scott, you can have your remedy against him, but you can only have it on these terms—you must enter into his bosom—you must dive into the reservoir of his heart—you must explore secrets known only to the Almighty—and you must not only learn what were his secret motives and intentions, and whether he was actuated by any malice to you, or by a general principle of hostility to mankind, but you must also bring proof of this before a jury! If you do this, you shall have justice—if you fail in doing

it, you shall be punished with double costs, for daring to complain of what you have suffered.[89]

Given its troubling legislative sequelae, *Wright* must be said to have an ambiguous status within indemnity jurisprudence. On the one hand, *Wright* would be cited in that other infamous indemnity trial, *Phillips v. Eyre*, as the only successful action brought against an indemnity act during a time of rebellion. On Justice Willes's reading of the case, the principle of *Wright* is simple and direct: "the defendant, in that case, acted from private malice and not for the public good."[90] Later jurists would formalize *Wright* even more, deriving from it a twofold test to define the sort of illegal acts that an indemnity could protect from prosecution. First, in what might be called the "objective" test (which, to be clear, predated *Wright*), the act must be necessary for preserving the *salus publica*: as in the jurisprudence of emergency more generally, the *casus necessitas*, or "necessities of the case," are the controlling principle for valid indemnification. In any given case, however, a given person's assessment of the "necessities of the case" will necessarily be confused, partial, and ad hoc. This is why, as Dicey would later write, a clear estimate of the necessities of the case can be formed only after the fact, by judge and jury, in conditions of peace and calm that are qualitatively different from, if not also both opposed to and enabled by, the situation of the magistrate whose duty it is to suppress riots and restore order without delay.[91]

In a basic sense, then, indemnification allows for ministers and servants of the government to break the law in situations where what Dicey calls the "moral duty" to protect the safety and security of the country comes into conflict with the legal duty to obey the law (or, put differently, under conditions where loyalty to the law alone would entail disloyalty to the safety and security of the public).[92] It is a crucial and decisive part of this convention that indemnity be both conditional and individualized. Dicey emphasizes that no indemnity shall be granted to any minister or servant whose illegal actions cannot be shown to have been committed "*bona fide* and solely with a view to the public interest" or can be shown to be excessive relative to the *casus necessitas* (the exigency or emergency) that required them in the first place.[93] The reason that this is important is that, taken together, these conditions—one "subjective" (the question of whether or not the official was acting in bona fide service to the public good), one "objective" (the question of whether the official's actions were excessive relative to the necessities of the case)—enable the indemnification convention to accomplish the goal of all conventions: the creation of harmony between political and legal sovereignty. It is an expression of political sovereignty because it allows officials to break the law in the name of the *salus publica* and, as such, positions the *salus publica* as the highest law.[94] It is an expression of legal sovereignty because it does not suspend any law at all (indeed, it leaves the writ of habeas corpus entirely in force) and maintains the principle that even ministers are individually accountable before ordinary courts (the criminal and civil guilt of a minister or official is the necessary precondition for an indemnity act). It is an expression of legal sovereignty above all, because its entire purpose is to restore the rule of law, to repeal the martial law that precedes it, and to ensure the return of juridical norms. Indemnity is therefore *the opposite* of martial law, because it is the legal means by which martial law is brought to a close.[95] But it is also its *supplement*: indemnity is that in the absence of which martial law would extend indefinitely, thereby permanently deforming the rule of law. Finally, and for this same reason, indemnity is essential for martial law if martial law is to retain its own internal coherence, for indemnity is that in the absence of which martial law itself could not perform its own stated objective, namely, restoring the rule of law.

The exceptional status of indemnity within Dicey's jurisprudence thus should be clear. The convention of indemnification not only allows for the reconciliation of the past of sovereign power *with its present* (by reconciling the residual monarchical principle of sovereign immunity, "The king can do no wrong," with one of the basic principles of the rule of law, i.e., individual ministerial liability). It also reconciles sovereign power to itself *in the present:* by striking a balance between, on the one hand, complete sovereign immunity (which on its own terms would violate the rule of law) and, on the other, complete exposure to prosecution and individual ministerial liability (which, on its own terms, would unfairly punish ministers and officials who broke the law to secure public safety in times of crisis), the indemnification convention allows for the reconciliation of the legal sovereignty of Parliament and the rule of law with the political sovereignty of the people. Its historical and theoretical significance, in short, hardly can be overstated: it heals two divisions in sovereign power at one and the same time. In the concluding passages of his lecture on parliamentary sovereignty, Dicey even will go so far as to claim that the custom of indemnification does nothing less than offer a solution to one of the constitutive problems of modern political theory. Indemnity, Dicey argues, "affords the practical solution which perplexed the statesmanship of the sixteenth and seventeenth centuries, how to combine the maintenance of law and the authority of the Houses of Parliament with the free exercise of that kind of discretionary power or prerogative which, under some shape or other, must at critical junctures [which Dicey defines as "times of tumult or invasion when for the sake of legality itself the rules of law must be broken"] be wielded by the executive government of every civilized country."[96] If we conclude, then, that the convention of indemnification is the keystone of Dicey's jurisprudence, this is not simply because only Dicey (as distinct from Hearn, Todd, Mill, or Bagehot) confers on indemnity such an important and exemplary status within the English Constitution (although this is certainly true). It is because it is the only example of a law in Dicey's text in which the three grand principles of the English Constitution—as Dicey defines it—converge with such elegance, simplicity, and apparent stability.

2.5 This same Constitution is, however, riven by a fundamental instability. In the indemnification convention as in other things colonial, Britain's experience in Ireland would possess a modular status.[97] In the century that would elapse between 1791 (with the first indemnity act passed in connection with the suppression of Irish uprising) and 1883–84 (when Dicey wrote and delivered his lectures), indemnities in the mold of *Wright v. Fitzgerald* would be repeatedly passed in the colonies. They were passed in connection with government suppression of anti-imperial rebellions in the Cape Colony (in 1836, 1847, and 1853), Ceylon (in 1848), St. Vincent (in 1862), Mauritius (in 1867), New Zealand (in 1860, 1865, 1866, 1867, 1868, and 1882), and, most famously, Jamaica (in 1865).[98] So regular was this convention that, in 1912, Dicey's friend Arthur Berriedale Keith, an orientalist and colonial jurist, could write, "As a matter of fact, it will be found that acts of Indemnity are *invariably* adopted after the exercise of martial law in the colonies."[99]

Significantly, the same could not be said of England itself. On the mainland, as Rossiter wrote in 1948, "the British cabinet has long been capable of any crisis action which Parliament would subsequently indemnify, no matter how dictatorial or unconstitutional it might be." Nevertheless, Rossiter observed, "this has not happened since 1766."[100] Martial law, he observed, "has not been instituted in England itself for over 150 years."[101] Indeed, as

Rossiter later notes, "[i]n the nineteenth century martial law as a legal concept or practical institution can hardly be said to have existed in England itself," yet "it was still a burning issue for the colonies and Ireland, and in this way martial law was kept alive as a product and a part, although an extraordinary part, of English law."[102] While Parliament did pass one indemnity act in 1920, relating to acts that were committed during World War I,[103] this was but the exception that proved the rule, and Parliamentary debate over the bill in May of 1920 (which included at least one reference to Dicey's definition of indemnity as "the highest exercise and crowning proof of the sovereignty of Parliament" and the "legalisation of illegality") bore witness to that status (with members calling the bill "revolutionary" and "unprecedented," "unjust" and "unfair").[104] In theory and juridical practice alike, the "habit of relying on a bill of indemnity," as Finlason put it, emerged not in London but only and precisely in the experience of colonial administration.[105]

We therefore confront what seems to be a paradox. In his 1885 text, Dicey reserves the purest expression of sovereign power within the English Constitution to a juridical measure that, for at least a century before Dicey wrote, had not been used in England at all, and whose paradigmatic juridical forms crystallized under conditions of imperial suppression of anticolonial rebellion. The convention of indemnification, which permits the central principles of the English Constitution to dovetail with harmonious unity, derives almost exclusively from and is applied almost exclusively to the peripheries of the British Empire.[106] At first glance, this strange, inside-out spatiality seems as though it might present a conceptual difficulty for Diceyan jurisprudence. It amounts to the claim, after all, that the *innermost inside* of the British Empire is constituted by a legal practice that exists almost exclusively at its *outermost limits*. On reflection, however, it becomes clear that this exteriorization of the interior is actually a mark of the extreme consistency and rigor of Dicey's jurisprudence. In Dicey's hands, the indemnification convention is more than just a solution to the juridical and political impasses of the English Revolution. Its *historical* merits (as a source of reconciliation between Crown and Parliament) are matched by its *geographical* merits (as a force of reconciliation between London and the dominions). As a legal measure that reconciles, on the one hand, colonial governments' illegal use of force against colonized populations with, on the other hand, those same governments' fidelity to the rule of law, indemnification is also, if not primarily, Dicey's solution for reconciling the tensions of empire itself.

It is the juridical form through which Dicey sought to smooth the inconsistency between the despotism of English colonial administration and the liberalism of metropolitan English legality. Interpreted within the horizon of Diceyan thought, it is the very keystone of imperial jurisprudence: it is the juridical form in the absence of which the structural integrity of imperial unity—not to mention the unity of *imperium*, of law itself—would be imperiled.

That indemnity would fail to perform this function, in South Africa above all, is thus no small matter. But the mode of its failure, the way in which it failed, is even more important. In the years following Dicey's death, his theory of "conventions" did not age well. Dicey argued that "conventions" were observed because their breach inevitably would bring their offender into conflict with the law (although not necessarily to trial as such) and moreover would be punished with political sanctions (such as electoral losses, loss of reputation, etc.).[107] Yet not only was it far from clear that a breach of a convention could also come to possess the status of a breach of law (for, even by Dicey's own account, convention and law are and must remain distinct), but, as H. L. A. Hart later would observe, the Diceyan tradition is arguably even incapable of providing a consistent classificatory distinction between laws and conventions—a distinction in the absence of which the coherence of Diceyan jurisprudence as a whole is threatened.[108] Above all, Dicey left wide open the question of the internal composition of the political sovereign whose ostensibly feared sanction was supposed to retain the power to keep Parliament, ministers, and the executive within the limits of a given convention. Dicey was more than a bit imprecise on this front, referring sometimes to the will of the electoral body, the electorate, and the majority of electors and sometimes to the will of the nation. In part because of this ambiguity, Dicey would be criticized by his contemporaries and by later generations of legal scholars over the question of whether there could ever be such a thing as an "effective" sanction for the departure from a convention.[109]

In colonial legal orders, where race and ethnicity assumed explicitly constitutional status, this criticism was especially pertinent. In South Africa as elsewhere in the British Empire, colonized populations were governed by parliaments whose members those populations were barred by law from electing.[110] Under these constitutional conditions, the possibility of "sanction" in Dicey's sense lay exclusively in the hands of a minority white population whose opinion alone constituted the "political sovereign."[111] Under conditions of colonial legal order, then, Diceyan jurisprudence would authorize a situation in which native populations would be internally excluded within institutions of sovereign power over which they had no legal check (because the conventions that were supposed to limit those institutions were not laws in the first place) or political sanction (because native subjects were precluded from the vote).[112]

This would have serious consequences for the indemnification convention in particular. The purpose of indemnity, in Diceyan jurisprudence, was to reconcile the divide between political sovereignty (in the form of the *salus publica*, the safety, welfare, security, or well-being of the people as expressed through parliamentary representation) and legal sovereignty (in the form of the revolutionary principles that parliament is supreme and that no one is above the law). For white populations, the repeated and even regular indemnities that were passed by the South African Parliament and the Rhodesian Parliament after 1948 not only reconciled this divide; they threatened to obliterate it altogether. Although Dicey's theory of conventions arguably applied in the case of the South African indemnities of 1914 and 1922 (in subsequent elections, those officials responsible for indemnification were voted out of office),[113] the same would not be true of later indemnities. If, under colonial law, indemnity acts were not conditional (as Dicey required), but "invariabl[e]" (as Keith put it in 1912[114]), under South African segregation they became "inevitable" (as Hahlo and Kahn wrote in 1961[115]). At this point already, and on this basis alone, the practice of indemnity under colonial and segregationist conditions departed quite markedly from the theory of indemnity as outlined by Dicey. Under apartheid, this departure became even more pronounced. The indemnity provisions of South Africa's Defence Act of 1957, like the more conventional Indemnity Acts of 1961 (South Africa), 1975 (Rhodesia), 1977 (South Africa), and 1986 (KwaNdebele), protected from prosecution police officers and other government officials who committed crimes in the name of preserving state order, and they sometimes even protected any person committing such crimes while acting under the authority or at the discretion of a police officer or government official.[116] These repeated indemnifications not only brought white populations and white parliaments into greater and greater proximity and alignment; because these legalizations of illegality were acts of parliament over which South African and Rhodesian courts had little to no check, these indemnities also collapsed the distinction between legal and political sovereignty. They allowed for extreme consistency between the rule of law, on the one hand, and illegal acts committed in the name of the *salus publica* of white minorities, on the other. And this, in turn, had an unintended consequence: where the rule of law no longer constrained the biopolitical—where repeated legalizations of illegality dissolved all distinctions between the sovereignty of law and the political supremacy of white populations—biopolitics no longer remained identical to itself either. Biopolitics, unconstrained by the rule of law, imploded into a kind of war.

Its theoretical coherence notwithstanding, the indemnity convention thus failed in practice in a most thought-provoking way. On Diceyan terms, the overarching purpose of indemnity was both historical (to reconcile the tensions between Crown and Parliament) and geographical (to reconcile the tensions between London and the dominions). But even though the colony was the one place where indemnity *was consistently applied*, the colony was also the one place where indemnity *could not be applied consistently*. Nowhere was this impasse more acute than in South Africa, whose unusually developed case law on martial law created the conditions for an unusually developed indemnity jurisprudence as well. Here, the very convention designed to prevent English monarchy or French despotism began to allow something different and worse than despotism or monarchy. By normalizing the legalization of illegalities performed in the name of the safety of white populations, indemnity jurisprudence in South African helped authorize the intolerable situation that the liberal South African philosopher R. F. A. Hoernlé called "race war."[117] Understood in this sense, indemnity was not an apparatus that worked by attempting to *reconcile* the tensions between Crown and Parliament and between London and the dominions; it worked, when it worked at all, by attempting to *export* the tensions between Crown and Parliament from London to the dominions. Whether or not this apparatus did in fact work as planned in London, a question that shall not detain us here, it certainly did not work as planned in the dominions. For one dominion in particular, the more regularly indemnity would be applied, the more impunity it would authorize, and the more it would release the brakes on "race war," all without renouncing fidelity to the "rule of law." Here, indemnity was not at all a keystone. It was an impossible machine.

Chapter 3

INDEMNITY IN CRISIS

3.1 In 1961, the South African right would realize one of its long-held aspirations. South Africa would shed its mostly ceremonial status as a British dominion and become an independent republic. The 1961 republican Constitution—the "high-point" of parliamentary sovereignty in South Africa[1]—coincided, however, with a growing impotence on the part of the apartheid state's juridical and political structures to contain the newly militant "extraparliamentary" political organizations that, in the prior decade, had formed in opposition to it.[2] The telltale symptom of this impotence— the apartheid state's increasing use of extralegal and extrajudicial violence, particularly its "massive deployment of the army and the police"[3]—was most acutely expressed in March 1960, when police officers opened fire on unarmed protestors who had gathered near Vereeniging to protest the apartheid state's pass laws, resulting in the murders of at least sixty-nine black South Africans, many shot in the back while fleeing police.

The Sharpeville Massacre is, for this reason, widely recalled as a turning point in the history of apartheid, up to and including the TRC, whose mandate used the events at Sharpeville to define the beginning of the period into which it inquired. But what's sometimes forgotten in this memorialization of Sharpeville is the specific sort of law that the apartheid state's newly sovereign Parliament would pass in its wake. Seeking to protect from litigation police officers who claimed to have killed in good faith and in the name of public safety, the new republic would inaugurate its parliamentary sovereignty in true Diceyan fashion, by passing, as its very first law, the most sovereign law of all: an indemnity act. This would not be the last time in the twentieth century that a "new" South Africa would come into being through an indemnity act. Nor, as we have seen, was it the first. By 1961, indemnity had become so predictable and normal a part of South African law that one

South African MP would even argue that the truly unprecedented event would have been for Parliament *not* to pass an indemnity act following the Sharpeville massacre.[4] "Are we going to govern ourselves by continuous Indemnity Bills?" Senator Aaron Berman (Cape Town) asked.[5] Particularly at a moment when South Africa was attempting to "turn over a new page" in its history, claiming to inaugurate a republic that was independent of British traditions of law and politics, and at a moment when the basic norms of international law and governance were becoming more postcolonial than ever before (as represented, e.g., by the changing membership and resolutions of the General Assembly of the United Nations),[6] it was symptomatic indeed that this "new" South Africa should try to mark its independence by passing precisely the same sort of deeply British legislation that prepared the way for Union government in 1909.

But while the new republic may have inaugurated its new sovereignty in paradigmatic Diceyan fashion, its use of indemnity also heralded a dynamic that, to the exact degree that it would turn indemnity into a norm of South African governance, would destroy from within Dicey's intricate jurisprudence of indemnity. Over the course of the twentieth century, most especially during the repressive period between 1960 and 1994, each of the components that combined in Dicey's thinking to produce indemnity would undergo a set of subtle but decisive crises. The cumulative effect of these interlinked crises would be to strip indemnity of all of the features that Dicey had attributed to it. Before returning to the TRC, in order to interpret it anew from the standpoint of its reiteration of indemnity jurisprudence, it thus will be necessary to take a last detour. Our aim this time will not be to understand indemnity jurisprudence on its own terms; it will be to recognize some of the specifically colonial dynamics that undid the terms of indemnity jurisprudence from within. To accomplish this aim, we will turn from a rereading of Diceyan texts to a rereading of select cases and laws from the apartheid era. This rereading won't repeat the usual criticisms of the apartheid regime; it will explicate and schematize the sense in which certain cases and laws are symptomatic of a deeper crisis in Diceyan jurisprudence.

3.2 Let's begin with the Public Safety Act of 1953, one of the earliest and most infamous of apartheid security laws. Best known for conferring broad emergency powers on the governor-general, this act also removed liability from those state agents who acted in the bona fide interest of public safety and security.[7] Like the Police Act of 1912 before it and Section 103*ter* of the Defence Act of 1957 after it, this act transformed what was, for Dicey, only a *convention* of the constitution (one that, as such, existed merely in the mode of an assurance or expectation) into a *law* on which the security forces could depend when making choices about its strategic and tactical conduct.[8] In Diceyan terms, this shift had a very precise significance. It not only integrated martial law into normal legislation, rendering martial law itself irrelevant and outmoded.[9] It also dissolved the intricate balance that Dicey attempted to achieve between law and convention. On Dicey's account, the essential difference between "good" British parliamentary sovereignty, on the one hand, and "bad" British monarchy or French *droit administratif*, on the other, was that indemnity was not a certainty but merely anticipated and regularly granted. Indemnification, in other words, could remain commensurable with the rule of law only insofar as it retained the status of a convention. Theorized as a convention, indemnity was thus strictly conditional and contingent.[10] Once indemnity became "inevitable"—as Hahlo and Kahn, writing in 1960, argued it had become in South Africa[11]—it acquired the character of a permanent and unconditional exception to the law within law itself and so ceded its difference from the French *état de siege*. As such, it dissolved from within the difference between the rule of law, on the one hand, and, on the other hand, the monarchical and French juridical forms in opposition to which Dicey identified the rule of law.[12]

Closely connected with this was a second shift in indemnity's temporal horizon. For Dicey, the indemnity convention could not reconcile the rule of law with the supreme law of the *salus publica* unless indemnity acts remained strictly retrospective in application. The illegality of an act first had to stand open and exposed to prosecution before it could be retrospectively legalized by Parliament. At numerous points in his writings, Dicey argues very clearly that in circumstances where ministers feel duty-bound to violate the law (whether on moral grounds or legal grounds or both), they must first engage in this violation and only afterward receive indemnification for their actions. This emphasis on retrospectivity also was clearly recognized in one of the key rulings in early South African security jurisprudence. Writing in *Krohn v. Minister of Defense* (1915), Judge Innes argued,

> The Parliaments both of England, and (so far as I am aware) of the self-governing dominions, while they have refrained from tying the hands of

those in authority, have refused to regularise *in advance* any departure from
the ordinary law, or to endow the Government with exceptional powers for
exceptional emergencies. The result has been to compel those responsible
for the safety of the State to act upon their own judgment *in the first instance,*
and to apply to Parliament for an Act of Indemnity *afterwards.*[13]

Behind this clear temporal priority, as we have seen, was a clear priority of
a juridical and political sort: any indemnification that is not retrospective
would undermine the principle of parliamentary sovereignty, for it would
remove the capacity of Parliament or courts to decide whether or not illegal
actions committed in the public's name were bona fide and warranted by
the necessities of the case, placing that capacity instead in the military com-
manders and executive branch, who then would stand as judges in their own
cause.[14] Absent these priorities, state officials would be able to break laws
with impunity. In a strict sense, then, indemnity acts that were not retrospective would not be indemnity acts at all. Here, too, they would lose any
distinction from the monarchical and French immunities Dicey wanted to
oppose precisely through his emphasis on indemnification.

This jurisprudential self-consciousness was absent in the indemnities
that were written into the 1976 and 1980 amendments of the Defence Act
(not to mention the emergency regulations of 1960 and 1985). Like the controversial 1906 Natal Indemnity Act that was their forgotten precedent,[15]
and almost like a secularized juridical version of the Calvinist doctrine of
predestined grace,[16] these measures indemnified security forces from civil
and criminal liability in advance of any action taken by them.[17] Not surprisingly, the meaning, basis, essence, and limits of indemnity jurisprudence
would be explicitly in question in debates over the Indemnity Acts of 1961
and 1977. In his introduction of the Indemnity Bill of 1961 to Parliament,
F. C. Erasmus, minister of justice, cited as precedents for this bill the Indemnity Acts passed by the Botha and Smuts governments in 1914 and
1922. Erasmus's parliamentary opponents quickly rejected this reasoning on
the grounds that the police in 1914 and 1922 faced armed mobs who had
set buildings on fire, whereas the victims of the Sharpeville Massacre were
unarmed protestors, many of whom had been shot in the back. Between
the two events, the opposition argued, there was simply no analogy.[18] Some
senators tried to justify the Bill by citing the precedent of the Indemnity
Act of 1920, passed in Britain to apply to actions committed by the Brit-

ish government during World War I.[19] Others disagreed, on the grounds that "[T]here is no real precedent for the circumstances in which this Bill is seeking to grant indemnity, because the Union is at peace. We are not at war. And the Union was not at war in the period which this indemnity covers."[20] This confused argument, which seems to have been premised on a conflation between a declaration of martial law and a declaration of war, was compounded by another, even more acute, confusion: a disjunction between the period of time covered in the Indemnity Bill of 1961 and the period of time covered by the government's own declaration of emergency. Whereas the state of emergency was declared only on March 30, 1960, the Indemnity bill proposed to indemnify police for actions beginning on March 21, 1960. This disjunction was a sign of a subtle but decisive dynamic, one that had roots in colonial jurisprudence,[21] but that would only become radicalized in the apartheid era. Increasingly, the apartheid state would disjoin indemnity acts from declarations of martial law, resulting in the monstrous spectacle of an indemnity act that legalized state illegalities *prior to* and *independently of* the apartheid state's own official declaration of a "state of necessity" in the Republic.[22]

To justify these measures, courts began seeking out new and different rationales for the creeping permanence of temporary emergency measures. In particular, courts began to have more frequent recourse to the Ciceronian principle *salus populi suprema lex esto*. After 1961, this principle would be stretched beyond its normal application, in situations of emergency and war, to provide a rationale for the exceptions to law that, normally, only such situations could justify.[23] Recourse to the principle would provide a way to avoid anxious questions about the mode, origin, and limits of internal conflict in South Africa; about the implications of the regularity of martial law and indemnity for the rule of law; and, indeed, about the essence and basis of a legal system in which law and war risked becoming coterminous. In the wake of the Soweto Uprising, this dynamic would be radicalized. By this point, when even National Party jurists themselves were questioning the overextension of Cicero's maxim, South African Party parliamentarians would begin to experiment with somewhat new justifications for indemnity—justifications that strained against the limits and conventions of indemnity as Dicey had formulated it almost a century earlier. In these debates, as distinct from the debates over indemnity in 1961 (which remained narrowly focused on departures from precedent), the very "principle of indemnity" itself (as numerous parliamentarians put it) was in question. Responding to Helen Suzman's argument that the Indemnity Bill of 1977 was flawed because it did not pertain to a "crisis in which a state of emergency or martial law [had] actually been declared,"[24] National Party representative H. J. Coetsee claimed that "the essence of the situation in 1976" required a departure from the very concept of the state of emergency that, in common law, traditionally formed the basis of indemnity acts.

> The essence [of the situation in 1976] is that a classic state of emergency as we knew it and on the basis of which the British developed their indemnity laws and state of emergency laws, simply no longer exists. The situation as we know it today prevails throughout the world and not only in South Africa. Various countries are coming up with various measures with which to deal with this situation, and states of emergency are never declared any more in order to promulgate emergency measures. It is well known, for example, that in a country like Germany the security situation is dealt with, *inter alia*, by questioning and detaining people until they have certain information. They do not declare a state of emergency if an embassy is taken over or an Olympic Games is disrupted. They have other methods of operation because in the face of this threat which menaces the entire world, namely terrorism and the specific methods of terrorism, it is impossible to take steps with regard to a state of emergency and act in accordance therewith, because one would then be living constantly in such a situation.[25]

Under conditions where it was no longer clear that states of emergency were defined by a distinct beginning and end, indemnity jurisprudence could not but enter into crisis as well. In the absence of a declared state of emergency or a declared martial law—in the absence, in other words, of the two central determinations of "necessity" in common law—on the basis of what understanding of the "necessities of the case" would indemnification proceed? On what grounds would it be possible to differentiate "necessary" and therefore legalizable illegalities from illegalities that were unnecessary and thus irremediably illegal? If one of the reasons that South Africa could no longer declare martial law was that its own normal laws were already an extension and prolongation of martial law (as Helen Suzman argued), then to what normal state of affairs would an indemnity now refer and return? If martial law no longer could be punctuated by an indemnity act that would mark its official end, how could either martial law or indemnity perform their own internal objectives, namely, protecting and restoring the rule of law?

The jurisprudential conditions for this crisis were most clearly articulated in an essay authored by Raymond Ruiter in Henry John May's thrice reprinted and often-cited 1935 collection *The South African Constitution*. After citing Dicey's famous formulation of indemnity acts, Ruiter reminded his readers that "there is a distinction [in indemnity jurisprudence] between acts as such done in good faith to suppress rebellion or maintain order and security, and acts in fact necessary for such purposes."[26] Wrongful acts that a person performs out of strict necessity, Ruiter then proceeded to argue, are in no need of an indemnity.

> By the strict necessity of the situation he takes upon himself and his officers and military courts the duty of maintaining order. Acts done by him in such circumstances are protected by the ordinary common law by reason of their strict necessity. Any person whatsoever who does an act with the object of preventing riots, murder, or arson, if that act were strictly necessary, is protected under the common law.[27]

Because acts undertaken out of obvious necessity were not in need of indemnity, Ruiter proposed, the indemnification convention as Dicey formulated it was intended to cover only acts that were not strictly necessary but were nevertheless bona fide. In contrast to illegal acts that are strictly necessary, Ruiter wrote, "it is not always certain that acts done by the authorities in good faith are strictly necessary."[28] These unnecessary but well-intentioned acts, Ruiter claims, are the true reason for indemnity.

> This, then, is the chief object of an act of indemnity: to protect acts done in good faith though they were not strictly necessary. Strictly necessary actions are protected by common law, but acts not strictly necessary, when done in good faith and in times of extreme national emergency, certainly merit protection. It is in order to protect such acts, to quieten doubts and to legalize any sentence of imprisonment imposed during the existence of martial law, that an act of indemnity is required.[29]

The erasure of the necessity requirement in South African indemnity jurisprudence had an alarming implication—particularly when, as in the case of the Indemnity Act of 1961, the indemnity act in question covered not only a very wide range of state officials and officials acting in official capacities but also the state president and the Executive Council and thus, in effect, the state itself (whereas in Dicey, as Hyman Miller dutifully noted, indemnification was supposed to apply only to individuals).[30] Over the bitter objections of parliamentary critics, the NP forced through the erasure of the "necessity" requirement when they passed the first act of the Republic of South Africa.[31] Crucially, in the absence of this "objective" limitation on state illegality, only the "subjective" limitation would remain: the indemnification of individual ministers or officials now would be conditional only on whether or not a given minister or official could be said to have acted in "good faith" in service to public safety and security. But this remaining limitation on indemnity was, at best, exceedingly vague, particularly after *Stanton v. Minister of Justice and Others* (1960). There, in a case involving a woman, Hanah Stanton, who had been detained indefinitely and without trial during the 1960 state of emergency, the Transvaal Provincial Court found that, on the terms of the 1953 Public Safety Act, police officers were not obliged to give reasons for their actions during states of emergency but only had to form a bona fide opinion about who constituted a threat or risk to public safety.[32] In the process of reaching its decision, the court rejected the notion that the Indemnity Acts of 1914 and 1922, which required police officers to prove that their acts were bona fide, provided any guidance. Because each indemnity act creates its own definition of what constitutes a bona fide motivation for an illegal act, the Court reasoned, precedent is of little assistance when the question is what constitutes a bona fide motivation for an act that was legal under the far-reaching powers of the 1953 Public Safety Act.[33] Under these conditions, the onus no longer would be on the police officer to prove that his act was bona fide; the onus now would be on the applicant to prove that a police officer's opinions were *male fide*. After *Stanton*, then, any act by a police officer, however violent or illegal, would be presumed bona fide, unless or until proved otherwise.

The alarming implications of this ruling would become even more apparent in *Mawo v. Pepler* (1960), when the court defended as misguided but nevertheless bona fide a police officer's belief that because unemployment could lead to public mischief, it was desirable to indefinitely detain young unemployed men under the 1960 state of emergency.[34] Yet even though the court's decision on this presumption was formed in opposition to the status of bona fide in the apartheid state's indemnity acts, it left the question of the scope of the indemnity act open, and precisely the same presumption quickly found its way into indemnity acts. In parliamentary debates of June 1961, preceding the passage of the Indemnity Act of 1961 (which protected police offices from liability in connection with the Sharpeville Massacre), the South African Liberal Party senator John Cope would argue that the language of the bill that required officers to have acted "in good faith" was not specific enough and that the bill should instead require that actions be "necessary, unavoidable, and responsible."[35] The minister of justice responded by arguing that the meaning of *bona fide* can be found in any handbook of constitutional law and that the government could be trusted not to indemnify anyone who could be proven to have acted in *male fide*.[36] This same language would reappear in the Indemnity Act of 1977 (which absolved police officers for murdering students in the Soweto Uprising). But, of course, as Helen Suzman would later say (reprising a classic argument dating at least to *Wright v. Fitzgerald*), proving *male fides* in a court of law is "something which every lawyer—even every non-lawyer—knows is impossible."[37] Therefore, even if the bill did, in a purely technical sense, place conditions on the protections it offered, and even if this indemnity did not technically rule out complete recourse to the courts, the very opposite was true, for all effective purposes.

Even this, however, was not the most radical departure from Diceyan indemnity jurisprudence that would be made by the Indemnity Bill of 1977. Despite the obvious crisis resulting from the situation of the Soweto Uprising, apartheid leaders famously refused to declare a state of emergency or martial law in the wake of that uprising's events. Not only would such extreme measures panic foreign investors, so the argument went, but South Africa faced a situation that was without precedent in the English jurisprudence that gave rise to martial law and the jurisprudence of emergency. Having rejected the traditional grounds in common law for thinking about the necessity of indemnification, parliamentarians in 1977 would offer indemnity on the basis of a new necessity: the unique and unenviable situation of the policeman in Southern Africa in general. The reason to indemnify police within South Africa, so the argument continued, was that they were forced onto a military footing by the warfare outside of South Africa. The necessities of the case here metastasized: the "necessity" justifying indemnity was not simply a specific emergency; nor was it the restoration of the rule of law, or even the safety and security of the republic. Indemnity, in this account, was necessary for the same reason that permanent martial law was necessary; but permanent martial law was necessary for the same reason that colonialism as such was necessary—because defending Christian civilization in "darkest Africa" was necessary.[38] In the parliamentary debates of 1977, in other words, indemnity explicitly became what it always already latently had been in Dicey's jurisprudence: a technique for the imperial suppression of anticolonial rebellion. In the process, indemnity jurisprudence gained a relative but nonetheless pronounced conceptual autonomy from the discourse of martial law. The justification for indemnity here no longer derived from the need to put an end to martial law; it now started to produce its own genre of coherence. No longer grounded in a reference to temporary exigencies, to a threat to law or even to state, indemnity here received its justification from a broader and deeper source: from the "necessity" of preserving "civilization itself."

Nasser Hussain has argued that under conditions of colonial governance, where English common law was modified in its applications by colonial powers' racial hostility toward colonized populations, the concept of "necessity" that had hitherto underpinned English martial law as a self-evident fact lost its obviousness and coherence and surfaced for colonial administrators as a source of considerable conceptual anxiety.[39] Apartheid South Africa was a colonial regime in precisely this sense. The disjunction its jurists enacted between "necessity" and the "state of emergency" prepared the grounds for an outright erasure of the "necessity" requirement from the indemnification convention as Dicey formulated it: by the state's own implicit admission, the Indemnity Act of 1961 covered acts that were not committed in a state of necessity.[40] In the absence of any clear test of the "necessities of the case," and with the burden of proof now placed on plaintiffs to show that the illegal acts of policemen and other state officials were motivated by bad faith, any illegal act committed without bad faith in the name of white supremacy could in principle be justified as necessary. As such, the indemnity convention in apartheid South Africa achieved the exact opposite of what it was supposed to achieve according to Dicey's jurisprudence. It did not legalize illegality; *it illegalized legality itself.* Under conditions where "necessity" was everywhere assumed and nowhere in need of proof, any torturer who tortured "honestly" or in "good faith" would qualify for indemnity (as parliamentarians pointed out in not only in 1961 but also in 1799).[41]

No one sounded the alarm about this reversal more clearly than did the Diceyan jurist Anthony Mathews in his 1988 critique of the indemnity provisions set forth in the apartheid state's 1986 emergency regulations.

> The combined effect of this regulation (if valid) and the censorship regulations [of the same 1986 regulations] is to free the security forces *in advance of action taken by them* from both legal and public accountability. Such immunity is disturbing in light of the ominous development in the Eighties of an increasingly lawless police power in the state. There appears to be enough evidence to convince an objective observer of the recent unrest in South Africa that the police "eliminate" troublemakers by shooting, that they support or turn a blind eye to vigilante attacks on activists and the torture is widely practiced on detainees. The growth of official lawlessness makes the scope and validity of the indemnity regulation an issue of the highest importance.[42]

Mathews then proceeds to observe the meaningless of the emergency regulations' limitation of indemnity to "bona fide" acts: "It is by no means clear . . . what *bona fide* means in this context. Does an official who knows that his actions are illegal but honestly believes that they are necessary to deal with the unrest situation, act in good faith? Can an official be said to act in good faith if what he has done is strictly not necessary for the suppression of the unrest?"[43] More than any other clause of the 1986 emergency regulations, Mathews would conclude, its indemnity provisions "enabled the police and military authorities, in the language of the notorious instruction sent to the Port Elizabeth police prior to Uitenhage [a police slaughter of over twenty people on March 21, 1985, the twenty-fifth anniversary of the Sharpeville Massacre], to 'eliminate' the law-and-order troublemakers. When the law enables the security forces to mete out their own version of street justice, it seems bizarre to talk about the requirements of the rule of law."[44]

Indemnity jurisprudence under apartheid South Africa was not, to be sure, completely evacuated of meaning. As Kathleen Satchwell observed in her 1989 analysis of South African indemnity jurisprudence,[45] even in the midst of the apartheid state's abuses of indemnity jurisprudence, there still somehow seemed to remain the slim possibility for indemnity to remain "conditional" and for the old mechanisms of "accountability" to continue to function. In *Damane v. Minister of Police* (1979), for example, a plaintiff successfully sued a policeman who did not intervene in an assault. The police officer claimed that he was protected by the Indemnity Act of 1976, but his chief witness was found to have given false evidence on his behalf, which helped persuade the court that the actions of the officer himself could not be qualified as bona fide.[46] In *Makhasa v. Minister of Law and Order, Lebowa Government* (1988), meanwhile, an indemnity act passed by the "Legislative Assembly" of one of the apartheid state's "independent homelands," was successfully challenged, but only because it was not a "necessary ancillary power" of National States Constitution Act 21 of 1971 (which created Lebowa as an entity of law).[47] In 1994, finally, the Ciskei Division Court would cite South Africa's new Constitution to overturn the Special Indemnity Decree of 1993, which was passed by the "Council of State of the Republic of Ciskei" to protect officials and policemen for their implication in the Bisho Massacre of 1992.[48] In each of these cases, one can discern the remnants of indemnity jurisprudence as Dicey defined it.

By and large, however, these were but isolated cases. By the late 1980s, when the apartheid securocrats were forced to wager on a *new* "new South Africa," indemnification was generally not an exception but a norm. Under these conditions, indemnity was no longer a convention at all: it no longer involved a careful calibration of uncertainty and certainty, a calculated anticipation, a deliberate imposition of anxiety over rights upon state officials and police officers. It was now, more than ever, an "inevitability." With courts unable and often unwilling to apply the "objective" test of indemnification, police faced almost no risk of or liability for illegal acts. What was, in Diceyan jurisprudence, a delicate mechanism designed to balance the rule of law with the supreme law of the *salus publica* now morphed into a "shield" whose main function was to protect the security police from law itself.[49] Despite some significant exceptions, indemnity under apartheid was no longer a convention for the limitation on illegal state activity (as it was for Dicey); it now was a generalized assumption that illegal activity could and would be authorized by the state as long as it was committed in good faith. Indemnity was here no longer the keystone of a parliamentary sovereignty grounded in the principle of ministerial liability. It instead showed signs of undermining the very rule of law it was supposed to preserve. Used more frequently than infrequently, indemnity introduced into the rule of law such a degree of lawlessness that the rule of law itself began to undergo a qualitative change, turning into its opposite. Rather than legalize illegalities, indemnity instead operated to illegalize legality itself. Theorized as a mere exception to the norm, indemnity now showed signs of becoming the norm itself, producing a situation where neither the exception nor the norm itself retained much meaning, and where the distinction between legal violence and illegal violence began to dissolve.[50] If, in this situation, indemnity ceased to function as Diceyan theory had planned, it was not, however, because its original meaning had been misapplied or perverted. To the contrary, indemnity jurisprudence entered into crisis under apartheid precisely because it *reverted to form*, excessively becoming what it always already was. Initially theorized under imperial conditions as a technique for the suppression of anticolonial rebellion, indemnity functioned under apartheid as a carte blanche endorsement for the police to wage "low-intensity war" against individuals and populations opposed to apartheid.[51] Its unacknowledged genealogical root thus reactivated and radicalized, indemnity jurisprudence began to authorize the very "culture of impunity" to which the TRC soon would attempt to put an end.[52]

3.3 Under apartheid, as Dennis Davis, Matthew Chaskalson, and Johan de Waal have argued, "South African constitutional law became a mixture of Diceyan constitutionalism and white majoritarianism, in which democratic rights were conflated with the rights of the majority of white people, or the majority of their parliamentary representatives. It proved to be a fatal brew."[53] Under apartheid, the indemnification convention ceased to be an exceptional instance of parliamentary sovereignty, as Dicey believed it should be. The apartheid state normalized indemnity to such a degree that it ended up undergoing a qualitative change. Theorized by Dicey as an antidote to the state's violation of the rule of law, indemnity jurisprudence under apartheid turned into the opposite: a justification for the state to commit crimes with impunity, and thus too, by extension, a juridical form that ended up rendering law itself "useless."[54] Functioning now less as an antidote to state lawlessness than as the poison itself, indemnity acts did not so much legalize occasional illegalities as illegalize legality itself, allowing "race war" to be prosecuted in the name of the "rule of law."

In the process, indemnity jurisprudence certainly did enter into crisis. Required by the contradictions of the apartheid state, yet no longer intelligible on the terms of Diceyan thought, indemnity jurisprudence under apartheid lost whatever coherence it once may have had. This same crisis, however, had an unanticipated effect: it loosened indemnity's relation to the martial law for which it was supposed to be a mere supplement. Precisely to the extent the apartheid state radicalized and disintegrated indemnity, it also released indemnity from its systematic place and function within Diceyan jurisprudence, freeing up its various component parts for new, different, counterintuitive, and unanticipated uses. An entrenched legal practice in search of a theory, indemnity now began to function in reverse, demanding new and ever broader justifications to the precise extent to which its now "inevitable" enactment manifestly lacked the justification Diceyan thought once seemed to provide for it.

Symptoms of this strange situation, this odd struggle to provide new theories for an otherwise increasingly incomprehensible legal practice, began to appear in the parliamentary and public debates surrounding indemnity bills. Among the most intriguing (because it was the weakest and most confused) of the attempts to produce a new theory for these indemnity acts that were no longer Diceyan came from Theo Aronson of the center-right South African Party. Aronson's speech in support of the Indemnity Bill of 1977 was, however rambling, governed by a submerged logic with contours worth explicating. Aronson's speech reduced the bill to its most basic purpose— self-preservation—in order to suggest that the bill would only achieve this purpose if coupled to a broader program: the reform of the apartheid security state into a free-market, liberal, capitalist economy. Aronson's speech remained well within the limits of Ciceronian reason and the defense of the white supremacist state (he would, it is worth noting, vote for the bill). But it also accomplished something else: it offered up, however inchoately, the contours of a new translation of the term *salus* in Cicero's maxim *salus populi suprema lex esto*. The apartheid state translated this maxim with reference to the logic of the raison d'état, where Ciceronian reason was made to emphasize the "security" or "safety" of the white population. Aronson, by contrast, reframed *salus* on the terms of neoliberal governmentality, where the production and circulation of "wealth" was understood to be the central purpose of governance and where the correct management of "human capital" was understood to be the central means to that end.[55] Under conditions where the high costs of maintaining the apartheid state's security apparatus were beginning to emerge as a counterargument to apartheid policies and where corporate capital itself was thus beginning to question the desirability of state-centered white supremacy,[56] Aronson produced a division internal to the concept of *salus*, opposing its securocratic iteration by retranslating it within the horizon of a newly neoliberal version of South African exceptionalism.

> The hon. the Minister is asking us to enact legislation to indemnify certain people retroactively, but in my humble submission there should, together with this law, go out a clarion call to all responsible South Africans that if we are to survive on the African continent, it can only be if we stand shoulder to shoulder in the fight for survival. . . . This Bill is a product of our time and it calls for the submerging of personal opinion and the emergence of a greater South Africanism of which I know our people to be capable. . . . [T]he wealth of our magnificent country does not lie in its gold, diamond mines or mining industry; our wealth lies in the quality of all our people. Harness that quality and we have the potential of becoming the greatest country in the world.[57]

For Aronson, indemnity was a juridical form that allowed the *implicit premise* of martial law (the notion that the *salus* of the republic is the highest law) to be turned against the *explicit application* of martial law (which, after 1960, was understood to be undesirable for the instability it created in global markets).[58] Not despite but precisely because of the uncertainty and ambiguity in this reasoning (indeed, the next speaker would note the self-contradictoriness of a speech that would argue for the apartheid government's radical indemnity act but against apartheid itself), we witness more than just the incoherence of the indemnification convention as Dicey defines it. The self-exculpatory power internal to indemnity—its capacity to exempt state officials from criminal and civil liability—here began to exceed the supplementary place and function allotted to it within martial law. Stripped down to the *salus* that was its first principle, indemnity in Aronson's iteration could be justified only with reference to a completely new understanding of the South African *salus populi*, one that would come into being only where the apartheid state's security apparatus would no longer artificially restrain the inherently harmonizing forces of free-market capitalism. Already in 1977, in other words, we see indemnity begin to be justified within the horizon of a neoliberal discourse on national reconciliation.

Nearly a decade later, meanwhile, Kathleen Satchwell would make a much different and stronger, but nevertheless commensurable, critique of the apartheid state's abuse of indemnity laws. After a detailed description of the Lebowa Indemnity Act of 1986, Satchwell would note that the act doesn't even achieve its own declared end: the protection of public safety. What is protected by this act, she argued, "is the coffers of the State and the physical freedom of the State's servants. Can the safety of the public be assured or public order be maintained or the state of emergency be terminated by not imprisoning or penalizing the criminals?" "On the contrary," Satchwell concluded, the effect of the law

> could well be to militate against the safety of the public or the maintenance of public order. The regulation is, in a sense, " . . . inimical to the protection of lives, person and property, in that it deprives persons of redress for unlawful killings, assault or damage to property." Surely the protection of lives, person and property is what safety of the public is all about? The regulation gives licence to servants of the State to perform actions which may endanger the public or disrupt public order.[59]

For Satchwell as for Aronson, the apartheid state's indemnity jurisprudence is so out of joint with itself that it could be criticized and opposed on the basis of the innermost premise of the jurisprudence of martial law itself—the Ciceronian principle that the *salus* of the republic is the highest law. As we shall see in section 8.2, this turning against itself by martial law would take on a truly unusual and unanticipated form: it would prepare the basis for a new and specifically pastoral discourse on the salvation of the South African state.

Perhaps the most unprecedented element of indemnity jurisprudence under apartheid, however, was its coupling with a second mechanism: the compensation committee, which was charged with identifying and compensating the "innocent victims" among the many injured and killed at Sharpeville. Particularly after the Sharpeville Massacre of 1960, South Africa was the object of censure by the very Western states whose civilization was the foundation for the "necessity" of the apartheid state's extraordinarily repressive measures.[60] Because of its export-oriented economy and because its regional power in Southern Africa depended in part on its continued military alliance with the United States under conditions of the Cold War, South Africa could not afford to ignore this censure completely. Consequently, the National Party added to its Indemnity Bill of 1961 what it understood to be an unprecedented innovation into indemnity jurisprudence: as part of what would eventually come to be called the 1961 Indemnity and Compensation Act, the South African Parliament authorized the apartheid government to create a committee to provide *ex gratia* payments to "innocent victims" who suffered police repression.[61] In 1961, *ex gratia* payment was proposed simply as a discretionary gesture on the part of the apartheid government, an act "of grace" or (as Helen Suzman later would put it) of "executive charity"[62] that the apartheid government extended not on the basis of legal obligation but simply "out of the goodness of its own heart,"[63] as a way to acknowledge that among the sixty-nine protestors killed by the police at Sharpeville were a number of individuals who were not at all deranged communist agitators hell-bent on attacking the police.

This acknowledgment immediately created a host of complicated juridical questions, not a few of which pivoted on a demand for greater administrative knowledge about the actual events of the Sharpeville Massacre. Were all or only some of those killed at Sharpeville innocent victims? If only some, by what criteria could one decide who was innocent? Who, precisely, would decide? What safeguards would there be for error in their decisions? And what would happen should inquiry into an injury or death begin to point to signs of a *male fide* intention on the part of the police? How, if at all, would that evidence be reconciled with the indemnity bill for which compensation was supposed to be the counterpart? These questions would return in parliamentary debate over the South Africa Indemnity Bill of 1977 and the Rhodesian Indemnity Bill of 1975, both of which established committees designed to disburse *ex gratia* payments and both of which cited the Indemnity and Compensation Act of 1961 as their precedent. Speaking once again with explicit reference to world opinion, South Africa's parliamentarians now formalized *ex gratia* payments to an even greater degree. Parliamentarians now spoke of *ex gratia* payments as a way to supplement the "grey area"[64] in indemnity jurisprudence, namely, those who were wrongfully killed by police (e.g., schoolchildren) but for whose killing no one was liable (because police had been indemnified). To differentiate these truly "heartbreak cases"[65] from the cases of those killed while rioting and agitating (with no heartbreak, apparently), a more sophisticated and independent version of the 1961 committee was established. New procedures and tests were established to define and understand what constitutes an innocent victim of political violence. Parliament accepted, more explicitly than in 1961, the premise that the state accept a modicum of responsibility—which is not to say liability—for the innocent victims harmed by those it indemnified. In 1977, MP W. V. Raw would sum up the new precedent in a formula: "Indemnify the policeman but provide simple machinery for compensation for the innocent victim."[66] MP D. J. L. Nel would articulate what he called the "principle" of the *ex gratia* payment.

> When an *ex gratia* payment is involved, the State takes upon itself the responsibility which individual members of the Force or the Public Service may have had. In other words, the State takes upon itself an additional function of protection in that it takes upon itself the responsibilities of individual members of the police or of other State officials. That is why the principle of an *ex gratia* payment must be upheld.[67]

Even though there are certainly precedents for the compensation of plaintiffs of indemnified officials (most notably in the case that Dicey himself treats as exemplary, the Morant Bay Rebellion of 1865), and even though each of the indemnity acts passed in 1900, 1914, and 1922 included "special tribunals" for the adjudication of various issues connected with indemnity, with compensation for victims set forth in Indemnity Act 15 of 1900 and Indemnity and Undesirables Special Deportation Act 1 of 1914 (as amended in 1919) as well, many parliamentarians nevertheless declared unprecedented their call for a committee connected to indemnity whose mandate was to disburse compensation to those it judged to be innocent.[68] The formation of this committee was announced in 1961.

> The Government has now decided, and I have already taken the necessary action, that where persons consider that they have a *bona fide* complaint, a committee under the chairmanship of the Government Attorney will go into such complaints thoroughly, investigate the claims which are made and then recommend *ex-gratia* payments to the Government.[69]

The political purpose of this proposal was clear: not only would the existence of the committee permit the government a response to the criticism from abroad that the South African government was persecuting innocent South Africans, but it also implied that not every person killed at Sharpeville was "innocent," thereby adding justification and legitimacy to the killings.

The opposition would object on three grounds. First, the government was both admitting liability (because it was acknowledging that, on its own terms, "innocent persons" were killed and injured by its police) and not admitting liability (because the government was doing this not out of obligations but purely out of grace or charity, out of the goodness of its own heart). To the opposition, therefore, *ex gratia* payments were either disingenuous or meaningless or both.[70] Second, the government was appropriating to the executive a function—the determination of innocence—that should properly be left to the judiciary.[71] This was all the more troubling to the opposition because the apartheid government was entirely unclear about the basis on which and means by which it intended to establish the difference between "genuinely innocent victims" it proposed to compensate and the rest of the "roaring mass of humanity" who (as W. H. D. Deacon put it in 1977) "only violence will stop . . . once a riot is underway."[72] Third and finally, the government was acting as judge in its own case. Because the Indemnity Act of 1961 protected not only individuals but also the state itself from prosecution, the state's interests were directly at issue in the compensation committee that the minister of justice had proposed.[73] Although the minority would vote against the bill on these grounds, it would pass, and a precedent would be created.

This act would be cited as precedent not only for the South African Indemnity Act of 1977 but also for the Rhodesian Indemnity and Compensation Act of 1975. In these laws, the rationale for the existence of compensation committees would be more developed (they were now understood to be supplements for the "grey areas" in indemnity jurisprudence, chances for the state to redress those "heart-break cases" in which police who were acting in good faith and hence were indemnified nevertheless killed innocent civilians);[74] the procedures for identifying innocent victims would become more elaborate and precise (involving determinations, this time, by an attorney and a supreme court judge); and the committee on whose authority compensation would be disbursed would be more "diverse," more reflective of South Africa's multiracial society (the committee would now consist of not only the minister of justice but also the secretaries for colored and Bantu administration and the secretary for social welfare and pensions). We would also see fresh arguments attempting to make sense of the new temporality of an indemnity act passed prior to the conclusion of the events it covered: the merit of a compensation board, as opposed to a civil court, was that it would not have to wait until conflict was over in order to provide recompense to those injured by the state.[75]

According to the emerging logic of *ex gratia* payments, then, the compensation board would not then amount to a removal of the right to courts; it would be a better and even speedier way to accomplish the same ends.[76] It certainly would be a way—as advocates of transitional justice might put it—to respond to the needs of "genuinely innocent victims" without the sound and fury of the adversarial process of the trial, a way to do justice to the "heart-break cases" in the absence of the courtroom's legal technicalities. But it above all would be, as its legal Latin indicates, an expression of sovereign immunity—the act of a sovereign that defines itself by its capacity to exempt itself from the same law it enforces. There was no legal obligation for the state to take upon itself the responsibility of compensating the losses of those who suffered at the hands of its officials and police officers. When the state acted as a proxy of this sort, it admitted no wrong; it acted on the basis of grace alone. In this respect, the *ex gratia* payment was not at all unprecedented. It marked the redoubled return of the monarchical maxim "The king can do no wrong" within the very institution—the sovereign parliament—that was supposed to have rationalized, constrained, and neutralized it.

3.4 In 1961—the same year that South African parliamentarians would cite Dicey on the topic of indemnification in order to exculpate the state for liability for murder and torture—the Israeli Supreme Court would cite Dicey on the matter of individual ministerial responsibility to reject Adolf Eichmann's plea that he was "just following orders."[77] Given this apparent divergence in the itinerary of Diceyan thought, it would be tempting to conclude that the South African government did nothing more than "pervert" or "abuse" a Diceyan jurisprudence that was, on its own terms, otherwise perfectly coherent and practical. But is this conclusion well drawn? To be sure, when liberal Diceyan critics of apartheid objected to the excesses of the apartheid state,[78] they were correct to argue that the apartheid state's indemnities were almost entirely without relation to the intricate measures Dicey described and prescribed between 1885 and 1915. But there is an important sense in which this defense of Dicey would betray Diceyan jurisprudence just as much as did the apartheid government when it radicalized indemnity's self-exculpatory powers. For Dicey, indemnity wasn't just the highest power and crowning proof of sovereign power; it was a juridical form that derived almost exclusively from and was applied almost exclusively to the colonies. The conclusion that the apartheid state perverted or abused Diceyan indemnity jurisprudence rests on the premise that Diceyan indemnity jurisprudence was at some point coherent in the first place; but this premise itself rests on the prior assumption that indemnity could be applied consistently under conditions of colonial governance. And this assumption, as we have seen, is questionable at best.

What is colonial administration, after all? In Southern Africa, as Mahmood Mamdani has argued, colonial administration involved a twofold bifurcation. It was split not only between *colonial citizens* (who governed themselves by representation in Parliament and enjoyed the same rights and privileges as their metropolitan counterparts) and *native subjects* (who could not be governed except by "custom" or "tradition" and were considered unable to survive absent the constraints of an autocratic chief) but also between *rural despotism* (the administration, through decentralized indirect rule, of "Native Areas" and, later, Bantustans) and *urban despotism* (the administration, through centralized direct rule, of "locations" and "townships").[79] Implicit in Mamdani's analysis is the understanding that native "uprising" was a permanent possibility that, in turn, exerted a constant pressure on the very structure of colonial administration itself.[80] To underline this possibility, it is useful to supplement the administrative distinction Mamdani outlines by underlining its accompanying indistinction: the systematic confusion between the civil category "subject" and the military category "national enemy."[81] An English subject but not an English citizen, the native was understood by colonial administration not only as a childlike barbarian whose errors could be corrected by means of law but also as a childish rebel whose incorrigible disloyalty needed to be anticipated and prevented by means of military force.[82]

At once a potential citizen (whose latent capacities could be developed through tutelage and trusteeship) and a potential enemy (whose manifest obedience to law concealed deeper hostilities and proclivities to violence), the native was a juridical and administrative figure who crossed wires in liberal jurisprudence that normally remained distinct. In the late nineteenth century, metropolitan jurisprudence was governed by a relatively recent distinction between the police (where a police officer was simply "a person who was paid to perform as a matter of duty acts which if he were so minded he might have done voluntarily" as an ordinary citizen[83] and who was unarmed, on principle, since the passage of the 1829 Metropolitan Police Act) and the standing army (which prior jurists had considered a threat to English freedom, an exception or anomaly in English history, or even an "excrescence" of the militia, but which Dicey, in an explicit reversal, was determined to consider a normal and necessary part of civic life).[84] This distinction rested, in turn, on a qualitative difference. The object of the police was to apprehend criminals whose acts may be illegal but whose lives were nevertheless protected by law (with rare exceptions, as in the case of self-defense) and who could not then be killed with impunity. The object of the military, by contrast, was to defeat enemies whose acts were legal (inasmuch as they obeyed the laws of war) but whose lives were generally not protected by law (with important exceptions, as in the case of the prisoner of war) and who could therefore be killed with impunity (for *inter arma silent leges*, "during war, the law is silent"). Whereas the police aimed at preventing mischief perpetrated upon the public from within, the military sought to defend it against aggressions from the outside.[85] Like most legal distinctions, the distinction between police and military was refined with continual reference to an ambiguous threshold case: the riot. In the riot, colonial jurists found a case where the clear *qualitative* distinction between police and military turned out to rest on a much less clear *quantitative* distinction.[86] Depending on the degree of its intensity, a riot could become a rebellion, and a rebellion could become a revolution; and depending on the amount of force necessary to suppress a given riot, the police could call the military to their aid. The criminal—the rioter—accordingly could shade into something much different: the rebel, which is to say, an "internal adversary" on whom the sovereign was allowed to wage war *as if* against an "external adversary."[87] As such, the riot was that event in which the *qualitative juridical distinction* between criminal and enemy and between police and military force had the potential to become confused by a *concrete quantitative indistinction* between the same.[88]

In the colony, where the *native subject* doubled as a potential *national enemy*, this confusion would become a systematic part of native administration.[89] Here the *qualitative differences* generated by late nineteenth-century racial theories produced, in turn, *quantitative differences* in the juridical distinction between riot and rebellion: because of the racial distinction between "Englishmen by birth and descent" and "foreign races," the colonial rioter always would be much closer to the rebel than was the metropolitan rioter. In the colonies, as distinct from the metropole, the specter of "race war" led writers such as William Francis Finlason to argue that it would be desirable not to wait until after actual rebellion occurred before declaring martial law but, instead, to declare it as a precaution, prior to any actual rebellion, at the mere sign of the "spirit" of rebellion.[90] For these jurists, race itself became intelligible as the cipher of a rebellion that was permanently imminent, the preparation for which was, all appearances to the contrary notwithstanding, always silently underway among racially marked populations. But from this, of course, it followed that there could be no foundation in the colony for the temporal limits, the discrete beginnings and discrete ends, that allowed the "state of necessity" to remain a mere exception to the rule of law in the metropole. Under colonial conditions, therefore, a racist hermeneutics provided the premise for the "state of necessity," this temporary exception to law, to become prolonged into a norm and for the distinction between rioting and rebelling to become structurally indistinct. But where this distinction dissolved, so too did the distinction between police and military forces and, above all, between criminals (who retained the right to be free from unjustified trespass and to sue for damages if this right is violated)[91] and enemies (who could and must be killed with impunity). Colonized populations, according to this logic, weren't simply "native subjects" whose riots were to be punished by the police forces led by autocratic chiefs; because colonized populations always already carried, in the view of colonial jurists, the indelible potential to double as "national enemies," their riots, not to mention their simple political activity, were signs of incipient anticolonial rebellion that needed to be defeated at any costs if the existence of the colonial state was not to be thrown into question.

In the Union of South Africa, the confusion of military and police force would be institutionalized beginning at least in 1913.[92] South Africa's national police force, in contrast to the unarmed bobbies called into being by the Peel Act, was modeled on the Natal Police Force, which doubled as a colonial occupation force vested with an expressly military aim.[93] "In the state built in 1902," Martin Chanock has observed, "law and order were secured by the creation of a paramilitary police force which was to combine the roles of policing and internal occupation."[94] But the converse was true as well. Section 76 of the Defence Act of 1912 allowed for the military to participate in the prevention and suppression of internal disorder, and in 1907, 1913, 1914, and 1922, the newly formed South African Defence Force was deployed to prevent and suppress internal disorder that the South African Police (SAP) could not contain.[95] In 1929, the permanence of "the native menace" would be formalized in the shape of the so-called Kafir Manifesto, a declaration of white political will grounded on the notion that "there is always the possibility of peril from the native."[96] In 1939, the liberal philosopher R. F. A. Hoernlé would describe this situation by declaring the obvious: "first and main function of the White Defence Force" was not to defend the Republic of South Africa against "external" threats but "to defend the White Community against a possible uprising of the Native peoples."[97] An apparatus in which the relations of police to "native subjects" were militarized and in which the defense forces of the military focused on "internal enemies" may be characterized by some as "despotism" and by others as "tyranny" or "totalitarianism."[98] But it might be better to formulate one's understanding of colonial administration in Chakrabartyian terms, by emphasizing the sense in which this apparatus was defined by aporias that exceeded from within the lexicon of political philosophy both classical (which gives us the terms *despot* and *tyrant*) and modern (from whence *totalitarian* derives). It might be better, that is, to locate the hallmark violence of colonial rule in a subtle but decisive vanishing point, a point where native subjects (always about to rebel) double as national enemies, where criminal acts (e.g., cattle thefts) double as acts of war, and where colonial government sustained itself with police forces that (as in the case of Natal) doubled as military forces (and vice versa).

From this perspective, the violence of the apartheid state becomes intelligible in its specifically colonial pathogenesis. "The aim of an army," Desmond Tutu wrote in 1999, "is to kill enemy personnel and knock out enemy equipment. It exists to destroy, to kill the enemy. As resistance to apartheid intensified in the 1980s, this philosophy was increasingly applied internally. Thus instead of apprehending suspects and culprits it became more and more the practice to eliminate them."[99] Not least because it is qualified with reference to a difference of degree (which, as we have seen, is the foundation in common law of the distinction in kind between military and police), it's hard to disagree with Tutu's claim about the confusion of police and military forces in waning days of the apartheid state. Not so hard to disagree with is a similar claim set forth in the *TRC Report,* where we read,

> With the intensification of conflict inside South Africa in the mid-1980s, tactics that had worked externally began to be applied on the domestic front.

The domestic application of an essentially military counter-revolutionary strategy was a significant landmark. Whereas the SADF had previously directed its military operations at external targets, it now began to play an increasing role in support of the SAP inside South Africa. The policing of internal resistance became militarized.[100]

This claim rests on a questionable presupposition: that there was ever a point in time when the SAP was not already thoroughly militarized. To trace this confusion only to the mid-1980s is to confirm the argument of critics such as Mahmood Mamdani, Colin Bundy, Deborah Posel, Mark Sanders, and Premesh Lalu, who argue that one of the decisive and troubling effects of the TRC is to have framed the problem of apartheid in such a way as to have foreclosed on the question of the apartheid state's own reliance on the theories and practices of colonialism.[101] Under conditions where colonial subjects always also remained potential enemies, one can see how the theoretical possibility that Dicey maintained on principle in 1885—that the early nineteenth-century distinction between police and military would dissolve and that a fully armed population, a citizenry fully transformed into a racially defined *posse comitatus*, would emerge in its place—would become a normal and regular part of South African governmentality.[102] From this perspective, the significance of agencies like the Bureau of State Security and, later, the Civil Cooperation Bureau is that they formalized and institutionalized the same confusions that inhered in colonial governance—between police and military, criminal and enemy, law enforcement and battle, inside and outside, and so on—only with reference not to riot or rebellion, much less to colonial occupation, but to "terrorism."[103]

To pay attention to the colonial conditions for the apartheid state's violence is not only, however, to achieve a better understanding of the limits of the TRC's account of that violence; it is also to understand the reasons why indemnity jurisprudence came into crisis during apartheid. Under conditions where the "state of necessity" tended toward indefinite prolongation and where martial law therefore tended to become permanent, the instant of indemnity theorized by Dicey—the point in time when indemnity could retroactively legalize illegality and, in so doing, restore the rule of law— never fully arrived. Applied to a colonial situation that bore the hallmark of a structural disappearance of quantitative distinctions between police and military force, indemnity jurisprudence could provide little to no basis for jurists to draw qualitative distinctions between legal military actions against external enemies, on the one hand, and illegal police violence against internal subjects and citizens, on the other. Indemnity jurisprudence entered into crisis in South Africa not because it ceased to work but because it worked under conditions that obliged it to work in overdrive, to work not as an exception but as a norm. From a genealogical perspective, the problem is not that the apartheid state abused indemnity jurisprudence, thus perverting an otherwise coherent doctrine. It is that it used indemnity jurisprudence with excessive loyalty, thus waking the incoherence that had lain asleep in indemnity jurisprudence from the very beginning. The indemnification convention failed to retroactively reconcile illegality and legality in South Africa not because it was misapplied, but because *the one form of government most responsible for applying indemnity*—the governmental apparatus of colonial administration, from which the "known disposition" to wage war, and thus wartime itself,[104] never completely disappeared—was also *the one form in which indemnity's basic concepts were fundamentally inapplicable.* And this impasse, this silent but decisive limit internal to Diceyan jurisprudence, was all the more reason why an unprecedented reiteration of indemnity would become not only desirable, but necessary.

Chapter 4

INDEMNITY IN THE TRC

4.1 Our detours complete, let's return now to our point of departure, and formulate in succinct terms the understanding of the TRC that results.

On the one hand, the apartheid state's deployment of indemnity jurisprudence not only put indemnity jurisprudence into crisis, but also produced the very conditions under which it became necessary to devise an institution like the TRC. In the 1992 speech that is widely considered to have introduced the very idea of a Truth Commission into South Africa's political transition, Kader Asmal argued against "the exoneration of those guilty of crime," observing that "time and again the apartheid state has bestowed immunities both prospective and retrospective, on police and military action, and in so doing has debased criminal law and encouraged state lawlessness."[1] Hardly has there ever been a more concise and precise summary of the crisis of indemnity jurisprudence under apartheid. If the main purpose of the TRC was, as José Zalaquett put it, to investigate "human rights violations which were ostensibly illegal under the laws of apartheid but were nevertheless committed by the regime to preserve the system,"[2] then the crisis of the indemnification convention has to be considered as a condition for the "culture of impunity" the *TRC Report* so unequivocally criticized.[3] The hallmark of this crisis—the illegalization of legality itself—authorized the debasement of law and the state lawlessness that, in turn, required the invention of an institution like the TRC.

On the other hand, however, indemnity jurisprudence *also* provided the TRC with the most direct and concrete precedents for the amnesties it offered. In its initial draft, the TRC Bill was a simple extension of what, in 1977, parliamentarians from all parties called the "principle of indemnity."[4] It was a classic Diceyan attempt to provide retroactive protection from civil and criminal prosecutions to those who violated the laws passed by the apartheid state's own sovereign parliament. That in the revisions of this legislation the ANC insisted that the TRC's mandate "extend beyond the issue of indemnity to harness 'the cleansing power of truth,'"[5] implies that the TRC's amnesty provisions alone were not sufficient to abrogate indemnity jurisprudence. As we shall see in what follows, the opposite, in fact, would seem to be true.

What then do we get if we put these two sides of indemnity jurisprudence together? Not only was indemnity jurisprudence *doubly critical for the TRC's genesis*; it also, as such, provides an interpretive standpoint that allows us *to dialecticize the TRC's practice.* Only by recalling indemnity jurisprudence do we become able to understand that *the TRC itself reused the very power whose abuse it criticized in the apartheid state.* To understand the genealogy of indemnity is to understand the limit at which the juridical "subject" that was the TRC (its legal status, that is to say, as a "juristic person" that was vested with the power to indemnify) entered into a relation of identity with the very same juridical "object" the TRC proposed to investigate, censure, and finish (namely, the "culture of impunity" the TRC as a whole sought to criticize and to end). And it is only with reference to this limit, in turn, that we become able to name the dialectical extremes that together defined the transitional mechanism at the core of the TRC.

From this perspective, the unprecedented audacity and even genius of the TRC was not at all that it discovered a "golden mean" between vengeance and forgiveness. Nor was it that the TRC charted a "middle way" between the "victor's justice" of Nuremberg, on the one hand, and Latin American blanket amnesties, on the other. *It was that the TRC attempted to put an end to indemnity jurisprudence by reiterating that same jurisprudence in an exceptionally salutary way.* It was that the TRC tried to turn a version of the techniques and juridical powers *proper to* martial law into the juridical basis for an *exposure and criticism* of the conditions under which it became possible for the agents of martial law to commit illegal, intolerable, and inhuman acts in the first place.

To this interpretative standpoint there corresponds, in turn, a new norm for evaluating the success or failure of the TRC. This is a norm that must be distinguished from the excessively normative discourse of transitional justice, which is derived from a mix of watered-down psychoanalysis (or rather what Freud would call "'wild' analysis"[6]), bleached-out theology (heavy on pieties and light on descriptive analysis), and symptomatic silence on questions of South Africa's colonial jurisprudence (preferring instead "comparative" analyses of various Truth Commission "models" that have been deployed around the world). It's a norm whose measure of best and worst derives immanently from the colonial juridical form that was doubly critical for the TRC's amnesty provisions. At best, "amnesty" as deployed in the Amnesty Committee will *not* have been just one more indemnity. It will have been an indemnity that called into question the colonial conditions under which indemnity itself became so normal a part of South African jurisprudence, and that thus too raises questions about the continued "necessity" of indemnity jurisprudence itself. It will have been, in other words, *an indemnity to end all indemnities*, an indemnity that had the power to render "defeasible" or "inoperative" the thoroughly colonial jurisprudence from whence it came. This same power, however, also will have been the locus of the Amnesty Committee's most definitive risk. By limiting itself to an implicit or even unselfconscious reiteration of indemnity jurisprudence, rather than by explicitly stating the conditions under which it would be possible to undo indemnity jurisprudence, and at worst by employing with little modification the same core mechanisms that defined indemnity jurisprudence under apartheid only now under a new name, the Amnesty Committee will have risked leaving in place the conventions of the same indemnity jurisprudence the TRC as a whole, in its *Report*, recommended the end of.[7]

From this perspective, the critical analytic question is not *whether* the TRC's amnesty is a reiteration of indemnity jurisprudence in the Diceyan paradigm (and therefore too, by extension, the martial law jurisprudence of which indemnity is, in the Diceyan sense, the supplement). It's first of all *the precise character* of that reiteration. Certainly, as we saw in section 3.3, a constitutive part of the crisis of indemnity jurisprudence was that it lost any capacity to recognize the very juridical forms it also set into motion. This loss was not simply negative; it was also generative. It produced the conditions under which new juridical forms could and perhaps even needed to come into being. But because these forms came into being in and through reiterations of indemnity jurisprudence, it's necessary to inquire closely and carefully into the precise relations that comprised those reiterations. Through what modes of repetition and difference, and through what relations of transposition and negation, condensation and displacement, reversal and opposition, substitution and supplementation, was indemnity translated into amnesty? How did it come to pass that the extralegal and quasi-juridical powers generated in and through past states of emergency—such as *ex gratia* payments from innocent victims of police violence—came to find their way into the extralegal and quasi-juridical powers of the PNR Act? What differences, if any, did the TRC seek to introduce into its repetition of these powers?

The purpose of this book is not to produce definitive answers to these questions. It is simply to put a finger on the questions that need to be posed if the TRC's unprecedented character—its character as an event—is to be adequately named at all. Reasonable people certainly will disagree about the precise way and degree to which indemnity jurisprudence figures into the origin of the TRC. But there should be little disagreement on the genealogical preconditions for that disagreement, or for that matter on the symptomatic silence on this genealogy with the scholarly field that so far has arrogated to itself the right to monopolize discourse on the TRC. Given its central place and function not only in the apartheid state's theory of parliamentary sovereignty, but also in the genesis of the PNR Act that established the TRC, indemnity jurisprudence provides a hermeneutic horizon for interpreting the TRC's self-exculpatory powers that is at once *concretely rooted in the TRC's most direct precedents* and *almost completely absent from transitional justice's ethical reflections on "forgiveness" within the TRC*. In what follows, we shall not attempt to settle the questions that emerge within this horizon. We shall simply demonstrate the possibility and desirability of the questions themselves, by reexamining some well-known features of the TRC now from the standpoint of the indemnity jurisprudence that the TRC at once inherits and, at best, opposes.

4.2.1 Let's begin with the Amnesty Committee. In its nuts and bolts, this committee's work was reducible to two mechanisms.[8] Charged with "the granting of amnesty to persons who make full disclosure of all the relevant facts relating to acts associated with a political objective committed in the course of the conflicts of the past,"[9] the Amnesty Committee evaluated the applications it received on the basis of two tests.[10] The first, the "political objective" test, required applicants to demonstrate that the purpose of their illegal acts was consistent with the mandate or mission of the organization of which they were a member (whether that organization was the ANC, the apartheid state, or some similar political organization). An important subset of this test was the "proportionality" requirement, which directed the Amnesty Committee to ask whether or not an applicant's illegal act was a suitable, necessary, and reasonable means to the end of accomplishing his or her stated "political objective."[11] The "full disclosure" test, meanwhile, required applicants to reveal "all relevant facts" related to the illegal act for which they were asking to be indemnified, up to and including the question of who in their organization's chain of command ordered or authorized the illegal act. According to the letter of the law, applicants for amnesty had to pass both tests: not only did they have to demonstrate that their illegal acts were committed as part of a political struggle (and not out of private malice or for personal gain) and that their acts were not out of proportion with the end for which they were a means; they also had to make full disclosure of their acts. On these grounds, an applicant was to have been refused amnesty if they fully disclosed an illegal act without a political objective; or fully disclosed an illegal act that had a political objective, but was an unsuitable, unnecessary, or unreasonable way to achieve that objective; or incompletely disclosed an illegal act that was both defined by and proportional with a political objective.[12]

4.2.2 According to the usual history of the PNR Act, these mechanisms originated in Section 6.5.2(a) of the report of the Groote Schuur Working Group ("Whether or not an offence is political depends on the facts and circumstances of each individual case. The question is thus approached on a case by case basis"), which in turn derived from a set of criteria called the "Norgaard Principles."[13] Drawn up in 1989 by Professor Carl Norgaard as part of the settlement plan between the South African government and the South West Africa People's Organization (SWAPO) for the establishment of an independent Namibian state, the Norgaard Principles outlined an approach to the definition of "political offences" that both parties could agree on (although it must be noted that South African negotiators opposed any distinction between criminal and political offenses)[14] and that accordingly served as the basis for retrospectively legalizing the illegalities committed not only by police and military forces (as in a standard indemnity agreement) but also by SWAPO militants, who, once retrospectively legalized in this manner, then could serve without fear of prosecution in an independent Namibian government.[15] Using European extradition laws that distinguished between political dissidents and political terrorists,[16] Norgaard settled on five criteria for the definition of a political offense: the motivation of the offender (whether political or merely venal), the political and military context of the offense (whether or not it was part of an uprising or political disturbance), the nature of the political objective (whether it was aimed at overthrow of the government or policy change), the legal and factual nature of the offense (with special reference to its "gravity" or "seriousness"), and the relationship between the offense and the political objective being pursued (whether or not the former was proportional to the latter).[17]

Although there can be no doubt that the Norgaard Principles directly informed the PNR Act of 1995, there is good reason to doubt those histories of the PNR Act that limit their analyses of the genesis of the Amnesty Committee to the Norgaard Principles alone. While the Norgaard Principles have been criticized for the specific way they distinguish between crimes and political offenses, there has been little analysis of the non-European conditions under which it became necessary for Norgaard to turn to European extradition law to draw these distinctions. To recall these conditions, it will be helpful to return to a forgotten precedent for the Norgaard Principles in South African colonial jurisprudence. In August 1900, in the midst of the Anglo-Boer War, the Parliament of the Cape of Good Hope entered into contentious debate over a bill that eventually would become Indemnity and Special Tribunals Act 6 of 1900. The object of the bill was to establish a special court to try the defeated rebels, one that could both prosecute and punish their ringleaders and integrate their rank and file into peaceful society by means of a policy of leniency and clemency (which, in the concrete, came in the form of a version of the Roman law penalty of a "loss of status" in the political community for a period of five years).[18] In his reading of the bill, James Rose Innes emphasized that the proposed legislation drew a distinction between, on the one hand, a person who joined the rebellion merely "for his own benefit and to please himself" and who may have committed ordinary crimes under the cover of rebellion and, on the other hand, an actual rebel whose crime was, Innes said, of a "political character" (which the bill defined as "any crime incidental to or forming part of political disturbances"). To explain the sense in which "political crimes" exceeded mere cases of treason, Innes explained that the source of the bill's definition of "political crimes" was English extradition law, particularly a case in which an English court refused to extradite to Switzerland a Swiss man who shot a Swiss member of government. As Innes explained, even if the murder "might have been the blackest murder in the world," it was "incidental to a political disturbance" and hence protected by the English common-law principle that "there could be no extradition for crimes of a political character."[19] Similarly protected were the "political crimes" that were at the center of the Indemnity and Special Tribunals Act. As neither conventional acts of treason, on the one hand, nor normal acts of crime, on the other, the "political crimes" for which indemnity was reserved had a very specific condition: "[t]here must be two contending parties, and the man must have taken part on one side or the other."[20]

Implicit in Innes's presentation of the category of "political crimes" was a swerve from indemnity jurisprudence in the strict Diceyan sense. The Indemnity and Special Tribunals Act of 1900 did not presuppose, as Diceyan indemnity jurisprudence presumed it could and should, a single or unified *salus publica* in the name of which an illegal action may be retrospectively legalized. Quite the opposite: it started from the assumption that no such *salus publica* existed, that there was no such thing as *a* South African public in the name of whose safety or security one could act. It assumed, to the contrary, that the only form of political allegiance that existed in the wake of the Boer War was allegiance to a faction. On the terms of classical political philosophy, the polity that is divided into factions is not a polity at all: it is a divided city, a city afflicted by the illness of civil war (or *stasis*). On these terms, the traditional antidote is not indemnity, but a very different power: amnesty. Whereas indemnity is an exceptional measure according to which an "already constituted" power protects itself from an existential threat, amnesty in the classical sense is an act of "constitution-making power," an expression of will that retroactively creates or produces the very political unity to which it also refers.[21] Whereas indemnity presupposes political unity in order to legalize illegalities committed to protect it, classical amnesty presupposes civil war in order to create or produce a political unity under conditions where no such unity yet exists. The Indemnity and Special Tribunals Act of 1900 undid these distinctions. In this Act, we see an indemnity (which presupposes a crime against an already constituted juridical order) that was made to function as an amnesty (which presupposes a situation of civil war and therefore the need to create a juridical order *ex nihilo*). This confusion was not, however, the product of a confused legal mind. It was a precise legal response to a confusing situation—a colonial war of conquest—the hallmark of which was a fluid and ambiguous "frontier," which in turn dissolved all of the familiar spatial, temporal, and juridical coordinates of warfare (e.g., the "front" and the "rear," wartime and peacetime, combatant and noncombatant, crime and battle). Because Innes found himself called on to apply indemnity jurisprudence under colonial conditions where, as we saw in section 3.4, it could not be applied at all, it was necessary for him to turn to "extradition law" to fabricate a concept of "political crime" that, in turn, could reconcile the presuppositions of indemnity with those of amnesty.

What holds for the confusion of indemnity and amnesty in 1900 holds for the same confusion ninety years later. Understood in a merely positivist sense, the Norgaard Principles certainly do derive from extradition law alone. But here, as elsewhere, positivism is not at all adequate for understanding the intricacies of colonial jurisprudence.[22] In 1990, as in 1900, the conditions under which it became necessary to cite extradition law to resolve a Southern African conflict did not derive from extradition law alone. In 1990, as in 1900, extradition law arrived in South Africa as part of an attempt to create explicit juridical clarity out of a conflict with a torque and thrust that were distinctly, if implicitly, colonial in character—where *colonial* is a name for, among other things, that vanishing point in jurisprudence at which military and police power become indistinct.[23]

4.2.3 The Norgaard Principles are not, of course, the sole source of the concept of "political crimes" in the PNR Act.[24] In addition to the genealogy of "extradition law" in South African jurisprudence, there is a second and even more important reason why we cannot consider the Norgaard Principles to be the most originary paradigm for "political crimes" in the TRC. Unlike the Namibian agreement, the Groote Schuur Minute (into which the Norgaard Principles were assimilated) was not directed at militants and guerrillas alone. It was drawn widely enough to include indemnities for government officials, and as the minute was developed into legislation by various working groups, one of the legal powers it established—the ability to stop prosecution—was located in differing strains of indemnity jurisprudence (particularly the Indemnity Act of 1990 and an indemnification clause passed as part of the Criminal Procedure Act of 1977, designed to enable the suppression of the Soweto Uprising).[25] Despite the introduction of the term *amnesty* in the postscript to the Interim Constitution, the National Party continued to demand that the terms and criteria of indemnity be recognized by the PNR Act as a trade-off for the ANC's insistence that the "proportionality" requirement be included in the PNR Act.[26] As a result, as Du Bois-Pedain has shown, key clauses from indemnity jurisprudence survived the negotiations over the PNR Act. But this, in turn, created the potential for a conflict over the definition of a political crime. "In the context of extradition law," Anurima Bhargava has pointed out, "political crimes have long been defined with little regard for the relationship between an individual and a political organization."[27] By contrast, Section 20(2) of the PNR Act, which "sets out the required connection—both person and in terms of mandate—between an amnesty applicant and the organization or institution to which he belonged," defined political crimes in just this manner: as Du Bois-Pedain rightly puts it, Section 20(2) "echoes the formulation of the link required between the defendant and the state in [the apartheid state's] early indemnity laws."[28] Although, as Du Bois-Pedain argues, the letter of the PNR Act backs away from the wide indemnity acts of the apartheid era, it also left unresolved the tension between, on the one hand, the merely "factual" approach to political crimes characteristic of indemnity jurisprudence and, on the other hand, the more stringent approach to political crimes set forth by the Norgaard Principles (which required as the necessary condition of any true political crime the "normative" principle that the illegal act in question not only must be committed in good faith but, quite independently of good faith, must be "proportional" to the political objective the act was intended to achieve).[29]

In practice, the Amnesty Committee resolved this tension in a manner that is, in genealogical terms, extremely significant: it completely dropped any evaluative or normative dimension to the "proportionality" requirement set forth by the Norgaard Principles.[30] In the Amnesty Committee, Jeremy Sarkin observes, "[t]he proportionality principle is not only ignored in decisions granting amnesty; it is sometimes also ignored in cases where amnesty was refused."[31] Perhaps because, as Du Bois-Pedain suggests, "strict adherence to the Norgaard principles would have been difficult to sustain if the amnesty scheme was to fulfill its political function as a politically inclusive amnesty process that could reach out to perpetrators from all sides of the conflict,"[32] the Amnesty Committee did not end up relying upon its proportionality principle in its decisions. Instead, as Du Bois-Pedain has shown, the committee limited itself to nonnormative, descriptive distinctions between political objectives and nonpolitical objectives.[33] And this is part of the reason why Du Bois-Pedain reaches her conclusion that the TRC's amnesty provisions remained shaped and governed by their roots in the indemnity acts of the past. "Despite their innovative character," Du Bois-Pedain writes, "the amnesty provisions in the TRC Act still betray their roots in a long legislative tradition that affords special treatment to (at least some) politically motivated crimes."[34] In their juridical form as in their administrative practice, the TRC's amnesty provisions remained animated from within by indemnity jurisprudence: the latter remained active and operative in the former in all but name.

4.2.4 Unintelligible though it may be when interpreted with reference to the letter of the legislation that created it, the practice of the Amnesty Committee is in fact intelligible in genealogical terms, when interpreted with reference to the indemnity jurisprudence that provides the Norgaard Principles with their forgotten precedent and to which the Amnesty Committee reverted when it quietly abandoned the Norgaard Principles. Indemnity jurisprudence depended on what jurists have subsequently called a "subjective test" and an "objective test." The "objective test," which dated at least to 1688, was the test of the *casus neccessitas*: an illegal act could be indemnified by Parliament insofar as the exigencies inherent in the tumultuous situation itself were such that an act of this sort was necessary for the restoration of the rule of law and the sovereign peace. The "subjective test," which dated to the 1798 case *Wright v. Fitzgerald,* placed emphasis less on whether a given illegal act was truly necessary than on whether the person who committed the illegal act was motivated by malice or personal gain or whether that person honestly and frankly believed that such an act was necessary to restore the rule of law and the sovereign peace.

Taken together, these two tests were structured by a fatal conceptual flaw. This flaw may have subsisted in silence, but, like Dicey's "conventions," it was no less substantial for this reason. In the absence of a clear resolution of the "cognitive problem" posed to law by the notion of "necessity" in the jurisprudence of emergency, indemnity jurisprudence increasingly relied on the subjective test alone, asking not whether the illegal act was "objectively" necessary for the defense of the *salus publica* but only whether the person who committed that act honestly believed that it was necessary for the *salus publica*, sometimes even placing the onus on plaintiffs to prove the opposite. During the parliamentary debate that followed Fitzgerald's trial in 1799, lawyers for plaintiffs against Fitzgerald underlined the potential abuse inherent in this use of the indemnification convention. One lawyer stated, "I think it impossible to enumerate all the outrages of man against man, or the crimes which might be committed without the perpetrator's being actuated by private malice."[35] In 1961, opposition parliamentarians would cite this same potential for abuse. "Hundreds of crimes can be committed *bona fides*," as MP P. C. Pelser put it in debate over the South African Indemnity Bill of that year.[36] Writing during the state of emergency of the 1980s, Anthony Mathews would criticize this same potential for abuse. Under conditions where bona fide belief alone is ground for indemnification, Mathews argued, "the torture of a detainee to discover the location of a cache of weapons would be protected if the interrogator genuinely believed that his actions were necessary to ensure the safety of the public or to bring the unrest situation under control."[37] Last but not least, it was this same potential for abuse that Lourens du Plessis criticized when he criticized the Further Indemnity Act of 1992 as "the self-amnesty of an illegitimate regime," singling out for special condemnation its "purely subjective approach," its focus on "political motivation" as "the sole criterion for establishing someone's entitlement to indemnity or release."[38] The innermost norm of indemnity jurisprudence—which was simultaneously also the source of its innermost pathology, its fatal conceptual flaw—was that Parliament would legalize illegalities that were committed in good faith to protect the *salus publica*, whether or not those illegalities were at all necessary.

Those who have studied the issue most closely—scholars like Sarkin and Du Bois-Pedain—agree that the Amnesty Committee failed to apply in their decisions the "proportionality principle" whose inclusion in the PNR Act was to have turned that Act into more than just yet another indemnity act, and whose prudent application rightly has been characterized as the key to the legitimacy of the TRC as a whole.[39] Absent the "proportionality" requirement that was supposed to have been the legislative counterweight to indemnity, the Amnesty Committee instead repeatedly decided cases on the basis of applicants' bona fide belief in the necessity of a given illegal act, however extreme, to accomplish a given political objective.[40] Now, the words *bona fide* or *good faith* or *honest* do not appear in the Norgaard Principles; at most, one could infer the test of honesty or good faith from the Norgaard Principle's "personal motivation" clause, insofar as all questions of personal motivation are questions of good or bad faith.[41] In indemnity jurisprudence, by contrast, the presence of bona fide belief in the necessity of an illegal act was the innermost norm for legalizing illegality. Given the frequency with which the Amnesty Committee ultimately ended up deciding ambiguous amnesty cases by the bona fide test alone, and given the absence of competing precedents, it is reasonable to ask whether the indemnity jurisprudence that governed the earliest drafts of the PNR Act did not survive, silently but substantially, in the implicit rules that provided what consistency there was in the Amnesty Committee's practice.

This is not, of course, to suggest that the Amnesty Committee explicitly cited any indemnity acts when arriving at its decisions. It did not.[42] But explicit citation is not the mode in which conventions, understood in the strict Diceyan sense, exist. Conventions, not unlike the "secondary rules" made so famous in the legal theory of H. L. A. Hart,[43] exist only in and through the unspoken rules with reference to which legal officials relate to and interpret the language set out for them in statutes, laws, and treaties. If despite the best efforts of the authors of the PNR Act, indemnity jurisprudence survived in and as the very practice of the Amnesty Committee, it did so by surviving through rules of this sort. Stated positively: the implicit rules according to which the Amnesty Committee ended up withholding or granting "amnesty" seem to have owed more to Diceyan indemnity jurisprudence than to extradition law as stipulated in the Norgaard Principles or amnesty as it has been articulated in international law.

4.2.5 A similar claim may be made about the Amnesty Committee's "full disclosure" requirement. As Du Bois-Pedain puts it, this test is "often considered the moral cornerstone of the amnesty process."[44] Not only was the full disclosure of gross abuses of human rights supposed to be the "good" part of a negotiation in which the "bad" part was amnesty for torturers and murderers, but, as Du Bois-Pedain points out, the Amnesty Committee's "full disclosure" test became even more important given the collapse of any normative component to its "political objective" test.[45] The elevated importance of full disclosure notwithstanding, its inner norms and criteria seem to have been no more clear or distinct than was the "political objective" test. As Sarkin notes, "What the requirement of 'full disclosure' meant is not immediately clear and has been a source of difficulty in interpretation by the Committee. There was no guidance in the statute or elsewhere as to what it meant or what non-compliance would entail."[46] In particular, Sarkin argues, the Amnesty Committee's application of the "full disclosure" test "periodically suffered, due to a lack of a system of precedent, which would have ensured consistency."[47] In the absence of such a system, we find that the Amnesty Committee conferred coherence on its "full disclosure" test in much the same way it conferred coherence on its "political objective" test: with tacit reference to the "secondary rules" specific to Diceyan indemnity jurisprudence. As with the Amnesty Committee's "political objective" test, this reference was not a simple repetition; it was an iteration, involving a reversal and an impasse.

The pivotal criterion in the Amnesty Committee's "full disclosure" test, like the subjective test of indemnity jurisprudence in the paradigm of *Wright* (and, indeed, like martial law more generally) was neither legality (for only illegal acts were considered) nor error (because the Amnesty Committee granted plenty of amnesties to militants and officials who acted in error but in good faith) but honesty: applications were rejected, Du Bois-Pedain reports, if applicants failed "to give 'an honest account of what actually happened.'"[48] But although the actual criterion at work in the Amnesty Committee's "full disclosure" test was therefore continuous with the standard criterion that had traditionally grounded the "subjective test" of indemnity jurisprudence, a significant nuance to this continuity complicates the conclusion that the Amnesty Committee was limited to a straightforward repetition of indemnity jurisprudence. South Africa's Indemnity Acts of 1961 and 1977, like the Irish Indemnity Act of 1800, placed on plaintiffs injured by state officials the onus to demonstrate that the actions of the accused were motivated not by an honest belief in the necessity of their actions but, instead, by malice or pecuniary desire. The Amnesty Committee's "full disclosure" requirement reversed this onus: it obliged applicants who wanted to obtain amnesty to demonstrate that their actions were both necessary and bona fide. In principle, amnesty was not granted to applicants unless and until that threshold was met. Amnesty in the TRC thus seemed to have been conditional on good faith in a much different way than indemnity in the tradition of *Wright* was conditional on good faith. But although *Wright* is exemplary within indemnity jurisprudence, it is not categorically definitive of indemnity jurisprudence, most particularly the indemnity acts that were passed in twentieth-century South Africa. In its "full disclosure" requirement, as with its reference to extradition law, the TRC's concept of "amnesty" assumed a form that was already in effect in the indemnity stipulated in the Indemnity and Special Tribunals Act of 1900. In this act, those accused of cooperating with the enemy were presumed guilty until they proved themselves innocent: the onus was on surrendered rebels, Innes argued in 1900, "to show some legal justification for their conduct." Innes then explained how, despite this departure from normal legal procedure, the Indemnity and Special Tribunals Act obliged former rebels to appear before the special courts it proposed: "Lists of those people [surrendered rebels] had been kept, and it was proposed that those lists should be posted in every ward in which those people resided. If they did not choose to come the penalty would be imposed upon them; if they did care to come they would get a fair hearing."[49] The Indemnity and Special Tribunal Act of 1900, like the PNR Act of 1995, was a policy of "carrots and sticks."

But here too, as before, there is no need to return to 1900 to find a precedent in indemnity jurisprudence for the "full disclosure" test at work in the TRC. There is another, more recent precedent for it, one that owes its provenance less to Diceyan indemnity jurisprudence in the strict sense than to the crisis of Diceyan jurisprudence that took place under apartheid, when the "exception" that Dicey believed indemnity to be was repeated to the point that it became a "norm." In her insightful analysis of the Amnesty Committee's ad hoc attempt to invent and clarify its own procedures for determining the meaning and limits of "full disclosure," Du Bois-Pedain observes that the committee was faced with two extreme interpretations of that test. Both interpretations sought to resolve a very difficult problem: how, if at all, could the TRC reconcile its procedures of individualized amnesty with the manifestly shared or common character of the political crimes it was charged with adjudicating? On the strict terms of the TRC's mandate, the more "political" a given political crime was, the more it qualified for amnesty. By definition, therefore, there could be no amnesty application that was strictly and exclusively individual in character: a purely individual illegality, an illegality unconnected to any claim to the political, would be not a political crime at all, but just a crime. The question before the Amnesty Committee was therefore how to adjudicate complicity—not in an ontological or moral sense, but in a strict juridical sense, as the category of conspiracy to commit a crime. This is the same question raised by earlier indemnity jurisprudence, which also turned to the concept of criminal conspiracy to differentiate those in a riot or revolution who had committed a political crime and those who had merely committed crimes for individual gain.[50]

The most restrictive interpretation, which was put forward by former state officials and their lawyers, proposed that the test of "full disclosure" be limited to the equivalent of the confession of a crime under the normal procedures of criminal law. On this interpretation, "all that should be required of [an applicant for amnesty] is to admit having performed the *actus reus* of a criminal offence with the required *mens rea*, and to explain the political background of their deed."[51] Not only would this interpretation have limited full disclosure to the actions of single applicants, foreclosing on any obligation of individual applicants to disclose the actions or omissions of their accomplices; it also would have limited the amount of information that applicants likely would have offered in exchange for amnesty, thus undercutting the rationale for the TRC as a whole.[52] Counterpoised to this approach was an interpretation that Du Bois-Pedain calls the most "expansive." Put forward by the famous antiapartheid lawyer George Bizos during the amnesty hearing of the Civil Cooperation Bureau, this interpretation departed markedly from the normal procedures of criminal law—despite, or rather because of, its explicit citation of a long-standing precedent in South Africa's infamously repressive criminal law. Bizos's claim was that applicants should be under an obligation to answer any and all questions put to them by the Amnesty Committee and should not be able to restrict their testimony at all, even and especially if their testimony ended up incriminating them in crimes they neglected to mention in their amnesty application.[53] To defend this departure from the right to remain silent, Bizos cited the indemnity provisions set forth in Section 204 of South Africa's Criminal Procedure Act of 1977. Section 204, like its precedent in Section 62 of the General Law Amendment Act of 1966,[54] marked an increase in prosecutorial power and a decrease in the rights of the accused. Its intention was to better allow prosecutors to make deals with witnesses who were accomplices to a crime but who had decided (or, more likely, been compelled) to testify on behalf of the prosecution. Deals of this sort were nothing new: as Bizos well knew, indemnity as a prosecutorial technique for breaking up conspiracies was used extensively and shrewdly in the Rivonia Trial of 1963–64 by state prosecutor Percy Yutar, in his attempt to convict Nelson Mandela and others on charges of conspiracy to commit sabotage.[55] Section 204, like similar indemnity provisions before it, held out to the witness the promise that "if he answers frankly and honestly all questions put to him, he shall be discharged from prosecution."[56] Unlike earlier indemnity provisions, however, the questions enabled by Section 204 were not limited to the *actus reus* and *mens rea*. As Du Bois-Pedain explains, "A 'section 204' witness is expected to answer all questions relating to the crime charged, and these can on occasion include matters which fall outside the specific offence for which the accused is prosecuted, but which may throw light on issues such as the accused's possible motive for the act."[57] In exchange, the witness "will be obliged to answer any question put to him, whether by the prosecution, the accused or the court, notwithstanding that the answer may incriminate him with regard to the offence so specified or with regard to any offence in respect of which a verdict of guilty would be competent upon a charge."[58] Anything less than "frank and honest" testimony would authorize the prosecutor to withdraw the offer of indemnity (which, in the Criminal Procedure Act of 1977, did not leave the witness liable for newly disclosed crimes). Section 204 was not, of course, unprecedented in South African law: the concept of "full and honest" disclosure stretches back at least to the 1939 case *Rex v. Nxumalo*. Its distressing novelty was due mainly to the way it was coupled with Section 208 of the same act, which normalized a controversial provision from the Terrorism Act of 1967 that decreased the number of witnesses necessary for conviction from two to one. Taken together, Sections 204 and 208 were part of an entire set of modifications to the English rules regulating witnesses that the apartheid state put into place in the years after the Sharpeville Massacre as an attempt to expand and intensify the apartheid state's already considerable prosecutorial and investigative powers.[59]

As Du Bois-Pedain suggests, Bizos's apparently extreme interpretation of the PNR Act's "full disclosure" provisions was not new. Nor, despite its departures from the normal procedures of criminal law, was it inconsistent with the spirit of the PNR Act, which, like the Indemnity Act of 1990 before it, expressly rejected the constraints and protections of ordinary criminal trials in order to institute an administrative body in which indemnity could be "exchanged" for the disclosure of politically motivated illegal acts. Indeed, as Du Bois-Pedain suggests, Bizos's reiteration of the indemnity jurisprudence of the apartheid state marked the widest possible interpretation of "full disclosure" that came before the Amnesty Committee during its existence. Had it been adopted by the committee, Bizos's interpretation of "full disclosure" would have yielded the greatest amount of testimony possible and the best possible "exchange" or "deal" of indemnity for truth. On principle, therefore, Bizos's approach to the "full disclosure" test was the interpretation of "full disclosure" that was most consistent with the aims of the TRC as a whole. That the Amnesty Committee quietly rejected Bizos's interpretation on the primarily administrative grounds of bureaucratic "efficiency" (as Du Bois-Pedain observes, Bizos's interpretation arguably would have produced an excessive amount of work for the committee)[60] does not remove the aporia implicit in Bizos's proposal. Interpreted in genealogical terms, Bizos's re-iteration of the "frank and honest" requirement from the indemnification provisions of the Criminal Procedure Act of 1977 is yet another paradoxical expression of the basic juridical impasse the TRC was forced to confront as the condition for its novelty. *The more loyal the Amnesty Committee would have been to the repressive indemnity jurisprudence of the apartheid state, the more consistent the Amnesty Committee would have been with the most basic mandate of the TRC as such.*

4.2.6 Nowhere in the TRC was indemnity jurisprudence reiterated with greater audacity and risk than in its Reparations and Rehabilitations Committee (RRC). Already in the South African indemnity jurisprudence of the 1960s and 1970s, we see a discourse on the tragic juridical figure of the "innocent victim," and we see the emergence, in response to and around this figure, of a strange administrative body, the compensation committee. This was a body that, like the TRC, was neither entirely judicial (because it was invented precisely to preclude recourse to the courts and because it derived its principles not from precedents of criminal justice but from precedents in insurance and liability law) nor entirely legislative (because, at least in its 1977 incarnation, it was composed of a lawyer, a supreme court justice, and "representatives of the natives"). Notably, it derived its authority not from the rule of law but from the highest form of exception to the rule of law, the sovereign right of grace, which it used to claim that its procedures for compensating innocent victims for their groundless suffering was superior to the contentious, adversarial procedures of courts of law. Above all, the compensation committee deployed an iteration of indemnity that was at once derived from Diceyan jurisprudence (because it was offered in connection with harms committed by apartheid police offers who had been protected by indemnity acts from criminal and civil liability) and yet, in its most pivotal juridical forms, no longer Diceyan in its jurisprudence (because it didn't refer to a legalization of illegality, but to a payment intended to compensate innocent victims for the loss or damage they incurred). It is, in this sense, one of the novelties churned up by the crisis of indemnity jurisprudence under apartheid.

The apartheid-era compensation committee exerted a clear influence on the TRC. The first paragraph in the first draft of the bill that eventually would become the PNR Act of 1995 clearly indicated its debt to the indemnity and compensation bills of 1961 and 1977. The purpose of the bill, according to this draft, was "[t]o provide for the granting of amnesty and indemnity from civil and criminal liability for acts committed with a political object; to provide for the compensation of persons prejudiced by the granting of such indemnity or amnesty; and to provide for matters connected therewith."[61] Subsequent drafts would modify this language significantly, though without the sort of open consultation with civil society that characterized other elements of the PNR legislation.[62] As a result, "reparation measures" of the PNR Act's Section 3(1)(c) and the Committee on Reparation and Rehabilitation created by its Chapter 5 were far more intricate than was the 1977 principle of and formula for *ex gratia* payments and the committee that was charged with disbursing them. This intricacy notwithstanding, the former nevertheless defined its concept of reparation in terms that were almost identical to the latter. The language of 1961 and 1977 that authorized the apartheid state to make *ex gratia* payments—language that came into being during two of the worst moments of apartheid state repression—persisted almost completely intact in the 1995 legislation that created the TRC.[63]

On the one hand, therefore, the PNR Act contained a host of continuities with the compensatory schemes of 1961 and 1977. Just as the compensation committee of 1977 explicitly cited the precedent of 1961 to define "compensation" as the "counterpart of indemnity," so, too, the framers of the PNR Act implicitly cited the precedent of 1977 when they defined "reparation" as an "essential counterbalance for amnesty."[64] In 1961 and 1977, we also see a clear recognition on the part of all official parties that the Commission of Inquiry, coupled with *ex gratia* compensation for innocent victims of state violence, would be much less expensive and time-consuming for the state than would be criminal and civil trials.[65] In his presentation of the Indemnity and Compensation Bill of 1961 to the Senate, for example, the minister of justice for the apartheid state, F. C. Erasmus, would make this argument quite plainly. Noting that there already had been lawsuits filed against the government over the Sharpeville Massacre, Erasmus argued that "it is a good thing that the State asks for indemnity," because the lawsuits "will probably cause the State unnecessary expense."[66] Erasmus and other National Party parliamentarians then proceeded to outline in detail the costs of the lawsuits and to cast aspersions on what they understood to be the pecuniary desires of the law firms organizing and filing them. To save the state from frivolous lawsuits, these men reasoned, indemnity was indispensable. Similar arguments would be made in 1977, but in a different register, with reference to the insidious tactics of guerrilla warfare rather than the insidious desires of the legal profession. As National Party parliamentarian D. J. L. Nel would put it, when the task of the police is, in effect, to wage war

> in the residential areas of South Africa, and when the aim of the inciters of internal disorder is specifically to act in the presence of the maximum number of people, and since the aim is to involve the maximum number of people in the action, we suddenly find that the potential accountability of the State becomes impossibly wide. We must bear in mind that the State takes this accountability upon itself in conflict with a principle which has been established over decades, because if we look at indemnity laws in other parts of the world, we can see that the principle of compensation, or the principle of *ex gratia* payment, is not in those indemnity laws as a matter of necessity because the principle of indemnity is so strong in all respects.[67]

Worth noting here is Nel's remarkable self-consciousness about the innovative character of South Africa's indemnity jurisprudence. To supplement indemnity in the Diceyan sense with a mechanism to indemnify innocent victims (now in the non-Diceyan sense of the word, where to indemnify is to compensate) and to establish administrative procedures for determining the identity and meaning of "innocent victims" in the first place is here recognized for the unprecedented step that it is. This innovation is quite important from a genealogical perspective. Not only did it come into being under conditions where indemnity jurisprudence already had entered into crisis—where, that is, it was already clear that classic Diceyan indemnity jurisprudence could not solve the problems put to it; it was also a juridical form that, reiterated under different conditions, would be deployed not to maintain the apartheid state, but to end it.

Indeed, whereas the compensation committee was deployed in an unequivocally repressive form by the apartheid state in 1961 and 1977, it would become, in the postapartheid state, the site of a fascinating set of juridical disputes, each of which implicitly would play out on a space marked out in advance for it by the genealogy of indemnity jurisprudence in South Africa. Explaining the constitutional basis for the TRC's power to nullify civil claims against the state in *AZAPO et al. v. President of the Republic of South Africa et al.*, Justice Ismail Mahomed would describe the socioeconomic inequalities bequeathed to the postapartheid state by its predecessor.

> The resources of the state have to be deployed imaginatively, wisely, efficiently and equitably, to facilitate the reconstruction process in a manner which best brings relief and hope to the widest sections of the community, developing for the benefit of the entire nation the latent human potential and resources of every person who has directly or indirectly been burdened with the heritage of the shame and the pain of our racist past.
>
> Those negotiators of the Constitution and leaders of the nation who were required to address themselves to these agonising problems must have been compelled to make hard choices. They could have chosen to direct that the limited resources of the state be spent by giving preference to the formidable delictual claims of those who had suffered from acts of murder, torture or assault perpetrated by servants of the state, diverting to that extent, desperately needed funds in the crucial areas of education, housing and primary health care. They were entitled to permit a different choice to be made between competing demands inherent in the problem. They could have chosen to direct that the potential liability of the state be limited in respect of any civil claims by differentiating between those against whom prescription could have been pleaded as a defence and those whose claims were of such recent origin that a defence of prescription would have failed. They were entitled to reject such a choice on the grounds that it was irrational. They could have chosen to saddle the state with liability for claims made by insurance companies which had compensated institutions for delictual acts performed by the servants of the state and to that extent again divert funds otherwise desperately needed to provide food for the hungry, roofs for the homeless and black boards and desks for those struggling to obtain admission to desperately overcrowded schools. They were entitled to permit the claims of such school children and the poor and the homeless to be preferred.

Mahomed concluded,

> [I]t is much too simplistic to say that the objectives of the Constitution

could only properly be achieved by saddling the state with the formal liability to pay, in full, the provable delictual claims of those who have suffered patrimonial loss in consequence of the delicts perpetrated with political objectives by servants of the state during the conflicts of the past. There was a permissible alternative, perhaps even a more imaginative and more fundamental route to the "reconstruction of society", which could legitimately have been followed. This is the route which appears to have been chosen by Parliament through the mechanism of amnesty and nuanced and individualised reparations in the Act. I am quite unpersuaded that this is not a route authorised by the epilogue to the Constitution.[68]

Critics of the TRC's compensation scheme have interpreted *AZAPO et al.* by focusing on the tragic irony of a successor state having to inherit the debts incurred by a predecessor it opposed.[69] But if anything, this critique risks understating the tragic irony at work in this decision.

From a genealogical perspective, the inheritance at stake in *AZAPO et al.* extends to include a reiteration of the very logic according to which the Constitutional Court justified the South African state's desire for self-indemnification. To be sure, in 1996, as distinct from 1961 and 1977, the reason for the South African state's self-indemnification was no longer the safety and security of the white minority, but the health and welfare of the postapartheid public. But in 1996, as in 1961 and 1977, the South African state justified its limited compensation scheme with reference not to the rule of law (in particular, the requirements of criminal or civil law), but to the exception to law demanded by a specifically fiscal declension of the *salus publica* (the intricate logic of which we shall investigate in greater detail in section 8.2). The Constitutional Court thus reiterated a juridical form it inherited from apartheid-era indemnity jurisprudence, repeating the legal limits interior to indemnity now with a political difference, under a new and different regime of political "necessity."

From its very inception, the TRC also struggled to reiterate this inheritance in a salutary way. It sought, from the beginning, to turn compensation into something more meaningful than just a "symbolic" payment to "innocent victims," seeking to structure compensation payments according to principles deeply held by the postapartheid state (e.g., development, healing, reconciliation, and cultural appropriateness).[70] It strove to respond to critics of the RRC, who faulted it for almost every aspect of its practice: its pace (it moved very slowly), the size of its grants (the amounts of which were at best modest and at worst insulting), its attempts at meaningfulness (its effort to avoid the word *compensation* and to speak instead of the symbolic "restoration of dignity"), and its breadth (its failure to function as part of the broader social justice for which the *TRC Report* seemed to call and its focus, instead, on a selected number of procedurally verified individual victims).[71] Acknowledging the truth of these criticisms, the TRC would, in its final report, become even more aggressive.[72] Led by Archbishop Desmond Tutu, who was especially outspoken on this point, the TRC proposed a number of fairly far-reaching measures that would have enabled victims to acquire compensation not only from the government but also from the corporate and personal "beneficiaries" of apartheid.[73] For all of these reasons, it cannot be said that the TRC's compensation program was nothing more than a simple repetition of the apartheid state's compensation schemes.

What can and indeed must be said is that the Mbeki administration's response to the TRC's proposals ruined the TRC's ability to differentiate itself from those schemes. In April 2003, the Mbeki administration would definitively repudiate the TRC's compensation proposals, setting aside the TRC's recommendation that total compensation to victims should amount to around $375 million, and instead agreeing to pay only around $74 million. Although this decision quickly would be criticized on moral, political, and economic grounds, its genealogical significance would be left in silence even by its most vociferous critics. When the Amnesty Committee ceased to use its proportionality test, and made its decisions mainly on the grounds of bona fide belief, it undercut the central difference between the TRC's amnesty provisions and the indemnity jurisprudence that provided those provisions with their most direct precedent. Absent this differentiation, nothing prevented the juridical forms of a colonial-era "convention" (in Dicey's sense of the word) from silently surviving in this Committee's practice. When the Mbeki administration rejected the RRC's innovative compensation proposals, the TRC was forced into a similar repetition: in the absence of supplementation by these innovations, the RRC lost the ability to differentiate itself from the compensation committees of the apartheid state.

4.3.1 Nothing in the discourse of transitional justice, it should be noted, stood in the way of this repetition. If anything, transitional justice prepared the conditions under which that repetition became possible in the first place.

Because the TRC was unable to think about its own juridical forms with reference to their colonial precedents, it wasn't able to pose as a question either for its theory or its practice the task of producing a postcolonial legal order. It wasn't able to ask, that is to say, the question of what it might mean for it to repeat, but now with a marked difference, the apparatuses of colonial sovereignty and governmentality it inherited by virtue of the principle of "legal continuity" that structured the South African negotiated settlement. Transitional justice didn't just occupy the vacuum left by this silence; it also sealed it up. The leading studies of the TRC within the field discuss at length events in European history and politics—ranging from the Athenian amnesty of 403 B.C. and the French Revolution, to the Nazi genocide and postcommunist regimes in Eastern Europe—while managing to remain almost perfectly silent on the history and politics of colonialism.

This silence is foundational for transitional justice's analysis of the TRC. The field's basic concepts depend for their continued validity on the prior absence of any truly critical inquiry into the juridical forms of colonial law and administration. Applied recursively to the TRC's repetition of colonial juridical forms, the field's basic concepts reproduce their silence, only this time in a different mode. The field's central analytic distinctions—vengeance versus forgiveness, truth versus justice, trauma versus healing, forensic truth versus narrative truth—not only lack the ability to validate the repetition of colonial jurisprudence as a problem for thought; worse, any rigorous application of those distinctions could not but *invalidate* that repetition as a problem for thought, externalizing the field's founding silence this time as a blind spot, as a self-confident sense that the postcolonial is obviously a *non*-problem for studies of the TRC, a question that isn't and shouldn't be relevant to the *real* questions raised by the TRC. This even though transitional justice formed its analysis of the TRC with remarkable haste, crystallizing its basic concepts before the TRC was even finished with its work, and even though in the decade since the TRC has finished its work it has refrained from radically criticizing or questioning those basic concepts. Even though, in short, transitional justice's analysis of the TRC came into being through an odd—and oddly unquestioned—metalepsis.

The fact that transitional justice has left unasked the question of the postcolony—despite the immanence of that question within the TRC's own theory and practice—points to the need for a set of critical questions about the adequacy and competency of the field of transitional justice itself.

These questions pertain, in particular, to the way that transitional justice has characterized the problem of "forgiveness" within the TRC. What should we make of the fact that, at *the very center* of *the best of the best* (the possibility of "forgiveness" that transitional justice found exemplified in the TRC), we find *the very same juridical forms* that, for at least a century, retrospectively legalized *the worst of the worst* (indemnity jurisprudence, that branch of martial law that functioned to retroactively legalize the illegalities of the apartheid regime)? Have the normative excesses of transitional justice led it to embrace and affirm a discourse on forgiveness that, in genealogical terms, is little more than a newly moralistic shell for an old legal kernel—for the legalization of illegality that was at the core of indemnity jurisprudence? In other words, is "forgiveness" simply the name that indemnity jurisprudence gives to its juridical forms under conditions where it is no longer able to recognize either itself or its by-products, where indeed its basic forms silently survive even as indemnity jurisprudence itself has been legally proscribed? If so, why is it that, despite so much insistence within transitional justice scholarship upon the importance of memory for any and all ethical reasoning about apartheid, so much transitional justice scholarship would seem to have consented to and replicated what seems to be a forgetting of the indemnity jurisprudence that is internal both to the TRC's amnesty provisions and, beyond that, to transitional justice's own discourse of "forgiveness" as well? How should we make sense of the remarkable failure of transitional justice to apply its own ethical imperatives about memory (imperatives like "amnesty, not amnesia," "forgive, don't forget," etc.) to the origins of the single legal power (the amnesty provisions of the PNR Act) that occasioned those imperatives and to which they were designed to apply?

Nowhere are the blind spots of transitional justice more pronounced than in the field's pious and self-confident deployment of its normative lexicon. The excessive emphasis on ethical problems within transitional justice, corresponding as it has to a deficit of genealogical work within the field, has had the regrettable consequence of leading those influenced by transitional justice to justify, using a newly acceptable set of imperatives ("amnesty, not amnesia," "forgive, don't forget," etc.), the very same self-exculpatory power that once was at the core of the apartheid state's indemnity jurisprudence. It is, of course, easy to criticize the operation of this power in a law like the Further Indemnity Act of 1992, where there is no attempt to conceal the brute and cynical face of self-exculpation. Much harder is to recognize

its effects in the *ex gratia* payments to victims that the apartheid state offered in connection with the indemnity acts of 1961 and 1977. These were
payments made to victims *out of* grace and *on the basis* of grace; they were
gratuitous acts uncompelled by any law and unmandated by any command.
But they also were a particularly twisted *exercise* of grace, an act of grace
aimed not at victims (whose innocence was explicitly asserted by the apartheid state and to whom any remission of penalty therefore would have been
a contradiction in terms), but rather at the apartheid state itself. By offering
these payments to the innocent victims harmed by its agents and officials,
the apartheid state exempted itself from the constraints of the rule of law: it
accepted a "higher" form of "moral" responsibility for the harm it caused, but
precisely and only insofar as that "moral" responsibility could operate as a
substitute for the legal responsibility the state's indemnities simultaneously
negated. In Hegelian terms: under apartheid, the moral discourse of the *ex
gratia* payment—of compensating victims out of uncompelled, gratuitous
goodness—was *the sublation* of the legal discourse of indemnity. It was the
expression—now in a form at once higher, canceled out, and distorted—
of the same self-exculpatory power that was directly in effect in the state's
indemnities.

That transitional justice gave voice to sublated forms of indemnity jurisprudence was quite apparent in 2003, at the moment when some in the
TRC sought to radicalize its proposals for compensation. By this point, of
course, the leading works of transitional justice already had been published,
and the field already had settled on the meaning of the TRC, even if this
meant that the field's understanding of the TRC now could be deployed
at cross-purposes to the emancipatory potential that some TRC committee members then were trying to actualize. Because the amount of state's *ex
gratia* payment was slight to the point of being insulting, transitional justice's
theories of "restorative justice," "healing," and "forgiveness" became essential
for explaining why, appearances to the contrary notwithstanding, these payments did in fact have a symbolic meaning. By providing the terms under
which the state's *ex gratia* payments could be said to signify new virtues like
"restorative justice," the discourse of transitional justice gave a redemptive
sense to a juridical form that, under apartheid, was unequivocally repressive.
But though the lexicon might have changed, the effect of the lexicon had
not: the figure of the "innocent victim" of state violence was in both cases
denied civil and criminal redress under the rule of law and instead offered a

menu of "moral victories" whose various advantages over the rule of law were theorized nowhere more fully than in the field of transitional justice. Just as a victim of state violence in 1977 was supposed to have been satisfied with an *ex gratia* payment, which signified the state's "heartbreak" over the loss of "innocent life," so too the victim of state violence in 2003 was supposed to have been satisfied with the knowledge that the state at least and at last had taken symbolic responsibility for their tragic and unnecessary suffering and had signified that responsibility with its *ex gratia* payment. When compared with the incalculable good of this "moral victory," any "innocent victim" who elected to question the precise amount of compensation on offer could not but seem calculating and petty, more impure than pure, less and less "powerless," and thus too less and less "innocent," and finally more and more out of joint with the sacralized image of the victim at the heart of so many works of transitional justice. It was almost as though the very category of "innocent victim" itself depended for its intelligibility on the prior, implicit requirement that the victim remain in a state of complete destitution—destitution unremedied by any restitution except the symbolic.

Of this, in fact, there was a subtle but decisive confirmation in the years between 2002 and 2004, when the TRC's compensation scheme would become the object of litigation by a group of victims who rejected the powerlessness and speechlessness associated with the category of "victim" and to whom Tshepo Madlingozi thus gave the ironic name "bad victims." "Bad victims," in Madlingozi's account, are victims who were not satisfied to rest content with the notion that it was "victory enough" to accept the sacred status connoted by the notion of the "innocent victim"[74] and who were unpersuaded by the denigration of courts of law and litigation that, by then, was a commonplace of transitional justice scholarship on the TRC. Filing suit in U.S. courts against U.S. corporations that profited from apartheid, the Khulumani Support Group used a law that was originally written to stabilize colonial markets and colonial trade—the Alien Tort Claims Act—to call into question certain U.S. corporations' own neocolonial profits from South African labor.[75] This lawsuit was consistent not only with the TRC's claims to be "victim-centered" but also with the *TRC Report*'s findings on the business community;[76] it also was arguably consistent with Mbeki's own deeply questionable anticolonial rhetoric (which around that time was playing such a significant part in his HIV/AIDS denialism).[77] Nevertheless, the Mbeki administration responded to the Khulumani suit by bowing to pressure from the Bush administration and filing an *amicus* brief, in a U.S. district court, in opposition to Khulumani's claims. The problem with the Khulumani lawsuit, the Mbeki administration claimed, was not its redistributive substance but its recourse to foreign courts, which violated the sovereignty of the South African state to deal with the problem of compensation in a manner consistent with the "well-being of our country" and "the perspective contained in our constitution on the promotion of national reconciliation."[78]

Understood from the perspective of indemnity jurisprudence, this response has a clear significance. In the bad old days of parliamentary sovereignty, indemnity was the most definitive act of sovereign power; it was, as Dicey argued, "the highest exertion and crowning proof of sovereign power." By treating simple sovereign power as the basis for its argument in support of its otherwise questionable compensation scheme, and against Khulumani's recourse to courts, the Mbeki administration revealed the sense in which indemnity jurisprudence was not simply the most direct precedent for the TRC's *ex gratia* payment, but also, in the last analysis, one of its most basic rationales.

Transitional justice didn't just remain silent on this repetition of indemnity jurisprudence; it provided the lexicon under which the repetition itself could be newly justified and explained. The field's criticisms of the rule of law, initially offered in the name of "restorative justice," "healing," and "forgiveness," at this point could begin to fulfill the same function for the postapartheid state that indemnity jurisprudence once had fulfilled for the apartheid state. This discourse allowed the compensation machinery of the TRC to repeat the indemnity jurisprudence and the compensation committees of old, only now in terms that could be praised rather than damned by outside world. With their *amicus* brief, the Mbeki administration revealed how transitional justice's discourses of "national reconciliation" and "innocent victims" could be deployed in a way that, far from emancipatory, was consistent with the discourse of "national interest" at work in the repressive jurisprudence the postapartheid state inherited from the apartheid state.[79] Here, in short, we see the genealogical risk immanent to the TRC—that it repeat rather than render inoperative paradigms of colonial sovereign power—play itself out, hidden in plain sight.

4.3.2 That transitional justice should have remained so consistently silent on the problem of indemnity jurisprudence is, in a sense, understandable. The genealogy we have sketched in fact provides a very good explanation of the fact that so many scholars have been able to write about indemnity without alarm or disquiet, without realizing that in so doing one is speaking about a branch of martial law jurisprudence. As we saw in sections 3.2 and 3.3, the jurisprudence of emergency became so normalized in twentieth-century South Africa that indemnity, doctrinally a mere supplement to martial law, became disjoined from martial law. Thus it was that the apartheid state would pass an indemnity act in 1977 with no declaration of martial law at all, and indemnities would be passed in 1990 and 1992 with no mention of martial law either. This disjoining was so complete that by the time transitional justice scholars began writing about indemnity and amnesty in the mid-1990s, it had become routine to refer to indemnity as if it had no relation whatsoever to martial law. But what is most remarkable about this forgetting is how clearly the paradigms of martial law nevertheless managed to persist silently within the very transitional justice scholarship that proceeded in oblivion of it. Transitional justice scholars speak often about the superiority of restorative justice and forgiveness over retributive justice and the criminal trial. From an ethical or therapeutic perspective, this discourse may or may not be persuasive. From a genealogical perspective, this discourse simply pushed through the open door toward which existing juridical forms pointed it. The jurisprudence of emergency, which required declarations of martial law to be followed by indemnity acts, already entailed a claim of this sort: by legalizing the illegalities of certain classes of persons, exempting them from criminal and civil liability, indemnity already exercised the exculpatory power that transitional justice praises (albeit in a different context and within a different lexicon). To interpret the amnesty agreement genealogically, as an exceptionally audacious iteration of the South African indemnity jurisprudence, is certainly to understand the TRC outside of the hermeneutic horizon of transitional justice. But it is, for this same reason, to better understand the genius and risks of the TRC itself. On the one hand, it is to see that there is a counterintuitive relation between the concept of "necessity" as it is cited in transitional justice discourse on the origins of amnesty in the negotiations at Kempton Park ("but for an amnesty agreement, South Africa would have dissolved into the civil war") and the concept of "necessity" as it operates in the jurisprudence of emergency. Both genres of jurisprudence refer to situations in which the very existence of the state itself is in question and in which "the necessity of saving the state from destruction" authorizes a swerve from or suspension of the normal procedures and practices of the rule of law.[80] This "similarity in function" is not, to be clear, a mere resemblance or homology. It is a concrete legal continuity that produces a relation of identity between the TRC and its moral opposite—the discourse of martial law, which both authorized and incited many of the gross human rights abuses the TRC was mandated to investigate. It is a genealogical sign that the emergency jurisprudence of the apartheid state was at the very heart of the paradigmatic institution of the postapartheid state, and that the worst of the worst in the old regime—its regularization of martial law—was transplanted into the new regime's attempts to enable the healing of the victims of the old regime.

From a genealogical perspective, then, it quite misses the point to analyze the TRC on the basis of oppositions like "forgiveness versus vengeance" or "truth versus justice." The critical opposition is rather between two potentially incommensurable modes of self-exculpation. The significance of the TRC was that it attempted to operate as a juridical mechanism in which the existing self-exculpatory powers of the apartheid state could be reiterated now in a new context. Whereas the apartheid state used indemnity not as an exception but as a norm, the postapartheid state used this normalized exception as an occasion to try to found a new norm. In the TRC, indemnification functioned to found a *Rechtsstaat* that expressed its most essential and basic norm, *ubuntu*, by reiterating indemnity/amnesty now as an unprecedented form of "forgiveness." If, in this reiteration, "forgiveness" appeared to have no relation to indemnity jurisprudence whatsoever, this was because the "amnesty" set forth in the PNR Act was itself an indemnity act of such radical size and quality that *it was no longer recognizable as an indemnity act at all*. The illegality that this "indemnity act" sought to legalize, after all, was no longer this or that particular crime (as was supposed to be the case in Dicey). *It was the criminality of the South African state as such*. Under conditions of political transition, the South African state found itself in such great need of legalization—or, more to the point, it found itself with such a great need to legalize its own fundamental illegality—that it could not avoid some variety of self-exculpation. But the precedents for self-exculpation that were most directly and concretely available to its jurists were neither valid nor desirable, not least because precisely these precedents had contributed so much to the very criminality the state now was seeking to legalize. At best, the Amnesty Committee was the final resting place for indemnity jurisprudence—its last gasp and dying breath, the place where the self-exculpatory powers of the old, criminal state went to die. At best, in other words, it was the place where the sovereignty of the apartheid state, which always had indemnity at its apex, perished in the forgiveness of the postapartheid *Rechtsstaat*, which, in effect, tried to extinguish the exceptional powers of its predecessor by redeploying those exceptional powers *one last time*.

But if this is true—if the TRC helped found the postapartheid state by repeating, with a difference, the self-exculpatory powers of the apartheid state—then we only begin to grasp the true genius of the TRC after we first set aside the reified binary oppositions of transitional justice (e.g. "restorative" vs. "retributive" justice). The essence of this repetition cannot be grasped with reference to Nuremberg or Latin America. It entails a movement between a well-defined paradigm of colonial sovereign power, on the one hand, and an as yet undefined paradigm of postcolonial sovereign power, on the other. From this perspective, the most important and critical test of the success or failure of the TRC is not its instrumental effectiveness in creating a transition to a functioning market economy (or what transitional justice calls "peace"). It is, more to the point, whether or not the TRC succeeded in rendering inoperative, sinking into desuetude, or "decommissioning" the very same colonial juridical forms from which the TRC itself emerged. The question that should interest us, in other words, is not whether the TRC "worked" in its attempt to create a process of national healing in and through which South Africa finally became the whole that it already, allegedly, incipiently was. It is whether or not the TRC's reiteration was sufficiently felicitous to institute a new mode of juridical reason—one capable of *completing* the crisis of colonial jurisprudence that occasioned the invention of the TRC to begin with.

Part 2

Chapter 5

WHAT IS A COMMISSION?

5.1.1 In addition to claims about its "individualized amnesties," there is another feature of the TRC that often is considered unprecedented and that, as such, lays claim to our genealogical attention. "What we have tried to do in the Bill," Johnny de Lange explained in his 1995 presentation of the PNR Bill Act to Parliament,

> is to place the victims at the centre. Again I want to say that this is unique in the history of the world. In most instances where atrocities like these have taken place, it has invariably been the perpetrators of violence, of those horrible deeds, who have been able to come forth and again bask in the glory of what they have done. They usually got off scot-free. To this extent I think this Bill is a great victory for the victims, and I think it is something that future generations will be grateful for.[1]

Speaking in 1999, Kader Asmal concurred, albeit with less hyperbole: "Unlike many truth commissions that preceded it, our own was not solely concerned with granting amnesty to perpetrators of human rights abuses. It in addition gave voice to victims and provided for reparation to and rehabilitation of victims."[2] "The alleged victim-centeredness of the truth and reconciliation process" was not only, as Du Bois-Pedain writes skeptically, "the TRC's dominant justificatory theme";[3] it was also, as the *TRC Report* itself emphasized, "the core of the Commission's work."[4]

Unquestionable though this claim to novelty has come to seem within the field of transitional justice, it becomes far less self-evident when considered with reference to a genealogy that is no less constitutive of the TRC but about which transitional justice is almost completely silent. Long before the emergence of the TRC—preceding and enabling even the Skweyiya and

Motsuenyane Commissions, the two commissions that the ANC instituted in the 1980s to investigate claims of torture in its own training camps—there was another, more prosaic name for the administrative organ tasked with listening to, evaluating, and archiving the voices of the victims of abuses of illegal state activity: the Commission of Inquiry.

The Commission of Inquiry is, as we shall see below, an administrative apparatus through which institutions of sovereign power pose questions to themselves about the scope, limits, and aims of governance, whether the governance in question be of populations, things, or goods. Although it has roots in medieval English politics, its constitutive place and function within English government would not be secured until the early nineteenth century, when royal commissions flourished in both metropole and colony alike.[5] In legal terms, the notion that the TRC was a Commission of Inquiry is a remarkable statement of the obvious: by its own account, the TRC was, of course, "set up as a commission of enquiry."[6] In genealogical terms, by contrast, the commission's administrative status is the point of departure for questions with answers that are anything but obvious.

As scholars have noted, and as the *TRC Report* suggests,[7] the apartheid state frequently had recourse to Commissions of Inquiry. In twentieth-century South Africa, commissions aimed at understanding "race relations" in South Africa (or what Adam Ashforth has called the "Grand Tradition" of "Native Question" Commissions in South Africa)[8] and, more important for the purposes of this book, commissions tasked with gathering information about acts of violence committed by state officials were not the exception but the rule. It was a Commission of Inquiry, the 1903–5 Native Affairs Commission (or "Milner Commission"), that solidified the epistemic field— the social scientific knowledge as well as the public opinion, the *connaissance* as well as the *savoir*[9]—according to which it was both possible and desirable for whites to govern South Africa while also excluding Africans from full citizenship.[10] It was also a Commission of Inquiry (or, to be precise, two such commissions) that produced the epistemic field within which apartheid policies would emerge and then dominate white public opinion during the late 1940s and 1950s: in 1947, the Sauer Commission would recommend "total apartheid between Whites and Natives," and in 1955, the Tomlinson Commission would plot out the industrialization of the "Black Areas" created by the 1913 Native Land Act. Later Commissions of Inquiry (e.g., the 1960 Commission of Inquiry into the European Occupancy of the

Rural Areas), following the precedent established by a long line of colonial Commissions of Inquiry,[11] would generate the policies of "location" and "native reserves" on which the apartheid state would come to rely in its use of "forced removals."[12] Still other Commissions of Inquiry would be deployed by the apartheid state to create the epistemic conditions for the creation of "Bantu Education" (the 1949–51 Eiselen Commission), the censorship of press and literature (the 1950–61 Press Commission and the 1954 Commission of Inquiry into Undesirable Literature),[13] the prohibition of antiapartheid student organizations (the 1973–75 Commission of Inquiry into Certain Organisations), and the persecution of churches opposed to apartheid (the 1984 Eloff Commission of Inquiry into the South African Council of Churches, which included considerable investigation into Tutu himself).[14] The list, unfortunately, could go on.[15]

The point of recalling these precedents is not, to be clear, to suggest that because the TRC deploys an administrative apparatus that was central to the very system it rightly declares evil, it is necessarily also "contaminated" or "tainted" by virtue of that sharing. That the nonracial 1996 Constitution is, like the racist 1983 Constitution that preceded it, also a constitution does not, after all, necessarily taint it. As the saying goes, *Ad abusu ad usum non valet consequentia:* one cannot conclude from the abuse of a thing that its use, too, is invalid. Nevertheless, whereas the abuse of the rule of law under apartheid gave rise to debates over the essence and basis of South African law (in the form of the South African Law Commission of 1973, which was established by a statute of Parliament), the same cannot be said for the Commission of Inquiry. There has been no Commission of Inquiry into the use and abuse of Commissions of Inquiry in colonial and apartheid South Africa.[16] Few scholars have reflected critically on its ways, means, origins, and power relations, more often preferring, instead, to adopt an uncritical attitude toward the "evidence" generated by various commissions, treating that evidence as unadorned fact that can just as easily undercut as support apartheid theory and practice. But just as legal theorists only become able to reflect on the difference between good law and bad law by asking the prior question of what law itself is, surely we can only hope to understand the TRC's relation to its precedents in the apartheid state once we have asked a similarly prior question of the Commission of Inquiry.

This sort of question may at first strike the reader as much less interesting than the grand questions that currently attract so much attention in the field of transitional justice. Can truth really be substituted for justice? To what extent and for whom is it healing or therapeutic to tell stories of trauma and pain in public? What sort of ethics of memory and narrative are appropriate when we listen to the stories that emerge from the TRC? These are the sorts of questions that transitional justice scholars have become habituated to answer and that we, in turn, have become habituated to ask of the TRC. But these questions all depend for their coherence on a decisive prior assumption: that the Commission of Inquiry is, as a technique of governance, nothing more than an empty container, a purely neutral and ahistorical form without a substance, content, politics, or genealogy of its own. In the end, this assumption cannot survive scrutiny.

The premise of this book is that only by first studying the colonial juris-prudence that is so decisive a part of South African law is it then possible to raise the ethical and epistemological questions or entertain the norma-tive claims that today dominate transitional justice scholarship on the TRC. In the case of victim testimony given before the TRC, as with the TRC's Amnesty Committee, the important question is not whether the TRC is anomalous with reference to a categorical set (the "Truth Commission") that is defined in and through an international learning curve that begins in Berlin, passes through Buenos Aires, and ends up being perfected in Cape Town. It is whether the TRC is anomalous with reference to a categorical set (the "Commission of Inquiry") that is incompletely theorized in London and aggressively imposed in the colonies, where its latent incoherence be-comes painfully manifest. Only through such an inquiry is it then possible to understand the audacity and even genius implicit in the TRC's attempt to place the victims of state violence at the center of its administrative work. However moving we may find the testimonies that the TRC made possible, the power of these testimonies is not, in the end, purely spontaneous. It is, in part, the effect of an administrative apparatus whose ways and means not only precede the TRC but also determine and even undermine the very experiences—above all, victim testimony—that apparatus seems merely to stage. That the Truth Commission derives from a governmental apparatus that was central to colonial domination again does not mean its repetition of colonial juridical forms is necessary or inevitable. But it does mean that the TRC's true novelty can only begin to be understood when we approach it as an institution and practice of postcolonial politics. To begin outlining that understanding, it is necessary to enter into a second genealogical detour.

5.1.2 The genealogy of the Commission of Inquiry, like the genealogy of indemnity jurisprudence, requires that we touch base with a premodern origin—not because we are antiquarians who value the past for the sake of the past alone, but because, per Chakrabarty, we are genealogists who want to understand how the impasses and crises that are implicit in modern political theories and practices manifest themselves in the way in which colonial governmentality explicitly posed its juridical questions for itself. It is, admittedly, quite difficult to generalize about Commissions of Inquiry in any sweeping way. The Commission of Inquiry is not only an extremely flexible technique of governance, one that can differ wildly depending on the wording of its mandate, but also a creation of law that, in its origins, objects, applications, and administrative power is extremely variegated: Judicial Commissions of Inquiry are, for example, not the same as Royal Commissions of Inquiry; and Royal Commissions of Inquiry are distinct, in turn, from Select Committees. Nevertheless, almost all commissions share a number of distinctive epistemic regularities that, given the symptomatic silence on the problem of the "commission" in "transitional justice," are well worth considering.

The Commission of Inquiry, as Oz Frankel has written, is "a remnant of the old regime. Its power rested, at least nominally, on the royal prerogative to delegate power to a group of subjects, a practice that may be traced back as far as the Doomsday Book of 1086."[17] In medieval England, where *commissio* was a synonym for the monarch's personal command, commissions were used as tribunals (to conduct hearings into legal guilt and innocence), as organs of investigation and detection (to acquire knowledge about conspiracies, sedition, treason, and confederacies within the kingdom), and as despotic instruments to persecute opponents of the Crown ("the king shall often send his commissioners in great force," wrote John Fortescue, who knew whereof he spoke, having himself served frequently in this capacity, "to repress and punish rioters and risers").[18] Gradually, however, their "inquisitorial function" (their use *ad inquirendum*, for the purposes of gathering knowledge about the kingdom) and their "inquisitional function" (their use *ad audiendum et terminandum*, for the purpose of hearing and determining cases), which were never entirely distinct in medieval England,[19] began to come under scrutiny and thence to separate. Already in the late sixteenth century, Francis Bacon noted that Parliamentary legislation was taking up many of the same problems and achieving many of the same objects and aims that hitherto had been achieved by royal commissions (e.g., the question of how to dispose of the goods of bankruptcies, the punishment of counterfeiters, the examination of riots, inquiries into unlawful hunting, the taxation and punishment of servant laborers, and the punishment of rogues and vagabonds).[20] If royal commissions later would come to be seen as challenges to parliamentary power,[21] this would be not least because the emergence of parliamentary power itself presented a challenge to the ways and means of the royal commission.

From the seventeenth century on, the Commission of Inquiry would retain a function within English governance that was less inquisitional than inquisitorial. Using the technique of the Commission of Inquiry, Holdsworth argued, the nascent state would "inform[] itself" in order "to solve the many problems of this new age [namely, modernity]."[22] In the sixteenth century, accordingly, Commissions of Inquiry would acquire information about the compounding of prisoner debts, felons, the reformation of canon law, relations between the town and university of Cambridge, the supply of corn in certain counties, and the regulation of provisions to still other counties.[23] In all of these domains, the aim of the Commission of Inquiry was quite distinct from the aim of law courts. Its objective was not to determine guilt or innocence, to apply existing laws to specific cases, or even to rethink existing laws and establish precedents on the basis of what some would today call "hard cases." It was to figure out how to better manage natural and social phenomena based on the discovery of the "laws" (or, better, regularities, norms, or equilibriums) intrinsic in those phenomena. It aimed at knowledge of proximate, immediate, and efficient causes as determined by instrumental reason, their necessary and sufficient conditions, and dependent and independent variables, as determined by the natural and social sciences (statistics chief among them). The goal of the Commission of Inquiry was not, then, to apply a preexisting norm to social and natural phenomena; it was to treat an event of social or natural aberration or excess (e.g., an epidemic) as an occasion to discover the norms intrinsic in social and natural phenomena themselves (e.g., the social vectors and biological processes by which smallpox communicates itself), in order to discern in them their innermost mechanisms and dynamics. Once these mechanisms and dynamics were thoroughly known, it then became possible to manage things themselves without recourse to the prohibitory form of the law. Government could achieve equilibrium and homeostasis (in the classic manner of instrumental reason) by making adjustments that used the dynamics internal to things themselves to cancel out any excesses or aberrations to which they might lend themselves (here, the technique of vaccination or inoculation—using a quotient of the disease to establish immunity from the disease—is exemplary). In this way, knowledge of natural and social phenomena could serve as a means not only to the end of achieving equilibriums and homeostases within those phenomena themselves but also, moreover, to the end of the creation and maintenance of a balanced and flourishing capitalist political order.

Michel Foucault has argued that the transformation of the medieval state into the administrative state of the fifteenth and sixteenth centuries amounted to a "governmentalization of the state," in which the state was primarily defined no longer by the territory it defended but, rather, by the felicity of its management of natural and social life.[24] The Commission of Inquiry was at the very center of this transformation. Not only did it come into being within the king's privy council (which, as Holdsworth observes, was the precursor to the modern executive branch); in its quest for information and knowledge, it also, as Holdsworth notes, served as one of the "germs" from which the machinery of the modern, rational and bureaucratic state would burst out of the husk of the medieval order.[25] Precisely because of its central place and function within British monarchy, in other words, the Commission of Inquiry also could be instrumental in the undoing of monarchy: the rationalization of its particular powers helped set into motion the rationalization of monarchical power more generally.[26]

In its modern iteration, the Commission of Inquiry would emerge as an administrative apparatus through which the sovereign (the Crown, but now in closer connection with "public opinion"[27]) could pose questions to itself about the scope, limits, and goals of the governance of its populations and territory. These were questions about government's epistemic and institutional limits, and the answers to them would provide the sovereign with empirical knowledge about what it is that government does when it governs and, above all, why and how it was that, in a particular case, government may have failed to govern. The conditions under which Commissions of Inquiry became necessary and desirable were therefore, despite the wide divergence in commissions' mandates, fairly uniform. Commissions of Inquiry almost always came into being on the occasion of some governmental scandal or crisis. Whether implicitly or explicitly, they were almost always appointed to restore public confidence in government. They almost always took as their point of departure some or another anomaly in or exception to government's normal administration of the population's health, wealth, welfare, and safety. They almost always concluded with findings that located, often with extraordinary detail, fault or blame (which is not to say criminal guilt) in one or several persons. Given those findings of fault or blame, they almost always sought, in their recommendations, to propose improvements to and for government's attempts to secure the health, wealth, welfare, and safety of certain populations—or, at the very least and in what often amounted to the same thing, to avoid a repetition or recurrence of the scandal or crisis in question.

It is not difficult to see, therefore, that the fundamental horizon within which the Commission of Inquiry posed the question of governance for itself was both "sovereign" (because the commission, even under conditions of parliamentary sovereignty, was created "by command" of the person of the sovereign[28] and, indeed, classified as a "command paper" within the taxonomy of parliamentary procedure) and "biopolitical" (because of the substance of the inquiries themselves). The Commission of Inquiry was not primarily, in other words, an organ of civic self-government, public debate or discussion, or political self-representation (though it did, of course, on occasion function in tandem with these techniques and institutions). It was more precisely an administrative apparatus in which a few dignified or charismatic persons (almost always led by male leaders or experts who were expected to imprint their "character" on a given commission and whose surnames frequently operated as metonyms for the commissions they led)[29] evaluated the relation between government and population on the terms of social scientific knowledge and natural scientific knowledge. It would be even more precise to say that the Commission of Inquiry was a device for the sovereign to pose for itself the question of why and how its biopolitical strategies had failed or were failing, in a recurrent attempt to calibrate and fine-tune those strategies, to adjust the relation between government and population in an endless effort to achieve a fit between the two, to understand the norms internal to a population by studying their pathologies and anomalies—in an endless attempt, that is, to administer the population's health, wealth, welfare, and safety in the most optimal way possible.

5.2 To this end, but also always within the limits of this sort of administrative reason, Commissions of Inquiry were not at all adverse to the notion that they should "open their ear" to the voices of the victims of colonial administrative violence. To the contrary, this openness was one of the primary, if inexplicit, contributions of Commissions of Inquiry to colonial governance more generally. The Jamaica Royal Commission was paradigmatic in this respect. Commissioned in December of 1865 by a command of Queen Victoria, the JRC was an attempt on the part of the government of the prime minister, John Russell, to calm a British public that had become outraged by news of Governor Edward Eyre's violent suppression of the Morant Bay Rebellion in October of 1865.[30] More specifically, the JRC was created by the Russell government to respond to a group of English radicals called the "Jamaica Committee," whose outrage was directed, in particular, at Eyre's claim for the legality, under martial law and indemnity acts, of the summary executions, tortures, and imprisonments he had ordered.[31] Although the Jamaica Committee had demanded "a searching Parliamentary inquiry into the past and present social, legislative, and political condition of Jamaica, and to promote measures for the future good government of the Colony,"[32] the resulting royal commission inquired only into "the origin, nature, and circumstances of the said disturbances, and with respect to the Measures adopted in the course of their Suppression."[33] In its pursuit of this mandate, the commissioners "collected a large body of evidence," including, among other things, "oral and documentary" sources.[34] In the sixty hearings it held, the JRC listened to the testimony of over seven hundred of those involved in the uprising and its suppression, recording that testimony in a publication over one thousand pages long.[35] Vested with the power to subpoena witnesses and take their examination upon oath,[36] the JRC nevertheless quickly found that, at least for a certain class of witnesses, subpoena powers would not be necessary. The readiness with which and extent to which their mostly native witnesses proffered oral evidence "proved at first a source of some embarrassment."[37] While the commissioners would have preferred, they wrote, to have kept each branch of the inquiry "separate and distinct," so that all evidence could be taken consecutively, the "irregularity in the attendance of witnesses," together with the sheer amount of evidence they received, forced them to modify their original plan.

> It then became necessary, in order to avoid expense and loss of time, and notwithstanding the inconvenience incident to the derangement of our plan, to take the evidence of such persons as were at hand, numbers of whom were

daily presenting themselves before us, especially from the lately disturbed districts, for the purposes of tendering their evidence.[38]

To solve this problem, the JRC settled on a compromise that should be of interest to students of the TRC. Because of its administrative inability to hear all testimonies, as it had planned, the JRC decided to give extra time to what one observer called "a selection of typical cases," ensuring that, in the words of legal historian R.W. Kostal, "it had garnered evidence on all the kinds of major transgressions in all the localities that had been under martial law."[39] Thus reassured that it had excluded no material evidence and neglected no material witness,[40] the JRC nevertheless encountered another difficulty, this one related not to the quantity but to the quality of native testimony: it found that it could not verify this "vast mass of evidence," especially that given by the three hundred witnesses examined in connection with "the graver cases."[41] Acting in the best tradition of the Royal Commission of Inquiry, the JRC commissioners thus took measures into their own hands and made "an official visitation of the lately disturbed districts, with a view to a report being made to us of the number and value of houses destroyed in the course of the suppression."[42] Even this, however, did not, in the end, resolve the doubts the JRC harbored about the testimony of victims. The paradoxical passages in which the JRC's report describes these problems are worth quoting in their unbroken continuity; their jagged non sequiturs are symptoms of the simultaneously open and closed way in which the commission lent its ear to the voice of the native victim.

> In many cases the witnesses manifested a singular ignorance of the nature and value of evidence, as well as a misconception of the proper scope of the Inquiry.
>
> As regards the negroes, it is enough to recall the fact that they were for the most part uneducated peasants, speaking in accents strange to the ear, often in a phraseology of their own, with vague conceptions of number and time, unaccustomed to definiteness or accuracy of speech, and, in many cases, still smarting under a sense of injuries sustained.
>
> Many of them, again, misconceived the object of the Commission, and came to tell their tale of houses burnt or property lost, in the undisguised hope of obtaining compensation. Some also heard of the money which was

being paid out of the funds at our disposal to those who travelled to Spanish Town to give evidence.

Even as regards the other witnesses, many even of the educated class could often scarcely be restrained from giving opinions in general and positive terms as equivalent to facts, or from stating as facts within their own knowledge matter communicated to them by others.

A considerable body of evidence, especially in relation to the state of the Island, was thus tendered, which, on being sifted by us, proved of but little value.

The result of these tendencies on the part of so large a number of the witnesses has been the accumulation of a vast mass of evidence, much of which is vague, unimportant, and remote from the subject of Inquiry.

Upon a review, however, of the evidence as a whole, and with a full appreciation of the gravity of the defects, in substance as well as in form, to which we have averted, we are nevertheless satisfied that all such defects are more than compensated by their collateral results.

If we have erred on the side of a too great facility in giving audience to all persons, of whatever class, at whatever stage of the Inquiry in which they might present themselves, and in receiving evidence in many cases but little pertinent or material, and if, moreover, in consequence, the evidence taken is more or less wanting in order and somewhat redundant, we have yet the satisfaction of feeling that the Inquiry has been both thorough in fact, and thorough likewise in the estimation of the persons most concerned.[43]

On the one hand, the JRC reports, most of the evidence given by natives was *without value.* Not only was this testimony disorderly, vague, incoherent, venal, and untrue; the mandate of the JRC required it to focus on a very specific point in law, not on the pain of natives. On the other hand, this same evidence, precisely to the extent that it could be received and published in a formless mass of raw testimonial material, was also *of great value.* Not only did hearing all comers enable the JRC to fulfill its mandate ("the ascertainment of the truth" through a "full and impartial inquiry"); it also allowed the JRC report to sustain the premise of colonial rule, producing an epistemic basis for colonial administrators to speak on behalf of the native victim, to make the case for the native victim with language and a reasonableness that were, on the terms of the JRC, unattainable for natives themselves. Jeremy

Bentham's epochal but ambivalent critique of Aristotle's definition of the human as the "political animal"—"The question is not, Can they *reason?* nor, Can they *talk?* but, Can they *suffer?*"[44]— provided one of the key premises for the humanitarianism of the Jamaica Committee. Precisely in its formless-ness and in the incoherence of the suffering it conveyed, the raw testimonial material that appeared in the JRC report allowed for the supporters of the British Empire, which included the members of the Jamaica Committee— above all, its most prominent leader, John Stuart Mill[45]—to assume that by speaking on behalf of the rule of law, they also were speaking on behalf of those who could suffer but not speak or reason.

The decisive point here, in other words, is not that the JRC commission-ers themselves were personally paternalistic or condescending or that the JRC itself was implemented in a way that was biased or flawed—that could have been more empirically accurate or materially inclusive.[46] It is that the JRC, precisely as a Commission of Inquiry in the best and most robust sense, was nevertheless structured by the same epistemic impasse that structured colonial rule in general and colonial Commissions of Inquiry in particular. On the one hand, it listened to all comers, turning away no material witness, no matter how incoherent or unverifiable. On the other hand, however, it heard almost nothing: concluding that Eyre should be faulted only for an excessive and unnecessary use of martial law, it resisted the conclusion that the coincidence of legality and cruelty in Eyre's person was symptomatic of the failure of the colonial civilizing mission more generally. The commis-sion engaged in this paradoxical endeavor not despite but precisely because of its representational apparatus, which obliged it to reach its conclusions through empirically verifiable knowledge, up to and including empirically verifiable knowledge about native suffering.

Although this impasse may find its extreme and exemplary illustration in the JRC, it was not at all limited to that commission. Adam Ashforth has argued that in apartheid South Africa, the "Grand Tradition" of the "Native Question" Commission of Inquiry involved the substitution of the voice of Africans with the voice of the "expert." Under political conditions defined by the exclusion of Africans from institutions of political representation, Ash-forth argues, the work of governance required regular commissions in which "experts" could speak on Africans' behalf.[47] While, as we soon shall see, the Commissions of Inquiry appointed under South African apartheid func-tioned very much in the way Ashforth describes, it is nevertheless worth underlining the point that the "inclusion" of African voices alone is no anti-dote to the political exclusion Ashforth rightly criticizes. After all, the JRC, which involved no "experts" of the sort Ashforth describes under conditions of apartheid, made a strenuous effort to include as much native testimony as possible, only to exclude much, if not all, of it as an epistemologically sound basis for their conclusions and findings.[48] In this empirical and material "inclusion" of voices, the JRC was, in effect, engaging in a form of epistemic "exclusion" that differed only in degree and not in kind from the "exclusion by expert" criticized by Ashforth. In colonial Jamaica as in apartheid South Africa, the Commission of Inquiry opened its ear to the victims of state violence, but always within the limits of a very specific epistemic field—one that sought to restore law, coherence, and order to colonial rule, while also rigorously foreclosing on the possibility that the colonized themselves should determine the extent and direction of this restoration.

This same paradox, this same strange mechanism of inclusive exclusion, structured the final report of the JRC. Aspiring to the schemata of administrative equilibrium that is the implicit premise of all Commissions of Inquiry, the JRC's recommendations and conclusions were evenhanded to a fault. Construing martial law as a "necessary evil" of colonial rule, it refrained from calling either colonialism or martial law into question. On the one hand, the JRC concluded that the Morant Bay Rebellion was not merely a riot but an incipient rebellion and that Eyre was not only justified in declaring martial law but deserved praise for the "skill, promptitude, and vigor" with which he implemented it.[49] On the other hand, the JRC criticized the cruelty that occurred under Eyre's authority, concluding that the punishments inflicted by Eyre under martial law were "far greater than the necessity required."[50] The JRC was silent, however, on the crucial question of whether Eyre and his lieutenants had committed culpable murder by executing George William Gordon, one of the leaders of the Morant Bay Rebellion. Reacting with fury to this silence, the Jamaica Committee undertook a heroic but ultimately futile effort to use the evidence generated by the JRC to establish the illegality of Eyre's declaration of martial law and indemnity.[51] In July of 1866, John Stuart Mill persuaded the Jamaica Committee to put a resolution before the British Parliament arguing for the prosecution of Eyre. Even though he had argued against Mill within the confines of the Jamaica Committee, the resolution was presented by Charles Buxton (son of the abolitionist Thomas Foxwell Buxton), then chair of the Jamaica Committee.[52] Buxton's resolution cited the commission's seventh conclusion, namely, "[t]hat the punishments inflicted were excessive. (1.) That the punishment of death was unnecessarily frequent. (2.) That the floggings were reckless, and at Bath [a town in Western Jamaica] positively barbarous. (3.) That the burning of 1,000 houses was wanton and cruel."[53] It called for, among other things, the compensation of those whose property was destroyed and whose loved ones were "put to death illegally," as well as for the punishment of civil, military, and naval officers who acted with severity or excess in their suppression of the "rebellion."[54] Speaking in support of the motion and on behalf of the Jamaica Committee, Mill argued forcefully that the findings of the commission warranted prosecution of colonial authorities on the precedent set by *Wright v. Fitzgerald.* Mill's reading of the commissioners' report is worth reprinting here at length. Not only was it "worthy of the occasion" (in the words of one of Mill's contemporaries),[55] but there is a definite sense in which it is the forgotten exemplar for the case that human rights jurists make today for the prosecution of state officials who commit crimes in the name of the state. This is because it comes from the thinker who is the "leading exemplar" of nineteenth-century British liberalism[56] and because, in the indemnification of Eyre, together with the inaction of the Derby government, Mill rightly recognized that the whole theory of modern liberal government hung in the balance.

> Now, if, after due investigation, the Government and the country generally had made up their minds that all these lives were justly and properly taken, and all these floggings and burnings justly and properly inflicted, there would have been no ground on which to require the Government to prosecute the agents and authors, though private individuals would be at liberty to do so if they pleased. The case, however, is far otherwise. Respecting the degree of culpability of these transactions there is a wide difference of opinion, but that there has been serious culpability no one now disputes. The events have undergone a minute inquiry, by Commissioners carefully selected and invested with full power to ascertain the facts, but not, I must remind the right hon. Gentleman, empowered to declare what is the character of those facts in the eye of the law. The Commissioners have emphatically condemned a large portion of the proceedings. They declare that many more persons have been put to death than ought to have been put to death; some of these on evidence which they declare to have been, so far as it ap-

pears on record, wholly insufficient to justify the findings, while in other cases, assuming the evidence to be unimpeachable, the sentences were not justified by the facts deposed to. The floggings they pronounce to have been reckless, and some of them positively barbarous: the flogging of women they reprobate under any circumstances, and in that I am sure the House will not differ from them. The burnings they pronounce wanton and cruel. There is no need to go one step beyond the verdict of the Commissioners. I am almost ashamed to speak of such acts with the calmness and in the moderate language which the circumstances require. The House has supped full of horrors throughout the speech of my hon. Friend. But we need not go beyond the dry facts of the Commissioners' summary. On their showing, the lives of subjects of Her Majesty have been wrongfully taken, the persons of others wrongfully maltreated; and I maintain that when such things have been done, there is a primâ facie demand for legal punishment, and that a court of criminal justice can alone determine whether such punishment has been merited, and if merited, what ought to be its amount. The taking of human lives without justification, which in this case is an admitted fact, cannot be condoned by anything short of a criminal tribunal. Neither the Government, nor this House, nor the whole English nation combined, can exercise a pardoning power without previous trial and sentence. I know not for what more important purpose Courts of Law exist than for the security of human life. Hitherto in this country the agents of the executive Government have had to answer for themselves in the same Courts of Law as the rest of Her Majesty's subjects. But if officers of the Government are to be allowed to take the lives of the Queen's subjects improperly—as has been confessedly done in this case—without being called to a judicial account, and having the excuses they make for it sifted and adjudicated by the tribunal in that case provided, we are giving up altogether the principle of government by law, and resigning ourselves to arbitrary power.[57]

It is important to note here, for the purposes of identifying the epistemic field set into motion by the JRC report, what Mill did *not* say. First of all, Mill did not make recourse to the more general enthymeme circulating in radical political opinion at the time, namely, that the real reason Eyre could be pardoned was because his otherwise unpardonable crimes involved "only Negro blood."[58] Mill did not treat the report as an occasion to speak against the assumptions of colonial rule.[59] Nor did Mill seek to call into question the premises of the JRC report itself; in this, he was quite unlike those other famous readers of nineteenth-century Commissions of Inquiry, Karl Marx and Friedrich Engels.[60] Mill, by contrast, followed Buxton in arguing from the premise of the government's own report. Mill's dialectic, quite unlike that of Marx and Engels, sought to turn the JRC report into the source of a greater consistency: a consistency between colonial despotism and the rule of law. This desire may have added a certain quotient of force and clarity to Mill's argumentation, because the JRC report (unlike the antiracism of certain members of the Jamaica Committee or the communism of Marx and Engels) was marked with the consent and seal of approval of Queen Victoria herself. But this choice of premise also weakened Mill's argumentation in a decisive way. Despite the cogency of Mill's argumentation, the JRC report was so rigorously evenhanded that it could not but create doubt for his claims on the premises he had chosen (i.e., "the dry facts of the Commissioners' summary"). The JRC report did not, in short, fully support Mill's characterization of its findings.

The JRC report, in fact, provided more than enough evidence for conservative and liberal members of Parliament to stifle Mill's call for prosecution. Speaking against the resolution, the undersecretary of state, Charles Bowyer Adderley (the "mouthpiece of the Government"),[61] argued, "[I]t is clear that what the hon. Member wants the House to do is to pick out of the Report of the Commissioners all that censures the authorities in Jamaica, and to omit all that praises their action or excuses in any way their excesses in suppressing the insurrection."[62] Was it not, Adderley asked, "the opinion of the Commissioners, and all the authorities who had been consulted on the matter, that martial law was fully and properly established, that it was fully justifiable, and proclaimed upon good reasons"? If so, Adderley argued, there was nothing illegal to prosecute.[63] Moreover, Adderley argued, any new action that Parliament might take based on the JRC report's revelations would either be redundant (the queen had already accepted many of the commissioners' revelations, and Eyre was already being tried) or at odds with the basic purposes of the House (which is not a judicial tribunal). Adderley did not, to be clear, see in the JRC report any grounds either to "pardon" or to "exculpate" Eyre (pardon is, as Mill suggests, predicated on guilt, and exculpation is impossible except in a court of law). In Adderley's view, the report should be read not as "cause" for legal action but as nothing more and nothing less than simple description, evidence: "We must take the evidence and the *Report* as given to us."[64] He viewed the JRC report as only that—a report, not a prescription.

Meanwhile, the colonial secretary, Cardwell, whose treatment of the Eyre situation the Jamaica Committee found "judicious"[65] (he at first praised Eyre's actions in suppressing the tumult, then voiced his concern at Eyre's continuation of martial law, and later removed Eyre from his governorship), adopted a different reading still, one that reiterated the commissioners' own ambivalent relationship with the archive of testimony they at once heard and ignored. Although Cardwell reported that his reading of the entire contents of the "ghastly volume" (and not merely the commissioners' thirty-four-page introduction) left him with "the deepest sorrow and regret," he also observed that "[i]t is the invariable effect of detail to influence the imagination and the feelings" and that he must prefer "the deliberate and careful finding of the Royal Commissioners, who heard and saw the witnesses" over "the complaints contained in the ponderous book which the Commissioners have prepared."[66] Although Cardwell could not be described as an unambiguous supporter of Eyre, his "judicious" skepticism of the testimony implied his consent to the same premises that grounded the explicitly racist arguments of Eyre's allies (who included none other than Thomas Carlyle):[67] because the negroes could not be trusted to represent themselves, their testimony, however detailed, could not be considered credible or reliable. Because the findings of the commissioners against Eyre were balanced out with praise for Eyre, Cardwell reasoned, he could not support the motion to prosecute. This did not, of course, mean that Cardwell was unsympathetic to the suffering of Eyre's victims; it only meant that his sympathy with their grief had a precise limit. In Cardwell's view, it seems, grief was acceptable insofar as it did not translate into legal or political grievance, insofar as it remained grief pure and simple—we might say, insofar as it remained purely human suffering in the strict Benthamite sense of the word, suffering that could not be given form by speech or reason.

To the reading strategies implied in the positions of Mill (*accuse*) and Adderley (*exonerate*), we must then add a third, that of Cardwell: *mourn.* For Cardwell, the purpose of reading the report of a Commission of Inquiry into alleged crimes by state officials was neither to prosecute nor to exculpate. It was to grieve, to lament, to experience a tragedy all the more poignant for the fact that it was, as all the available evidence clearly showed, unavoidable. This, as we shall soon see, would become one of the dominant paradigms for the reading of the reports of Commissions of Inquiry—one of the dominant ways of resolving the ambiguous relation of Commissions of Inquiry to courts of law. Tragedy here emerges as a discourse of power: it becomes a poetics of government, a mode, at once graceful and profoundly euphemistic, by which institutions vested with considerable administrative and discretionary power might "humanize" themselves by "regretting" or "lamenting" the fact that they would not and indeed perhaps even could not act on the knowledge communicated to them—in this case, that Eyre was plainly and publicly known to have murdered and tortured in the name of the Crown. Tragedy, in short, here becomes a mode in which government construes the juridical status of those among its officials who kill with impunity.

In the end, the slightly different positions of Adderley and Cardwell carried the day against the more radical position of Mill, whose repeated attempts to prosecute Eyre would fail[68] and who would lose his 1868 campaign for reelection to Parliament largely because of his stand on Eyre.[69] Even though the Compensation Commission would, in 1867, award £2,426 to those who suffered "damages" from the government's suppression of the disturbances (which, by the Compensation Commission's own calculations, came to £10,136), no prosecution of Eyre would be forthcoming.[70] "The House would weep over these atrocities [committed by the Eyre against the queen's "negro subjects"] but it declined to punish the authors of them," Edward Underhill would write in 1895.[71] "It is unnecessary to go over the sickening story again," he continued, "but it was resolved [by the House] that, so far as the Government and Parliament could determine, the guilt of the perpetrators should go unpunished, and the terrible injustice pass away unavenged. For the astounding catalogue of crimes recorded by the Commissioners, there should be no judicial or even political remedy, though not one tittle of the facts was denied or disproof attempted."[72] Yet even though Underhill rightly decried the way in which Parliament would leave the matter of Morant Bay, we are obliged to observe that, in its form if not in its content, Underhill's own narration is in fundamental agreement with the action of the House by his own description: a "tragedy," as Underhill titled his 1895 account of the Morant Bay events, is nothing if not a lament, and "lament" is precisely what the House did when it "wept without prosecuting."

Accuse, exonerate, mourn—here, then, are the principal historiographical modes in which the suffering conveyed in the commissioners' report was interpreted by its readers and, indeed, addressees in Parliament. None can be said to be a misreading. In particular, the report did not at all exclude the possibility of prosecuting Eyre and his cronies for the suffering they caused. To the contrary, the epistemic field it produced carefully left that possibility open, and numerous indictments were laid as a result of the evidence it produced.[73] At the same time, however, and especially in the case of Eyre himself, it painstakingly neutralized that same possibility, compensating for its allowance of one reading of its findings by pointedly opening up the possibility of a reading opposed to it.[74] The report did not, then, *rule out* the possibility of prosecution. It produced an epistemic field that *canceled out* that possibility. It hosted the possibility of accusation—a calling to account—but it equally hosted the possibilities of exoneration and, differently, of depoliticized suffering. The report was written as if its purpose was to validate all three historiographical modes at one and the same time, each compensating for the other through a carefully calibrated latticework of weights and counterweights—as if the governmental task of restoring equilibrium *to* the colony could only be accomplished if the principle of equilibrium first governed the report on disequilibrium *in* the colony. Thus did the JRC's report establish a subtle but decisive paradigm for the interpretation of the victims of colonial violence. Judicious without also being judicial, it accused without prosecuting, exonerated without pardoning, and mourned without fury or rage.

5.3 Paradigmatic of the constrained epistemic field within which Commissions of Inquiry sought to give voice to the suffering of natives, the Jamaica Controversy was also paradigmatic of the incoherence of imperial rule, particularly the failure of Victorian jurists to reconcile the despotism of colonial administration with the liberal principles of the metropolitan rule of law.[75] The Commission of Inquiry—whose "reports" were, for Hannah Arendt, the exemplary text of colonial bureaucracy[76]—contributed to this failure in a subtle but decisive manner. From the very beginning of its modern refashioning, the Commission of Inquiry would be deployed in England's administration of its colonies.[77] Starting with a secret report issued by the Commission of Inquiry tasked with understanding tumults in Ireland (1798), the Crown would create similar commissions in Australia (1834), South Africa (1835), Ceylon (1848), Mauritius (1848), and Jamaica (1866), to investigate, in particular, the causes of anticolonial riots and rebellions, as well as the justification of their violent suppression.[78] This practice intensified with de-colonization in the twentieth century, with various Commissions of Inquiry publishing reports on disturbances in Trinidad (1903 and 1937), Ireland (1914), Palestine (1921), Zanzibar (1936), Barbados (1937), Rhodesia (1940), Mauritius (1943), Uganda (1945 and 1960), the Gold Coast (1948), Eastern Nigeria (1949), Southern Sudan (1955), Sierra Leone (1956), Kanpur (1961), and India (1967).[79] Crucially, when these Commissions of Inquiry looked into the "causes" of a colonial riot or a police massacre, the concept of "cause" at issue was understood not in a juridical sense, as *causa* (a controversy or dispute that could and should be remedied in a court of law), but in a noso-logical or diagnostic sense, as a "source of ailment" (a malady or disorder that can and should be remedied through informed administrative measures). In the same way that colonial administrators would want to prevent a shortage of grain, a contamination of water, a potato blight, or the spread of disease, so too would they want to take measures to prevent the recurrence of antico-lonial notions and emotions among the restless natives. In cases where those notions and emotions did end up exploding into riots, they would want to know exactly how much force could be used to restore order, and the correct measurement of that amount often (though not always) required the minute investigations of a Commission of Inquiry. Within a biopolitical horizon, a riot or rebellion—like unsanitary water, inefficient distribution of grain, a wasteful expenditure from the public purse, or an epidemic—was, in other words, nothing more and nothing less than the mark of a disequilibrium within the health, welfare, and safety of populations. It was a phenomenon that was to be understood not legally but etiologically, and it was something that colonial governments should seek to prevent in the future through cor-rections to governmental policy, by implementing governmental measures that would be more capable of maintaining order to the precise degree that they were grounded on reliable empirical knowledge about the populations they administered. Almost invariably, this knowledge would seek the ori-gin of the riot or disturbance in direct and detailed social scientific knowl-edge about race and ethnicity. All biopolitics entails race difference as one of its constitutive and central polarities, and the Commission of Inquiry, as a biopolitical apparatus, was no exception.[80] Commissions that were concerned, in particular, with riots and disturbances posed the question of the failure of governance not only in demographic and economic terms (births and deaths, nutrition, disease) but also in psychological and anthropological terms (grievances, misunderstandings, perceptions, beliefs, and customs). They invariably concluded by proposing governmental measures for mitigating the conflict between various racial and ethnic populations—techniques for better managing or administering the equilibrium between races and ethnicities, for preventing the recurrence of hostility and conflict within colonial settlements. In their pursuit of this aim, Commissions of Inquiry proved to be remarkably effective apparatuses for the articulation of inequality, suffering, and injustice. What they almost never produced, however, were proposals for self-government: as it was deployed under colonial conditions, the Commissions of Inquiry was, above all, a device for the *displacement* and *deferral* of political self-representation, a device that allowed for the representation of the health, safety, and welfare of populations who were, in paradigmatic colonial manner, understood to be unable to represent themselves.

In a sense, then, it is a small wonder that Commissions of Inquiry would be so regularly coupled with the indemnity jurisprudence that, as we saw in Part I, was so constitutive a part of colonial governmentality. After all, a fundamental demand for knowledge is structured directly into indemnity jurisprudence. Whereas *Wright v. Fitzgerald* established limitations for the indemnification of state officials who acted illegally to suppress riots and rebellions, *Rex v. Pinney* (1832) established the conditions under which it was also illegal for state officials *not* to suppress riots and rebellions. The fine line between too much force and not enough force was determined by the principle of necessity, which, in turn, depended on two other criteria: honesty and reasonableness. On the theory that martial law was, in effect, the law of necessity and that illegal acts committed by state officials under martial law could only be indemnified to the extent that they were necessary for the *salus populi*, indemnification, like martial law, depended on the acquisition of knowledge.[81] In many cases (though by no means all), the only way for the Crown to determine whether illegal acts were honestly "necessitated" by the case at hand was through an extensive and detailed inquiry into the causes and facts of the riot or disturbance itself. Because of the sheer complexity of the event and the sheer number of persons affected, such an inquiry could not be undertaken by any court of law, but which, once it was undertaken by a Commission of Inquiry, which seemed uniquely fitted to this purpose, nevertheless led to insoluble juridical impasses.

As its genealogy shows, the Commission of Inquiry is a technique of governance with an indeterminate relation to the rule of law. Commissions of Inquiry were routinely criticized throughout the eighteenth and nineteenth centuries for the way their premodern tribunals violate key principles of the rule of law—indeed, for the way in which their administrative practices lent themselves precisely to the monarchical despotism that the rule of law was designed to displace and extinguish. Nevertheless, Commissions of Inquiry were not completely eradicated by the emergence of the rule of law: they remained a residual force within English governance, a site of ongoing struggle between Parliament and the Crown, and it was left to individual commissions to reconcile their administrative practices with the principles of the rule of law, adopting into their procedures, in a sometimes ad hoc and piecemeal manner, some of the modes and principles of common law and the modern judiciary.[82] The JRC was, as R. W. Kostal has shown, exemplary in this regard.[83] But for this same reason, there was no clear way to translate the report generated by any given commission into the terms and practices of English courts or even into Parliament. Even though, as a contemporary jurist has observed, the entire purpose of a Commission of Inquiry was "to establish the facts so that action may be taken,"[84] it was certainly unclear—and in the case of the JRC, it was somewhat unclear[85]—precisely what that action should be.

To begin, the commissioners who wrote these reports were not elected but appointed to their positions, so they could not be said to speak or act with the sort of representative legitimacy specific to democratic institutions.[86] Moreover, even though commissions could, in principle, give rise to prosecutions, they were more often substitutes for prosecutions. The procedures through which evidence emerged in Commissions of Inquiry (without due process of law) and the evenhanded conclusions they consistently sought to produce had the distinct effect of creating difficulties for (or even precluding) later prosecutions.[87] Those Commissions of Inquiry that seemed to disclose possible criminal wrongdoing, particularly crimes by state officials, thus strayed into the indeterminate zone (or, if you will, the epochal scar tissue left over from the English revolution) between the rule of law and the royal *commissio*. The point of a commission was not, after all, to seek justice for the violation of rights or the loss of life. It was simply to seek full and impartial information about the origin, nature, and circumstances of that violation and loss and to communicate that information to the Crown. The domain of the commission, then, may have overlapped with that of the courts and Parliament, for the commission took as the object of its inquiry many of the same objects that were also under dispute in the courts and Parliament. But even where the commission allocated fault, blame, and responsibility for actions that otherwise would have constituted "cause," its report would painstakingly distinguish itself from a legal discourse on criminal or civil guilt and even from a political discourse on self-representation.[88] Even, especially, in its most juridicalized form—such as the JRC—the Commission of Inquiry thus remained, at root, a biopolitical apparatus, the primary concern of which was not law but the administration of populations. Even when its discourse pertained to rule of law—as in the case of the JRC—it spoke about the rule of law in terms that were not derived from the rule of law, that not only preceded but also often precluded the rule of law. Because the Commission of Inquiry was a residual technique of premodern, personalized governance that was antagonistic with and indeed remained incompletely assimilated into the impersonal institutions and practices of the modern rule of law, the commission left open the question of how to interpret and act on a report of a Commission of Inquiry within the courts and the Parliament. Even, especially, when the content of the report was colonial massacre.

This indeterminacy became especially acute when, as with the JRC, the Commission of Inquiry in question operated in tandem with indemnity jurisprudence. Internal to indemnity jurisprudence was a procedural incommensurability between the modes of action, temporalities of reflection, and hermeneutic horizons proper to the institutions of the executive branch, on the one hand, and those of the judiciary, on the other. This incommensurability, which had roots in early modern political philosophy,[89] was addressed by the second and most conclusive of the two tests that jurists would derive from *Wright* (which we may call the "subjective" test). Here, as we have seen, the question was not whether or not the magistrate's illegal act was, "in reality," necessary for preserving the peace (the answer to this question hinged, to a large extent, on whether one posed it within the hermeneutic horizon of the executive or that of the judiciary). It was a much different question, one that neatly avoided the incommensurabilities of thought and action that divided the executive from the judiciary, the compromise question of whether the magistrate or person honestly believed that breaking the law was necessary (where honesty was understood with reference to the test of the "reasonable man," or, as Finlason put it with his characteristic flair for tautology, as "something reasonably honest as opposed to anything so reckless or ir-rational that no sensible man could honestly imagine it reasonable").[90] Any act in excess of this test could not be indemnified—but, of course, it is very difficult to imagine an act that would exceed these limits.

Particularly if, as in the Indemnity Act of 1800, Parliament placed the onus on the plaintiff to prove bad faith. For Dicey, therefore, the lesson of *Wright* was much more equivocal than it was for Willes. It was not that indemnification was conditional on service done in good faith to the public good. It was that "[e]verything depends on the terms of the Act of Indem-nity," which "may be either narrow or wide."[91] As bland as this lesson may seem, the simple fact that *Wright* contained any terms at all was actually decisive, for it enabled Dicey to cite the case in support of his argument against Frederick Pollock over the essence of martial law: whereas Pollock argued that indemnity was redundant and superfluous because it was always already presupposed in advance by any and all declarations of martial law, the fact that *Wright* placed conditions on indemnity allowed Dicey to argue that indemnification had a juridical status independent of martial law, as an uncertain and contingent convention that, however slightly, was nevertheless capable, in principle, of restraining the discretionary power of the execu-tive.[92]

After *Wright*, as we saw in section 2.4, the question for courts reviewing claims brought against indemnity acts was not whether law had been violat-ed but whether the lawbreaking person honestly believed that breaking the law was necessary. It is critical to point out here that the honesty and neces-sity tests in this emergent jurisprudence had a subtle but decisive function: they gave shape to the doubtless disorienting anxiety that confronted those tasked with the suppression of riots and rebellion. As apartheid's apologists would never tire of repeating, the position of the police officer faced with a riot was an unenviable one, for the twin imperatives of the rule of law and public safety, of the sovereignty of law and the law of sovereignty, some-times did oblige him to preserve public safety by breaking the law and to do so, importantly, without any guarantee or promise of indemnification. This anxiety was there by design: the police officer was *supposed* to suffer it. Its implicit purpose and function was to remain unwritten in order to inscribe itself all the more profoundly in the officer's conduct. But while uncertainty was indispensable if the indemnity convention was to function as a convention—uncertainty was its mode of being, just as surely as writing is the mode of being of statute law—*too much* uncertainty could throw off this delicate calibration, paralyzing the officer and endangering public safety. The *Wright* test was implicitly designed to get the dose right. After *Wright*, officials and magistrates remained bound (as they were before *Wright*, on the terms of *Rex v. Pinney* [1832]) to use the force they honestly believed to be necessary to suppress tumults and uprising. Now, however, given the new limits for parliamentary protection for acts committed in excess of "honestly necessary force" and, hence, for "honestly necessary force" itself, the anxious question of the juridical status of the acts performed under conditions of martial law was displaced: it became a question that could only be answered afterward, by judge and jury, and their answer might differ substantially from that formed by the magistrate and official.[93]

To be sure, then, indemnity jurisprudence entailed an administrative demand for the production of historical truth about the uses and abuses of martial law. Not only did indemnity cases oblige judge and jury to evaluate and determine the *casus necessitas* (the exact nature of the emergency situation) and how the "reasonable man" would act in that situation; they also were obliged to retrospectively infer from the acts of a given person (as in other areas of the law) whether or not that person's intentions were malicious or genuine. Because the question of bona fide intention presupposed a resolution of the prior question of the necessities of the case, the only way to determine what qualifies as bona fide was through inquiry into the essence and basis of emergency. Because this, in turn, required a knowledge of emergency that was at once detailed (what was the meaning of a specific utterance?), totalizing (was the emergency really an emergency or simply a perceived emergency?), specialized (involving knowledge of weaponry), and serious (involving threats to the existence of the state itself), it is clear why, as Chamberlain put it, the "grave and serious examination" demanded by a challenge to an indemnity act would not necessarily be best undertaken by a court of law, if it could be so undertaken at all. The indemnity convention, as we saw in section 2.3, was designed to heal the conflict between the two sources of the English Constitution: *the sovereign power of law* (the "rule of law") and *the law of sovereign power* (as exemplified by the maxim *salus populi suprema lex esto*). But the sort of detailed historical knowledge that was required in order to adjudicate indemnity could not be produced by either of the two political institutions that derived from these sources: the judiciary, on the one hand, and Parliament, on the other. To the extent the indemnity convention was able to reconcile this division, it thus also needed to exceed it: its capacity to reconcile the rule of law with the demands of public safety was predicated on a form of knowledge that neither the judiciary nor the executive could fully provide.

Internal to indemnity jurisprudence, therefore, there stirred an administrative demand for knowledge, a subtle but decisive demand that helps explain why, in a former colony like South Africa (where martial law was the norm and where the army would frequently be called out to suppress riots, rebellions, strikes, and other tumults), indemnity acts would be so consistently coupled with the Commission of Inquiry, this apparatus whose relatively unlimited powers of investigation seemed to be particularly well fitted for the work of scrutinizing the essential minutiae that alone could retroactively distinguish necessary from unnecessary violence. In 1914, 1922, 1923, 1961, 1977, and 1986, indemnity acts of varying scope would be coupled with Commissions of Inquiry of varying mandates tasked with the investigation of uses and abuses of martial law of varying severity. Sometimes this coupling even would take place while martial law was still underway. In 1900, for example, Kitchener's legal adviser Richard Solomon would cite the final report of the JRC to clarify martial law's concept of "necessity," to argue that Alfred Milner should administer martial law with an eye toward a future Commission of Inquiry, and to recommend indemnity for any illegal acts committed in bona fide defense of the colony.[94] More often, however, Commissions of Inquiry were organized to investigate the "necessity" of illegal acts committed under martial law only *after* an indemnity act had already legalized those acts.[95]

However uniquely fitted it may have seemed to produce precisely the knowledge demanded of it by indemnity jurisprudence, the Commission of Inquiry also frustrated the imperial desire—to reconcile the violence of colonial despotism with metropolitan theories of the rule of law—that provided that jurisprudence with its most active and essential energy. Because of the biopolitical terms that defined its epistemic field, the Commission of Inquiry was uniquely allergic to posing the question of culpability for the violent suppression of native riots or disturbances in terms of legal justice. Even when Commissions of Inquiry into riots and disturbances were not coupled with indemnity acts that were passed with the express intent of protecting from liability the police and officials who suppressed those riots (as they were not only in Jamaica but also in Ceylon and Mauritius), and even where, as in the case of the JRC's 1866 report, these commissions found fault with colonial authorities, their biopolitical presuppositions—prior even to their various mandates, which, given their occasional character, necessarily differed from one another quite drastically—still predisposed them toward the exculpation of those who killed, maimed, and tortured in the name of empire. As would become painfully evident under apartheid South Africa, the more that Commissions of Inquiry would be created to investigate state massacres, the less they would produce public debate and discussion (as apparently was the case in the metropole),[96] and the more they would reduce public debate, by obfuscating or even concealing altogether the ways and means of state crime.[97] Here, the Commission of Inquiry was not a fact-finding device; it was a "whitewashing" machine.

Chapter 6

THE RISE AND FALL OF THE
TUMULT COMMISSION

6.1.1 In colonial Southern Africa, the Commission of Inquiry would operate much differently than it did in the nineteenth-century metropole. Beginning at least with the 1823–35 Commission of Inquiry into the Condition and Treatment of Natives in Southern Africa, the purpose of the Commission of Inquiry was to enable the emergence of colonial government within the unfamiliar political space of the colonial territory. In 1852, the lieutenant governor of Natal appointed a commission to prepare for the "future government of the native tribes" in the district and, to this end, mandated the commissioners to perform a census of natives (registering populations using the names of chiefs), to distinguish between aboriginal natives and emigrating natives, to track the causes for the emigration of natives, to gather information about native chiefs and their powers to better understand native laws, to consider the "expediency of the proposal of removing the natives," and to look into "the causes of the want of labor, and the remedies applicable to ensure labour."[1] A similar, if more precise, set of questions would be posed in 1878, following Britain's annexation of the Transvaal: the House of Commons would debate a motion to appoint "a Commission for the whole of South Africa" in order to inquire into "[t]he great question as to what sort of government should be established in South Africa."[2] Although the motion failed (in part because it was thought that the very appointment of a commission would excite the natives and cause unrest), the questions and aims it posed (the problem of polygamy, of native law, of liquor among the natives) would reappear intact first in the 1883 Cape Colonial Commission upon Native Laws and Customs (the recommendations of which resulted in the Transkeian Territories Penal Code) and then again in the mandate of the infamous 1903–5 South African Native Affairs Commission (which, as Chanock rightly notes, simply followed the precedents of earlier Commissions of Inquiry).[3] From the very beginning, the Commission of Inquiry in South Africa was not then merely a neutral source of information; it was a technique of governmentality that was deployed as a means to the end of securing and normalizing colonial conquest.

Michel Foucault has argued that *government precedes the state* and that the abstract entity we have become accustomed to casually calling "the state" was only able to come into being under conditions that first were constituted as a problem for governmentality.[4] To this must be added: *the Commission of Inquiry precedes government.* It maps out in advance the sorts of things, goods, and populations whose preservation and equilibriums the sovereign will need to manage, administer, and oversee; it seeks to foresee the problems government might encounter as it undertakes a given program of administration; it examines, in retrospect, the failings and scandals that marked similar attempts to establish government in the past; it poses the questions government will need to answer if it is to achieve its optimal thresholds of credibility and efficiency. Like any liberal practice of governmentality, the Commission of Inquiry fulfills a manifestly critical function: it points out the inapplicability of given models and paradigms to actually existing things and populations; it recapitulates and provides historical narratives of errors in government's own policies and procedures; it presents and names that which in government is not working well and which can and ought to work better; it is a locus within the state to object to, in order to fine-tune, the ways and means of state power. In short, the Commission of Inquiry's investigations prepare the conditions under which government based on knowledge—a government in and by instrumental reason, based on manipulating things and populations to the end of the *salus populi*—could not only come into being but also endure.

For the same reasons that indemnity would become more normalized in South Africa than in England, the Commission of Inquiry would become more normalized in the colony too. In modern England as well as in America, Commissions of Inquiry were a technique of liberal governance: they provided a salutary way for government to relate, develop, civilize, and improve the lives of populations (e.g., Native Americans, the illiterate, women, former slaves, prisoners, the working class) who were presumed to be unable to represent themselves in formal institutions of political representation (such as Congress or Parliament).[5] In South Africa, this same technique would be deployed for the same purpose but to a greater degree—to a degree demanded by the "permanently temporary" condition of colonial trusteeship. Under these conditions, the Commission of Inquiry became one among many administrative techniques for *economically including* native populations within colonial government as sources of cheap labor power and as objects of uplift and improvement while also *politically excluding* those same populations as subjects or agents in the modern sense of the word—as beings capable of self-legislation. This technique was not, to be clear, unnuanced. Even in its apartheid phase, the liberal-colonial origins of the Commission of Inquiry remained active. As with trusteeship more generally, the apartheid state's declared purpose in including natives in government as objects of commissions while also excluding them from government as self-legislating subjects was precisely so that natives "eventually" could develop into self-legislating subjects (but, of course, "along their own lines") while colonial authorities took responsibility for their health, welfare, safety, and security "in the meantime."[6]

In twentieth-century South Africa, as elsewhere in the British Empire, there was an intensification of the practice of appointing Commissions of Inquiry following violent state suppression of riots or disturbances. Beginning with the commission appointed in 1836 to inquire into the murder of King Hintsa by Governor Benjamin D'Urban,[7] commissions of this sort even began to become something of a norm. Under the authority of, first, Section 5 of Transvaal Ordinance 30 of 1902 and, later, Commissions Act 8 of 1947, the Union and then the Republic of South Africa would create around two dozen commissions to acquire information about the causes and circumstances of a given riot, disturbance, or commotion.[8] To be sure, not every instance of state killing in nineteenth- and twentieth-century South Africa would become the object of a Commission of Inquiry, despite sometimes emphatic demands from organizations like the African National Congress.[9] But those that did were investigated with reference to a set of generic consistencies and administrative continuities that, despite their many obvious differences, allow them to be grouped together in a loose yet coherent unity. These commissions together comprise what, for heuristic purposes, we will call the "Tumult Commission."[10]

Like the "Native Question" Commission with which it was concurrent, the Tumult Commission was tasked with understanding and managing "race relations,"[11] that is, with the monitoring, adjustment, and modification of relationships between South Africa's constituent racial and ethnic groups. Again like the "Native Question" Commission, the Tumult Commission defined this task for itself by rendering African biopolitics intelligible on the trope of a machine or an organism susceptible to afflictions by certain "frictions" or "diseases" in and between its constituent ethnic and racial "components" or "organs."[12] On these terms, sedition was a "poison" or "fever" to which the body politic was always exposed and for which the Tumult Commission needed to find a "remedy" (as its recommendations were sometimes called).[13] But, of course, whereas the "Native Question" Commission studied race relations with an eye toward "the *avoidance* of racial strife,"[14] the Tumult Commission studied race relations under conditions where it already was too late to avoid racial strife, where racial strife already had manifested itself in violence and repression, and where the aim of the Commission of Inquiry was consequently to present remedies for avoiding the *recurrence* of racial strife (or, at least—and indeed more often—the avoidance of its *expression* in the form of violence).[15] Yet despite its different point of departure and conclusion, the Tumult Commission nevertheless shared with the "Native Question" Commission an intense empirical interest in the relationships between native land, native labor, and native populations, more often than not tracing the "remote" causes of tumult to precisely the same biopolitical dynamics studied in depth by the "Native Question" Commission (e.g., polygamy).[16]

In its recommended remedies as well, the Tumult Commission coincided and overlapped with the "Native Question" Commission.[17] In biopolitical terms that were just as racial as were the mandates of the "Native Question" Commission, the Tumult Commission took up the abiding problems of the *salus populi*, such as health and welfare (water pollution, leprosy, influenza, dysentery, tuberculosis, venereal disease, mental hospitals, mixed marriages, deviate children), wealth and commerce (labor, poor whites, unemployment, the eight-hour workday, insolvency, the cost of living, war pensions, the shoe and boot industry, candle production), and safety (assaults on women [which also were listed under the heading "Black Peril"],[18] secret organizations, assassinations, police and military forces), alongside newer and more specifically colonial questions about the conquest, division, and appropriation of land and natural resources (electricity supply, irrigation, drought relief, flood relief, wool production, pipelines, hydrobiology and fishes, meat, ostrich feathers, deciduous fruit, wine production, grain elevators, railways, and harbors).[19] Whether to avoid racial strife (in the case of the "Native Question" Commission) or to prevent its recurrence (in the case of the Tumult Commission), the Commission of Inquiry posed questions of race within an epistemic field that was, in its approach to population as a sort of "raw material," fundamentally biopolitical. Therefore, on Friday, July 5, 1878, shortly after the end of the Third "Kafir War," one Mr. Geard would put a motion before the Cape Legislative Council requesting the governor-general

"as soon as practicable, after the present hostilities on the frontier are ended, to appoint a commission to inquire into and report upon the causes of the late outbreak, the condition of the native tribes immediately within and beyond the frontier of this colony, and the best means of securing their future good government." The hon. member remarked that he felt he need offer no apology for submitting this motion, as the management of the native tribes was a most important subject. The colony had just passed through a serious and devastating war. This was the third native war which had broken out within his experience. They had caused an immense loss of valuable lives, and had caused much distress upon the frontier, and he thought it would be of great assistance to the Government, in regulating its future proceedings with respect to the natives, if the causes of the late war could be ascertained. His object in bringing forward this motion was not to reflect upon the Government. No feeling of a want of confidence in the Government had induced him to move in this matter. He thought that the hon. gentlemen who were now in office were men of large experience, but the subject was a large one requiring serious investigation as to the causes of the war, and the future Government of the natives. Whatever might be said by some people who boasted of their knowledge of the colony, that it would be better if the natives could be improved off the face of the earth, he believed that, with good Government, the natives could be made a real source of wealth, and he *therefore* held it was important to obtain all the information with respect to them which was available, in order to guide them in these matters. He wished it to be clearly understood that he had no want of confidence in the Government, or had any desire to embarrass it in settling affairs upon the frontier, but his own opinion was that the late war need not have happened at all, with a proper management of the people.[20]

Within the epistemic field the Tumult Commission shared in common with other, more explicitly managerial Commissions of Inquiry, in other words, native populations were understood not on the model of European humanity (centered on the rational subject who was, in principle, capable of self-legislation and political self-representation) but on the model of a nonhuman natural resource, like water or "human livestock." On these terms, the native was valued only as a valuable resource—a "sacred trust"—to be administered intelligently, with care and even caution, for just as the mismanagement of water reserves could result in the "pollution" or "scarcity" of an otherwise good, abundant resource, so, too, the mismanagement of "native reserves" could lead to hostility and thence to riot, rebellion, and even war.[21]

6.1.2 Because most of the South African Tumult Commissions were appointed not by the queen but by the South African governor-general (who is the "representative of the Crown" in the dominion),[22] most were not technically Royal Commissions of Inquiry. Nevertheless, most adopted the Royal Commission of Inquiry as their model, both implicitly and explicitly,[23] and repeated a few of the more specific techniques and practices we see exemplified in the JRC. Like the JRC, most of the Tumult Commissions went to great lengths to publicize their hearings and to invite all comers to testify, only to express considerable doubt and sometimes even scorn regarding the veracity, credibility, and reliability of the resulting testimony (which commissioners repeatedly found to be filled with lies, inconsistencies, and excessive narration).[24] Most, but not all, of these commissions were, like the JRC, mandated to investigate the question of the necessity of the use of police and military force in suppressing riots and rebellions; and like the JRC, some of these commissions did end up finding fault with the military and police authorities for their actions.[25] But in each case where a commission ensured that the violent acts of colonial authorities were, as Mill put it in 1866, "so deservedly but so mildly condemned,"[26] that condemnation would almost always be qualified in familiar ways. In some cases where state officials were found to have committed crimes, Tumult Commissions did end up recommending prosecution.[27] More often, however, nothing happened at all.[28] Like the JRC before it, the Tumult Commission carefully calibrated condemnations of police not only with criticisms of the natives themselves but also with praise of the promptness and even the severity of authorities' responses.[29]

This carefully calibrated "evenhandedness" would become so formal and regular, would become such a hallmark of the Tumult Commission's epistemic field, that it would determine even the grammar of certain Tumult Commission reports.[30] The existence of this rule is confirmed by the exception to it. In its 1949 *Report of the Commission of Enquiry into Riots in Durban*, the apartheid government would put a name to the Tumult Commission's habitual evenhandedness (in which "the truth lies somewhere between").

> Public disorders break out, run their course like fevers and come to an end either by being overcome or by destroying their host, the State. Owing to negligence on the part of the authorities, a foreseeable and preventable disturbance may occur; because of further neglect an outbreak of insignificant proportions may denigrate into riots with consequences of national importance. Again, partisans in the disturbances may be aided and abetted by the authorities or by other instigators, and a small flame may thus be fanned into a serious conflagration. For lack of a better word we call such causative factors "concomitant causes."[31]

Particularly because the Durban Riots Commission then would proceed to reject the concept of "concomitant cause," this commission's aggressive distance from the typical Tumult Commission positions it as the explicit exception that proves the implicit rule: in general, the epistemic field of the Tumult Commission would be structured, with surprising consistency, precisely by narration of a "concomitant cause" type. In this, as in other matters, the Tumult Commission did not drift far from the paradigm established for it by the JRC. Whereas the JRC carefully arranged its several and various findings so that, in the end, the interrelation between each of them canceled the others out, the Tumult Commission tended to arrange *each one* of its findings as internally self-canceling mechanisms. First in the JRC in 1866 and then in many of the Tumult Commissions in the twentieth century, we see the emergence of a grammar and a logic in which innocent bystanders could be killed with impunity because *everyone* was to blame.[32] Already in the JRC, we saw how tragedy could be made to function as a discourse of power—as the "literary" mode through which colonial bureaucracy spoke about its officials who killed with impunity, the poetics through which police officers—stranded as they were on a knife's edge by *Rex v. Pinney*—could be both scapegoat and hero. The Tumult Commission, like similar commissions elsewhere in the British Empire,[33] would turn this too into a norm. Commissioners regularly would narrate "disturbances" like massacres and riots explicitly as a tragedy in which violence enacted or permitted by the police could be called both intolerable and unavoidable.[34]

Nowhere was this more pronounced than in the South African government's response to the 1923 report of the Bondelzwart Commission. Speaking in Parliament on May 22, 1923, on the occasion of the publication of the report, General Jan Smuts praised the commissioners for the detailed and painstaking way their report represented an almost century-long cleavage in South African public opinion, between the realism of the colonist and the idealism of the missionary. The commission's rendering of this strife was so perfect, Smuts argued, that "[t]he report is part and parcel, if I may say so, of the soul of South Africa, and we shall not get further—on this point [i.e., the strife of missionary and colonist] we shall always differ to some extent."[35] He then went on to address a criticism made by Labor Party leader Colonel F. H. P. Creswell about the multiple and reciprocal misunderstandings between the government and the Bondelzwarts and the effect this criticism might have on its reader, particularly its readers at the League of Nations (which, in 1920, had conferred on South Africa the mandate for administering South West Africa).[36]

> Colonel Creswell asked about the form of the report, but the Commission must have thought that this was the best way of setting out the whole case. It does read like a Greek play. The movement seems to be smooth; and all at once there is a pull up—just like South Africa and its politics. I ask the hon. members and the public to read this report, which for me is a sufficiently honest and sincere attempt to grapple with the difficulties of the situation. There is a difference in the report as to how this trouble took place, and the events which led up to the culminating tragedy. But I do not think it is necessary to go into the details now.

Instead of going into the details, Smuts proceeded to offer a specifically colonial declension of the narrative trope of "tragic *misunderstanding*" to explain and justify the "tragic *inevitability*" of the government's slaughter of Bondelzwarts by airplane.

> The Bondelzwarts are a native people with simple minds—they misunder-

stand things and exaggerate others, and in one way or another a whole psychology grows up in their minds which in the end bursts forth in a rebellion. Their psychology has been so worked up that this state of affairs became inevitable, but hon. members must agree with me that these things could not possibly justify a rebellion. . . . I have a certain amount of sympathy with them. I can understand that with their psychology, their past and their character, how they came to view things in the light they did, but even so they were not justified, and that, I take it, is the result that the majority of the Commission has arrived at, and that Commission was influenced by very real sympathy with them. You could not but come to the conclusion that they were hopelessly wrong, and rendered the punishment which was ultimately inflicted on them inevitable.[37]

The purpose of classical tragedy, according to one particularly influential tradition of aesthetic thought, is to present its spectators with a turning point in which a simple misunderstanding between actors sets into motion a series of events that unfold in such a way that they cannot be altered by the thought, will, or action of the very actors who initiated them. Understood thusly, tragedy is a fatalistic discourse that functions to establish insuperable limits to the possibility of determining human responsibility for grievous actions. Articulated in Parliament, by the prime minister of an imperial power, the discourse of tragedy becomes a powerful way for colonial government to admit to the illegality and inhumanity of imperial slaughter while at the same time articulating the impossibility of accepting legal guilt or even just legal responsibility for that slaughter. Hewing rigorously to classical tragedy's coupling of misunderstanding and inevitability, Smuts here powerfully mobilized that coupling to present an almost unanswerable claim on the part of the sovereign power of the Union to massacre the natives entrusted to their administration, in the absence of legal justification before the fact or legal penalty after the fact. After receiving a "moderate censure" from the Permanent Mandates Commission, the Union would learn from the Assembly of the League of Nations that the latter "regretted" the massacre and hoped that "future reports of the mandatory power would allay all misgivings."[38] Reiterated within the epistemic field of the Tumult Commission, the tragic here acquires a very definite status: it is the paradigmatic administrative mode in and through which the colonial regime would refer to its own power to kill with impunity. Although contemporary academic disciplines tend to separate law and literature, even and especially when they "combine" them, it is important to underline this point: a certain declension of the "literary" (the tragic) is here, prior to any interdiscliplinary blurring, already internal to a certain declension of the "legal" (the Tumult Commission), as the narrative form with reference to which colonial government tried to justify the massacres that contradicted its most basic self-understanding and mission.

At the same time, already in Smuts's reading of the Bondelzwart report, one can see how the tragic spills into and is informed by another hallmark of the Tumult Commission paradigm. Perhaps the most surprising feature of the Tumult Commission is how intensely its inquiries focus on questions of the psyche or soul—the "feelings," the "state of mind," the "passions"—of those who engage in riots and disturbances. Like the JRC, which sought to isolate and evaluate the causes for the unrest and discontent of the "negro part of the population" (the origins of their "feelings of hostility toward political and personal opponents"),[39] almost every Tumult Commission Report was, in effect, a *history and taxonomy of hatred*. The reports of these Commissions were texts which were almost therapeutic in their intense interest in the gradations and thresholds internal to hatred, in their curiosity about exactly where the purple of suspicion, resentment, and antipathy shaded into the crimson of rage, about the precise threshold where discontent, grief, and disappointment flare into uncontrollable fury.

This curiosity was not, of course, politically neutral; its intensity derived from its colonial conditions, and here, as elsewhere, the specter of colonial rebellion was decisive. War, for English political philosophers such as Hobbes, did not consist in "actual fighting" but, rather, in the "known disposition" to fight—in the very declaration or signification of "hostilities."[40] The Tumult Commission's interest in hatred must be interpreted in these terms: it was, at root, a concern with the return of war, with *re-bellatio*, in a moment of colonial conquest that never quite ended (and where, as Albie Sachs put it, the state violence of the twentieth century was intelligible as the return of the "frontier wars" of the nineteenth century).[41] The knowledge it acquired (about the secondary or proximate causes for anger and fury) was valuable for this reason: it allowed the colonial administrator to manage hatred, to decrease the conditions under which hostility may manifest itself in open war or rebellion. It is no accident, then, that in the historical narratives that were such a standard feature of every Tumult Commission, the unusually alert attentiveness to the causes, degree, and quality of hostility are narrated so regularly in demographic terms, as hostility between South Africa's officially designated ethnic and racial groups. Often, this hatred seemed as though it was difficult to discern: certain Tumult Commissions found that they needed to arrange their historical narratives in a way that allowed them to adjudicate the fallacy *post hoc ergo propter hoc*. From a mass of impassioned and confused testimony, they sought to differentiate *causal relations* from *temporal relations*, clarifying and distinguishing the two domains in order to better isolate and analyze the proximate and distant causes that produced violence in the first place. But even where this did not occur, the Tumult Commission still went to great lengths to trace the emergence of ill will, hostility, or antagonism in a given population or between given populations, in order to argue that riots and disturbances had as their *proximate* or *immediate cause* a feeling of hostility or ill will that, in turn, was caused by the *remote cause* of some social, juridical, political, or economic structure.[42]

Because the Tumult Commission was thus, for reasons of colonial administration, a *history and taxonomy of hate*, its adoption of the terms and tropes of therapeutic discourse—its diagnosis, for example, of the "symptoms of unrest"[43]—cannot be understood as disinterested psychology. The Tumult Commission turned to psychology in its histories of hate as means to the end of administering relations between populations whose "natural frictions" with one another were understood to be always already at risk of heating up into open hostility. Here, again, it's instructive to make reference to the Bondelzwart Massacre. In 1919, Lord Buxton (then governor-general of the Union of South Africa) visited South-West Africa shortly after the Union annexed the territory from Germany. He explained in a memorandum that martial law and the improvement of the natives (who had been mistreated under the "harsh conditions" of German rule) were related goals. Thus, even though conditions of martial law pertained, and even though British authorities would not alter the pass laws set into place by German authorities, he wrote, "[M]agistrates and police officers are warned that the indiscriminate prosecution of Natives for offences against the Masters and Servants Laws are calculated to defeat the object of securing a better state of feeling between master and servant, and putting an end to the deplorable attitude assumed by the one toward the other."[44] Given this goal, the Bondelzwart Commission would gently criticize the military's decision to bomb the natives with airplanes, arguing, in conclusion, that "[t]he most pressing need," in their view, was "to establish a satisfactory and if possible a friendly relationship between [the Bondelzwarts] and the Administration."[45] As apartheid commissioners would observe in 1951, because "unrest" may be defined as a "state of mind," and because "disturbance" is the "outward active manifestation" of that state of mind, all recommendations should be aimed at creating the administrative conditions in which the native could achieve "inner peace" while the Union could achieve "peace and quiet."[46] The goal, in each case, was to arrive at "a possible solution of the Native problem in South African [that would be] in the interests not only of the Natives but also of the European population, because black and white will necessarily have to live together in this country and should adjust their mutual relations in such a way as to promote the beneficial development of South Africa."[47] In light of this necessity, *all* Tumult Commissions needed to function as "reconciliation" commissions.

The Tumult Commission's therapeutic language—its discourse on peace not only in the polity but also in the soul—cannot, then, be taken at face value. Not despite but precisely because of the commission's tendency toward therapeutic ministration, toward a "care for the soul" not just in individuals but across entire populations, the epistemic field of the Tumult Commission remained, at base, biopolitical. Therapeutic and psychological though their terms sometimes may have been, the Tumult Commission's discourses on "aroused passions" and "considerable feelings"—these complicated computations of the degrees to which certain populations had sympathy, suspicion, goodwill, or resentment toward others, as well as the conditions under which others remained susceptible to excitement, resentment, discontent, enthusiasm, and anger—remained *commensurable with* and even *determined by* the more explicitly administrative horizon of openly biopolitical Commissions of Inquiry (with their dry statistical calculations of the thresholds of arable land, cullable cattle, power supplies, taxes, etc.). The proof is in the pudding: the grievances of this or that population were consistently, in the reports of Tumult Commissions, understood to be interpretable on the basis of more fundamental biopolitical matters (which often appeared in the pages of the Tumult Commission under the rubric of the *remote causes* that needed attention if native grievances and thence native hostilities were to disappear).[48] Within the epistemic field of the Tumult Commission, in other words, the "feelings" that may have caused this or that riot or disturbance were yet another sort of raw material to be governed wisely; the fact that this governance happened to have assumed the form of the therapeutic should not distract. The therapeutic aim of the Tumult Commission (its psychological dimension, to calm the hostile passions that otherwise could lead to *re-bellatio*) remained subordinate to its fundamentally governmental aim, that is, its need to pose and answer the question of how "to keep the peace" between various populations under conditions of nonrepresentative, colonial government. Therapeutic discourses within the Tumult Commission, on the "soul" specific to this or that race, were a means to this end: this discourse helped colonial government "fit" laws and policies to the temperament, mind, and character of various populations, under conditions where those populations were presumed not to have the temperament, mind, or character to govern themselves.

6.1.3 Biopolitical in content, the Tumult Commission was also biopolitical in form. Biopolitics, as Foucault argued, is not simply a technique that disinterestedly attempts to discover the equilibriums that govern individuals, things, and goods; it is an apparatus that inquires into those equilibriums as a means to the end of "keeping the peace" within a given population. Even the very creation, through *commissio*, of a Tumult Commission was often itself a self-consciously "performative" act that, prior to any finding, was designed to produce peace and order in and between certain hostile populations. The 1865 JRC was appointed, as we have seen, in part to quell public outrage over Eyre's massacres. After the 1893 Featherstone Commission, meanwhile, the parliamentarian B. Coleridge would even recommend the appointment of Commissions of Inquiry on all occasions "where the military came into conflict with civilians with injury to life or limb"—not in order to prosecute military officials, however, but in order to "assuage the bitter feeling" left by such injuries.[49] Because, as countless Commissions of Inquiry would report, it was precisely "bitter feelings" that gave rise to riots and disturbances in the first place, the very act of appointing a commission could therefore be understood as an attempt to intervene into and redirect the mood of a given population. That this intervention could go horribly wrong—that the appointment of a Commission of Inquiry could just as easily "excite" as calm the natives[50] and that the creation of a Commission of Inquiry, if not coordinated with other domains of governance, could just as easily "undermine" as supplement government's legitimacy[51]—does not refute but confirms the sense in which the Tumult Commission was not merely an occasion for the historical representation of hate (its proximate and remote causes, its shades and hues, etc.), but—equally and at the same time—a technique for actively managing, deferring, and dissipating it.[52]

And yet, it hardly could be denied that the Tumult Commission also sometimes created the conditions for a repetition of the very violence it ostensibly sought to quell. Under conditions where commissions found that authorities' "negligence" in suppressing a riot was a "concomitant cause" of violence and bloodshed, the clear implication was that authorities must be, in the future, much more prompt in the discharge of their duties. This responsibility was both legal (on the terms of *Rex v. Pinney*, officials needed to hit that fine line between acting too aggressively and too passively) and, in a counterfactual and counterintuitive sense, moral (prompt and vigorous violence was sometimes said to be "merciful" for its prevention of the bloodshed that did *not* occur).[53] The legal and moral implication of the "concomitant cause" line of argumentation was not only that police officials needed to suppress riots by acting more promptly in the moment. It was, more radically, that state officials needed to prevent violence before it even happened, by removing not only the "immediate" or "proximate" causes of tumults (which, in the Durban Riot Commission, as increasingly under apartheid, located in native intellectuals and other agitators who "exploited" feelings of hostility), but also their "remote" or "distant" causes (the governmental policies, laws, and practices that engendered hostility in the first place). Created to restore the peace, the Tumult Commission thus also accomplished the opposite: it reinforced the premises according to which the ongoing suppression of perpetually incipient rebellion should be the normal paradigm of colonial government as such.

6.2.1 The Tumult Commission was, in this sense, an apparatus that allowed for the management of one of the constitutive impasses of colonial rule. It provided colonial officials with a device for mitigating and containing the juridical crises that emerged from colonial rule, without also, at the same time, conceding political self-representation and self-legislation to colonized populations. In the Bondelzwart Rebellion Commission, as in the JRC, the Tumult Commission functioned as a machine available to the colonial administrator for dealing with state officials who (like Eyre) were found to have illegally killed subjects of the Crown (like Gordon) but who, despite such findings, were not prosecuted according to the rule of law (the principle of ministerial liability in particular). The Tumult Commission mitigated these situations by narrating juridical-political impasse in terms of tragedy, achieving the mode of balance implicit in the tragic (understood as a genre of narration in which everyone and no one was to blame). Here, tragedy was both a juridical logic (a way of speaking about legal aporias where guilt and innocence seemed to coincide and coexist in one and the same person) and a juridical poetics (a discourse on the lamentable, regrettable, and unfortunate but unavoidable and, indeed, "necessary" status of illegal state killing). In his critique of the place and function of archival evidence within South African historiography, Premesh Lalu argues, "The colonial archive should not be seen merely as composed of techniques of governmentality but as a narrative strategy in its own rights, one that is capable of organizing our reading."[54] In the discourse of the Tumult Commission, as in the JRC, the tragic was the narrative strategy through which colonial governmentality posed the question of its own juridical impasse—its own inability to extend the civilizing element of rule of law without also itself violating, suspending, and neutralizing that same rule of law. It allowed colonial governmentality, in other words, *to encounter its own limits* (the lexicon of the tragic allowed colonial administrators to recognize that they were authorizing or committing acts that created suffering and violated the very rule of law that justified colonialism) while also simultaneously *disavowing those same limits* (arguing that, as regrettable, lamentable, and evil as its violence was, that violence was nonetheless "necessary," that juridical conditions of the colony "could not be otherwise"). Even in the "best-case" scenario, therefore, the Tumult Commission was designed to foreclose on a number of more radical possibilities for the narration of the event of colonial violence. The creation of the JRC, for example, foreclosed not only on the possibility of a robustly liberal position like Mill's (which argued for the prosecution of Eyre exclusively on the grounds of the rule of law) but also on the even more radical antiracist, abolitionist, and anticolonial discourses of the time (which argued for the prosecution of Eyre on the grounds of racial equality) or, of course, the revolutionary discourse of a Marx or Engels.

Given these foreclosures, it hardly should come as a surprise that, beginning with Gandhi's boycott of the Indian Enquiry Commission in 1914[55] and running through to the mass rejection of the Cillié Commission of 1979, the Tumult Commission frequently would be rejected and avoided by the very populations whose tumultuous conduct it was tasked with understanding, more often than not leaving Tumult commissioners in a solipsistic, self-justifying, and impotent conversation with the South African Police.[56] We will not, then, risk retroactively condoning the desirability or necessity of the Tumult Commission by saying that the apartheid government pushed the Tumult Commission to and perhaps even beyond its already despotic limit. Like the indemnity convention (to which it was closely related), the Tumult Commission entered into crisis and dissolution in the apartheid state. Under apartheid, the Tumult Commission was no longer *mainly*, as it was under colonial conditions, a governmental technique for the management of populations that *also*—in the course of its self-criticism of state violence—happened to justify the "lamentable necessity" or "necessary evil" of violent state action. It now became *mainly* a discourse through which the state justified its violent repression of agitators to its critics abroad, and only *secondarily* served as an attempt to inquire into populations in order to manage them, and as the source of a tragic narrative on the regrettable inevitability of violence as a part of that management. This was not an *epistemic break* (in which the Tumult Commission assumed an entirely new way of knowing) but, rather, a *shift in emphasis*, a diminution in one function of the Tumult Commission and an augmentation of another—a shift that was, to be precise, marked by a change in the way the Tumult Commission addressed its implied metropolitan reader. One sees here, in particular, a new declension of the tragic mode, in which the stress was less on the reciprocally terrible consequences of miscommunication and misunderstanding for all parties involved and more on the sense in which the police officer was unfairly at risk of becoming figured as a scapegoat, a flawed hero in whom collective guilt could be concentrated and at whose expense the public could absolve its own conscience.

6.2.2 This development was signaled quite openly in the difference between the Indian Enquiry Commission of 1914 (tasked with investigating the 1913 strike led by Gandhi in Natal, which police suppressed by killing nine and wounding twenty-five) and the Durban Riots Commission of 1949 (mandated with reporting on the causes of the January 1949 riots in which 142 were killed and 1,087 were injured). The former, like the latter, would exonerate the police from any allegations of violence and abuse: both commissions would find that the police's use of deadly force was justified by the necessities of the case.[57] The Indian Enquiry Commission expressed annoyance with Gandhi for advising Indians to boycott the commission.[58] Yet not only did it recommend that he be released from jail in order to facilitate the commission's inquiry,[59] but it also organized its report as a point-by-point response to Gandhi's letters written to the minister of the interior on June 30, 1913, and January 21, 1914. In its fourteen recommendations, meanwhile, the commission included reforms that, in effect, conceded the truth of many (but by no means all)[60] of Gandhi's grievances about South African laws and policies relating to "Asiatics."[61]

The Durban Riots Commission, by contrast, went out of its way to identify the highly tenuous sense in which Indian agitators motivated by identical Gandhian principles (the report derisively mentions "soul-suffering" and "soul-force" in particular)[62] were actually to blame for the disproportionate number of Indian casualties in the riots.

> Certain sections of the Indians have attempted to unite the Natives and the Indians into a united front against the Government, and have in doing so not scrupled to invoke outside assistance from abroad and there to dissemi-nated [*sic*] distorted and malicious accounts of South African conditions and events. In the process they cause a feeling of unrest and dissatisfaction to stir amongst the Natives, always a dangerous course with a section of the community not yet ripe for responsibility. In the result the Indians were hoist with their own petard.
>
> In the recent passive resistance movement in Durban the Indians ostentatiously contravened the law of the land, attracting as much attention as they could to the fact that they were flouting authority. The example did not escape the notice of the Natives. . . . [C]ontempt for the law increases like a vice, and the effects of a bad example are not limited by the proportion or heinousness of the precedent. By using these high-sounding terms ["soul-suffering" and "soul-force"] some Indian witnesses attempted to sublimate their bad example into a virtue. It is not. It is not. . . . The method proved successful elsewhere, but not because of its transcendental spirit. . . . Shorn of its quasi-philosophical trappings, passive resistance in Durban was defiance of the law and of constituted authority; it set the Natives a bad example.[63]

Whereas Indian participation in the riots was said to be due mainly to the circulation of "ideas" (of course, "bad" ones, "quasi-philosophical" ideas that ended up recoiling on those who conceived them), native participation was attributed mainly to "increasing lack of discipline."[64] Unlike the Indian (who has "nimbler wits than the Native" and "tried to prevail by using his wits"), the native "is inclined to assess merit in terms of physical strength and is inclined to have recourse to physical suasion."[65] Unlike civilized Europeans, whose understanding of forgiveness and the rule of law presumably enabled them to outgrow the habits of "noxal dedition," of vendettas and blood feuds, the native "is inclined to observe a kind of *lex talionis*, a phenomenon we find in ancient Roman and Germanic laws: an eye for an eye, irrespective of the culpability of the person who causes the loss of that eye."[66] Through openly racist argumentation of this sort, the report could shift considerably from the standard sort of reasoning, based on "concomitant cause," that predominated in prior Tumult Commissions. It could also manage a remarkable argumentative strategy: even though the report acknowledged that the "frictions" between natives and Indians over racial inequalities in housing, social standing, population growth, intermarriage, transportation, labor, economic competition, and pass and liquor laws provided "combustible material" for the "explosive force" of the riots, the report also concluded that no blame could be put on the government that enforced these inequalities as a matter of law and policy.[67] It placed the blame instead on those Indian intellectuals who, in their attempt to oppose apartheid policies through "satyagraha" and solidarity with natives (this was two years after the "Doctors' Pact" between Dr. Alfred Xuma of the ANC and Dr. Monty Naicker and Dr. Yusuf Dadoo of the Natal and Transvaal Indian Congresses), suffered the "natural" biopolitical punishment of their misguided ideas and actions: uncomprehending native vengeance. For the Durban Riots Commission—as for the Witzieshoek Disturbances Commission, the Cillié Commission, and the University of Zululand Violence Commission after it—the causes of racial "hatred" were not to be investigated or solved by eliminating the underlying conditions of legally enforced racial inequality; they were to be investigated and solved by eliminating the agitators, intellectuals, and "radical student groups" who persist in calling racist laws into question.[68]

This is not, of course, to imply, that the Indian Enquiry Commission did not fault Gandhi for the strike in Natal or even that the Martial Law Inquiry Judicial Commission did not call out certain "revolutionaries" by name as the proximate cause of the 1922 Rand Riots. It is only to point out that in 1914 as in 1922, the history of riot was still narrated in the mode of "concomitant cause," with blame being apportioned "judiciously" not only between lawbreaking strikers and lawbreaking authorities[69] but also between direct causes (an inflammatory utterance, a disobeyed command, the setting of a fire, a sign of disrespect) and indirect causes (a tax increase, a harsh marriage law, low wages). Put simply, in 1914, liberal governmentality was still the dominant frame in and through which the colonial commission of inquiry sought to pose to itself the question of "tumult." That changed in 1949, when the Durban Riots Commission unconditionally exonerated the police for their inaction and their action alike and openly rejected the claim, set forth by Dr. Lowen of ANC and the South African Indian Congress, that "horrible slum conditions, for Indians and Africans alike, are at the bottom of this."[70]

It is also relevant that, in a command paper written under conditions of empire, the Indian Enquiry Commission addressed itself to the British Parliament in both form (it is "presented to both houses of Parliament") and content (its fourteen recommendations list actions that only Parliament could undertake). The Durban Riot Commission, on the other hand, was written under much different conditions. At a moment defined not only by early signs of divisive relations with the Commonwealth[71] but also by the emergence of sharp criticism of South Africa within a United Nations newly committed to the postcolonial (criticism coordinated, in its earliest phases, by none other than Gandhi himself),[72] the manner in which the Durban Riot Commission addressed itself to the British Parliament changed both in form and in content. In their 1949 report, the commissioners not only blamed disturbances in South Africa on outside influences but also concluded with a direct address and retort to its critics in the Commonwealth and the United Nations about the justice and necessity of apartheid governance.[73] In this, however, we must recognize the paradoxical continuity between pre-apartheid and apartheid Commissions of Inquiry. In 1878, members of Parliament argued that a Commission of Inquiry was needed in South Africa to investigate "a question of the broadest kind: What was the nature of the Government we should establish in South Africa?"[74] In 1949, the Durban Riots Commission would ask a more explicitly biopolitical (and therefore also more explicitly racial) iteration of this same question. In a retort to foreign observers who criticized South Africa for refusing rights to Africans, the commissioners argued,

Such abstract notions as a good form of government and a claim at natural law to exercise public rights exist only in the mind of the visionary. A form of government and the privilege (and obligation) of exercising public rights cannot be *per se* either good or bad. A form of government can be good only if it is in harmony with the mental outlook, character and moral fibre of the people concerned. Because it suits his temperament and moral fibre, the publicist, especially of British Stock, is inclined to regard the vote as the *everriculum omnium malitiarum*, the panacea for all social and economic evils.[75]

There hardly could be a more explicit statement of the biopolitical presuppositions that implicitly underlie the Commission of Inquiry tradition as a whole—up to and including its liberal iteration. The question of the relation between law and population is here not abstract or theoretical; it has nothing to do with universal or even only transcendent principles. It is a concrete and empirical question about the form of life to which law must conform. Just as liberal legality was the form of law that conformed to populations and individuals of British "stock," so, too, the legality of the Bantustan system was appropriate to populations and individuals of African "stock." Under these conditions, the measure of good governance was not whether South Africa's various populations had achieved the rights to self-determination and political representation but whether, in their relations with one another, they could attain the form of equilibrium the commissioners called "xenobiosis,"[76] which is to say, in a manifestly biological sense, "a form of symbiosis among ants in which two colonies of different species live together on friendly terms without rearing their broods in common."[77] On these manifestly organicist terms, which were also a constitutive part of the "Grand Tradition" analyzed by Ashforth, the commissioners would argue that hostility between Africans and Indians was caused not by the *introduction* of apartheid policies and the government's own hierarchical segregation of Africans and Indians but, rather, by their *absence*—by the very "racial frictions" for which apartheid policies claimed to be the solution, such as miscegenation between Africans and Indians, or, put differently, Africans' envy of the "explosive fecundity" of Indians in Natal.[78]

6.3.1 The shift in the Tumult Commission announced in 1949 soon would proceed in an unpredictable direction. In 1961 and 1977, following the Sharpeville Massacre and the violent suppression of the Soweto Uprising, the apartheid regime would appoint Tumult Commissions that, by all appearances, seemed to return to the paradigm of "concomitant cause," balancing out blame for state killing between protestors and police alike. But the excessive evenhandedness in the conclusions of these commissions—the strained way in which first the Wessels Commission and later the Cillié Commission would force the paradigm of balance on events in relation to which the presumption of balance could not but itself become unbalanced—reveals a second decisive change in the operation of the Tumult Commission. With the UN General Assembly's increasingly aggressive attention to the question of apartheid from 1960 onward, the departure of South Africa from the British Commonwealth in 1961, the global economic crisis in 1972–74, and the revolutions in Angola, Mozambique, and Zimbabwe, the apartheid regime deployed the Tumult Commission under conditions that were fundamentally inimical to its most basic premises. In the 1970s, the Tumult Commission was, in effect, a colonial apparatus that was trying to prolong its existence at a moment when the basic norms of global governance were, at least nominally, becoming postcolonial. Under these conditions, the Tumult Commission's narration of "concomitant cause" became more important, if also more abstract and forced, than ever before. The evenhanded apportionment of blame for massacres "both" on rioters "and" on police was now less a device for persuading a British public that the rule of law applied in metropole and colony alike and more a mechanism for projecting calm, stability, and fairness to foreign investors who desired political stability in South Africa but who also wanted to disavow the repressive apparatus in and through which the apartheid regime achieved that stability. Under colonial conditions, the Tumult Commission sought to convince a metropolitan public that occasional administrative massacres were no counterargument to the continued validity of the imperial rule of law; under apartheid, it sought to persuade foreign investors that occasional state massacres were no reason not to continue with neocolonial business as usual.

This approach extended to the very act of creating a Tumult Commission. In the nineteenth century, the act of establishing a Commission of Inquiry was itself an act of governance. Because publicity was just as integral to the operation of a commission as was information gathering,[79] governments announced commissions with an eye toward the way in which the creation of a commission would "send a message" to a given public. The creation of a Tumult Commission in particular, by publicly signaling a government's intention to air any and all of the powerful grievances that typically were associated with tumult, doubled as a preemptive strike against the political energy latent in those grievances: the very creation of a formal governmental space where passionate grievances could be aired, prior even to any formal inquiry into the facts surrounding those grievances, was an administrative gesture that, by deferring, dissipating, and redirecting passions of hatred and anger, itself participated in the governmental work of restoring a normal state of affairs following a riot, rebellion, strike, or disturbance.[80] Before the disclosure of any facts or information, in other words, the very act of creating a Tumult Commission had affinities with the work of policing: it was a technique for restoring law and order, for keeping the peace, for reducing conflict, for maintaining public safety.

Under apartheid, the creation of Tumult Commissions not only shared the repressive character that defined the apartheid regime more generally;[81] it also took place under global conditions where repression itself assumed a very different character than under empire. The international response to Sharpeville, which included large-scale capital flight and an unprecedented condemnation of South Africa by the UN, unsettled a National Party that relied on foreign direct investment for its stability and that used its police forces to supply the stability that foreign direct investors demanded in turn.[82] Especially here, at the height of its strength, the apartheid state found itself obliged to respond to a genre of international censure with which it was, by then, well familiar.[83] At the same time that it embarked on an unprecedented phase of political repression, the apartheid state also announced a Judicial Commission of Inquiry to investigate the events at Sharpeville. The creation of this commission was an attempt, on the part of a regime whose control over the judiciary was at that point extensive,[84] to avoid the even more profound disruption to apartheid that would have occurred were foreign investors to become spooked by the specter of political instability and to panic and withdraw capital.[85]

What is curious about the Wessels Commission is not, however, that it was repressive (this is to be expected) but, rather, how excessively and forcefully it returned to the paradigm of "concomitant cause" that the Durban Riots Commission had so aggressively rejected. At the same time that Wessels claimed to be impressed by the "sincerity" of the grievances that led the Pan-African Congress to protest pass laws,[86] his report did not hesitate to describe those protestors by using the language of the South African Police, which construed the PAC as a "frenzied mob."[87] At the same time Wessels expressed "mild criticism" of the SAP commander who ordered his men to fire on PAC protestors, questioning whether a fusillade was really necessary to disperse the crowd, he also "agree[d] with the police that they had been confronting a hostile assembly," finding that the police's massacre was at least partly prompted by the actions of the assembly itself.[88] Above all, Wessels refused all findings of police culpability. Concluding that the shootings were neither justified nor unjustified, he speculated that they might even have prevented further loss of life.[89] As usual, therefore, state massacre turned out (upon examination not only of the facts but of the counterfactuals) to have a counterintuitively merciful dimension to it; and in the end (also as usual), everyone and no one was to blame for the "tragic occurrences" (as Wessels called them) that took place on March 21, 1960.[90] Readers of the report were predictably paralyzed by the discourse of "concomitant cause" and the poetics of tragedy. As G. J. Suttor said of the final report of the Wessels Commission, during Senate debates over the Indemnity Act of 1961: "I sit, Sir, with a report that leaves me no better off than I was. The Judge does not say the police were right or the police were wrong. He does not say the Natives asked for it or they did not ask for it."[91] Its findings were, in short, as Philip Frankel notes, "a mixed blessing": "[V]iewed through the ideological spectacles of the South African government and its apartheid supporters, they appeared to exonerate the state. But seen from a more humanitarian perspective, the self-same pronouncements also could be interpreted as a general condemnation of the police and the system of social relations that their behavior upheld."[92]

In the Wessels Commission, we thus see the return of the standard Tumult Commission schema of "truth as balance"—only now in a framework where governmentality, the work of coordinating things, goods, and populations, demanded calculation, equilibrium, and a program of persuasion with a scope that was no longer imperial (grounded with reference to the civilizing influence of the rule of law) but now global (grounded with reference to markets in the United States and Europe, the political institutions of the United Nations, and the totalizing alliances of the Cold War). Here, the value of "truth as balance" did not correspond to an actual state of affairs: obviously, the "balanced" findings of the Wessels Commission could not be considered a faithful or loyal account of the events of Sharpeville. Nor was it valuable for the conventional reasons of colonial governmentality: the apartheid state's reaction to Sharpeville, up to and including its investigation of the events, only hardened the resistance to apartheid and thus failed to achieve the classic goal of the Tumult Commission, the relaxation of racial tensions. It was valuable because of the claims to justice it implied. Wessels' "judicious" finding was that, although a few specific police officers were wrong for firing into the backs of fleeing protestors, there was ultimately blame to be had on "both sides," for the PAC had used inflammatory language prior to the events; that Sharpeville was therefore less a crime than a lamentable and regrettable tragedy; and that the government was not violating rights with impunity but was criticizing the individual excesses committed by specific police officers while also compensating innocent victims. This "balanced" conclusion gave South Africa's apologists abroad grounds to argue for the bona fide good intentions of the apartheid government as a whole, while also condemning the "unforgivable" racism of particular individuals.[93] This, in turn, gave European and American investors confidence that levels of race "hostility" in South Africa were sufficiently low that their shares in gold and diamond mines would not be "nationalized" by black revolutionaries anytime soon. With the Wessels Commission, in other words, one of the standard aims of the Tumult Commission—to write a history of racial hate in a way that also, therapeutically and performatively, decreased that hate, such that a multiracial society could be more easily managed and administered at the subpolitical or prepolitical level—acquired a new and different function. In conjunction with the state's redoubled powers of censorship, security, and detention, which stifled dissent internally, the Tumult Commission decreased the perception of racial hatred abroad—a double strategy designed to allow the apartheid state to mitigate its own governmental contradictions and to sustain the foreign direct investment demanded by its domestic and regional policies.

6.3.2 Much the same was true of the 1979 Commission of Inquiry into the Riots at Soweto and Elsewhere, a one-man commission headed by Supreme Court justice Petrus Malan Cillié and colloquially known as the "Cillié Commission." The Soweto Uprising, following on the heels of the dockworkers' strikes of the early 1970s, helped create the conditions for the terminal crisis of the apartheid state.[94] Because the Tumult Commission was a constitutive part of apartheid governance, the crisis of the apartheid state implied significant shifts in its practices and techniques as well. Some of these shifts were quite pronounced. In a departure from standard practice, for example, the Cillié Commission was not appointed *after* the events into which it was mandated to inquire but *during* those events—indeed, only two days after the onset of the Soweto Uprising.[95] Given the genealogy of the Tumult Commission, other shifts were entirely predictable. Like most of the other Tumult Commissions in South Africa (but only now to a greater degree), the Cillié Commission was boycotted by those who opposed it politically.[96] Again like most of the commissions in South Africa (but now more openly than before), the Cillié Commission was therefore informed mostly by the perspective of the police, and, not surprisingly, it narrated the plight of the South African policeman with great understanding, sympathy, and insight.[97] But while there was ultimately no doubt that the Cillié Commission was, like other Commissions of Inquiry appointed by the apartheid government to look into police abuses, a "sham and a charade,"[98] its report is still worth reading and, indeed, has been the object of insightful readings by scholars from a range of disciplines.

One reading, in particular, will be useful to consider in detail as a way to underline the path of a specifically genealogical approach to the Cillié Commission. In his detailed account of the that commission, Richard Price argues that there were two contradictory themes at work in its report: besides the report's main claim that the Soweto Uprising was the result of "outside agitators" directed by the USSR, there was also, Price argues, the secondary claim that apartheid policies themselves established the conditions for the uprising. On Price's read, the Cillié Commission's report presented apartheid "as part of the South African problem rather than the solution."[99] Together with the 1979 Riekert Commission, Price suggests, the Cillié Commission "became part of an evolving program of urban reform, incorporating both the physical upgrading of the townships and an alteration in the legal, economic, and social status of township residents, particularly those of African descent."[100] The fact that the government's own commission could reach these conclusions is, for Price, a "dramatic indicator" of the degree to which Soweto undermined the basis and force of apartheid rule.[101] By interpreting the Cillié Commission genealogically—as a repetition, though with a difference, of the paradigm of the Tumult Commission—the reader may reach a similar conclusion, only now by a much different route. Unlike Price and more like literary scholar Aubrey Mokadi or historian Helena Pohlandt-McCormick, the genealogist would question the very root of the recommendations and findings of the Cillié Commission.[102] On this read, the report of the Cillié Commission no longer could be divided up between, on the one hand, "inaccurate" (ideological, and propagandistic) blame of agitators (which cannot be taken at its word) and, on the other hand, its "accurate" (social scientific) diagnosis of the actual crisis of the apartheid state (which can be taken as its word). But it also would not suffice to criticize the Cillié Commission only for "misrepresenting" or "inaccurately representing" history. Though, in the general sense, this criticism is not wrong, it is nevertheless off the mark on a more fundamental and counterintuitive point. There is, after all, a paradoxical sense in which the Cillié Commission's distortions are ultimately a sort of *accurate* expression—not, of course, of the violent events of Soweto, but of the impotence underlying that violence, namely, the impotence of apartheid as a mode of government, or, put differently, the fact that the apartheid regime presided over a situation that *in concreto* was "ungovernable." The apartheid state's inability to inquire into its own limits and impasses, its own abuses and scandals, is in this sense a sign that the program of apartheid was, by the late 1970s, no longer capable of supporting the sort of self-criticism that was constitutive of governmentality in general and of colonial governmentality in particular.

On this read, in other words, Price would be on the mark to argue that the open distortions of the Cillié Commission, together with the degree to which it was openly contested and rejected both in South Africa and abroad, are indeed signs that, as Price would have it, apartheid governance was then entering into crisis—only a much different mode or sort of crisis than the one Price names. The distortions of the Cillié Commission were signs that governmentality was at that point breaking down, that the apartheid government could not pose and answer the question of governmentality with its full force. They signaled that the standard inquiry of governmentality—what are the norms and equilibriums intrinsic in and immanent in things themselves, and how should law conform itself to those norms?—was becoming mutually exclusive with the preservation of apartheid itself. A full inquiry into the Soweto Uprising, one imagines, would have revealed that equilibrium in South Africa was no longer possible, not even by police or military force, since state coercion itself had by then revealed itself not as an antidote to governmental disequilibrium but as one of its primary sources. The Durban Riots Commission rejected the standard form in which the Tumult Commission had generally posed the problem of racial equilibrium. In the Cillié

Commission, by contrast, equilibrium became a *form without content*. The Tumult Commission abandoned any pretense to find equilibrium in the "things themselves." It instead generated a purely formal equilibrium, a "concomitant cause" argument that was so painstakingly balanced, but so clearly without any foundation in the modes of evidence that the Tumult Commission had traditionally called its own, that the only real source of what shred of credibility it did possess was the sheer momentum of the administrative mechanism that produced it. The degree to which the Cillié Commission forced the form of equilibrium, however, is itself a true sign: it is a symptom of the real fact that equilibrium was an impossibility for colonial governmentality at that point. In this respect, the Cillié Commission marks the same sort of degradation and decline in the genealogy of the Commission of Inquiry that one sees in the genealogy of indemnity (to which the Commission of Inquiry is indeed closely related). Just as indemnity ceased to function as a calibrating mechanism between sovereignty and law and began to function as that juridical form through which the apartheid state could absolve itself for the war it was then waging on its own populations, so too did the Commission of Inquiry cease, in the 1970s and 1980s, to function as an attempt to fit law to population, beginning instead to function as an apparatus for openly falsifying that fit, an occasion for the apartheid state to narrate to itself, but only to itself, the normality of its own governance.

This understanding leads to the genealogist's second and third objections to Price's reading of the Cillié Commission. Although Price rightly observes that the reforms of apartheid proposed in the late 1970s were measures intended, in part, to avoid revolutionary onslaught, he argues that those measures were "contradictory" with the other theme of the Cillié Commission (that the Soweto Uprising was, in effect, directed by Moscow). But, to the contrary, the two measures are completely consistent, not only with each other, but also with prior Tumult Commissions (particularly the Durban Riot Commission). The Cillié Commission's findings point to the need to eliminate both the primary cause of the riots ("agitators") and the secondary causes (the "conditions" for agitation). Both aims were rigorously anti-Communist, and even though the two aims would seem to have much different manifestations—one cruel ("elimination" of key activists through assassination, banning, imprisonment, and torture) and one lenient (relaxation and reform of apartheid polices)—they both derive from one and the same biopolitical program. The Cillié Commission, exactly like the Durban

Riot Commission before it, pointed to the need to eliminate both the social conditions that gave rise to unrest (as a state of mind) and the agitators who converted that unrest into actual disturbances (acts). A final genealogical objection to Price's reading is that he omits the strange section of the report in which the commissioners declare that race relations in apartheid South Africa are, despite widespread disturbances, just fine. The Cillié Commission would, like other similar commissions, begin with a historical narrative that traces the way in which "exceptional tension" surrounding Afrikaans language instruction first developed into "fury" and then erupted into "riots."[103] The Cillié Commission would then analyze, like many other Tumult Commissions before it, the degree to which the "frustration" or "dissatisfaction" generated by various apartheid policies (homelands policy, influx control, group areas, ethnic grouping, the Immorality Act, discrimination) served as direct or indirect cause of the riots.[104] But its analysis of this history was so euphemistic as to be unintelligible. The commission found that "[d]iscrimination, which has always been considered unjust, has engendered not only dissatisfaction but also a great hatred in many. This dissatisfaction and hatred were some of the main factors that created the milieu and the spirit of revolt."[105] It also, however, concluded that it "cannot find that race relations as such were a cause of the riots, but the extremely bitter hatred which some of the rioters felt for Whites, probably because they were regarded as the oppressors, was a direct and contributory cause of the riots. This hatred was sometimes fanned and exploited by the agitators."[106] Aside from the scholars' "great hatred for racial discrimination" and "bitter hatred for whites," in other words, race relations "as such" did not affect the events of 1977; that is, in the absence of a few agitators, race relations "as such" would have been just fine. The category of "race relations as such" here undergoes a remarkable torque. It comes to exclude everything that prior Tumult Commissions had included under the category of race relations (hatred, anger, dissatisfaction).[107] With the small exception of *the basic substance of race relations as established by every previous Tumult Commission*, the Cillié Commission would thus have us believe, race relations were *not at all at issue in the riots*. The concept of "race relations," ostensibly the main object of apartheid laws and policies, here became so emptied of content that it no longer contained any reference to the problem of race relations at all. In the Cillié Commission, the concept of "race relations" was thus both *applied* and *not applied* (because, aside from hatred, dissatisfaction, and fury, "race relations as such" were not involved), and the main categories of the Tumult Commission were turned inside out, making sense only insofar as the categorical set to which they referred (e.g., "race relations" or "riots") contained anything but their own contents ("race relations" and "riots").

Critics of the apartheid state were not wrong to call this incoherent discourse "doublespeak" and "euphemistic," or, put differently, "absurd" and "surreal." But we should not lose sight of the sense in which this nonsensical language, paradoxically, had a very serious genealogical meaning as well. The incoherence of the Cillié Commission was a sign of the terminal crisis of the Tumult Commission more generally. The colonial Tumult Commission, as exemplified by the JRC, was designed to convert incipient hostility into relative equilibrium: in its investigations of colonial massacres, its conclusions almost invariably balanced out criticisms of excessive force by police with criticisms of unruly natives. The apartheid state's Tumult Commissions, by contrast, pushed this scheme to its limit, pursuing the norm of equilibrium to such an extreme that the Tumult Commission turned into its opposite: a mechanism of disequilibrium. The careful calibrations of the Tumult Commission, to be sure, always involved a trace of contradictoriness: this apparatus always had functioned to invite otherwise mutually exclusive truth claims to coexist and coincide with one another. Taken to the extreme, however, this balance became unbalanced, collapsing, in the Cillié Commission, into open contradiction and incoherence.

Since at least the JRC, which was accused by English radicals of being a "whitewash,"[108] the Tumult Commission's pursuit of equilibrium functioned not only to reveal but also to conceal the brutality of colonial massacre. But in a world context where colonialism was a normal mode of governance, those who questioned the colonial premises of the Tumult Commission (e.g., George Padmore, who, in 1937, published a book criticizing the Union of South Africa for its handling of the "Bondelzwarts Affair")[109] could be marginalized in institutions of international governance for their aberrant or extreme opinions. The Union's 1923 massacre of the Bondelzwarts could become a cause célèbre in the League of Nations, but because the latter had explicitly mandated the South African occupation of Namibia, the Commission of Inquiry that reported on that massacre in evenhanded terms (in the discourse of "concomitant cause" and the poetics of "tragedy") could be interpreted by the league not as a farce but as a reason for "regret" and as the basis for calls for improved colonial administration. Once it was reiterated in a world context defined not by colonialism but by decolonization, not by Victorian racism but by universal human rights, not by trusteeships and mandates but by the increasingly postcolonial character of international law, this same administrative machinery, deploying the same regime of truth, now appeared openly farcical: not only was injustice done; it now was seen to be done. Operating under conditions where international law and world opinion no longer openly affirmed colonization as a norm of global governance, it was no longer the critics of the Tumult Commission who were seen to be aberrant or extreme (in the 1940s and 1950s, in fact, criticisms of Padmore's sort would become the norm in the UN General Assembly's discourse on South Africa).[110] The pathology was now the Tumult Commission itself, this bizarre administrative machine that proposed to inquire into "both sides" of the event of colonial massacre. The Wessels Commission and, even more so, the Cillié Commission were now publicly understood to conceal more than they revealed, to increase more than decrease hostility, to produce more than reduce instability. No longer an effective mechanism of colonial governance, the Tumult Commission now had become little more than an empty ritual, a legal husk that continued to repeat colonial truths under postcolonial conditions, conditions in which those truths openly appeared to be untruths. The Tumult Commission thus finally became what, latently, it always already was: an administrative means to the end of maintaining a colonial rule founded, in the last instance, on a militarized police force. Even so, this terminal crisis was not without its own subtle but decisive recoil. Not despite its collapse, but precisely because of it, the Tumult Commission's various constituent components now lay available for new forms of deployment, new principles of arrangement, and new political aims—for experiments with truth that were at once necessary, desirable, and unprecedented.

Chapter 7

A TUMULT COMMISSION OF
A SPECIAL TYPE?

7.1.1 In its strongest iteration, the argument on behalf of Truth Commissions within transitional justice assumes a form at once dialectical and critical. Against those who would criticize Truth Commissions on the assumption that criminal prosecution is the only or best paradigm of justice, transitional scholars deploy two arguments. The first and most well known is equal parts epistemic and ethical. Against those who claim that Truth Commissions are merely the "second-best" option for successor regimes who are unable to carry through on their desire to prosecute the crimes of their predecessors, transitional justice scholars argue that Truth Commissions actually provide an epistemic space that is, in many ways, *superior* to that of the criminal trial. Criminal trials tend to arrive at their truths through the intense and often hostile or even humiliating practices of cross-examination. Witnesses whose stories of suffering often involve vulnerabilities and uncertainty under cross-examination find their narratives of pain sliced up before their very eyes, retranslated into a legal lexicon that not only bears little to no resemblance to their own idioms, but that also seems designed to destroy the fragile kernel of truth in the words they have to offer. When victims of state violence are spared this ordeal, when the testimony of victims is allowed to unfold uninterrupted by the acidic skepticism of lawyers and by the criminal trial's stringent limitations on what counts as "admissiable evidence," not only do victims benefit from a form of remedy that is both different from and deeper than the remedies of the criminal trial, but there is also a greater likelihood that—over time, through the gradual accumulation of victim narratives—the basic facts of authoritarian pasts will come to light. If the goal of a Truth Commission is to provide a space where traumatized individuals and collectives can come to terms with and work through the unavowed pain and suffering in their own past, not only is the criminal trial not the best or only means to this end, but it is second best to the Truth Commission, whose freer epistemic space is much more likely to enable the "healing truth" or "restorative justice" that, in turn, allows for the recovery of traumatized individuals and collectives alike.

Alongside this well-known argument is a second that, perhaps because it is merely administrative in character, has not received nearly the same sort of the attention as the first, even if there are some readers for whom it is even more compelling. Against those who would claim or assume that criminal prosecutions are the only or best form of justice in cases of state violence, transitional justice scholars point to the sheer expense involved in even a single criminal trial (e.g., to take the obvious example from South Africa, that of Eugene de Kock).[1] There is, after all, an economy to law: it is expensive and time-consuming to prove guilt beyond a reasonable doubt, to protect the rights of the accused and (if necessary) witnesses, to select and (sometimes) to sequester a jury, to hear all appeals, and to observe all procedures, no matter how technical or apparently petty. When these expenses are multiplied by, say, twenty thousand, one can see why the argument on behalf of Truth Commissions is so strong: in some cases, criminal prosecutions are not only epistemically and ethically undesirable (because of the way they fragment and retranslate the stories of victims) but also administratively impossible (because of the sheer expenses and overwhelming complexities that are involved).

For reasons both qualitative and quantitative, therefore, Truth Commissions are understood by transitional scholars to have virtues that make them not only more desirable but also more feasible than criminal prosecutions. Their weaknesses turn out to be strengths; their vices turn out to be virtues. To authoritarian crimes—these crimes that can be neither forgiven nor punished—there is, of course, no perfect remedy. But among the many imperfect remedies known to us, the Truth Commission is, at least according to transitional justice, the least imperfect. In contrast to the "Nuremberg model," in other words, there is thus a good case for the "South African model," particularly when the case in question is made by so eloquent and charismatic a leader as Archbishop Desmond Tutu.[2]

So successful have these arguments become in transitional justice that they are the basis for a broad consensus within the field today. It is virtually unthinkable to make sense of Truth Commissions in general and the TRC in particular without first rehearsing the various ways in which the TRC is the antithesis of the criminal trial. Each of the main analytic oppositions that govern the interpretation of the TRC within transitional justice—truth versus justice, vengeance versus forgiveness, retributive versus restorative justice, Nuremberg versus South Africa—derive from the hermeneutic horizon opened up by these oppositions. Yet precisely this success prepares the conditions for a subtle but decisive failure. By making sense of the TRC mainly or even only in opposition to the juridical forms at work in the criminal trial, transitional justice scholars allow themselves to avoid serious scrutiny of the juridical forms at work in the administrative apparatus of the Commission of Inquiry. From the transitional justice perspective, all that seems significant about the Commission of Inquiry is that it is not a criminal trial (that it is not contentious, expensive, formal, forensic, etc.). It is as if the Commission of Inquiry were nothing more than a neutral and empty juridical form, had no epistemic field of its own, and placed no constraints or limits of its own on the voices of victims; it is as if administrative efficiency in response to the victims of state violence were without precedent or strategy. None of these suppositions are well founded; yet only by presuming their validity is it then also possible to construe the Commission of Inquiry, as transitional justice scholars habitually do, as nothing more than an especially accommodating backdrop, an innocuous setting that allows for the staging of the dramatic and sometimes miraculous testimonies with which the TRC has now become associated.

Above all, by focusing our curiosity on the question of how the TRC relates to its "antithesis" in the criminal trial, transitional justice has authorized us to remain uncurious about another question: *how the TRC is antithetical to its precedents in colonial and imperial jurisprudence.* This is, however, not simply one among many questions. Not only is it the indispensable condition for any coherent discussion of postapartheid law in general, as Martin Chanock has argued; it also happens to be the one question that alone can reveal the submerged, inner logic that links transitional justice's own two strongest claims on behalf of the Truth Commissions. The genealogy of the Tumult Commission, even in the schematic form in which it appears in this book, contains telling precedents that link the epistemico-ethical argument for the TRC (that it provides a space for the stories of those who have suffered state violence) with the administrative argument for the TRC (that commissions are more efficient than are courts of law for getting to the facts of mass state violence). It even contains precedents for the very antithesis that today remains so central for the field of transitional justice itself. The distinction between courts of law (where witnesses are litigiously cross-examined) and Commissions of Inquiry (where witnesses are only asked about facts) was a standard feature of the self-understanding of the Tumult Commission itself.[3] The genealogical question, in short, turns on its head transitional justice's account of the phenomena of the Truth Commission. By leaving in silence the question of how the Commission of Inquiry functioned as a technique of colonial governmentality, transitional justice not only becomes undialectical (for it is thereby obliged to leave in silence the question of the TRC's relationships with its most intimate and therefore most radical antithesis); it also becomes uncritical (for it is likewise obliged to assume the neutrality and ahistoricality of a governmental technique that is, as we have seen, anything but).

7.1.2 To raise this question, even in a preliminary way, is to encounter a host of additional questions—questions that are essential for understanding the TRC but that cannot be asked within the hermeneutic horizon of transitional justice. What does it mean that one can find so many of the defining attributes of the TRC operating under conditions defined not by democratic transition but by colonial and even apartheid governments? The TRC's extensive solicitation of the voices of the victims of state violence is repeatedly said to be one of the features that made the TRC unique in the history of the world. How, then, should we think about the equally extensive solicitation of victim voices that took place in the JRC? Is there not, in the JRC as in the TRC, an administrative attempt to listen to and to catalog the stories of as many victims of government violence as possible, treating those voices and narratives as the raw material and primary source for the fullest and most complete narrative possible—one that is, in each case, not at all uncritical—of the use of extralegal government violence?

One might object that the TRC, in stark contrast to the JRC, is obviously not at all dismissive of the voices to which it lends its "ear of power." But is this contrast really all that obvious? From the beginning, after all, some of the scholars who have made the most careful studies of the TRC have argued that the TRC was plagued by an excess of unverifiable and ambiguous testimony and that many stories offered by victims were incomprehensible and unreliable.[4] In the case of the TRC, no doubt, the incomprehensibility and incompletion of this testimony was not rendered intelligible according to the old tropes of colonial anthropology, where the metropolitan social scientist advocated on behalf of the irrational, passionate native who was presumed to be unself-conscious about the ways and means of rational discourse. It was, instead, rendered intelligible in the new tropes of "trauma studies,"[5] as the symptomatic speech of someone whose suffering has caused her to unconsciously say more than she knows, whose unsymbolizable suffering is at once the very source of her common humanity, and interpretable only by a qualified analyst. Isn't it here, then, still the case that the victim of state violence is assumed to be unable to independently represent her suffering and so must depend on a trained expert to be represented, only now under slightly different conditions, where the metanarrative for this incapacity for self-representation is not the condescension of cultural anthropology but the overextension of psychoanalytic therapy (whose subject is, in the TRC as elsewhere in its history, a woman)? Hasn't the field of trauma studies today accomplished the same end—the production of experts who are confident about representing the otherwise incomprehensible speech of the victim—that used to govern the cultural anthropology of the nineteenth century? Similarly, what else is "dialogue truth"—this ostensibly new administrative genre designed to allow for the possibility of a truth that is somewhere "in between" the opposing claims of political adversaries[6]—except a new name for precisely the same paradigm of "concomitant cause" that was so systematic a part of the Tumult Commission? Is it really so surprising that the TRC would pursue "evenhandedness" to such an extreme (irritating, in the process, Kader Asmal, because of the legal and even moral parity it established between, on the one hand, a comparatively small and ineffective guerilla army and, on the other, a nuclear-armed garrison state equipped with sophisticated military, naval, and air force units)? Inasmuch as the TRC did not explicitly differentiate its epistemic field from the paradigm of the Tumult Commission, what other sort of conclusion was available to it? What juridical forms other than "concomitant cause" were available to it for producing "as complete a picture as possible" of the violence of the past? Given the TRC's genealogical precursors in prior Tumult Commissions, wouldn't the truly unprecedented event have been for the TRC *not* to have issued neutral and neutralizing findings and *not* to have habitually referred to the violence of the apartheid era as a "tragic" conflict?[7]

To give voice to these questions is not, to be clear, the same as arguing that the TRC is nothing more than a simple repetition of the forms, theories, and practices of the colonial and apartheid Tumult Commission. Nor is it, of course, to imply that any juridical theory or practice in the TRC that is not absolutely new and unprecedented (in the mode of the French Revolution) is, by definition, complicit with apartheid by virtue of its simple contact with the apartheid past. It is only to suggest that the indispensable condition for evaluating claims about the TRC's representation of the voices of the victims is a grasp of the epistemic field of the Tumult Commission—this unusual administrative apparatus that was so constitutive a part of colonial and apartheid rule and that provides the TRC with its most intimate and most distressing precedents. Accordingly, the point of this chapter is not to *settle* the question of the relation between the Tumult Commission and the TRC but merely to *open* it. Here, as in section 4.2, we will not attempt to resolve each and every question that emerges within the space of this relation. We will simply demonstrate the possibility and desirability of those questions by reexamining a number of texts that, taken together, exemplify the TRC's reiteration of the epistemic field of the Tumult Commission. What understanding of the TRC's genius and risks might we receive were we to understand its techniques and practices not in opposition to the criminal trial but in opposition to the Tumult Commission that preceded it? In what sense, if any, did the TRC simply repeat the epistemic field it inherited from the Tumult Commission? In what respect, that is to say, did it operate as *a Tumult Commission of a special type,* a governmental apparatus that, despite the best intentions of its architects and participants, ended up performing little more than an unusually extensive whitewashing of an unusually extensive and violent period of martial law (what Richard Rive once called the "normal emergency")? Or, on the other hand, in what sense did it repeat the forms of the Tumult Commission but now with a difference? And if this was the case, what then was that difference, and what difference might it make for the way we think and speak about the event of the TRC today?

7.2.1 Let's begin with the strongest argument that the TRC did in fact break with the epistemic field it inherited from the Tumult Commission. This requires close consideration of a concept that, from Aristotle to Hegel, has been closely connected with the tragic: catharsis, particularly the concept of catharsis as it figures into the thinking of Kader Asmal in the early 1990s, at the moment when he first called for a Truth Commission in South Africa. Asmal's earliest remarks on catharsis appear alongside his reflections on the Gramscian concept of the "interregnum,"[8] and when we read Gramsci over Asmal's shoulder, it is not difficult to understand Gramsci's appeal at such a juncture: in the tumultuous days of the mid-1990s, Gramsci could provide precisely the "granular" theory of political transition that the ANC and the South African Communist Party (SACP) otherwise lacked. Although rumors of the SACP's influence within the ANC surely are overstated, it is nevertheless sound to say that the SACP was, in general, the "theoretical wing" of the ANC. In the early 1990s, at precisely that moment when it ought to have been poised to take power, the SACP instead found itself without a coherent theory of political transition. The early 1990s were thus a paradoxical moment for the SACP. Whereas most communist parties around the world started to lose supporters after the fall of the USSR, the SACP gained supporters, not only among youth, but also among its former critics. Yet at this very moment, the SACP's theoretical deficit left it unprepared to lead. Within the SACP, the dominant theory of political transition derived from the SACP's more general political theory of South African apartheid, namely, the concept of a "colonialism of a special type" (CST).[9] Yet by the late eighties and early nineties, the CST theory seemed as epistemologically unsound as it was politically shortsighted.[10] At such a crossroads, as Harold Wolpe argued, it became vital to "open[] up the question of the specific class content of variant formulations of policies aimed at dismantling the structure of racial domination."[11]

Joe Slovo's 1991 critique of the CST theory did precisely that. In his 1989 paper "Has Socialism Failed?," Slovo took the collapse of state socialism as an occasion to question, first and foremost, the notion of the "dictatorship of the proletariat" at the core of Marx's theory of the transition to socialism.[12] In a subsequent paper, Slovo not only returned to the problem of transition but also questioned "the truly indigenous theory of the South African revolution based on its conception of colonialism of a special type."[13] Writing at a moment of crisis for the concept of transition to socialism in general, Slovo suggested that "perhaps the time has come for more emphasis to be placed on the class content of the continuous quest for national liberation."[14] At the very moment that there was, on the part of the ANC and the SACP, a desire to win state power, on the theory that the assumption of state power would be a means to the end of economic and social transformation, there was, therefore, a pronounced lack of theoretical agreement on precisely what it would mean to transform the state itself.

Under these conditions, it makes sense that a certain rereading of Gramsci (focusing, as Martin Legassick has argued, on the concepts of the "war of maneuver" and "hegemony") would gain momentum on the South African left.[15] Gramsci's concept of catharsis would be one of the concepts at stake in this rereading. In one of the more enigmatic passages of his 1929–35 *Prison Notebooks*, Gramsci gave the name "catharsis" to "the starting-point for all the philosophy of praxis."[16] Catharsis, in Gramsci's view, would be achieved through a synthesis of feeling and intellect that, in turn, would prepare the way for the "organic cohesion" that Gramsci would call the "ethical state": it would produce the subjective preconditions for a new state in the absence of which any state would remain a merely bureaucratic and formal order.[17] As distinct from the old doctrine of raison d'état, Gramsci's "ethical state" did not construe the state as an end unto itself; instead, it treated the state as a means to the end of the progressive civilization of its populations through the extension and intensification of their philosophical and moral consciousness.[18] Against Benedetto Croce's suggestion that the purpose of *katharsis* was to restore spectators' passions to the calm of a prior equilibrium, Gramsci followed the early Marx's argument that ideas themselves could produce material effects, above all the effect of transforming the social relations of production.[19] This, in fact, was the core of catharsis for Gramsci: to subsume the domain of apparent objective economic necessity under the domain of subjective ethico-political freedom.[20]

Law had a decisive place and function in this theory. Early in the *Prison Notebooks*, Gramsci would suggest that the very "common sense" (or, in an older lexicon, the *doxa*) that grounds and defines a given culture also consists of the residues and traces of past laws.[21] The reverse held as well: common sense, in Gramsci's view, already hosted the revolutionary potential that every individual could become a legislator and could govern themselves in and through autonomous freedom.[22] This potential was neither natural nor ahistorical; nor was it without uncertainties and dialectical limits of its own. Precisely because common sense, in Gramsci's view, included the remnants of past laws, its revolutionary potential was constrained in advance by a very definite risk: that its "spontaneous" actualization in and through revolution would turn out to produce not a new order but simply the return of prerevolutionary juridical forms, the forms of domination and tradition, only now under a new name. This was the risk, in short, that self-legislation grounded in unreconstructed common sense would give rise not to freedom but to voluntary servitude.

Catharsis, for Gramsci, was an antidote to this risk. It was integral to the transition from a capitalist to a socialist economy, because only its educational force, its intensification of philosophical and moral consciousness, could purge common sense of the traditional juridical forms that threatened to constrain its revolutionary actualization in advance and from within. In particular, common sense needed to be purged of the retrograde assumption that the productive potencies of human personality could and should be subordinated to the impersonal laws of the market. Socialists, Gramsci wrote in 1917,

> must not replace order with order. They must bring about order in itself. The juridical norm that they want to establish is the *possibility of the complete realization of one's human personality for every citizen*. With the realization of this norm all established privileges collapse. It leads to maximum freedom with a minimum of constraints. It wants the rule of life and allocations to be potential and productivity, to be independent of any traditional scheme; that wealth be not an instrument of bondage but, belonging to everyone impersonally, it provide all the means for the maximum possible well-being.[23]

As a part of this cathartic dynamic, it would be essential that all past activities must remain open for review and criticism.[24] The cultural policy under such conditions, Gramsci suggested, should be primarily negative: it should take place as a critique of the past that aims at "erasing from the memory and at destroying."[25] The reason for this is clear: before the revolution could release populations from their external constraints (the market, the economy, relations of production), it first needed to release them from their inner constraints (the residues or traces of old laws within their common sense). Catharsis, Gramsci's name for this release, was thus the subjective precondition for the autonomous and free determination of the objective economy—for the "complete realization of the human personality"—that only socialist order could provide.

7.2.2 One can see why Gramsci's theory of catharsis would hold a certain appeal in the South Africa of the early 1990s, under conditions defined by the crisis of existing theories of political transition. In the 1992 speech that first introduced the notion of a Truth Commission to South Africa, Kader Asmal would cite, as one of the nine arguments he advanced for a Truth Commission, "the argument that comes from Gramsci. If the old order is dying and the new is not yet born, can there be reconciliation simply through an assertion that new structures and new arrangements will be set in place?"[26] Interpreted against the backdrop of Gramscian thought, Asmal's concept of catharsis emerges as his answer to this question. Catharsis, Asmal argued, obviously should not serve the purposes of a "white-washing" that would produce "a past mysteriously purged of apartheid."[27] Nor should it take the form of the lustration laws passed in Czechoslovakia in 1991.[28] Not only would lustration be, in Asmal's opinion, "a convenient way of avoiding the Kafkaesque word 'purge' with its historical undertones,"[29] but, as others have frankly explained, the ANC had not yet trained a class of civil servants, particularly judges, capable of immediately replacing existing apartheid bureaucrats. Lustration was thus as strategically impossible as it was politically undesirable. Finally, Asmal counseled, catharsis should be distinguished from the unlawfulness of violent "liquidation."[30]

Yet if the catharsis in question would be none of these things, what *would* it be? Writing with Louise Asmal and Ronald Suresh Roberts in his 1995 *Reconciliation through Truth*, Kader Asmal would offer further clarification. The catharsis that will have been enabled by the apparatus that, by then, had been given the name "Truth and Reconciliation Commission" would take place only through a transvaluation of the "ethical" values of apartheid. Asmal, Asmal, and Roberts explained,

> Reconciliation requires an acknowledgement of wrongs committed and a re-evaluation by their perpetrators of the morality which lay behind them. Only then can reconciliation trigger real catharsis, a word which, in its original Greek meaning, contains the ideas of purification and spiritual renewal. Reconciliation, accurately conceived, must bring about a rupture with the skewed ethics [*sic*] of apartheid, and so upset any possibility of smooth sailing on a previously immoral course.[31]

Catharsis, in this schema, would be the task of "defining properly what dirtiness means. That task—paring the clean from the unclean parts of the past—is in fact at the heart of that much misused concept, 'reconciliation.'"[32] The "process of historical catharsis" that results would take place "as the previously excluded speak at last for themselves, and the privileged caste joins the South African family for the first time."[33] "Historical catharsis" would be a purge in the sense that it would get rid of the unclean ethics of apartheid, up to and including the ethics of speaking for those who are presumed to be unable to speak for themselves. But in another sense, it would not be a purge at all: neither whitewashing, lustration, nor liquidation, historical catharsis would not be violent, exclusionary, or a way of forgetting the political order with which it breaks. Defined, above all, by the inclusion of the speech of the subaltern into the very center of a state apparatus hitherto distinguished by its exclusion, historical catharsis would create, precisely, a new "common sense"—a common sense that will have been purified of all traces of the old regime's laws. In Gramscian terms, the "historical catharsis" identified by Asmal, Asmal, and Roberts was designed to create the subjective preconditions (the "spiritual renewal") that, by their mere existence, would constitute the "novelty" of the new South Africa (much more, in fact, than any objective, material transformation, the extent of which was all too limited by the terms of the negotiated settlement). A *purge without purge*, this historical catharsis would be, in short, the most active and radical catalyst of South Africa's "revolution without revolution" (or what Gramsci would call a "passive revolution").[34]

Interpreted in relation to the crisis of the Tumult Commission, the audacity of this turn to Gramsci becomes particularly clear. Historical catharsis, as Asmal, Asmal, and Roberts construe it, marks an attempt to redeploy the broken apparatus of the Tumult Commission, only now as a means to an end at which no prior Tumult Commission had ever aimed. No longer a "whitewashing" machine, as the Tumult Commission became especially under apartheid, the Truth Commission would be a space where the speech of the subaltern would educate the privileged classes about the unethical essence of apartheid "ethics." No longer a warehouse designed for the efficient stockpiling of unverifiable stories of native suffering, as was the Tumult Commission beginning at least with the JRC, the Truth Commission would treat those stories not only as sources of truth but also as the moral basis for a revolutionary new "ethical state." Whereas the Tumult Commission investigated the question of the "necessity" of police violence, concluding more often than not in the affirmative, the Truth Commission would declare that police violence was not necessary, above all because it was committed in the name of a legal order that was itself illegitimate and immoral (arguably indeed not even a legal order at all). The Tumult Commission was most often used *against* revolutionaries (as in, e.g., 1922 and 1949) to restore a *prior order*. The Truth Commission, by contrast, would be used *for the purpose of revolution*, to create the "break in time" and "founding legends" that are the hallmarks of the modern revolutionary tradition of creating *new* order.[35] Whereas the Tumult Commission worked according to the principle of a sort of thermodynamics, operating as a mechanism for "letting off steam" or "venting" to no purpose (in precisely the manner that Frantz Fanon warned against in his critique of catharsis),[36] the Truth Commission would have as its purpose an aim at once clear and distinct: the transformation of the South African "soul."

It certainly then would not be far off the mark to say that the originality of Asmal, Asmal, and Roberts was to add a fourth modality—catharsis—to the three existing historiographical modes that defined the paradigmatic Tumult Commission (accuse, exonerate, and mourn). But even this would ultimately understate their most decisive intervention. When they redeployed the Tumult Commission within a horizon defined by the aims of Gramscian catharsis, they radicalize a potential that was latent, all along, in the Tumult Commission's systematic dependence on the lexicon of the tragic. The genius of their concept of a commission that would produce historical catharsis was not that it "reconciled" Gramsci's discourse on catharsis with the apparatus of Tumult Commission or that it inserted the political "contents" of historical catharsis into the Tumult Commission's otherwise neutral administrative "container." It was that they reiterated the innermost poetics of the Tumult Commission under new conditions, in a way that made the tragic signify the very opposite of what it had signified for the Tumult Commission. Whereas the Tumult Commission mobilized the language of the tragic to explain the "necessary evil" or "lamentable necessity" of state repression, the Truth Commission would redeploy that same language to signify *emancipation* from a repressive state—to produce a historical catharsis in which the unethical basis of the apartheid state itself, independently of its violent acts of self-defense, would become self-evident to one and all. This is not to suggest, however, that these two declensions of the tragic are commensurable. To the contrary, the Tumult Commission presupposed a very different understanding of the illegality of state violence than did Gramscian thought. Whereas the Tumult Commission operated on the presupposition of individual ministerial liability and, as such, sought to personalize, to particularize, and, thus, to limit any question of illegal state violence, Gramsci inherited the early Marx's suspicion of the way that, particularly in cases of "partial revolution," claims about "universal offenses" actually functioned as *false* universals (as universal offenses whose implicit framing serves particular class interests) and, thus, also concealed a more radical illegality.[37] Whereas the Tumult Commission was inclined toward a meticulous and detailed historical inquiry into the excesses of particular illegal actions by specific state officials, Gramsci was inclined toward a critique of the very idea of concentrating on this or that "notorious crime": to do so would be to risk mistaking part for whole and, thus, to *impede* emancipation from a repressive state.

7.2.3 This incommensurability shoots through the TRC's 1998 report like an exposed nerve. The "historically cathartic" aim of the TRC (to narrate, as the common sense of the postapartheid state, the retrospective history according to which apartheid *as a whole* was a crime against humanity) sat uneasily with the TRC's aim as a paradigmatic Tumult Commission (i.e., to investigate whether or not *particular* illegal acts by the government and by the liberation movements were committed with a bona fide belief that those acts were really politically necessary). This tension was, from a very early point, quite apparent.[38] The TRC was not mandated primarily as an attempt to respond to the criminality of apartheid *as a whole*, and the *TRC Report* did not hide the fact that it regarded as a vexed issue the sense in which apartheid itself was a crime.[39] But at the same time that the *TRC Report* explicitly condemned apartheid as an intrinsically evil crime against humanity,[40] it also, because of its limited mandate, explicitly excluded apartheid from the restricted category of "gross violations of human rights" that it heard, investigated, archived, judged, and, under certain conditions, indemnified.[41] The consequence was a paradox internal to the report's juridical reasoning. The crime of "apartheid itself" appeared in the report as a conceptual set that, defined rigorously, could not include its own members, for the various notorious *parts* of apartheid that the TRC was mandated to investigate (i.e., "gross violations of human rights") were legislatively precluded from sharing a juridical status with *the whole* to which, according to the logic of "historical catharsis," they ought to belong (i.e., the "crime against humanity" that is apartheid itself). The resulting impasse is explained well by Jacqueline Rose.

If you spread accountability too wide by flattening out the differences between the state and its opponents, then oddly, symmetrically, it will also start to shrink, as the crimes of apartheid become more and more the acts of individuals, less and less the machinery of the unjust and illegal apartheid state ("the violence of the law," in the *Report*'s own words, pushed over the legal edge). Once it has been individualized, the act stands out in bold, plucked out of its context. In fact the more inhuman and outrageous the act . . . the more drastically it curtails the Commission.[42]

The *TRC Report* worked hard to reconcile this impasse. It tried to reconcile the tension between, on the one hand, the *indemnifiable particulars* of the crimes committed under apartheid and, on the other hand, the sense in which the crime of apartheid itself was, as Asmal himself held, *condemnable as a whole*. It is not clear whether it succeeded in this endeavor. On the one hand, it made an effort for its accounts of the various "gross violations of human rights" committed under apartheid to appear *sufficiently extreme* so that those violations would come *to exemplify* the sense in which apartheid as a whole was indeed a crime against humanity.[43] On the other hand, exactly as Rose suggests, these same accounts tried to avoid appearing *so extreme* that they would come to present those violations as *exceptions* to apartheid as a whole (as was the case with "bad apples," such as Eugene de Kock, who, not despite but precisely because of their pathological monstrosity, risked the appearance of having no relation whatsoever to apartheid as a whole and indeed, by contrast, normalized its underlying criminality).[44] As a means to this end, the report deployed both of the paradigms of state criminality it inherited during the period of its genesis. On the one hand, the report certainly did repeat the classic Tumult Commission logic of "concomitant cause" narration (concluding, to the great dismay of Asmal, Asmal, and Roberts, that "both sides of the struggle" were to blame).[45] On the other hand, it emphatically departed from this logic (concluding, as Asmal did in 1978, that apartheid was a "crime against humanity").[46] Theorized as a purge without a purge, the report thus reached conclusions that were extreme without being extreme. It tried to provide enough exceptional examples of apartheid state criminality so that the exceptions could exemplify the normal criminality of the apartheid state as a whole. It tried to damn apartheid as an unequivocal evil while also construing the struggle against it in a balanced, evenhanded way. It tried, we might say, *to illustrate* the criminality of the apartheid state as a whole (by amassing "typical cases" of state criminality) without also, in the process, *lustrating* the criminality of the apartheid state as a whole (by allowing its concentration on "typical cases" to become so excessive that it has the perverse effect of "cleansing" or "purifying" apartheid itself). If, in the end, this curious dialectic ended up producing a report that was less than fully consistent, it cannot be said that the report was completely inconsistent either. Like the negotiated settlement of which it was a metonym, the *TRC Report* is best read as a disjunctive synthesis of incomplete repetitions and insufficient differences, as an acutely unstable composite of incommensurable epistemic demands.

7.3.1 The instability of the synthesis in the *TRC Report* would become particularly apparent in a popular text published in 1998. Even more than the 1998 *TRC Report* itself, Antjie Krog's *Country of My Skull* seems to have become *the* canonical book about the TRC (especially after 2004, when the book was turned into a twelve-million-dollar Hollywood film called *In My Country*, starring Samuel L. Jackson and Juliette Binoche).[47] Although its filmic iteration would seem to allow *Country of My Skull* to be described as the story of an Afrikaner reporter who experiences a nervous breakdown and has an extramarital affair while covering the TRC hearings, the written text's painstaking attempts at metafiction throw this description into question. The narration of the book self-consciously multiplies the persona of its narrator, referring to its voice alternately with the names Antjie Krog, Antjie Samuel, Antjie Somers, and sometimes just Antjie. This, in turn, suspends any possibility of reading the book rigorously as autobiography.[48] Many critics have faulted the text for the allegedly unethical character of this self-conscious suspension of self-referentiality; but at least on the text's own terms, the resulting impasses are at the very core of what this text seems to think is its ethical teaching about the TRC. The conceit of *Country of My Skull* is that, in its structural unverifiability (i.e., in the inability of the reader to decide whether the narrator's extramarital affair is fact or fiction), it loyally exemplifies the structural unverifiability of testimonies given before the TRC (i.e., the inability of the commission to decide whether victims' and perpetrators' stories are, in forensic terms, fact or fiction); in so doing, it underlines the need for an ethics of reading that no longer founds itself in simple divisions of true from false.[49]

Country of My Skull has been praised and damned for this gambit; that dispute is not our concern here. From a genealogical perspective, what's interesting about this text is the way that, precisely because of its self-conscious fidelity to the TRC's administrative discourse, it ends up incorporating into its own narrative voice the disjunctive synthesis that is the hallmark of that discourse. It is not, after all, unprecedented to interpret as unverifiable the testimony of those who have suffered the violence of colonial regimes. This is, to the contrary, a standard feature of the Tumult Commission, beginning at least with the JRC. Nor is it unprecedented to repeat in a formless and unprocessed mass, as Krog often does, the transcriptions of those testimonies.[50] Here too, as any reader of the appendix of the JRC's report will see, one finds the telltale traces of the Tumult Commission paradigm. Nowhere, however, is *Country of My Skull*'s redeployment of administrative discourse more pronounced than in the way the figures of the "victim" and the "perpetrator" emerge in Krog's text. *Country of My Skull* is, as its critics have noted, at pains to identify with the administrative rubric of "victim" as it is defined by the TRC.[51] Whether in the text's dedication ("for every victim who had an Afrikaner surname on her lips"), in its narrator's nervous breakdown (in which the persona of Antjie begins to embody the symptoms of the trauma victim), or in its conclusion (in which the narrator writes "for us all; all voices, all victims"),[52] *Country of My Skull* confers on its narrator the attributes and status of the figure the TRC would call "the victim."[53] At the same time, however, the book also invites its reader to recognize its narrator in ethnic terms, as an Afrikaner, which is to say, on the text's own terms, necessarily complicit in the crimes of the apartheid regime. Although there is no sign within the book that the narrator herself has committed any crimes against humanity as defined by the TRC mandate, the text imagines the project of moral responsibility to consist in the fantasy of having participated in such crimes by virtue of demographic categories alone.

This is most apparent in the odd allegory that appears toward the closing of the South African edition of *Country of My Skull*. This allegory presents the reader with a scene in which the narrator confesses to her husband that, while covering the TRC, she has had an affair with an unnamed colleague.[54] Although, in strict conformity with the demands of metafiction, the book disavows the verifiability of this affair (presenting the reader with a passage in which the narrator admits to her editor that the affair is not fact but fiction[55]), it does not disavow the desirability of the affair as a literary device for personifying the psychological underpinnings of the TRC.[56] To the contrary, it seems to think it useful to ask its reader to consider bourgeois heterosexual infidelity as an allegory for understanding the gross human rights abuses considered by the TRC. On the terms of this allegory, just as perpetrators need to ask forgiveness of their victims for acts of torture, the narrator needs to ask forgiveness of her cuckolded husband for her acts of infidelity.

This allegory is, needless to say, not without its own juridical forms. It is curious, to say the least, to imagine that the infidelity of adultery is in some way akin to the inhumanity of torture, as if one should be obliged to ask forgiveness for an extramarital affair in the same way that a torturer should ask forgiveness for a crime against humanity. In the filmic iteration of the book (not to mention the American book edition, from which key metafictional doubts have been purged[57]), this fantasy becomes even more questionable. Because *In My Country* unfolds largely as a romance between Samuel L. Jackson's Langston Whitfield and Juliette Binoche's Anna Malan, infidelity here becomes interracial infidelity, and the "crime against humanity" for which Malan must ask forgiveness from her husband aligns, perversely, with the prohibition of "illicit carnal intercourse" as defined first by Immorality Act 5 of 1927 and then by Immorality Amendment No. 21 of 1950. Even though *Country of My Skull* wants this allegory to exemplify the psychological dynamics of reconciliation in postapartheid South Africa, the offense at its center—extramarital interracial sex—derives a quotient of its transgressive charge from its silent repetition of a category of offense defined by preapartheid legislation.

In order for Krog's allegory to remain consistent with itself, in other words, it needs to assume that extramarital interracial sex is a crime just as gross and inhuman, just as "immoral" and in need of forgiveness, as are the crimes against humanity confessed by perpetrators before the TRC. But this same assumption points to the threshold at which the book's moralistic censure of apartheid recoils upon itself and turns into its opposite. At the same time that the book imagines crimes against humanity being carried out mainly by those defending the racial laws of the apartheid state, its allegory implies that the immorality of those crimes shares a quality with the "immorality" of sex crimes as defined by the racial laws of the apartheid state. Whereas the *TRC Report* tried to make torture exemplify the crime against humanity that was apartheid itself, Krog's allegory allows extramarital, interracial sex—an act prohibited by apartheid law—to exemplify the "torture" for which "the perpetrator" must ask forgiveness. The allegory here acquires unwanted momentum and volatility; it doesn't so much illuminate the ethics of the TRC's "pardon machine" as it does short-circuit that machine. Here, the narrator who asks forgiveness for her infidelity ends up asking forgiveness for a "crime" that, sensu stricto, was only a crime under apartheid (and then only up until 1985, when the Immorality Acts of 1950 and 1957 were repealed). The voice of this narrator, at least in this scene, is not, then, the voice of a "victim" (who suffered a crime against humanity), nor is it only the voice of a "perpetrator" (who confesses a crime against humanity); it is, rather and, again, sensu stricto, the voice of the subject of apartheid, someone whose fantasy of moral guilt is the "trace" or "residue" of legal guilt as defined by apartheid law.

If *Country of My Skull* allows its narrator to speak in the voice of the victim, so too therefore does it permit that same narrator to speak in the voice of a perpetrator. Interpreted in genealogical terms, this doubleness has a very specific provenance. When *Country of My Skull* presents the reader with a narrative voice that seeks to reconcile within itself the attributes of both innocent victim and guilty perpetrator, its main accomplishment is to discover the possibility of narrating the TRC from within an epistemic field the innermost norm of which was "tragic" (that state massacres were "concomitantly caused" by policeman and multitude alike, that everyone and no one was therefore to blame, and that massacres thus entailed coincidence of complete guilt and complete innocence). In genealogical terms, however, this discovery is more properly understood as a *re*-discovery: its effectiveness derives from its reactivation of a juridical form derived from the Tumult Commission and undone by the TRC only incompletely. On these terms, the significance of *Country of My Skull* is not that it unethically engages in metafiction rather than in direct and unmediated representations of victim testimony; nor is it that its literariness self-consciously exemplifies the problem of ethical responsibility as it presents itself in the TRC's Human Rights Violations Committee. It is that its narration is only able to make sense to the extent that it unself-consciously repeats a form, at once juridical and literary, that already was internal to the administrative discourse of the Tumult Commission, dating at least to the JRC.

The problem with *Country of My Skull*, from this perspective, is not that it is self-conscious about its own narrative voice in relation to the testimony of victims. It is *the way* the text understands *the work* of self-consciousness, or, better still, the implicit form of self-consciousness with reference to which it understands the ethical self-consciousness for which the event of the TRC calls. There can be no doubt, after all, that the book remains loyal to the part of the TRC's lexicon—the declaration of apartheid as a moral evil—that would seem to be most decisive to Asmal's Gramscian redeployment of the Tumult Commission. But the administrative terms through which *Country of My Skull* tries to perform that loyalty lead it to redeploy, as the very form of literary self-consciousness itself, one of the key juridical forms the TRC inherited from the Tumult Commission. In this way, the extreme self-consciousness of this work of postapartheid metafiction becomes one and the same with an unselfconscious reification of the administrative discourse of the apartheid-era Tumult Commission.

The path for this repetition is prepared in advance by *Country of My Skull*'s heavy reliance upon the theoretical paradigms of testimony that emerge from trauma studies. The book is self-conscious about victim testimony given before the TRC in the same way that the field of trauma studies has counseled readers to be self-conscious about testimonies to the traumatic reality to the Holocaust. But what Nuremberg is for transitional justice's account of the precedents of the TRC, the field of trauma studies is for assumptions about testimony in *Country of My Skull*. It is a theory of the relation between speech, pain, and thought that derives its inner schema from events in European politics and history. Applied unmodified to what it takes to be the raw empirical material of the colony, this theory not only replicates well-known relations of imperial knowledge production but also directs self-consciousness away from the TRC's most intimate and distressing precedents—testimony as it emerges within the theories and practice of the Tumult Commission.[58] Prior to any integration of psychoanalysis within the administrative apparatus of the TRC, after all, the Tumult Commission already itself interpreted the etiology of political conflict within a manifestly therapeutic horizon, searching for the psychological antidotes that colonial administrators could apply to dissipate the "fevers" of hatred that always were at risk of swelling into open rebellion. The field of trauma studies produces its interpretations of the TRC only after first uncritically receiving support from the presupposition that politics can and perhaps should be medicalized. But this turn to the therapeutic is anything but novel; to the contrary, it reactualizes the therapeutic discourse already at work in the apparatus of the Tumult Commission, only now in a different idiom, by inviting individuals and collectives alike to self-identify as trauma victims— dependent beings who require "advocates" or even "saviors" to speak on their behalf.[59] Krog is certainly prepared, perhaps even overprepared, to theorize the TRC using the lexicon of trauma studies; but for this same reason, she is underprepared for the ease with which this lexicon describes its object—for the way this very theoretical language itself fits so neatly, with so little resistance, within the existing epistemic field of the Tumult Commission. In the process, "historical catharsis" is left to the side, and the unstable equilibrium internal to the TRC capsizes into a simple repetition.

7.3.2 In the afterword they appended to the 1997 republication of their 1995 book *Reconciliation through Truth*, Asmal, Asmal, and Roberts would come to recognize the limits of their notion of "historical catharsis." Writing under conditions when it was becoming clear that "historical catharsis" was nothing more, but also nothing less, than a utopian desire, they no longer attempted to define catharsis as a revolutionary paring of the clean from the unclean. They suggested, instead, that in the context of an institution that grounded its claim to truth not in juridical or empirical rules of evidence but in essentially unverifiable testimonies,

> the catharsis of revelation shifts away from pieces of paper, however important documents remain as a secondary or corroborating force; truth becomes dependent upon the stories that perpetrators and victims are willing to tell, on the extent to which they will relax and open up in acknowledgement. It is therefore interesting that the South African Defense Force chose to coordinate its contributions to the Truth and Reconciliation Commission by way of a centralised "Nodal Point," a single point, suggesting a clenched sphincter, through which all information is meant to pass. Consistent with this constipated approach, the depersonalized voice of the Nodal Point opens its submission by saying that "No attempt has been made to analyse or evaluate information with the benefit of hindsight. It may therefore not be a complete version of SADF actions, or a correct reflection of all SADF members' points of view." What kind of person's voice is this, the sound of a Nodal Point?

With this argument, Asmal, Asmal, and Roberts began to shift footing to a slightly different lexicon for describing the cathartic work of the TRC. By construing the SADF's submission to the TRC on the trope of a "constipated" or "clenched sphincter," Asmal, Asmal, and Roberts not only here have recourse to a classic diagnosis of anal-retentiveness as a symptom of the "authoritarian personality";[60] they also imply that uncensored free speech, which they earlier had connected to the cathartic expression of the voices of the previously excluded, would somehow share a quality with defecation and excretion (the corporeal opposite to the SADF's "anal retentiveness").

This language may seem playful or even outrageous, but the bathetic turn of Asmal, Asmal, and Roberts away from the "grand style"[61] of classic tragic catharsis has a very serious dimension. It is the archipelagic tip of an entire "aesthetics of vulgarity"[62] that was in circulation in the late 1990s, alongside and underneath the more dominant and palatable discourse of trauma studies, as a way to speak about the work of the TRC. Thus it was that Jane Taylor's brilliant 1998 theatrical production *Ubu and the Truth Commission* opened with a "Pschitt!!" that translated into Afrikaans the "Merdre!" ("Sheeyit!") that set the tone for Alfred Jarry's protosurrealist 1896 play *Ubu Roi*.[63] Much the same language, meanwhile, was used by the offstage TRC administrators who were charged with the responsibility of processing the 20,400 applications to testify before the commission.[64] To visit the backroom offices of the TRC during 1998 was to find that the shorthand idiom for speaking about the work of the TRC was anything but sacred. Someone asking about the purpose of the commission was likely to meet with such responses as "To get the shit out in the open," "To get rid of that shit," and "To get this shit out of our system."

Strange though it may sound, this language—the language of the *vulgus* (the "common people"), profane language uttered outside of the Truth Commission's public temple and inside its administrative entrails, language not of the sacred but of the *sacrum*—does justice to the event of the TRC with much greater precision than do the humanistic pieties and social scientific taxonomies that have come to characterize transitional justice. We can understand how if we turn from tragedy to comedy, from Krog's commissioned discourse on the TRC to an uncommissioned text on the same. The comedy in question, a play called *Past Imperfect*, was staged at the 1998 Grahamstown Arts Festival by drama students at the University of Natal, under the direction of Greig Coetzee.[65] Unlike Krog's *Country of My Skull*, which has been the subject of numerous reviews and scholarly articles, *Past Imperfect* has received no scholarly attention; unfortunately, it has not even been collected in the recent publication of Coetzee's collected works.[66] The quantitative difference in readerships between these two texts is symptomatic of a much more fundamental qualitative difference. Because Krog's *Country of My Skull* tried to make sense of the TRC using the TRC's own administrative lexicon, it could be easily assimilated within transitional justice scholarship on the TRC. *Past Imperfect*, by contrast, was an obscene comedy whose scatological and slapstick character left it not only unassimilable but also unintelligible for transitional justice scholarship. Yet, if the very idea of the literary implies the fundamentally democratic right to say everything,[67] then it must be said that *Past Imperfect* exercised this right much more fully and radically than did Krog's book. Whereas Krog's text, despite its apparently limitless capacity for pastiche, ended up obeying the constraints of the TRC's own administrative discourse, *Past Imperfect* opened up a desacralized discourse on the TRC's inquiry into the "dirtiness" or "messiness" of the past—one that, precisely because of its unself-censored quality, presents a metalanguage for talking about the TRC that, however obscene, is ultimately much more capacious and precise than is Krog's excruciatingly self-conscious metafiction.

The play's first scene is extremely short. A multiracial cast gathers at center stage. The audience hears the sound of an auto accident. Scene 2 begins.

SIMON: What the hell was that?
more comments, post crash moans
MRS RIDGEWAY: Whats that smell?
MAVIS: Yini le enugayo
Where is it coming from, *looking for the smell*
STIX AND SAM: I think its them . . .
JU: Don't be a racialist.
argument brews
DLAMINI: Wait, wait, wait
   (*gets control of the situation*)
   Lets just take this back . . .
THEMBI: Rewind.[68]

With Thembi's "Rewind," the actors mime the movements of a recording device moving in reverse. This simple allegorization of the TRC machinery marks a transition to scene 3, which, with slapstick irreverence, compresses into forty-five seconds at least a decade of South African politics and history.

There are two cars (two groups). The whites have formed a BMW and are on stage right. The blacks have formed a taxi and are on stage left. The BMW hums along. The taxi tries to start kli kli kli . . . on the second time it starts.

BMW: It was a normal day.

TAXI: A normal day.

BMW: I was driving along in my 7 series BMW

TAXI: BMW?

BMW: Blacks must walk.

TAXI: And there we were in our

STIX: over populated

DLAMINI: under developed

THEMBI: 3rd world 16 seater

TAXI: skoro-skoro

ALL: when suddenly we saw it

SIMON: There in the middle of the road

MAVIS: It came from nowhere

MRS R: It was big

DLAM: It was huge

JU: It was massive

STIX: It was gigantic

SIM: It was brown.

Everyone looks at him . . .

SIM: Well wasn't it?

ALL: It was brown.

JU: We were heading straight for it at 100 kilometers per hour

STIX: OK 120 kilometers per hour

ALL: Alright, we were going fast

SAM: It was a free way

THEMBI: Free for who?

MRS R: The way you people drive it was free for all!

DLAM: We had to stop.

BMW: Quickly

ALL: Very quickly

TAXI: We swung to the left

BMW: We swung to the right

STIX: I slammed on my previously disadvantaged brakes

MRS R: It was then that our Pirelli

SAM: Low profile

JU: All weather

SIM: Fully imported

MRS R: Euro centric tyres

ALL: Hit a patch of black oil

DLAM: At the same time our Soweto necklace

MAVIS: second hand retreads

TAXI: slipped on the white barrier line

ALL: This was a State of Emergency

BMW: For the first time ever we lost control

STIX AND THEMBI: Our taxi turned over and over and began a
rolling mass action

JU AND SAM: Our political wind bags automatically inflated

ALL: That's when we hit it.

MRS. R: The big

DLAM: huge

JU: massive

STIX: gigantic

SIM: brown pile of

ALL: SHIT!!!

The cast reenacts the crash, this time in slow motion. Everyone rolls around, stands up, and then takes the positions that begin scene 4.

SAM: We're in the shit

SIM: No shit

MAVIS: Who left this huge pile of shit in the middle of the road?

STIX: Shit happens

MRS R: Well, it must be somebodies responsibility. I have to make an
insurance claim.

JU: It could be God. I mean that it is a cosmic pile of shit.

THEMBI: If its God you're not covered.

DLAM: Well you're covered but not by insurance.

MRS R: Well. It has to belong to someone.

ALL: and that's when we saw him.

THEMBI: Qongqothwane

SIM: Who?

MAVIS: Qongqothwane.

DLAM: The dung beetle

STIX: The healer of the road

SIM: Look, this is no time for all that jungle bunny nonsense—this is
serious.

JU: We have to do something about this shit.

SIM: What is he doing?

STIX: He's a dung beetle.

SAM: Right! A shit shoveller

THEMBI: A Waste Management Expert

SIM: A Fast faeces forwarder

MRS R: Maybe we should follow Quong . . . Konkontane

THEMBI: Qongqothwane.

MRS. R: Konkatane.

MAVIS: Qongqothwane.

MRS R: . . . the dung beetle's example.

DLAM: What do you mean?

SIM: Well while we're arguing about the shit he's getting rid of it

JU: Look at that, he's rolling it away in little balls

SAM: I'm not touching anyone else's shit

STIX: Well, maybe we need to get a closer look at it to see whose
shit it is?

MRS R: What do you mean?

DLAM: I mean lets really look at this shit

SIM: What is in this shit?

ALL: What is this shit?

Thus framed as an inquiry into "this shit," the play maintains a madcap pace,
peppered with gags and jokes about racial irreconcilability at every turn.
Twenty scenes later, the players seem no closer to reconciliation than they
were at the outset (even though, of course, the drama's very form, in which
all and one cooperate in a comedic narration of a history in which mutual
suspicion and hostility still reign supreme, is perhaps already itself a form of
reconciliation). The final scene opens.

THE ENDING
The cast come together in the same positions as earlier

SAM: Oh shit, so its our shit
STIX: Its your shit
MAVIS: No its our shit
MRS R: Simunye, we are one
The cast all groan and argggh
SAM: Well, I suppose we'd better clean it up then!
Ju makes as if she is leaving
Sam pulls her back
SAM: Hey, if I can clean it up so can you
MAVIS: (*picks up a piece*): What can we do with this shit?
TH: We could make a shitman?
Stix picks up a bundle and looks ready to throw it at the whit[e]s. They all
hide behind Simon.
The cast then click on to Stix's idea, each pick up a bunch and throw it at
the audience.
ALL: ITS YOUR SHIT TOO!

At this point, when the cast throws the shit at the audience, nothing is actually thrown at the audience. The actors merely mime the throwing of shit. Yet it would be off the mark to say that they *truly* throw nothing. The nothing they throw is *not*, in fact, nothing. It really is *the shit itself*, where "shit" refers to the difficulty of referring to apartheid, to the hateless in between, that defines ostensibly postapartheid public space. The shit the actors throw, this shit that hits us and contaminates us, is precisely "our" shit. It is precisely the common "defect" that at once separates and unites "us," that indeed is the uncivil condition of possibility for saying "we" in the civil space of that theater. Importantly, if this "shit" is "our shit" too, then the "we" this play presupposes and posits, addresses and implicates, are neither "victims" nor "perpetrators." "We" are political animals of a very particular sort. "We" are precisely dung beetles who roll the shit of the imperfect past into little balls in order to get rid of it. "We" are *qongqothwanes*, click beetles. "We" are the ones who work for our imperfect reconciliation, for what community it is possible to attain in postapartheid South Africa. This work is real work: it is dirty work, "shit work," work that is neither valued nor recognizable, and that is, above all, recurrent work. That there remains leftover shit to throw even at play's end is a sign that apartheid's "past imperfect"—its continuing or nonfinite past—continues, such that especially now and here, in the presence of this theater, there is too much shit even for a multitude of *qongqothwanes* to roll away.

But even if *Past Imperfect*, like *Country of My Skull*, leaves us with impasse, something "clicks" here—certain things suddenly become more clear and understandable. The play's genius is to have revealed a much different impasse than we find either in *Country of My Skull* or in the *TRC Report*—one that passes beyond and, in that same motion, illuminates the inner limits of the TRC's administrative lexicon. Not despite but because of its scatological vulgarity, its postcolonial beetle, and its slapstick profanity, *Past Imperfect* describes, more precisely than transitional justice itself, the "dirtiness" and "messiness" driving the "cleansing" agency internal to the "historical catharsis" that, at least according to Asmal, was the most definitive kernel of the TRC's work. Hidden in plain sight in *Past Imperfect*, despite or perhaps because of the brilliance of its displacement of TRC's sacralized tragedy with the desacralizing energies of comedy, we find "apartheid itself," not so much "passed" or "past" as *transubstantiated*. No longer racial capitalism, no longer a set of grand or petty social practices, no longer a body of law, no longer colonialism of a special type, certainly not an epistemic formation, apartheid now refers to nothing more than a generalized vile substance. Captured within the regime of abstract equivalence that defines civil society and liberal legality at its best, apartheid is now only intelligible as a raw, uncivil material that interferes with the *interesse* of, or space between, persons who, in the necessary fiction of constitutional *Rechtsstaat*, are formally, if not materially, equal in the eyes of the law. However virtual it may be, apartheid here is not then immaterial. It causes a car crash, and the actors relate to it as though it possessed the properties of a "thing" (occupying its own space). But it is a most curious sort of thing. Apartheid is, in this comedy, nothing more than matter out of place: it is dirt, displaced matter that sometimes interferes with otherwise normally civil mediation. The question of "apartheid," now out of focus and utterly intangible, returns as nothing more than an ill-defined substance that threatens to contaminate the same community on whose exclusion it is founded. The eschatological hope informing the scatology of *Past Imperfect* is that this community already has arrived; that it is already somehow in place as the fundamental horizon of a new, unnamed common sense; and that the repetition of uncivil jokes in a civil way dramatizes something other than naked aggression.

Chapter 8

OUT OF COMMISSION

Salus or *Ubuntu?*

8.1.1 On the terms set forth by the TRC, the type of community we find enacted in Greig Coetzee's *Past Imperfect* would have a very specific name: *ubuntu*. Translated sometimes as "humanity," "compassion," and "recognition of the humanity of the other"[1] and sometimes simply as "caring for the community,"[2] *ubuntu* is most often interpreted within transitional justice in opposition to the basic concepts of liberal legality: it is understood to prioritize symbiosis and cooperation over competition between individuals, social harmony and forgiveness over punishment, restorative justice over adversarial litigation, and duties to the collective over individual rights.[3] It's in this sense that *ubuntu* is usually understood to "permeate" the 1996 Constitution[4] and to be central to the lexicon the TRC attempted to set into place to dissociate the postapartheid state from its predecessor.[5] Despite this centrality, however, scholars of the TRC seldom have posed the term's translation as a problem for thought. Instead, *ubuntu* is most often translated in the manner that Dipesh Chakrabarty has called, in the double sense, "rough"—a translation that is careless, hasty, or even abusive and whose very inaccuracy or imprecision is precisely what makes it most useful for the language of command, for the "rough-and-ready methods of colonial rule."[6]

It's not by accident, then, that the less roughly one takes the task of translating *ubuntu*, the more thoughtfully and carefully one considers its grammar and logic, the more one is led to question the assumption, so widespread in postapartheid jurisprudence, that *ubuntu* does nothing more than, as Mark Sanders has put it, "regulate[] and limit[] the rights of the individual in favor of the collective."[7] It is not, in other words, by accident that the scholars who are most mindful of the history of colonial anthropology also have been the most inclined to doubt the wisdom of translating *ubuntu* on the assumption that African traditions are uniquely suited to reciprocal, harmonic, forgiving, and communal ways of life.[8] Other readers, perhaps for similar reasons, have preferred to arrive at their understanding of *ubuntu* through careful and methodical philological work, deriving from the Zulu proverb *umuntu ngumuntu ngabantu* formulas that are downright Kantian in their austerity (e.g., "a person depends on other persons to be a person" or "a person is a person through other persons").[9] But while such renderings may be more accurate than the blunt conversion of *ubuntu* into the newest communtarianism, even they are not without their own sort of errancy. To begin, as Sanders observes, the very assumption that one could translate *umuntu ngumuntu ngabantu* in the imperative, as if it were a Kantian maxim regulating the conduct of moral persons, is already off the mark: this is, Sanders seems to suggest, to mistranslate into the familiar terms of modern moral philosophy a phrase whose grammar suggests, if anything, an ontological *dis*propriation of the moral person.[10] Even a translation of *ubuntu* that is accurate in a philological sense, in other words, is thus no guarantee that one will have thought the term beyond the limits of colonial reason.

If anything, in fact, philology is not so much an antidote to "rough translation" as a more erudite version of it. As Valentin Mudimbe has shown, contemporary African philosophers have long criticized the colonial underpinnings of the ethnophilosophical practice of trying to reconstruct an "African *Weltanschauung*" or "unconscious philosophy" from philological analysis of isolated utterances passed down from oral tradition.[11] In Mudimbe's view, the extremely detailed translations of the "*ntu* vision of the human being" that one finds in the work of scholars like Alexis Kagame or Tshiamalenga Ntumba owe much to the discipline of colonial philology.[12] For Mudimbe, consequently, the indispensable condition for contemporary African philosophy is a critique of the colonial epistemes that enable scholars to arrive at "accurate" knowledge of "Africanicity."[13] These epistemes are, in Mudimbe's account, not at all limited to open condescension: they range from the reduction of African thought to a "mirror" for rediscovering the truths of Western philosophy, to the exoticizing generalizations of colonial anthropology, to the exacting particularizations of colonial philology. The most careful thinkers of *ubuntu* are aware of this: they are alive not only to the silent agency of colonial epistemes but also to the cunning and interdisciplinarity of those epistemes, and they take steps, accordingly, to differentiate their postcolonial iterations of *ubuntu* from the concept's predecessors in colonial philology and ethnophilosophy as well as its equivalents in Christian theology.[14] But such efforts are the exception to the rule: in the appropriation of *ubuntu* by transitional justice, as in its appropriation in marketing, public relations, and management,[15] the question of the colonial episteme generally remains unasked.

8.1.2 This silence is especially pronounced when *ubuntu* is translated, again roughly, with the Latinate noun *person*. This rendering not only revives a dominant convention of nineteenth-century colonial philology;[16] it also reduces *ubuntu* to a screen on which one of most vexed questions of contemporary jurisprudence then externalizes itself, acquiring, in the process, a coherence it lacks when examined on its own internal terms.

Before Gaius divided Roman law into *actiones, res,* and *personae,* ancient Greek philosophers and poets already had spoken in deeply ambiguous ways of the *prosōpon,* which designated not only the "mask" donned by actors in order to allow their audiences to glimpse something of their countenance and character but also the "face" that we present to the gaze of others and that marks us as specifically human.[17] For early Christian theologians such as Augustine and Thomas Aquinas, by contrast, the concept of the "person" would become central to the Trinitarian dogma that God, Spirit, and Man subsisted in a single, sacred "hypostatic union"—a doctrine the poet, theologian, and jurist John Donne would call the "three-personed God."[18] As if the theatrical, juridical, and theological declensions of the "person" were not each already complex enough on their own terms, the path the term *person* would take through modern thought would end up being shot through with even more superimpositional drifts and subterranean grafts. After Hobbes affirmed the necessity of sovereign power by explaining how it operates as a *prosōpon, persona,* and Person,[19] Hegel would refer to these same juridical and theatrical dimensions to criticize the status acquired by the "person" in ancient and modern law (even as the concept "person" would remain at the very center of his own symptomatically incomplete account of the master-slave dialectic).[20]

English imperial thought, meanwhile, like the Roman Law to which it constantly compared itself,[21] would be predicated on the notion that "persons" have certain rights and privileges, among which are *dignitas* and *libertas.*[22] But just as every "person" is not necessarily a living being (as is the case with corporations and colleges), so too not every living being, not even every member of the species *homo sapiens,* is necessarily a "person." In Roman Law, the concept of the "person" was limited only to free Roman citizens, a *fictio legii* that gained its coherence only insofar as it could be opposed to another concept, the slave (understood as a form of living property or "thing"). To make matters more complex, Roman Law also recognized numerous "gradients" of a person (pertaining not only to race, nationality, domicile, and age, but also to sex and marriage, senility and minority, age and nonage, competence and incompetence, lunacy and reason, prodigals and absentees, legitimate and illegitimate children, etc.). As a result, the "law of the person" never failed to taper off into an manifestly administrative discourse, an evaluative framework that, despite being founded on a fundamental *qualitative* distinction between "persons" and "things," nevertheless also entailed complicated *quantitative* distinctions of "statuses" or "ranks" internal to the concept of the "person."

This framework, upon which the entire jurisprudence of the ancient "law of the person" was founded, would survive, albeit in very different ways, in the modern "law of the person." English common law would distinguish between "persons" and "minors" (those under the age of twenty-one, who could not be expected to be in full command of their faculties, and who therefore required a parent, trustee, guardian, or curator to manage their interests).[23] In colonial jurisprudence, particularly in the political thought of J. S. Mill, the concept of the "minor" would provide a key rationale and justification for the creation of despotic governments that were vested with the paternal authority to manage the interests of entire "races" whose "backwardness" qualified them as "nonage" and disqualified them from the exercise of liberty.[24] This was especially true in nineteenth- and early twentieth-century international law, where the legal fiction of "native personality" was the very crux of European jurists' internal exclusions of colonized populations within the *jus publicum Europæum*.[25] Under the mandate system of the League of Nations, the concept of "native personality" provided the conceptual framework for a hierarchical taxonomy of the relative degrees of "maturity" specific to various colonized populations, which, in turn, allowed the league to monitor and manage each population's specific rate of "development" or "coming of age" into proper, mature sovereign "persons" (a norm exemplified by European states).[26] In English colonial jurisprudence, to say nothing of American common law, the "law of the person" was more than just a cornerstone of modern rights. It was one of the cornerstones of legalized racism.[27]

At the same time that the term *person* is foundational for many areas of contemporary public law, for important traditions of critical and political theory, and for our very concept of humanity itself, it is thus also brimming with latent impasses and contradictions. A disjunctive synthesis of juridical, theatrical, and theological genealogical drifts that push together categories usually opposed to one another (e.g., the archaic and the modern, the theological and the secular, the aesthetic and the political, the individual and the collective, the legal and the living, freedom and repression), the term *person* is shot through with hairline fractures, unstable fault lines, and contingencies that have been welded into false necessities and artificial coherence.

Nowhere is this more important to remember than when human rights discourse invites us to treat the "person" as a synonym for the "human being" who is vested with rights. At least since the 1948 Universal Declaration of Human Rights (UDHR), which recognized the inherent dignity, freedom, and equality of all human beings and stipulated the right of one and all to be recognized as a "person" before the law, the concept of the "person" has functioned as a simple synonym for the "individual" or "human being" who bears the rights of the human.[28] Many readers today may in fact find this synonymy to be so obvious and necessary that to inquire into it would be to enter into tautology. But as Joseph Slaughter has shown, the self-evidence of this synonymy is simply the most powerful effect of a prior literary device (a "machine," as Slaughter calls it)[29] that is anything but self-evident. This machine is a literary genre, the *Bildungsroman*, or coming-of-age narrative, a "didactic story of an individual who is socialized in the process of learning for oneself what everyone else (including the reader) presumably already knows."[30] In the *Bildungsroman*, the reader tracks the progress of specific persons (usually white, male, middle-class citizens of European nation-states) who actualize the potentiality of their human personality by incorporating themselves within the political community of which they are a part. It is decisive for the proper comprehension of this genre, Slaughter insists, that we understand the "person" neither as an "individual" nor as a "human being," but rather, in a rigorously Latin sense, as a "legal fiction," a remarkably elastic and empty rights-bearing unit, a "mask" worn by the living being to which specific juridical communities may add (or subtract) rights at will.[31] Only by understanding the sense in which the "person" at the heart of the *Bildungsroman* is already a juridical form can we then understand, in turn, the sense in which the "person" at the heart of human rights law is, for its part, already implicitly "literary" in character. If, in other words, it was possible for the drafters of the UNDR to assert the existence of rights that were at once self-evident and nonexistent, that obviously and necessarily should attach to each and every person, but that in 1948 had yet to attach to most persons, the very possibility of this assertion was provided to them, in advance, by a specific sort of narrative—a narrative according to which the rights of each and every person would, precisely, "come of age" in and through the political community of which one and all persons were presumed to be a part.

The emphasis on community within the *Bildungsroman* reveals the falsity of the standard "communitarian" critique of human rights discourse (i.e., that it is individualistic, atomistic, and abstract rather than social, collective, and concrete). To the contrary, as Slaughter shows, human rights discourse presupposes from the very beginning that "no man is an island."[32] In Slaughter's view, in fact, the dominance of the *Bildungsroman* narrative, its widespread influence among the otherwise bitterly opposed framers of the UDHR (ranging from liberals and nationalists to communists), is the answer to the question of the famously "missing" sovereign of international law (which, according to so many Hobbesians, is the reason why international law is "unenforceable").[33] For Slaughter, the various temporal expectations and recollections that the *Bildungsroman* allowed its reader—the plot development according to which the reader could assume that it was natural, inevitable, and necessary that the individual person would "incorporate" himself or herself within the political community that preceded him or her—was itself, in terms of its own quasi universality as a "secondary rule" among the lawyers and intellectuals who framed the UDHR, its own sort of surrogate or proxy sovereignty.

Other thinkers, sharing Slaughter's attention to the residues of Roman law in the UDHR, have emphasized a different limit to the synonymy between "person" and "human being." In the view of philosopher Roberto Esposito, the freely self-determining sovereignty that is the hallmark of the rights-bearing "person" can come into being only by presupposing the agency of a very specific sort of apparatus. The "self-mastery" of the "person" always implies to some degree a prior "mastery" over the "living being" that is the silent support of that "person" (regardless of whether the "person" in question is an individual or a community). Before one can fully qualify as a "person," it is thus necessary to "master" this "living being," to get control of it, to determine its destiny, instrumentalize its internal movements and processes, to use it in the right way—in short, to reduce it into a mere living tool, an organic instrument, or what in the Aristotelian lexicon would have been called a "slave."[34] As such, every "person" who has managed to qualify as an independent "person" will have depended upon the operation, however inconspicuous, of a special sort of apparatus—an apparatus that is able to manage life only and also to the precise degree that it first can depersonalize life, to reduce life to a "thing." The necessary condition for speaking intelligibly of the concept of the rights-bearing "person"—even and especially where, as in the discourse of human rights, the "person" has become a synonym for the "human being"—is the ability to trace the "person" to the apparatuses of "depersonalization" on which it depends.

Whereas most philosophers who discuss the place and function of the "person" within the UDHR concentrate exclusively on the *positive qualities* it implies (e.g., identity, dignity, respect, rights, and obligation),[35] Esposito thus directs our attention to the *quantitative distinctions* silently entailed in those qualities—the administrative hierarchies that differentiate the self-mastery of full "persons" from the incomplete self-mastery of partial, developing, or minor "persons." For Esposito, any truly consistent insistence on the dignity and respect owed to the person *must by definition* entail an intricate taxonomy of living beings who are not yet capable of dignity, who do not yet deserve respect, who cannot yet be said to have an identity, and to whom the community of "persons" owes little or even nothing (except sometimes, in the most incorrigible cases, "civil death").[36] To render the UDHR synonymous with the rights of the person is thus to aspire to all-inclusive rights only at the cost of a host of internal exclusions: any and all attempts to universalize the person as the foundation of right will rigorously reproduce the apparatus on which the concept of the "person" silently depends—an apparatus that both demands and justifies practices of separation, rank, and subordination.

We receive a particularly jarring reminder of this impasse when we recall the centrality of the concept of the "person" for that other jurisprudence—the antithesis of the UDHR—that was born in 1948. Writing in 1960, the prominent South African jurist Herman Robert Hahlo would declare the South African law of persons to be one of the most conservative areas of South African jurisprudence. "There are few branches of South African law," Hahlo suggested, "where the principles of the original Roman-Dutch law have been so faithfully maintained as in the law of persons and family relations."[37] Hahlo then proceeded to define the law of the person in South Africa by referring it to its European origins:

Following the lines of traditional European jurisprudence, South African law defines a legal *persona* as any being or entity capable of rights or duties, and distinguishes between natural and juristic (or artificial) persons. Every human being is a person in law, having the capacity for rights and duties, but there are considerable differences in status between persons of different class and condition. The main factors determining a person's legal status in South African law are race, nationality, domicile, and age.[38]

Elaborating upon this point, Hahlo then proceeded to summarize the "four main racial groups" between which South African law then distinguished. "The differences in legal status between these four groups are considerable," he reported, "especially as regards the franchise, employment, movement, residence and the capacity to own or occupy immovable property."[39] Only after setting these premises into place did Hahlo then describe the aim of the "present policy of 'apartheid'": "to set aside separate areas for residence by members of the different racial groups, and to provide the different Bantu peoples with their own national homes."[40] Today we might be inclined to view apartheid as one of the paradigmatic violations of the rights of the person. For Hahlo, however, the very opposite was true. Apartheid was not inconsistent with the law of the person; it was a *subset* of the law of the person.[41] It was an extension, into the division and distribution of land and labor, of the hierarchies of legal status that, in empires both ancient and modern, always have been a part of the law of the person.

In the Roman-Dutch Law of the apartheid state, as in the English common law of colonial jurisprudence, one sees the despotic precursors for contemporary normative claims about the "aspirational" quality of human rights. In the latter as in the former, the concept of the "person" authorizes a discourse on the living being's "permanently incomplete" transition into a full rights-bearing "person." In the latter as in the former, the living being is always already on the way to "developing" into the sovereign, self-determining "person" it already latently is, all while perpetually never fully actualizing the potential to bear rights. From this perspective, the self-mastery promised by the concept of the "person" is less a foundation for human rights than a trapdoor within human rights: it is the hinge in and through which every positive affirmation of the rights of the human will risk pivoting into an administrative discourse that turns the human inside out, cutting up and distributing the plane of living being it presupposes into lesser and greater quantities, using fine distinctions to classify it into shades and grades of rights-bearing substance.[42]

8.1.3 The more one examines the concept of the "person," in other words, the more one has cause to question the "rough" translation of *ubuntu* into the lexicon of the "person." This translation presupposes a concept that, explicated on its own terms, turns out to host the stark antithesis of everything the principle of *ubuntu* would seem to want to represent. Whereas *ubuntu* proposes the maxim that "a person is a person through other persons," the maxim of the person, particularly in its despotic declension most relevant to the postcolony, is that "a person becomes a person only to the extent it first *depersonalizes* the living being." Whereas *ubuntu* marks the unity of the institutions of nonracial democracy in postapartheid South Africa, the apparatus of the "person" historically has functioned to justify the internal exclusion of colonized populations by apparatuses of colonial command. Whereas *ubuntu* is a principle of national reconciliation and healing, the concept of the "person" has consistently given rise to administrative discourses of rank and hierarchy. Whereas one of the cardinal achievements of *ubuntu* jurisprudence has been to ground arguments against capital punishment in postapartheid South Africa,[43] the concept of the "person," especially in the Enlightenment thought of Immanuel Kant, is the very basis for claims about the morality of capital punishment.[44]

Here, too, the examples could be multiplied; but the point should be clear. To translate *ubuntu* "roughly" into the colonial-era lexicon of the "person" is to risk transferring *ubuntu* into terms with a genealogy and structure that undercut the very juridical questions *ubuntu* jurisprudence most wants to pose. To translate *ubuntu* "unroughly," by contrast, another sort of work will be necessary: the equivalent, in jurisprudence, of Mudimbe's genealogical critique of the relation between colonial anthropology and anticolonial ethnophilosophy. Here, the task will not be to discover the "pure" African meaning of *ubuntu*; it will be to understand *ubuntu* in its *metonymy with* and *displacement of* the juridical forms that precede it in the apartheid state.[45] The aim of this understanding will not be simple satisfaction with a new term whose very Africanity supposedly leaves it self-evidently unrelated to and untainted by the Roman law concepts that were so central to the apartheid regime. It will be a specific form of critical vigilance, an alertness to the iterability involved in the translation of a term like *ubuntu*, an awareness that the felicity of this sort of translation will be measured not by its accuracy or correctness, but rather by its performative force, its ability to breach the epistemic horizon within which it emerged. By this measure, the most infelicitous translations of *ubuntu* will be those that do not *displace* the term's colonial precedents, but merely *replace* them, silently repeating their unacceptable logic and grammar, only now in the newly acceptable rhetoric of the "*ntu* vision of humanity." In this case, as with the rough translation of *ubuntu* into the lexicon of the "person," the ability of *ubuntu* to cause in us a desire for the unprecedented—for a postapartheid jurisprudence—will have been subverted, subtly but decisively, in advance. At its most felicitous, however, the translation of *ubuntu* jurisprudence will accomplish the opposite: it will render the precedents for *ubuntu* inoperative, sinking them into desuetude, or, in the language of H. L. A. Hart, leaving them "defeasible."[46] In this case, *ubuntu* will have been the centerpiece of a machine, the TRC, whose primary function will have been not to make impossible things possible (to perform "miracles") but, rather, to have made one very specific thing—colonial jurisprudence—impossible. On this read, in other words, the most important event to have come out of the TRC will not have been "healing," much less "reconciliation." It will have been a desire for new juridical forms, a desire for the unprecedented, a desire to put apparatuses of colonial sovereignty and governmentality *out of commission*.

8.2.1 Of the various precedents for *ubuntu*, there is one in particular that requires our attention here. Martin Chanock has argued that apartheid jurisprudence is characterized by a myopic attempt to generate laws and policies for the governance of modern Southern Africa by dwelling cognitively as much as possible in the theories, terms, and juridical habits of classical Roman law.[47] Nowhere is this more true than in Cicero's maxim *salus publica suprema lex esto* (the safety of the state is the supreme law).[48] As we have seen throughout this book, the concept of *salus publica* was a regulative ideal not only for the sovereign power of the apartheid state (grounding the indemnity jurisprudence that was the "highest exertion and crowning proof" of its sovereign parliament) but also for its techniques of governmentality (framing the sorts of equilibrium and the types of knowledge sought by the apparatus of the Tumult Commission). At first glance, it would thus seem counterintuitive, to say the least, to suggest that Cicero's maxim is in any way relevant to the interpretation of *ubuntu* in postapartheid South Africa.

Ubuntu jurisprudence, it would seem, would be better characterized as the very antithesis of Ciceronian political reason: whereas the latter was one of the most important maxims for the constitutional reasoning of the apartheid state, the former is one of the founding values of the postapartheid state. But the conciliatory work of translation does not take place under conditions of our choosing and does not always proceed in predictable or even desirable directions, either. Because "legal continuity" was one of the structuring principles of South Africa's negotiated settlement, it should not come as a surprise that remnants of *salus populi* reasoning would survive in the *ubuntu* jurisprudence of the postapartheid state or that, depending on the way that *ubuntu* is translated in postapartheid jurisprudence, it can and indeed does retain the traces of its predecessor.

Especially in the more communitarian translations of *ubuntu* (e.g., "I am because we are, and since we are, therefore I am"),[49] there is a clear emphasis on the priority of the community over the person, whose formation and existence is in turn understood to depend upon that community. This translation of *ubuntu*, which stresses its uniquely African character, gains part of its intelligibility from an unwanted and unexpected source. In the Aristotelian episteme that provided the grid for the earliest translations of the "*ntu* vision of the human being,"[50] there is also, already, a clear relation of strict and logical priority between the part and the whole. For Aristotle, just as a hand cannot survive without the body, so too the single human cannot survive in the absence of the political community.[51] To translate *ubuntu* into these terms, innocuous though they may seem, is to bury within it a logical fulcrum that, in turn, allows *ubuntu* to pivot into agreement with its antithesis. If it's the case that the rights of the human person depend for their existence on the community of which the person is a part, and if the community is thus the prior condition in the absence of which there can be no rights of the person, then threats to the community will be tantamount to threats to the person itself, and the safety and security of this community will be the prior condition for the rights of the person itself. Before the rights of the person can be defended, *in order for* the rights of the person to be defended, the safety and security of the community must be defended, even if this sometimes means violating the very rights of the person the community is meant to enable.

The irresistibility of this reasoning, the obviousness or self-evidence of its Aristotelian premises, is precisely what makes it so amenable to the jurisprudence of emergency. In 1981, speaking in parliamentary debate over whether to extend by another year the state of emergency that had existed in the country since 1965, Zimbabwe's deputy minister of local government and housing responded to critics who claimed that another renewal of the state of emergency would jeopardize the rights of individuals.

> Indeed, we need to protect the rights of the individuals and the State of Emergency should not unnecessarily derogate from those rights of individuals. But if the State of Emergency is not strong enough to protect the rights of the individuals, those rights will become useless because the State itself cannot protect them. The State needs to strengthen itself in order to be able to protect the rights of the individual and this is what the Minister is seeking to do.[52]

Even though this sort of logic is sometimes understood to be one of the primary roots for political evil,[53] it would be a mistake to assume that it is merely or exclusively the provenance of authoritarians, tyrants, autocrats, and totalitarians. Centuries before Cicero's maxim was cited by the high priests of raison d'état, it functioned as one of the main principles in the name of which modern revolutionaries asserted their right to resist and even overthrow monarchies and tyrannies (particularly by the founders of the same tradition of English legal liberalism that was so influential for Dicey).[54] In this iteration, Cicero's maxim was not limited to cases of illiberal politics; it was the innermost norm of the claim to the "public good" that enabled liberal juridical orders to limit, constrain, and even overthrow the monarchical and tyrannical regimes they opposed.[55] At the same time that *salus populi* named *the law of sovereignty*, as that maxim that allowed institutions of limited sovereign power to differentiate themselves from the tyrannies they understood themselves at risk of becoming (as in Locke), it was also the foundation, at least in the early modern English political philosophy, for *the sovereignty of law* (in Locke as in Hobbes, the supremacy of law derives from its capacity to give expression to the natural right of self-preservation, to the need for law to protect man against the wolflike animal that man sometimes can become). To limit one's interpretation of Cicero's maxim to its application to states of emergency *alone* is thus to disavow the sense in which *salus populi suprema lex esto* is *also* the norm governing *all* exercises of sovereign power, not merely the most pathological ones.[56] Should one pass beyond this disavowal, one reaches a more sobering impasse still. What *ubuntu* jurisprudence inherits from the episteme that precedes it is neither norm nor exception. It is the deadlock of a maxim that can just as easily justify exceptions to the rule of law as it can justify the norm of the rule of law itself, and that, as such, is a limit internal to liberal legality where the apparatus of liberalism begins to short-circuit, misfire, and collapse.

8.2.2 That this deadlock, which would express itself so violently in the apartheid state's deployment of Cicero's maxim, is nevertheless deeply rooted within Western political reason becomes clear from a schematic review of Michel Foucault's lectures on governmentality and biopolitics during the mid- to late-1970s. One of Foucault's desires in this period was to understand the odd way that the modern state depends for its coherence on a justificatory framework that seems repeatedly to exceed, from within, the very institutions and practices that framework also founds.[57] Foucault noticed that the safety, security, well-being, health, and welfare of populations was at once *central to* the modern state and, at the same time, *at odds with* the laws that give the modern state its essence.[58]

To explain this impasse, this strange antinomy between law and sovereignty, Foucault traced the modern state to its origins in an apparatus he calls "pastoral power." Pastoral power, Foucault argued, was quite distinct from the sort of power envisioned by classical political reason. Whereas classical political reason framed its objective with reference to the figure of the helmsman whose specific skill was the ability to steer the "ship of state" into safe harbor, pastoral power understood its aims with reference to the figure of the shepherd whose specific skill was to care for his flock as it moved from place to place.[59] Pastoral power accomplished this not by using commands to ensure that the many cooperate and function as one, but instead through an intense, soul-searching inquiry into the truth and life, the quality and experience, of each individual member of the flock.[60] By inciting individuals to examine their consciences, to bare their souls, and to account for their lives through practices of confession and attestation, and by caring for these individuals in the aggregate in the same way a shepherd would care for a flock, pastoral power sought "to constantly ensure, sustain, and improve the lives of each and every one."[61] If the aim of classical political reason was the creation of unity through command, the objective of pastoral power was the salvation (*salut*) of souls through knowledge.[62] Although pastoral power was therefore primarily an individualizing power, it did not lack an expressly distributive dimension. The pastor's aim was to save souls—in the plural. Pastoral power was a care for "all and one" (or, as Foucault would put it elsewhere, *omnes et singulatim*) that was organized by an internal logic that was very different than the logic of the one and many in classical political reason. In contrast to the figure of the helmsman, whose subjects are unified to the extent that they share a common destiny and fate (or, as it were, are "all in the same boat"), the shepherd's relation to his flock involved the distinct and ever-present possibility of sacrifice. This sacrifice obeyed a logic of reversibility: it involved the willingness and ability to sacrifice any sheep who (for whatever reason) could compromise the whole, but it also involved (if need be) the willingness and ability of the shepherd to sacrifice himself for the sake of the flock.[63] So complete was the obedience that emerged in and through this sacrificial relation that pastoral power not only released the flock from its obligation to obey earthly commands but, indeed, considered those commands to be obstacles to the salvation that should be the source of any true obedience. Pastoral power, Foucault consequently argued, is antinomian: it acquired its very form and coherence in opposition to the concept of law as such.[64]

According to Foucault, the collection of institutions and practices that we today recognize as "the state" came into being under conditions where, under the influence of new nonteleological natural sciences, pastoral power was obliged to translate its old objectives now into the language of calculative, mechanistic instrumental reason.[65] From this perspective, Foucault argued, the state is "a modern matrix of individualization, or a new form of pastoral power."[66] This was not, however, the same as saying that the modern state "secularized" pastoral power in any direct or straightforward sense, as if all political concepts necessarily came into being by simple analogy to theological concepts.[67] Foucault's point was rather more nuanced than that: it was that the modern state derived its coherence, in part, from its translation of a paradigm of law and sovereignty that both preceded and exceeded the self-understanding of the modern state itself. Unlike pastoral power, which led individuals to salvation in the next world, the modern state sought to ensure salvation in this world. "And in this context," Foucault wrote, "the word 'salvation' takes on different meanings: health, well-being (that is, sufficient wealth, standard of living), security, protection against accidents."[68]

To this retranslation, there corresponded a whole series of epistemic shifts. Once concerned mainly with the truth of the mind and the soul, the pastor's knowledge of his flock now focused on calculations and measures of the body.[69] The *singulatim* and the *omnes* that once characterized the old powers of the "pastor-sovereign" here became scientized.[70] What was once the pastor's intense curiosity into the soul of the single member of the flock now became a steady and constant gaze into the minutiae of the individual's conduct (or what Foucault calls "discipline"). What used to be the pastor's care for the flock overall now became the state's duty to manage the safety, security, health, and well-being of its whole population (or what Foucault would come to call "biopolitics").[71] Above all, while the modern state certainly did deploy pastoral power now to a new end—summarized by the doctrine of raison d'état, the principle that the state must be strong enough to win its wars against its enemies—the modern state also carried forward the old modes of antinomianism and sacrifice that characterized pastoral power. Whenever the state's laws happened to begin to constrain the state's fostering of the health and welfare of its populations, the institutional and administrative forces responsible for maintaining that health and welfare (the police and various ministries) would not hesitate to repeat the antinomianism of pastoral power, suspending the law.[72] When the security or safety of the state's populations was endangered by any one of its parts, the state would not hesitate to repeat the sacrificial violence of pastoral power, purging the part for the good of the whole. In short, the ambiguous *"salus"* that was at the core of the modern state's deployment of Cicero's maxim *salus populi suprema lex esto* translated into the apparatus of the modern state a paradigm, the salvation [*salut*] of pastoral power, that both informed the modern state and was incommensurable with its own self-understandings and self-justifications.[73]

For the purposes of thinking about the translation of *salus* in South African law, there are two important lessons to take away from Foucault's lectures. The first is that Foucault's genealogy of pastoral power is, in effect, a genealogy of the jurisprudence of emergency. The *salus* of the jurisprudence of emergency, like the "salvation" [*salut*] that grounded pastoral power, is antinomian: it demands exceptions to the laws of the modern state. But Foucault's genealogy of pastoral power does not allow us to rest content with moralistic condemnations of the pathological quality of raison d'état (its tendency, e.g., to suspend the normal rule of law, its constant need for war and enemies). It teaches us, to the contrary, that such pathologies are already immanent to the norms of the modern state itself. *Salus* is the norm of all norms: its constituent polysemy, its fecund untranslatability, guides each of the various fields of the state's biopolitical interventions (the state's maintenance of the health, welfare, safety, and security of its populations).[74] From this perspective, we can see plainly that the same logic of part and whole that manifests itself as martial law during times of "political necessity" (when the safety and security of the people, as the highest law, trumps the protections and promises written into the normal rule of law) amounts to little more than an unusually extreme expression of the standard aim of the modern state (which justifies its continued existence in large part with reference to the living standards of its populations). To presuppose *salus* as the basic norm of the liberal state—as do, to anticipate our point, certain translations of *ubuntu* in postapartheid South Africa—is thus already to concede the latent possibility and even desirability of the very doctrine, raison d'état, that liberal legality considers anathema.

From this follows a second lesson. According to its own self-understanding, the neoliberalism of the early and mid-twentieth century was an attempt to protect the rights of the person and property from the "totalitarianism" that, in the view of the neoliberals, was the inevitable result of "collectivism" and "big government."[75] Reacting to the racism and militarism of these governments, neoliberal thinkers like Ludwig von Mises and Friedrich Hayek proposed a revival of nineteenth-century liberalism, particularly its principles of "the market" and "the rule of law," as the best way to establish limits on raison d'état from within.[76] Understood genealogically, however, neoliberalism was not at all an antithesis to the logic of raison d'état. It was a refinement and intensification of that logic, a strategy for the state to manage the health, welfare, and safety of populations indirectly rather than directly, by extending techniques of "governmentality" beyond the formal limits of government itself.[77] Under conditions established by the unpredictability of the market, on the one hand, and the predictability of the rule of law, on the other, individuals and populations are not, of course, free in any substantial sense. Rather, their conduct is governed by the discipline of the market and the constraints of competition, which produce a milieu in which the "rational self-interest" of individuals and populations dictate that they conduct themselves as "entrepreneurs of the self"—as "persons" who relate to themselves, precisely, as "corporations"[78]—whose "human capital" must be prudently developed and invested as a precondition for any chance at survival.[79] Whereas raison d'état managed populations as a means to the end of strengthening the state into a force capable of waging and winning war, neoliberalism shifts emphasis from the political to the biopolitical. No longer concerned with managing the *salus populi* as the means to the end of defeating an enemy, neoliberalism began to treat the *salus populi* as an end unto itself, weakening the state into nothing more than a coercive means to the end of achieving higher "living standards" for one and all, while also giving property rights and the rule of law a new function as the formal limit upon administrative attempts to satisfy the constitutively limitless pursuit of the *salus populi*. In this way, at least in theory, the neoliberal state would be immune to the sorts of administrative excesses that characterized the regimes that neoliberals liked to call "totalitarian." But neoliberalism has broken neither with pastoral power's antinomianism (which it has reiterated in the discourse of the "deregulation of markets" and the removal of society's "defenses" against disease and risk), nor with its concern over knowledge of "the flock" (which it pursues by means of detailed studies of the "living standards" of various populations), nor finally with its emphasis on sacrifice (which it practices by abandoning populations to death and disease under conditions where achieving the health and safety of those populations would place property rights or the rule of law into question). Most of all, neoliberalism systematically failed to think through the despotic, administrative apparatuses that were central to the very nineteenth-century liberal thinkers—such as J. S. Mill and A. V. Dicey—whose revival in the twentieth century was, in their view, supposed to liberate the West from the racist bureaucracies of the totalitarian regimes.[80] As explicitly neocolonial as it was implicitly theological, neoliberalism was not, then, the antidote to repression it imagined itself to be: translating a set of premodern religious problematics (not only the "salvation" of pastoral power, but also the "providence" of *oikonomia*) into the unerring laws of late modern "economic science," neoliberalism remained unthinkingly guided by the same *salus populi* whose excesses it opposed in its fight against "totalitarianism."

8.2.3 These two points are important to keep in mind in order to understand why, at around the same time that Foucault was lecturing on *salus populi* in Paris, the same concept was coming into question in Pretoria—albeit in a symptomatically incomplete manner that Foucault, precisely, helps us understand. In a 1977 law review article titled, simply, "Salus reipublicae suprema lex," François Venter, Potchefstroom University law professor (and, later, advisor to the apartheid government in their negotiations with the ANC in the Convention for a Democratic South Africa), undertook a systematic examination of the ways in which this maxim had figured into South African jurisprudence, English common law, and Roman law. The main aim of Venter's article was to address the criticism that the apartheid state's concept of *staatsveiligheid* (state security) remained undefined. Tracing its historical correlation to the various key concepts of war legislation ("public safety," "state of national emergency," "security of the state," and "state interest"), Venter concluded that the word has developed to mean "the opposite of the overthrow or destruction of the state" (die teenoorgestelde can die verwoesting of omverwerping van die staat), or, put positively, "maintenance of the constitutional status quo."[81] Writing in a moment of national emergency that was defined by the very maxim whose coherence he was questioning, Venter argued that the translation of *salus populi suprema lex esto* by (as one Afrikaans-English legal dictionary had it) "the security of the people or population is the highest law" (die veiligheid van die volk is die hoogste reg)[82] was vague in an important way. Not only did *veiligheid* have the potential to refer to any number of threats, however perceived or real, but its conceptual ambiguity both correlated to and, indeed, authorized its own administrative or institutional counterpart, namely, the apartheid state's sprawling and diffuse security apparatus, which considered everything from literary fiction, film, and television to dissident wings of the Dutch Reformed Church to be a threat to this ill-defined substance or entity called *veiligheid*. As an antidote to this administrative ambiguity, Venter recommended that the apartheid state's sprawling and diffuse security apparatus be consolidated, brought under judicial review, and coupled to the Constitution of 1961. In contrast to his improbable Parisian contemporary, however, who placed the term *salus* into question and traced its iterations in contemporary discourses on health, welfare, and well-being to its premodern sources in salvation, Venter remained silent on the arguably more exigent philological question that was at the core of this institutional or administrative incoherence. Even as he recommended the reform of the apartheid state's security apparatus, he thus avoided the truly anxious question at its core. Under conditions where the task of the apartheid jurist was to reconcile the rule of law not only with the supremacy of a minority white population but also with an internal and external war against an increasingly revolutionary black majority, what exactly did it mean, after all, to say that the *salus* of the people or the population was the highest law? Under conditions where the "total war" the state was waging against black populations was more and more dissolving the very health, welfare, safety, and security in the name of which it claimed to be fighting, what could *salus* possibly mean?

A decade later, writing under conditions of an unprecedented nationwide state of emergency, another Afrikaner jurist would take up the philological task Venter left to the side. Like Venter, J. L. Pretorius scrutinized Cicero's maxim during a moment of national emergency that was justified by the very maxim whose coherence he was questioning. Unlike Venter, however, Pretorius questioned the adequacy and even desirability of translating Cicero's Latin phrase *salus publica* with the Afrikaans *staatsveiligheid* (state security). In his short but decisive article, Pretorius argued that Cicero's maxim could not be interpreted in isolation from the other principles of Ciceronian political reason with which *salus publica* was connected. Once interpreted in a hermeneutic context alongside Cicero's understanding of *communio utilitas*, Pretorius argued, it became clear that the true idea of the *salus publica* referred not to "state security" alone but to an inclusive set of national and communal interests—indeed, to the "general interest" conceived as the sum of the juridical convictions of the whole society (or, as Pretorius puts it, the *consensus juris*).[83] Pretorius then proceeded to suggest that the mistranslation of *salus publica* as a dogma of state security and no longer as the ethical-political ideal it was for Cicero was a specifically modern corruption: beginning with Machiavelli and then, permanently, in Bodin, Pufendorf, and Locke, the translation of *salus publica* as "public safety" and "public security" allowed the sovereign authorities of the state to legitimate almost any action.[84] What was lost in this rigid translation, Pretorius observed, was the classical sense in which *salus publica* was more the equivalent of "general interest" and "juridical consensus" than "state security." The painful, concrete result of this loss, Pretorius concluded, was the false and sterile dualism that gripped South Africa even as he wrote, in which two sides of a single principle that, in its classical iteration, used to be united—state security, on the one hand, and human rights and justice, on the other—now faced off against one another in brutal opposition.[85]

A year later, Pretorius's claims would be taken up and developed to their logical conclusions by yet two more "*verligte*" Afrikaner jurists who questioned the coherence of Cicero's maxim under concrete juridical conditions ostensibly justified by it. In their now almost completely forgotten 1988 book *South African Constitutional Law*, Deon Basson and Hendrik Viljoen set for themselves the task of formulating for the crisis of South African legality a constitutional solution that would put an end to apartheid while also saving South Africa from revolution.[86] Accordingly, their desire was to offer a "normative reinterpretation" of South African legal history and theory. Their argument in chapter 5 ("The Principle of the Law State [*Rechtstaat*] and the Doctrine of Fundamental Human Rights") was especially symptomatic of the way in which the crisis of the apartheid state in general amounted to the crisis of the concept of *salus publica* in particular. Their more general project was to reinterpret South African legal history and theory within the framework of what they call a "value-oriented approach to constitutional law,"[87] which would break from the Diceyan tradition of the "rule of law" and (following such authors as John Dugard, Gustav Radbruch, and Johann Van der Vyver) replace it with an emphasis on the *Rechstaat* and human rights, such that government action no longer would be arbitrary or uncontrolled but would remain bound by certain "legal values" shared by subjects.[88] Under conditions where, as the authors wrote, law had fallen into disrepute because of its service to the preservation of racist political order, the conditions were ripe for revolution, and far-reaching constitutional reform was the only other alternative.[89]

As part of this project, Basson and Viljoen turned the concept of *salus publica* into the basis for *a critique* of the security legislation predicated on it. Citing Pretorius at length, Basson and Viljoen called their readers' attention to a decisive indeterminacy in the most pivotal term of that legislation.

> Pretorius indicates a totally different dimension to the Roman maxim "*salus (rei)publica(e) suprema lex*" which usually, as has been indicated, implies the maintenance of state security. He refers to Cicero's writings (*De Legibus* 3.3.8) and declares that the *salus publica* in Cicero's thoughts was meant to reflect the idea of an optimal equilibrium of interests, and not to isolate state security in particular. In time, however, the interests of the subject were made subordinate to those of the state: "In the sixteenth century and later the principle '*salus publica suprema lex*' was, however, transformed to a juridical dogma which had to express the fundamental precedence of, in particular, state interests and in the beginning, in particular, state security. When Machiavelli refers to this principle, it is not Cicero's broad and comprehensive ethical and political ideal that he has in mind, but in fact the state's exemption (regarding its technique of control) from all juridical considerations, which he supports (*Discourses* 3, 40–42). In the legal theory

of Bodin, Pufendorf, Wolff, and even Locke, the principle 'salus publica suprema lex' was developed into a legalism with the purpose of legitimizing the contravention of all material legal limits by the sovereign government power." According to Pretorius this is the state absolutist variant of the legal maxim which has been established in the South African legal tradition and this has then mainly been responsible for the fact that the maintenance of state security has to a large extent been divorced from material and juridical restrictions.[90]

The clear implication of Pretorius's critique, particularly as developed by Basson and Viljoen, was that the political crisis of the eighties in South Africa was also, or perhaps even primarily, a crisis of translation. It was the crisis of translating *salus* not in its classical sense, as the ethical and political ideal of attaining the best possible harmony of interests between lawmaker and subject, but only in a merely legalistic or positivist sense, as nothing more than state security. To restore *salus* to its fullest possible sense, as Pretorius, Basson, and Viljoen all seemed to recommend, would be not to abandon the maxim *salus publica suprema lex esto*, but to rethink the sense and scope of *salus* in a way that allowed it to serve as the basis for the critique of the apartheid state itself. On these terms, the very concept of the state of emergency was a crisis born of infidelity to the true meanings of Latin sayings, a crisis born of the modern betrayal of Ciceronian republicanism. It would follow from this that the task of restoring the Republic of South Africa to itself would require not only a constitutional reform that gave the judiciary checks on the power of the executive branch and the security forces. It would also entail a much more radical project, an intellectual reform that returned the republic to its root in Roman law. The harmony of the republic, Basson and Viljoen take Pretorius to argue, depended vitally on the retranslation of *salus publica*.

> In the spirit of Cicero's approach he [Pretorius] declares that the essence of the state as *res publica* makes it clear that there is no public interest which does not bind government and the subjects of the state mutually: "When the maintenance of state security is held above all essential and effective control of lawfulness, then public confidence in the law in general, and the interest that government and subjects have (in solidarity) in the maintenance of constitutional integrity of office, in particular, are sacrificed to the security

needs of the government." Pretorius makes a valuable contribution here—especially to ensure, with the balancing of interests[,] that the *interests of the subjects* are taken account of properly, particularly since this maxim does not only serve the interests of the state but also emphasizes that of the subjects in order to establish a proper equilibrium of interests.[91]

Following Pretorius, Basson and Viljoen thus offered a forthright response to the dire political and legal conditions under which they wrote: they called into question the translation of the very maxim justifying those conditions. Like Pretorius, Basson and Viljoen proposed to deliver the South African body politic from political division in a specifically Roman manner: they would save the republic by saving the sacredness *at* and *of* its foundation.

Especially because of its attempt to salvage the aura of the Roman example,[92] this is a highly instructive response to the crisis of *salus* as a principle of political reason. Reinhart Koselleck has argued that the basic concepts of political reason may be said to enter into crisis when their meaning becomes so broad that they can encompass anything or everything.[93] The approach taken by Basson, Viljoen, and Pretorius, and even that taken by Venter, suggests that by the late 1970s and 1980s in South Africa, Cicero's maxim was a basic concept in exactly this sense: it justified not only the apartheid state's war against its own populations but also the "affirmative critique" of that war on the part of Afrikaner jurists who understood the incoherence of this justification.[94] The attempt by Basson, Viljoen, and Pretorius to save South Africa from its tendency toward anomie by saving *salus* from its specifically modern opacity indicates that by the late 1980s, if not already by the late 1970s, the concept of *salus* had become unintelligible, that *salus* had become estranged from its wide range of possible meanings—health, welfare, well-being, public good, or even security and safety—when it was transformed by the apartheid state's securocrats into a justification for the racist state to wage war on the populations whose interests it paternalistically claimed to represent. This same "affirmative critique," as we saw in section 3.3, was already implicit in the very different critiques of the apartheid state of Theo Aronson and Kathleen Satchwell, who, despite their very different political orientations, both saw that the legislative means by which the apartheid state was pursuing the *salus publica* were antithetical to the end of the *salus publica* itself. Basson, Viljoen, and Pretorius expressed the same crisis as did Aronson and Satchwell, only in a much different register. On the basis of the protocols and discipline of classical philology, rather than on the basis of neoliberalism (Aronson) and jurisprudence (Satchwell), the writings of Basson, Viljoen, and Pretiorius indicated that, by the late 1980s, the term *salus* had become sufficiently incoherent that it no longer possessed the glow of familiarity or obviousness that prior apartheid jurists had found in it. Before Basson, Viljoen, and Pretorius were able to pose the comprehensive retranslation of Cicero's maxim as an urgent task for jurisprudence, the term *salus* must necessarily already have been stripped of its self-evident meanings and transformed into a question. While Basson and Viljoen attempted to resolve the problem of the state of emergency by turning to Pretorius's salvaging of the word *salus*, by seeking to restore Ciceronian spirit to the word's now dead letter, the question they posed also opened up the possibility for a very different line of inquiry. Precisely the anxious philological care that Basson and Viljoen exercised in their handling of this ancient text— their attempt to salvage from *salus* a sense of the integrated whole to which it once presumably referred—was the best sign that the concept was at that time disintegrating like sand through their fingers.

Read against the grain, however, the writings of these *verligte* Afrikaner jurists reveal the conditions for another translation. After the maxim *salus populi suprema lex esto* slipped through the fingers of those most concerned to hold onto its original meaning, its constituent polysemy would enter into the grasp of another concept, indeed, another jurisprudence altogether. The terminal crisis of the concept of *salus populi* in the late 1970s and 1980s posed an implicit question—what could it possibly mean to speak of the *salus populi* in South Africa, this exemplarily divided polity?—to which Ciceronian republicanism could no longer respond on its own terms, out of its own lexicon and using its own conceptual resources. The apartheid state, after all, had reduced the constituent polysemy at work in the maxim *salus populi suprema lex esto* to securocratic terms, translating *salus* with emphasis on "security" and "safety" not only at the expense of other senses (e.g., "health," "well-being," "wealth," "welfare," or "salvation") but also in justifications for permanent internal conflict against South Africa's own populations.

By displacing the "safety" and "security" of *white* South Africans with the "healing" and "salvation" of *all* South Africans, *ubuntu* answered in non-Ciceronian terms the question posed by the crisis of Ciceronian republicanism. It allowed for a neopastoral discourse that would be just as antinomian as its predecessor but that would turn that antinomianism now in a more salutary direction. In *ubuntu*, the "political necessity" in the name of which the normal rule of law was to be set aside (e.g., in the TRC's suspension of Section 22 of the Interim Constitution) would no longer derive from the exigency of "saving" *certain* populations from the threat of internal enemies. It now would derive from the exigency of "healing" *all* South Africans from the internal conflict that had interiorized methods and practices of warfare that normally would be directed to the exterior.

The principle of *ubuntu* would come into being, in short, by dividing the principle of the *salus publica* against itself—by pressing a salutary translation of *salus* (emphasizing the "healing" and "salvation" of all) past the inner constraints established by its predecessor (which emphasized the "safety" and "security" of some). In the interests of the health of South Africa, in the interests of saving one and all from the disease of internal conflict, the safety and the security of populations could no longer be the highest law. Because, taken to the extreme, the *suprema lex* of safety and security had turned into its opposite—internal conflict, *stasis*—this "highest law" revealed that it needed another law, a law whose force derives not from being placed "*even* higher" than the *suprema lex* of the *salus populi* but, rather, from being *immanent within* that *suprema lex* itself, as the principle of its nonidentity with itself. This law would be the law of the self-negation of the *salus publica*, the law according to which *all* apparatuses of public safety and security risk reproducing the very danger and harm for which they propose to be the antidote.

Inasmuch as *ubuntu* is a name for this law, its novelty cannot be said to consist only in its "inclusion" of hitherto "excluded" populations under a preexisting form of political rationality. That novelty instead should be sought in the way *ubuntu* pushes *salus* past its own internal limits, dividing it against itself and only in this way—only, paradoxically, in and through this division—producing a new name for reconciliation, for relations between sovereign power and populations, between person and community, that could exceed the deadlocks of the *salus publica*. At its best, to be sure, *ubuntu* will have rendered inoperative or defeasible the logic as well as the episteme that were the driving force of Cicero's maxim. But to the extent that *ubuntu* acquires its singular sense and force from its translation of the *salus publica*, it cannot be said that the desire for which *ubuntu* is a name is, simply by virtue of its non-Latin name alone, completely emancipated from the episteme from which it emerges and to which it is opposed. At its worst, indeed, *ubuntu* jurisprudence will not *displace* Ciceronian republican reason at all; it will merely *replace* it, reproducing the same premises within postapartheid jurisprudence as Cicero's maxim did in apartheid jurisprudence. To translate *ubuntu* "unroughly" is to keep one's finger on the pulse of this difference—to take care that, in the reiteration of *salus* in and through *ubuntu*, the work of difference outlasts the inertia of repetition.

8.3 South Africa's 1996 Constitution, a document pervaded by and founded in *ubuntu*, expressly eliminates a number of laws premised on the *salus publica*. Its Section 34 lists a long set of rights that are nonderogable even in times of war, and it places strict thresholds on the suspension of rights in times of emergency.[95] Its Section 82, meanwhile, frames executive power in such a way as to exclude entirely the prerogative powers and declarations of martial law that characterized the apartheid state. Above all, the 1996 Constitution establishes a mechanism for adjudicating the violation of rights that intentionally rejects any relation to Cicero's maxim.[96] Under apartheid, as Basson and Viljoen wrote, "[t]he only justification for the violation of rights of subjects . . . is necessity or self-defense, as contained in the constitutional law maxim *salus reipublicae suprema lex* which was supported in the Roman, English, and Roman Dutch legal systems."[97] The 1996 Constitution, by contrast, removes the grounds on which the state may suspend the fundamental rights of citizens, even in a state of emergency.[98] Limitations of rights are now governed by a "limitations clause" that places the onus on the state to demonstrate exactly how and why the abrogation of rights is not only reasonable and justifiable in an open and democratic society but also consistent with the basic values articulated in the Constitution's principles, preamble, chapter 3, and epilogue.[99] With this, the suspension of rights is no longer constitutionally possible or valid, and the limitation of rights is no longer discretionary; it is proceduralized and constitutionalized. The *ubuntu* Constitution was, in short, carefully designed to undo the jurisprudence of emergency that, under apartheid South Africa, had become so refined, developed, and excessive.

It has not, however, eliminated the juridical problematic in response to which the modern state adopted Cicero's maxim in the first place: it hasn't eliminated the obligation of the state to seek the salvation of both one and all, to maintain the health, welfare, security, and safety of the community, sometimes at the expense of the rights of the person. Nor has it necessarily eliminated the "conventions" (as Dicey would call them) or "secondary rules" (as Hart would call them) on which law depends for its intelligibility and over which law itself has little to no direct influence. For this, only a specific kind of work, a particular sort of translation, will suffice: if *ubuntu* is to put the apparatus of *salus* "out of commission," it will be necessary to displace the episteme that corresponds to it and that tarries with it like its shadow, threatening to convert *ubuntu* into nothing more than an African equivalent for the Latin *salus*.

Consider Pumla Gobodo-Madikizela's 2003 book *A Human Being Died That Night*, a narrative of her prison interviews with the South African state assassin Eugene de Kock. On the face of it, the primary influence in Gobodo-Madikizela's text would seem to be not *ubuntu* but psychoanalysis. Gobodo-Madikizela is careful, for instance, to foreground her own symptoms (by comparing her encounters with de Kock to *Silence of the Lambs*, exposing her own projective fantasies), and she draws on the tragic framework that is latent in all psychoanalytic thought in order to interpret de Kock both as a scapegoat for and as a symptom of apartheid as such. But even though Gobodo-Madikizela's text does not mention *ubuntu* once, the "primary application" of *ubuntu* is in "the field of political reconciliation,"[100] and the mode of juridical reason Gobodo-Madikizela deploys in her text, not to mention her own self-description of the text as a work of political reconciliation, qualifies it as an exemplary instance of *ubuntu* thinking. Like the *TRC Report* itself, Gobodo-Madikizela confronts the impasse of connecting the TRC's argument about the criminality of apartheid as a whole (that the system itself was intrinsically and essentially evil) to the particular crimes committed in support of apartheid (Eugene de Kock's eighty-nine convictions). The text's concluding proposal, that de Kock ought to be pardoned,[101] negotiates this impasse in a manner worthy of comment. The proposal in question is not, to begin, openly theological, even though Gobodo-Madikizela does indeed argue for "forgiveness" of a sort (hence the subtitle of the text's first edition, *A South African Story of Forgiveness*, which was subsequently, and tellingly, changed to *A South African Woman Confronts the Legacy of Apartheid*). Neither, more important for our concerns, is it Ciceronian. Because pardoning de Kock certainly would let a mass murderer loose in South African society, Gobodo-Madikizela's recommendation to this effect cannot be said to be governed by the principle of public safety or security. It is, indeed, a logic that presses beyond the limits of pastoral power, for Gobodo-Madikizela's proposal is precisely to let a "wolf" back into "the flock." Her argument for a pardon for de Kock amounts to the proposal that postapartheid society live with, rather than repress, the evil and illegal actor and the evil and illegal acts that were symptomatic of apartheid as such.

Read as a translation of *ubuntu*, this proposal implies not only a suspension of the very possibility of distinguishing between part and whole; it implies, as well, a retranslation of the way that person and community enter into relation in postapartheid jurisprudence, a retranslation that seems to proceed without reference to the distinction between part and whole that was so characteristic of Ciceronian republicanism. The "community" into which de Kock "the predator" returns is no longer the "community" we find in the logic of *salus publica*, where the purpose of law is to immunize the community from its exposure to the predations of certain "wolves" within itself. It is a very different kind of community, one that not only does without the death penalty and thus the assumption, fairly consistent within modern political philosophy, that any law that really is a law should be backed by the threat of death; it also, seemingly on principle, invites the "wolf" into itself, as if the juridical apparatus that proposes to immunize the community against the "wolf" somehow posed a greater threat to the community than did the "wolf" itself. It is on these grounds that Gobodo-Madikizela's pardon expresses the antinomianism, although now in the mode of a pardon rather than emergency, that was so regular a part of the *salus publica*. But if, in Ciceronian republicanism, it was a simple *contradictio in terminis* to speak of a "community" that would not also use lethal laws to secure itself from its internal predators, then the paradigm of community implied in Gobodo-Madikizela's pardon cannot be translated on the basis of the Ciceronian episteme of the *salus publica*. The same would hold true as well for the way that Gobodo-Madikizela relates to de Kock "the person." On the terms of the early modern political philosophy of (say) John Locke, de Kock would be depersonalized, construed as an animal and an enemy to humanity, treated as a wolf to be executed.[102] In Kantian moral philosophy, meanwhile, the person of de Kock would provide the very basis for the community to reassure itself of the morality of its execution of his depersonalized animal being.[103] Implicit in the way that Gobodo-Madikizela treats de Kock, by contrast, is a very different approach to the "person," an approach that is almost as catachrestic as the sort of "community" she seems to presuppose. It's as if, in this text, a person could be a person only by deactivating the apparatuses of depersonalization on which the person depends. But just as a community that does not make a point of immunizing itself from the wolf within would no longer be recognizable as a "community" in the sense familiar to the discipline of modern political philosophy, so too would a person unsupplemented by depersonalization no longer be recognizable as a "person" on the terms of modern jurisprudence. In this case, as in the case of the "community" Gobodo-Madikizela seems to imagine, not only is "ubuntu" not translated roughly into the terms of Ciceronian republicanism, but we would seem to find a paradigm of ubuntu that strains from within against the legal Latin assumed by even the most self-critical juridical and political thinkers, a paradigm whose very untranslatability spurs us to confront the impasses and deadlocks internal to Ciceronian republicanism. On this translation, ubuntu would be less a noun ("personhood" or "humanity") or adjective ("compassionate" or "generous") than a sort of an intransitive verb, an ongoing activity that would have no object other than the sustained rethinking of received epistemes of modern political and legal thought. In an essay published in 1944 in the Johannesburg magazine *The Democrat*, South African psychoanalyst Wulf Sachs dreamed of the postracial social order that would come into being once societies had cured themselves of their desire to seek out and expel scapegoats as the cure for what ails them.[104] The iteration of ubuntu one finds in Gobodo-Madikizela would seem to be a fulfillment of this wish.

At the antipode of Gobodo-Madikizela's mobilization of ubuntu is the very different iteration of ubuntu offered by Anton Lembede, a Johannesburg lawyer and founding president of the ANC Youth League, which is quoted with great praise and emphasis by Alex Boraine. According to Lembede, who Saul Dubow describes as "the principal theorist of 'Africanism'" in South Africa,[105] precolonial African society was inherently socialist: the African in general

> regards the universe as one composite whole, an organic entity, progressively driving towards greater harmony and unity whose individual parts exist merely as interdependent aspects of one whole realizing their fullest life in the corporate life where communal contentment is the absolute measure of values. His philosophy of life strives towards unity and aggregation, toward greater social responsibility.[106]

In Lembede's early articulation of ubuntu, we find few conceptual resources for *ubuntu* to resist operating in precisely the same way that *salus* operated under apartheid. There is little basis in this rendering, in other words, to block the operation by which the part is sacrificed to the whole that is prior to the part and that confers on the part its value and its sense. Where *ubuntu* is construed in these terms, it seems fated to lend itself to the same raison d'état that characterized the worst of the worst under apartheid. Here as elsewhere, in other words, we encounter the classic deadlock of anticolonial nationalist consciousness: almost to the precise degree that *ubuntu* is separated from its status as a critical metonym for *salus publica*, almost to the precise degree that its wholesomeness and wholeness is instead construed as a pure antonym for the corrosive "individualism" of the West, it paradoxically will open itself up to a repetition of one of the most nihilistic premises of Western political reason. This would seem to be the result whenever translators seek, as it were, to "deurbanize" *ubuntu*—to find in it a "pure" African concept that is and must remain untainted by the corrupting "individualism" of Western law.[107] To resurrect Lembede's translation of *ubuntu* is, in short, to render the logic of *ubuntu* commensurable with the logic of *salus publica*.[108]

Most translations of *ubuntu*, including some of the most well known, fall somewhere in between these two extremes. The principled indistinction between part and whole that we see clearly articulated in Gobodo-Madikizela is certainly visible in Desmond Tutu's iteration of the concept of *ubuntu* in his 1999 book *No Future without Forgiveness*. Here, Tutu sought to define the concept in order to clarify why, in his view, so many South Africans were taking the opportunity offered to them by the TRC to forgive their oppressors rather than to demand retribution from them in courts of law. But because Tutu is here seeking to clarify the way in which "the third way of conditional amnesty was consistent with" *ubuntu*, we should be mindful of the sense in which *ubuntu* in his formulation is already proximate to *salus* in the Diceyan tradition (as we saw in sections 1.2 and 4.2.2–4.2.5, "conditional amnesty" is very much a reiteration of "indemnity" in the Diceyan tradition). Whereas "indemnity" in the Diceyan tradition was supposed to protect from lawsuits those who committed crimes in honest and necessary defense of the *salus publica*, Tutu turns to *ubuntu* to offer an interpretation that explains why South Africans who have been the victims of such crimes might prefer not to press lawsuits against their perpetrators. But what's striking about Tutu's pastoral declension of *ubuntu*, in contrast to Gobodo-Madikizela's implicitly psychoanalytic articulation of the same concept, is the extent to which Tutu occasionally translates *ubuntu* using the terms of the pastoral power that is the genealogical precursor to and perhaps even the still-operative unthought of *salus* in Western political reason. At certain points, Tutu seems to disallow any possibility for turning the *ubuntu* of the postapartheid state into the functional equivalent of the *salus publica* of the apartheid state, but at other points, he thus runs just that risk.

> *Ubuntu* is very difficult to render into a Western language. It speaks of the very essence of being human. When we want to give high praise to someone we say, "*Tu, u nobuntu*"; "Hey, he or she has *ubuntu.*" This means that they are generous, hospitable, friendly, caring and compassionate. They share what they have. It also means my humanity is caught up, is inextricably bound up, in theirs. We belong in a bundle of life. We say, "a person is a person through other people." It is not "I think therefore I am." It says rather: "I am human because I belong." I participate, I share. A person with *ubuntu* is open and available to others, affirming to others, does not feel threatened that others are able and good; for he or she has a proper self-assurance that comes from knowing that he or she belongs in a greater whole and is diminished when others are humiliated or diminished, when others are tortured or oppressed, or treated as if they were less than who they are.
>
> Harmony, friendliness, community are great goods. Social harmony is for us the *summum bonum*—the greatest good. Anything that subverts or undermines this sought-after good is to be avoided like the plague. Anger, resentment, lust for revenge, even success through aggressive competitiveness, are corrosive of this good. To forgive is not just to be altruistic. It is the best form of self-interest. What dehumanizes you, inexorably dehumanizes me. Forgiveness gives people resilience, enabling them to survive and emerge still human despite all efforts to dehumanize them.[109]

Here, Tutu's discourse on *ubuntu*, which is very plainly a discourse on the relation of *omnes et singulatim*, is so proximate to the principle of *salus* in classical political reason that he even goes so far as to translate *ubuntu* into legal Latin as a *summum bonum*. While we would not, of course, want to overread this translation, it would be a mistake to underread it as well. It occurs, after all, in a chapter of Tutu's text that begins by placing itself in dispute with classical political reason (Tutu begins his chapter with a critique of Aristotle's concept of human personality and the living slave) and that uses legal Latin elsewhere (to refer to the function of Tutu's own *persona* in the TRC).[110] We may therefore interpret Tutu's discourse on *ubuntu* in Ciceronian terms, as a *summum bonum* that competes with, displaces, or even replaces one of the other "greatest goods" Cicero mentions in his *De Legibus*, the *salus publica*.

Interpreted in this way, Tutu's translation of *ubuntu* generates a decidedly mixed set of possibilities. When Tutu translates *ubuntu* as "I am human because I belong," he situates the concept squarely in the very tradition of classical political thought that, by his own account, he both admires and critiques. In the same passages of the *Politics* where Aristotle sets forth his concept of man as a "political animal," he also states that unless one belongs to the *politeia*, one is not a human—one is either a god or an animal. On this political ontology, the whole is clearly prior to its parts: the whole, the *politeia*, confers upon the animal its human essence, and in the absence of the *politeia*, that human essence—Tutu would seem to be saying—does not exist. Much the same holds true for Tutu's claim that "[s]ocial harmony is for us the *summum bonum*—the greatest good" and that "[a]nything that subverts or undermines this sought-after good is to be avoided like the plague." Anyone who has read Tutu's 1984 testimony before the U.S. House Foreign Relations Subcommittee (in which he argued that the Reagan administration's policy of "constructive engagement" toward South Africa was tantamount to complicity with Nazism), or who has followed Tutu's criticisms of the postapartheid South African government understands that he is one of the most courageous examples of dissent in our time. One can also see the consistency between Tutu's moral dissent and his claim that social harmony is the *summum bonum*: the various governmental policies and practices he has criticized over the years are precisely, in their most concrete effects, *destructive* of the possibility of social harmony—or at least "social harmony" understood in the highest and best possible sense. But the trouble with Tutu's translation of *ubuntu* in this way is that it elevates "social harmony" to a level where, like Lembede's "communal contentment" or, indeed, Cicero's *salus publica*, it can serve as the basis for the expulsion or suppression of precisely the sort of dissent that Tutu himself so fully personifies. Tutu's interpretation of *ubuntu*, like any iteration of social or political "peace," would seem to be marked by an iterative volatility that exceeds his own intentions: brought into line with "social harmony," *ubuntu* can, like the *salus publica* before it, just as easily serve as grounds for liberal legality as it can serve as the premise for the most repressive actions of police forces whose main task is simply to "keep the peace."

Symptomatic, in this regard, are the four examples of *ubuntu* in action that Tutu provides in his book: Jomo Kenyatta's policies in postindependence Kenya; Robert Mugabe's 1980 election speech that emphasized reconciliation, rehabilitation, and reconstruction; Namibian independence in 1989; and the tendencies for communities to respond with unity to the effects of natural disasters.[111] In each of these cases except Namibia, *ubuntu* in action turns out to take place under juridical conditions that, in the concrete, are defined by the jurisprudence of emergency. Mugabe's amnesty and indemnity laws, which continued similar measures under Ian Smith's government, coincided with the torture of independent trade unionists on the basis of "emergency power" regulations he also derived from the white minority Smith regime.[112] President Kenyatta used emergency legislation in the North Eastern Province and then in the Northern Frontier Districts, in connection with the so-called *Shifta* War of 1963–67.[113] In classic Diceyan fashion, this legislation was then followed by the passage of an indemnity act. Much like the worst of the worst South African indemnity acts, the Kenyan Indemnity Act of 1972 protected government officials (mainly soldiers) from lawsuits for illegal acts committed between 1963 and 1967.[114] As in postapartheid South Africa, the Kenyan Indemnity Act was helped along by criticisms aimed at those who wanted prosecution and compensation in courts of law (who were enjoined to move beyond the "bitterness" of the past).[115] Last but not least, Tutu speaks about *ubuntu* in situations of natural disasters. But here too, at least on the terms of Dicey's student E. C. S. Wade, who argues that "natural disasters" are one of the conditions for states of emergency,[116] Tutu's example of *ubuntu* refers to a concrete situation that an earlier jurisprudence, the jurisprudence of emergency, would have called a "state of necessity." With one exception, Tutu's own examples of *ubuntu* thus show how the term can be deployed as a homologue of, even a synonym for, the *salus populi* that was so central to the jurisprudence of emergency. In genealogical terms, this consistency is neither a surprise nor an accident; it is a reminder that when *ubuntu* is translated into the jurisprudence of the postcolonial state, its capacity for difference and for the unprecedented is constrained or even undercut by the epistemic conditions of its utterance, up to and including the terms it replaces without also displacing.[117]

Surely the most counterintuitive reiteration of *salus* in *ubuntu* takes place in situations where the problem is not the state's exercise of the legal power to take life but the neoliberal economy's exercise of the biopolitical power to let die. In his 2002 book *We Are the Poors*, Ashwin Desai argues that the indeterminacy of the 1996 Constitution's "limitations clause" poses the question of whether the "struggle for the new South Africa"—particularly the struggle for the socioeconomic rights that are arguably the constitutional vestige of South Africa's revolutionary tradition—can be conducted on the basis of the Bill of Rights.[118] Writing months before the Constitutional Court's decision on *TAC v. Minister of Health*, Desai answers his question in the negative. Desai begins the conclusion of his discussion of Thulisile Christina Manqele's lawsuit over the August 1999 disconnection of her electricity by noting, "The energy, mobilization, and time put into the Manqele case raised the issue of whether activists can acquire any gains from the practice and language of 'human rights.'"[119] He continues,

> While a lot more creative litigating could be done in conjunction with mass struggles, the way the "limitation clause" in the Constitution is being trotted out on a range of decisions in the courts, these rights are appearing less and less "fundamental." With the Constitutional Court's doctrine of not interfering with policy decisions that are rational and *bona fide* (in essence, for them, a procedural enquiry), our era of constitutionalism is difficult to distinguish from the apartheid 1950s. Then too, the highest court in the land merely sent the National Party back to convene a proper meeting to take rational decision to remove colored voters from the common voters' roll in the Cape. The only difference is that the parliamentary sovereignty of those days has been replaced by a sort of executive sovereignty now and the ideology of apartheid as a political determinant replaced by the ideology of the market.[120]

Because the "limitations clause" was one of the constitutional mechanisms that, particularly when guided by the spirit of *ubuntu*, was supposed to have enabled a more "optimal equilibrium" between person and state than did the *salus publica* of old, Desai's criticism reveals one of the paradoxical ways the latter has survived in the neoliberal order that was supposed to negate and dissolve it.

Writing in the final days of the apartheid state, under conditions of emergency rule, the author Richard Rive noted that it was necessary in apartheid South Africa to distinguish between two sorts of "emergencies." On the one hand, Rive observed, are the "special emergencies," the legislative emergencies that are declared by competent authorities and that have a discrete beginning and end. On the other hand, however, are the "normal emergencies" that "continue" even and especially when the "special emergencies" are lifted.[121] These "normal emergencies," the juridical status of which is sometimes pointedly obscure in Rive's work, become acutely clear when Rive is read retroactively alongside Desai. Desai's point, in effect, is that measures such as the "limitations clause" have the worrisome potential to put an end to the "special emergency" without also putting an end to the "normal emergency." On these terms, the *ubuntu* Constitution certainly could, by turning "special emergencies" into the object of rational juridical procedures that obey the principle of the rule of law, limit and diminish the possibility of using the *salus publica* as a basis for exceptional legislative measures. But with this same gesture, it also stands a very definite chance of producing the conditions for the persistence of a certain experience of "normal emergency," one that the *ubuntu* Constitution—not despite but because of its commitment to the rule of law—paradoxically could risk normalizing even more than did the openly illegitimate regime that preceded it. Under juridical conditions defined by neoliberalism's unthinking opposition to bureaucracy as such, even administrative mechanisms that reiterate the *salus populi* in an unprecedented way are bound to seem obviously or self-evidently illegitimate, for no reason other than their nonconformity with the rule of law. But as effective as the rule of law may be for negating conditions of "special emergency," its genealogy under conditions of colonialism points unmistakably to the fact of its own nonidentity with itself, its own consistent coexistence with the despotic bureaucratic apparatuses it takes to be its antithesis. Not only is the rule of law a juridical form that is unlikely to address or redress the problem of the "normal emergency"; it is, in its colonial and neoliberal declensions alike, the very condition for the "normal emergency" itself.[122] Contempt for the rule of law may have been one of the hallmarks of the apartheid state's jurisprudence of emergency. But the rule of law alone will not translate the end of the "special emergency" into a life that is something more than just a "normal emergency."

EPILOGUE

Toward a Critique of Transitional Justice

In the closing paragraphs of the preface to his 1821 *Philosophy of Right*, G. W. F. Hegel offered a pithy and justly famous observation about the nonidentity between philosophy and the real present—the "actuality"—that philosophy desires to think. "The owl of Minerva," wrote Hegel, "begins its flight only with the falling of the dusk."[1] If Hegel's remark is not off the mark, then thought will be quite limited in its ability to think its own present. It will acquire the ability to think its present for the first time only afterward—only belatedly, only at dusk, only once events have faded away into their "grey on grey." Our second thoughts, from this point of view, are more than just afterthoughts; they are, to the contrary, the only way we begin thinking at all.

By this standard, it must be said, there is not much thought in the account of the TRC we receive from transitional justice. This is a field that generated its understanding of the TRC with notable haste, consolidating its basic concepts, its theoretical lexicon, its methodological habits, and its constitutive disputes well before two of the TRC's most important bodies, its Amnesty Committee and its Reparations and Rehabilitation Committee, even finished their work. While this rush may have been desirable within the limited horizon of the academic "marketplace of ideas," given the overwhelming strength of the demand for knowledge about the TRC during the late 1990s, it is not desirable within the horizon of thought. There is, in fact, little reason why future scholarship on the TRC should continue to take place in the "conceptually simplistic" terms quickly established for it by transitional justice over a decade ago.[2]

Writing in 2004, the late Nigerian philosopher Emmanuel Chukwudi Eze observed that "transitional justice" has a name that is "strange and highly ambiguous." At the same time that the name implies a reference to some sort of "limit" (for "transitional justice" clearly does *not* refer to a situation in which justice is self-identical with itself), Eze argued, it nevertheless fails to clearly pose the question of the limit to which it *does* refer.[3] This book offers a belated response to Eze. Our claim has been that, in the case of the TRC, genealogy can speak even more illuminatingly than can transitional justice itself about the internal limit that transitional justice at once presupposes and fails to explicate. Because, as Heinz Klug argues, "the history of constitutionalism in South Africa could be summarised as the rise and fall of parliamentary sovereignty,"[4] and because, as Dicey argued, indemnity acts are the "supreme instance of parliamentary sovereignty,"[5] it makes sense that the parliamentary sovereignty of the apartheid republic, which opened with the Indemnity Act of 1961, should end with an indemnity act as well. But indemnity jurisprudence did not come to an end in the TRC. Reiterated under the rubric of "amnesty," indemnity jurisprudence contributed to the legitimation, if not also the foundation, of the very Constitution that was expressly designed to abrogate the theory and practice of parliamentary sovereignty. Indemnity not only exemplified the sovereignty of the old regime; a version of it also, at the same time, enabled the overthrow of that regime. As such, indemnity disjoined the old from the new: reiterated now as "amnesty," it enabled a "new beginning" and a "break with the past." Crucially, however, this disjunction doubled as a junction: as a convention that silently guided amnesty decisions, indemnity jurisprudence continued on internally within the very power that was supposed to have discontinued the regime indemnity exemplified. Indemnity was, in short, a pivot point: it allowed parliamentary sovereignty to become nonidentical with itself, to turn into its opposite. The "limit case" of parliamentary sovereignty itself, indemnity was also the hinge that permitted parliamentary sovereignty to transition out of existence (and perhaps, in the process, to silently allow for the survival of the juridical forms that conferred its substance on it).

Indemnity is not then just one among many problems for the study of the TRC within transitional justice. To the contrary: it exemplifies precisely the "limit" that, in Eze's account, transitional justice needs to but cannot think. Transitional justice *needs* to think this limit if it is to answer its own question, and to understand the concrete juridical conditions under which South Africa's old regime of parliamentary sovereignty could transition into its new *Rechtsstaat*. But, by that same token, transitional justice also *cannot* think this limit: to bring indemnity jurisprudence fully within the horizon of its inquiries, transitional justice would have to acknowledge the sense in which it shares its very own object of study—the problem of how to restore the rule of law after a period in which the rule of law has been negated, suspended, or violated—with a branch of jurisprudence, martial law, that transitional justice rightly understands as its direct antithesis. For this reason, the silence within transitional justice on indemnity is not simply one among many silences. It is a symptomatic and necessary silence, an unthinking silence that transitional justice needs to maintain if its empirical and historical descriptions, on the one hand, and ethical and therapeutic prescriptions, on the other, are to retain any validity at all. Transitional justice cannot then think indemnity jurisprudence: the latter is, in every sense, the *dead center* of the field's horizon of self-understanding. In the case of the TRC, it would seem, transitional justice derived a quotient of its intelligibility by reinscribing the traces of a palimpsest that it itself was unable to read.

To understand the TRC outside the horizon of transitional justice—or, in what amounts to the same thing, from the standpoint of the genealogy that is internally excluded within its horizon—does not, to be clear, entail a despairing interpretation of the TRC. Quite the opposite: the melancholic consensus today that the TRC was an impossible *machine* (a frustrating machine, a machine that didn't work) is the deflated double, and dialectical counterpart, of the inflated expectation, produced in no small measure by transitional justice, that the TRC would be an *impossible* machine (a machine that made miracles). The perspective we have outlined in this book, by contrast, implies a strategy for exiting this bipolar oscillation. If this book's genealogy is not off the mark, and if the TRC's own juridical powers and administrative techniques did come into being by reiterating the forms of colonial sovereignty and governmentality whose excesses the TRC also exposed and criticized, then it should be possible to treat that reiteration as occasion for a new and different measure for evaluating the TRC's success or failure as an apparatus.

On the terms of transitional justice, the TRC's success or failure was measured with reference to the norms and assumptions of Eurocentric historiography and the "technicism" of a certain highly instrumental and depoliticized understanding of law.[6] Was the TRC more or less effective as a transitional mechanism than the Nuremberg Trials? Did it really generate reconciliation and enable the disclosure of truth? Or did it open new wounds without also healing them? From a genealogical perspective, by contrast, the test of the success or failure of the TRC is neither its instrumental effectiveness in creating a transition to a functioning market economy (what transitional justice calls "peace") nor its relation to the putative "retributive justice" of the Nuremberg Trials. It is whether or not the TRC succeeded in putting "out of commission" the apparatuses of colonial sovereignty and colonial governmentality from which it emerged. The question here is not whether or not the TRC made impossible things (such as miracles), but the extent to which it made one thing in particular—colonial jurisprudence—impossible. The dominant narrative of the TRC's "accountable amnesty" or "conditional amnesty" within transitional justice is that the existence of this power is anomalous when considered with reference to a class ("amnesty") defined in and through international law.[7] From a genealogical perspective, by contrast, the TRC's amnesty is anomalous when considered with reference to a class ("indemnity") defined in and through colonial jurisprudence, up to and including its iteration under apartheid South Africa. From this perspective, what should interest us is not whether the TRC "worked" in its attempt to create a national catharsis in which South Africa finally healed itself and became the holistic nation it always already, allegedly, incipiently was, or whether its "forgiveness" is morally or ethically preferable to the trials of postwar Europe. It is whether the TRC's reiteration of colonial forms was sufficiently felicitous to institute a framework of juridical reason that renders "defeasible" or "inoperative" the colonial machinery from whence the TRC itself most directly sprang.

This is, or at least should be, a noncontroversial claim. There is no reason why the TRC, as distinct from every other creation of contemporary South African law, should somehow be exempt from Martin Chanock's observation that the juridical problems faced by the postapartheid state derive their unique form and shape from the coconstitutive relation between empire and the discourse of the rule of law.[8] There is no reason to suppose that the TRC somehow remained untouched by the paradoxes of "legal continuity" that defined every other point of transition between the apartheid state and the postapartheid state (and which, as Heinz Klug has demonstrated, are the indispensable horizon for any analysis of "transitional law" in South Africa).[9] Finally, it should not be unthinkable that indemnity jurisprudence would function as a "hinge" for the undoing of apartheid (since, beginning in at least 1969, Nelson Mandela and other political prisoners would cite precedents of indemnity in South Africa as a legal basis for their own release).[10] This is not to say, of course, that there are only continuities between the TRC and its colonial and imperial precedents. It is only to say that the TRC's unprecedented character, as well as the significance of its concrete function as a transitional mechanism and the measure of its success or failure, are most illuminatingly named once we understand its operation with reference to its reiteration of—its repetition of as well as its difference from—its precedents in colonial and imperial jurisprudence.

If this hermeneutic horizon is "more illuminating" than the horizon that defines transitional justice, it is because it permits us an understanding of the TRC that is both *more affirmative* and *more critical* than the latter. It is more affirmative because the genealogy of the TRC we have explored in this book teaches us that the TRC is, in fact, much more audacious and daring than transitional justice would have us imagine. The genius of the TRC, more latent than manifest, was to have attempted to reiterate a set of manifestly colonial juridical forms as part of an endeavor to prescribe a postcolonial political order. It was to have attempted to turn existing precedents of state domination back on themselves in order to put those precedents to rest. Immanent in this genius, however, was a risk that was much different and much greater than the sorts of risk transitional justice is capable of acknowledging (such as, e.g., that TRC's amnesties were "perpetrator friendly," that the TRC's mandate was too narrow and its discourse too individualized, or that its reparations fell short of redistribution and social justice). Transitional justice does not—and cannot—grasp the sense in which the TRC's attempt *to use* forms of colonial sovereignty and governmentality might not render those paradigms *unusable* but might allow for their survival, reproducing what is worst in colonial jurisprudence under cover of a new, and newly acceptable, lexicon.

Nothing in this perspective, it should be said, requires that we deny the fact that, as Tom Lodge put it, the framers of the TRC were "inspired partly by the Latin American experience."[11] It simply focuses our attention on the prior condition for this turn to the Latin American experience. If the framers of the PNR legislation had no other choice but to search outside of South African jurisprudence for paradigms for the adjudication of systematic state crimes, this was because the precedents in South African jurisprudence most fitted to this task were not simply incoherent but also an enabling condition for the very state crimes in question. While there's no doubt of the extent to which a "turn to Latin America" was decisive for the genesis of the TRC, it is also necessary to recognize that the crisis of colonial jurisprudence was already silently inscribed in the "turn to Latin America," as its condition of possibility. This crisis was the prior epistemological and juridical condition on which the Latin American paradigm could become dominant: because jurists could not turn to South African precedents for clear and distinct examples of adjudicating state crimes, it was desirable or even imperative to consider similar examples from other settings.[12] To point this out, however, is not to oppose the ostensible "internationalism" of transitional justice scholarship (i.e., the narrative that situates the TRC as the culmination of an international learning curve that begins in Nuremberg and Latin America) on the basis of a forgotten "national" past (i.e., the troubling legal history of indemnity acts within South Africa itself). It is simply to prioritize the very different internationalism—British imperialism—that informed the modes of colonial sovereignty and governmentality that defined South African law, up to and including the TRC, but that has been foreclosed upon by the reassuring origin story that transitional justice has told about the TRC.

* * *

So far is it from being the case that transitional justice explains the event of the TRC, then, that in fact the very opposite now seems to hold: what most needs explaining is how this field came to dominate the study of the TRC in the first place. By speaking of "qualified or conditional amnesty," doesn't transitional justice obscure the question of whether this amnesty functions— and, more important, does *not* function—like the colonial indemnification convention it at once displaces and repeats? By letting its attention be distracted by the TRC's neon-light concepts (truth, forgiveness), doesn't transitional justice overlook the more modest but nonetheless powerful administrative apparatus of the commission itself and, consequently, the question of whether the TRC operates—and, again, does *not* operate—like the Tumult Commissions of the bad old days? By narrating the emergence of the TRC mainly or even exclusively with reference to the juridical paradigms of Nuremberg and Latin America, doesn't the field of transitional justice allow us to avoid altogether the rather more anxious question of the TRC's own potential continuities with the very jurisprudence with which it was to have enabled South Africa to have broken? If so, won't it obscure our understanding of the very apparatus it claims to most want to understand?

Although this book has posed these questions to transitional justice only in connection with that field's study of a single case, the TRC, there is reason to believe those questions pertain to the field more generally. To the extent that the TRC is, in a Kuhnian sense, the paradigm or exemplar for the field of transitional justice as such,[13] the blind spots we find in its analysis of the TRC may exist in other of its analyses as well. It's striking, in this respect, that of the twenty-five different Truth Commissions Priscilla Hayner lists in her pathbreaking book *Unspeakable Truths*, all but four took place in former European colonies, while every single one of Hayner's five "strongest" commissions took place in former European colonies.[14] It is thus reasonable to say that not only the TRC but also Truth Commissions *in general* have been overwhelmingly postcolonial affairs: the vast majority of them, after all, have come into being and operated in political spaces that are all—in one way or another, according to contingencies and specificities that would have to be determined through further genealogical study—former European colonies. The reasons for this striking correlation are not difficult to infer: Eqbal Ahmad, among others, has shown how the political, juridical, and economic conditions specific to postcolonial systems of power tend, in general, to accelerate the sorts of human rights abuses that Truth Commissions investigate.[15] Yet if this is the case, why has there been so little inquiry into problems of coloniality and postcoloniality in transitional justice literature on Truth Commissions?[16] Why has there been so little analysis within transitional justice about the empirical regularity with which Truth Commissions and postcolonial orders correlate? Why have most transitional justice scholars instead interpreted these commissions according to the standard pattern of Eurocentric knowledge production,[17] in which empirical raw material taken from the colonies is transported to the "laboratories" of European theory, where it is then processed with reference to European juridical paradigms? Why is it that so few transitional justice scholars seem to be worried about this division of labor between European paradigms and postcolonial case studies? How do we make sense of the remarkable absence of curiosity within transitional justice regarding the possibility that its theoretical paradigms might be leading us to misunderstand the realities of postcolonial political transformation?

Given these questions, it must be pointed out that the continuing credibility and validity of transitional justice as a field derive—at least in part, and perhaps even in the main—from sources that are not primarily epistemological in character. The field's rapid institutionalization, which certainly outpaced its self-theorization, took place during the decade that nation building arrived at the forefront of U.S. foreign policy. The discourse that held up the TRC as the model for other countries to imitate and (with modifications for local context) use for their own "miraculous" transitions to democracy cannot then be separated from the geopolitical interests specific to the United States after the Cold War, from the neoliberal economic policies associated with the Washington consensus, or from the extension of U.S. sovereignty to enforce those interests and that consensus.[18] For a long time now, there has been, indeed, a specifically geopolitical imperative to produce experts who can claim a social scientific ability to "make miracles"—to conjure new democratic life from the corpses of authoritarian bodies politic, without simultaneously giving voice to "old" desires for revolutionary transformation. This imperative is a high priority for quasi-official federal agencies like the United States Institute of Peace, which has been a leader in the modularization, methodologization, and instrumentalization of Truth Commissions. The same imperative is also a high priority for elite institutions such as Harvard University's Project on Justice in Times of Transition and the International Center for Transitional Justice (conveniently located just around the corner from Wall Street). Under these conditions, we should not be at all surprised that, as Desmond Tutu wrote in 1999, only half kidding, "the study of forgiveness is a growth industry,"[19] or that, as Jonathan Tepperman, senior editor for *Foreign Affairs*, giddily concluded in 2002, "the truth business, in short, is booming."[20]

Booms, however, have a way of turning into busts, and the truth business is no exception. The truth about the "truth business" is that it was a bubble comprised largely of cliché: "Close the book," "Turn the page without closing the book," "Wipe the slate clean," "Shut the door on the past," "Come to terms with the past," "Deal with the past," "Heal the wounds of the past," "Heal the nation," "Put the past behind us," "Freedom from the ghosts of the past," "The past is a foreign country," "Revealing is healing," "The truth will set you free," "Amnesty not amnesia," "To forgive but not to forget," "Move forward," "Never again," "Closure." These worn coins, which have such currency within transitional justice, don't supply what so many have earnestly demanded of the field: an understanding of the sense in which, despite everything, the TRC was still an event, in the very best sense of the word. To speak of this event without also speaking of colonial jurisprudence is to participate in, derive intelligibility from, and indeed enact the very "amnesia" that "transitional justice entrepreneurs" propose to oppose when they repeat their tired imperative: "Above all, do not forget."[21] Because it's improbable that a discourse so heavily invested in imagining itself as the moral anti-dote to authoritarianism would be able to admit that its cures partake of the same stuff as the poison itself, it seems unwise to hope that this field will be able to undo its motivated forgetting of the colonial apparatuses out of whose bowels was born the violence of the apartheid state and the ma-chinery of the TRC alike. In all likelihood, the "truth business" will continue to monopolize discussions of the TRC. But those who do business with it will be obliged to buy in at a very high cost. A field that grounds its sense of piety on remembering, while also exempting its very own discourse from its imperatives against forgetting, is itself the first and best accountant of its own imminent bankruptcy.

Notes

INTRODUCTION

1. William Verwoerd, "Towards the Recognition of Our Past Injustices," in *Looking Back, Reaching Forward: Reflections on the Truth and Reconciliation Commission of South Africa*, ed. Charles Villa-Vicencio and Wilhelm Verwoerd (Cape Town: University of Cape Town Press, 2000), 156.

2. Wendy Orr, "Reparation Delayed Is Healing Retarded," in Villa-Vicencio and Verwoerd, *Looking Back, Reaching Forward*, 240.

3. *Truths Drawn in Jest: Commentary on the TRC through Cartoons*, ed. Wilhelm Verwoerd and Mahlubi Mabizela (Cape Town: David Philip, 2000), 8.

4. See, for example, Charles Call, "Is Transitional Justice Really Just?" *Brown Journal of World Affairs* 11, no. 1 (Summer/Fall 2004): 101–13; Bronwyn Leebaw, "The Irreconcilable Goals of Transitional Justice," *Human Rights Quarterly* 30, no. 1 (February 2008): 95–118; Rosemary Nagy, "Transitional Justice as a Global Project: Critical Reflections," *Third World Quarterly* 29, no. 2 (2008): 275–89; Robert Meister, *After Evil: A Politics of Human Rights* (New York: Columbia University Press, 2011), 20–49.

5. Claire Moon, *Narrating Political Reconciliation: South Africa's Truth and Reconciliation Commission* (Lanham, MD: Lexington Books, 2009), 2–5ff.; Tshepo Madlingozi, "On Transitional Justice Entrepreneurs and the Production of Victims," *Journal of Human Rights Practice* 2, no. 2 (2010), 210–11, 225.

6. Madlingozi, "On Transitional Justice Entrepreneurs and the Production of Victims," 209. See also Michael Neocosmos, "Transition, Human Rights, and Violence: Rethinking a Liberal Political Relationship in the African Neo-Colony," *Interface: a journal for and about social movements* 3, no. 2 (November 2011): 359–63.

7. Peter Parker, "The Politics of Indemnities, Truth Telling, and Reconciliation in South Africa," *Human Rights Law Journal* 17 (1996): 1–13.

8. Florian Kutz, *Amnestie für politische Straftäter in Südafrika Von der Sharpeville-Amnestie bis zu den Verfahren der Wahrheits- und Versöhnungskommission* (Berlin: Berlin Verlag Arno Spitz, 2001), 29–64; Antje du Bois-Pedain, *Transitional Amnesty in South Africa* (Cambridge: Cambridge University Press, 2007), 17–59; Louise Mallinder, "Indemnity, Amnesty, Pardon, and Prosecution Guidelines in South Africa" (working pa-

per no. 2, Beyond Legalism: Amnesties, Transition, and Conflict Transformation, Institute of Criminology and Criminal Justice, Queens University, Belfast, 2009), 139.

9. Alfred Venn Dicey, *Introduction to the Study of the Law of the Constitution*, 8th ed. (London: Macmillan, 1924), 48.

10. Thomas Hobbes, *The Elements of Law, Natural and Politic*, ed. J. C. A. Gaskin (Oxford: Oxford University Press, 1994), 172; Thomas Hobbes, *A Dialogue between a Philosopher and a Student of the Common Laws of England* (Chicago: University of Chicago Press, 1971), 61, 63, 152–53.

11. Dipesh Chakrabarty, *Provincializing Europe: Postcolonial Thought and Historical Difference* (Princeton: Princeton University Press, 2000), 4. See also Partha Chatterjee, *Nationalist Thought and the Colonial World: A Derivative Discourse?* (Minneapolis: University of Minnesota Press, 1993), 28, 43.

12. Chakrabarty, *Provincializing Europe*, 8.

13. Chakrabarty, *Provincializing Europe*, 16, 43–45. Valentin Mudimbe adopts a similar approach, focusing not on dichotomies between tradition and modernity, orality and the written, and rural and industrialized economies but on the "intermediate space" between "so-called African tradition" and "the projected modernity of colonialism." The point of this focus is not, of course, to understand this space as a reason to affirm "hybridity" as such (which has its own genealogy in colonial race theory) but, rather, to treat it as the "locus of paradoxes that call[] into question the modalities and implications of modernization in Africa." See V. Y. Mudimbe, *The Invention of Africa: Gnosis, Philosophy, and the Order of Knowledge* (Indianapolis: Indiana University Press, 1988), 5, 195.

14. Michel Foucault, "Nietzsche, Genealogy, History," in *Aesthetics, Method, and Epistemology*, vol. 2 of *The Essential Works of Michel Foucault, 1954–1984*, ed. James D. Faubion, trans. Robert Hurley et al. (New York: New Press, 1998), 369–92.

15. Michel Foucault, "Truth and Juridical Forms," in *Power*, vol. 3 of *The Essential Works of Michel Foucault, 1954–1984*, ed. James D. Faubion, trans. Robert Hurley et al., (New York: New Press, 2000), 6–89.

16. In fact, only in the famous case *Phillips v. Eyre* (1869), which dealt with the legality of the Jamaican Indemnity Act of 1867, does one find the word *legalize* used in the sense that Dicey will use it in his famous theory of indemnity (an act that "legalizes illegality"). Cf. Dicey, *Introduction*, 8th ed., 48, 408, 554; Phillips v. Eyre, 1869 LR 4 QB 225, at 241. For an extended analysis of *Phillips v. Eyre*, see R. W. Kostal, *A Jurisprudence of Power: Victorian Empire and the Rule of Law* (Oxford: Oxford University Press, 2005), 432–59, esp. 456–58 (on Dicey's relation to the case).

17. The genealogy of indemnity jurisprudence, in other words, confirms Eqbal Ahmad's insight that European colonizing powers "export[ed] to the colonies the social and political tensions produced by the shift from feudalism to capitalism." Ahmad explains, "The ability to export the tensions associated with social change made possible the growth of liberal democracies involving a subtle and complex balance between institutions of coercion and consensus" ("Postcolonial Systems of Power," in *The Selected Writ-*

ings of Eqbal Ahmad, ed. Carollee Bengelsdorf, Margaret Cerullo, and Yogesh Chandrani [New York: Columbia University Press, 2006], 138). The genealogy equally confirms Nasser Hussain's related claim that the colonies are "the site for both the manifestations of contradictions embedded in the British constitution and the alternative locale for elaborating on these questions of power and restraint" (Nasser Hussain, *The Jurisprudence of Emergency: Colonialism and the Rule of Law* [Ann Arbor: University of Michigan Press, 2003], 24).

18. The best example of this passion is Dicey's enthusiastic statement of support for war against "Boer aggression" in South Africa. In this statement, Dicey defined imperialism as a "political religion" that cannot be comprehended on the basis of the utilitarian philosophy to which he otherwise by his own account adhered, and he likened British military intervention to the conduct of the North in the U.S. Civil War: "The war in South Africa was as surely waged by England and her self-governing colonies to maintain the unity of the British Empire as the war against the Southern States was waged by the Northerners to maintain the unity of the United States." See Alfred Venn Dicey, *Lectures on the Relation between Law and Public Opinion in England during the Nineteenth Century* (New Brunswick: Transaction, 1981), 455, 457.

19. Hussain, *The Jurisprudence of Emergency: Colonialism and the Rule of Law*, 31.

20. Antony Anghie, *Imperialism, Sovereignty and the Making of International Law* (New York: Cambridge University Press, 2005), 6–7, 37, 311–12.

21. See, on this distinction, H. L. A. Hart, *The Concept of Law*, 2nd ed. (Oxford: Oxford University Press, 1994), 94.

22. Truth and Reconciliation Commission of South Africa, *Truth and Reconciliation Commission of South Africa Report*, 7 vols. (vols. 1–5, London: Macmillan Reference, 1999; vols. 1–7, Cape Town: Juta), vol. 5, chap. 6, ¶101; chap. 8, ¶72 (hereafter cited as *TRC Report*).

23. H. L. A. Hart, "The Ascription of Responsibility and Rights," *Proceedings of the Aristotelian Society* 49 (1949): 175.

24. Yasmin Sooka, one of eighteen commissioners to have served on the TRC, explains, "While the NDPP is not empowered to provide amnesty to serving prisoners he is empowered to effectively indemnify others against prosecution, a power previously conferred on the TRC's Amnesty Committee. The net result is the same: impunity" ("Prosecutions," in *Truth and Reconciliation in South Africa: Ten Years On*, ed. Charles Villa-Vicencio and Fanie du Toit [Claremont, South Africa: David Philip, 2006], 17–22). Heinz Klug, meanwhile, has observed, "While the [TRC] was designed to address the legacy of past impunity, the Constitution continues to be buffeted by the high levels of violence and impunity that have characterized South African life" (*The Constitution of South Africa: A Contextual Analysis* [Oxford: Hart, 2010], 2).

25. Needless to say, the Khulumani Support Group was right to oppose it. See William Mervin Gumede, *Thabo Mbeki and the Battle for the Soul of the ANC* (London: Zed Books, 2005), 362.

26. Daniel Herwitz, *Race and Reconciliation: Essays from the New South Africa* (Minneapolis: University of Minnesota Press, 2003), 101; Ashwin Desai, *We Are the Poors: Community Struggles in Post-Apartheid South Africa* (New York: Monthly Review Press, 2002), 149; Tom Lodge, *Politics in South Africa: From Mandela to Mbeki* (Bloomington: Indiana University Press, 2003), 92, 253 (but cf. 162); Gumede, *Thabo Mbeki*, 161–65; David Dyzenhaus, "The Pasts and Futures of the Rule of Law in South Africa," in *After Apartheid: Reinventing South Africa?*, ed. Ian Shapiro and Kahreen Tebeau (Charlottesville: University of Virginia Press, 2011), 251–59.

27. Lodge, *Politics in South Africa*, 176.

28. André du Toit, "Experiments with Truth and Justice in South Africa: Stockenström, Gandhi, and the TRC," *Journal of Southern African Studies* 31, no. 2 (2005): 440n76. See also Richard Wilson, *The Politics of Truth and Reconciliation in South Africa: Legitimizing the Post-Apartheid State* (Cambridge: Cambridge University Press, 2001), 33; Paul Gready, *The Era of Transitional Justice: The Aftermath of the Truth and Reconciliation Commission in South Africa and Beyond* (New York: Routledge, 2011), 28–32. Neocosmos, meanwhile, notes the absence within transitional justice of any analysis of the state in general, and the colonial state in particular. See Neocosmos, "Transition, Human rights, and Violence," 367. This holds true even for the most extensive discussions of administrative reason within transitional justice, which remain rigorously focused on European examples. See, for example, Ruti Teitel, *Transitional Justice* (Oxford: Oxford University Press, 2002), 149–89.

29. Michel Foucault, *Security, Territory, Population: Lectures at the Collège de France, 1977–1978*, trans. Graham Burchell (New York: Macmillan, 2009), 66, 75, 108–10.

30. Hannah Arendt, *Origins of Totalitarianism* (New York: Harcourt Brace Jovanovich, 1976), 198; Michel Foucault, *The History of Sexuality*, vol. 1, *An Introduction*, trans. Robert Hurley (New York: Vintage Books, 1990), 140–44.

31. For this argument, see Alain Badiou, *The Rebirth of History*, trans. Gregory Elliot (New York: Verso Books, 2012), 38–41, 94–95.

32. Kostal, *Jurisprudence of Power*, 81.

33. Kostal, *Jurisprudence of Power*, 126.

34. Anghie, *Imperialism*, esp. 196–244; Mark Mazower, *No Enchanted Palace: The End of Empire and the Ideological Origins of the United Nations* (Princeton: Princeton University Press, 2009), esp. 149ff.

35. Premesh Lalu, *The Deaths of Hintsa: Postapartheid South Africa and the Shape of Recurring Pasts* (Cape Town: Human Sciences Research Council, 2009), 4–7, 26.

36. Regina v. Bekker and Naude, 1900 CTR 443, at 448. Or, as Alfred Milner put it in a government minute of July 15, 1900, "Martial Law should undoubtedly only be resorted to at times of extreme danger to the State, when the doctrine salus reipublicae suprema lex applies, and when restrictions upon the ordinary rights and liberties of the citizen become necessary for the defence of the very constitution, on which all those rights and liberties rest." See, on this point, Alfred Milner, Minute No. 184, "Cape of

Good Hope, Papers Relating to Martial Law in Certain Districts of the Colony, July 1900," CGR Series, 2/1/155, 29218, Cape Town Archives Repository, Cape Town, 20.

37. Antjie Krog, "The Choice for Amnesty: Did Political Necessity Trump Moral Duty?" in *The Provocations of Amnesty: Memory, Justice, and Impunity*, ed. Charles Villa-Vicencio and Erik Doxtader (Trenton, NJ: Africa World Press, 2003), 117.

38. This language occurs in the epilogue to the 1993 Interim Constitution, which establishes the constitutional grounds for a "mechanism" of amnesty, and it is also (indeed, perhaps even more so) the language of South Africa's Constitutional Court, which confirmed the constitutionality of the TRC as just such a "mechanism." See Republic of South Africa, Constitution of South Africa, Act 200 of 1993, chap. 16 ("To this end, Parliament under this Constitution shall adopt a law determining a firm cut-off date, which shall be a date after 8 Oct 1990 and before 6 Dec 1993, and providing for the mechanisms, criteria and procedures, including tribunals, if any, through which such amnesty shall be dealt with at any time after the law has been passed"). For an elaboration on this language, see AZAPO et al. v. President of the Republic of South Africa et al. 1996 (8) BCLR 1035 (¶¶3, 14, 19, 21, 22, 36, 37, 46) (CC).

39. *An Intermediate Greek-English Lexicon, Founded upon the Seventh Edition of Liddel and Scott's Greek-English Lexicon* (Oxford: Clarendon, 1987), 512.

40. Sarah Ruden, "*Country of My Skull*: Guilt and Sorrow and the Limits of Forgiveness in the New South Africa," *ARIEL: A Review of International English Literature* 30, no. 1 (January 1999): 176.

41. Catherine Cole, *Performing South Africa's Truth Commission: Stages of Transition* (Bloomington: Indiana University Press, 2010), 26.

42. Audrey Chapman and Hugo van der Merwe, "Introduction: Assessing the South African Transitional Justice Model," in *Truth and Reconciliation in South Africa: Did the TRC Deliver?* (Philadelphia: University of Pennsylvania Press, 2008), 12–17.

CHAPTER I

1. Priscilla Hayner, *Unspeakable Truths: Facing the Challenge of Truth Commissions* (New York: Routledge, 2002), 43; Priscilla Hayner, "Same Species, Different Animal: How South Africa Compares to Truth Commissions Worldwide," in Villa-Vicencio and Verwoerd, *Looking Back, Reaching Forward*, 36. See also *TRC Report*, vol. 1, chap. 4, ¶25; Desmond Tutu, *No Future without Forgiveness* (London: Rider Books, 1999), 24–34; Wilson, *Politics of Truth and Reconciliation*, 23. For a succinct account of the scholarly consensus on the novelty of this approach, see Elizabeth Kiss, "Moral Ambition within and beyond Political Constraints: Reflections on Restorative Justice," in Rotberg and Thompson, *Truth v. Justice*, 76.

2. *TRC Report*, vol. 1, chap. 4, ¶59; Tutu, *No Future without Forgiveness*, 33–34; Alex Boraine, "Truth and Reconciliation in South Africa: The Third Way," in Rotberg and Thompson, *Truth v. Justice*, 143.

3. *TRC Report*, vol. 1, chap. 5, ¶98.

4. Barbara Cassin, "Amnistie et pardon: Pour une ligne de partage entre éthique et politique," in *Vérité, Réconcilliation, Réparation*, ed. Barbara Cassin, Olivier Cayla, and Philippe-Joseph Salazar (Paris: Seuil, 2004), 41.

5. This is a familiar refrain within transitional justice. See, for example, Tutu, *No Future without Forgiveness*, 120–21; Jeremy Sarkin, *Carrots and Sticks: The TRC and the South African Amnesty Process* (Antwerp: Intersentia, 2004), 3–4.

6. See, on the amnesty laws of 1949 and 1954, Norbert Frei, *Adenauer's Germany and the Nazi Past: The Politics of Amnesty and Integration*, trans. Joel Golb (New York: Columbia University Press, 2002), 5–26, 67–92.

7. Tony Judt, *Postwar: A History of Europe since 1945* (New York: Penguin Books, 2005), 46–48.

8. See, in general, Nicole Loraux, *The Divided City: On Memory and Forgetting in Ancient Athens*, trans. Corinne Pache with Jeff Fort (New York: Zone Books, 2002).

9. Loraux, *Divided City*, 245.

10. Much the same is true of the amnesty deal offered by South African prime minister Louis Botha to quell the Afrikaner Rebellion of 1914. In a decree of November 12, 1914, Botha declared, "All persons who do surrender will not be criminally prosecuted at the insistence of the Government, but will be allowed to return to their homes and remain there on condition that they take no further part in the rebellion, give no information or any other assistance whatever to the rebels, and do nothing or say nothing whatever which is likely further to disturb the peace or to prolong the rebellion. This amnesty will not, however, apply to persons who have taken a prominent part in the rebellion, or who while in rebellion have committed acts in violation of the rules of civilized warfare. The Government reserve their authority to deal with these cases on their merits." Found in Union of South Africa, *Report on the Outbreak of the Rebellion and the Policy of the Government with Regard to Its Suppression* (Pretoria: Government Printer and Stationary Office, 1915), 45-6.

11. On the commensurability of the legal form of the trial with public or civic education, see Lawrence Douglas, *The Memory of Judgment: Making Law and History in the Trials of the Holocaust* (New Haven: Yale University Press, 2001), 1–11 and (on catharsis) 109–10.

12. On the sense in which the TRC's public hearings were intended to be a "powerful medium of education for society at large," see *TRC Report*, vol. 1, chap. 6, ¶36.

13. "In essence," Stéphane Leman-Langlois writes, the Nuremberg myth in postapartheid justice "contributed to the transformation of a large set of objective but meaningless potentialities and uncertain, overly complex, contradictory or unclear notions into a very small range of valid options and proper attitudes. It was of great help in reducing the appearance of arbitrariness in decision making and it created post-transition South Africa as a series of easily identifiable, specific necessities that had to be met while solving unanswerable, paralyzing questions by eradication. The Nuremberg myth al-

lowed this reconstruction by providing key elements of a new discourse, used to convince a critical mass of the population of the reasonableness of a drastic departure from what is conventionally accepted as justice in criminal matters." See "Constructing a Common Language: The Function of Nuremberg in the Problematization of Postapartheid Justice," *Law and Social Inquiry* 27, no. 1 (2002): 96–97.

14. For an overview of these amnesties and attempts to question them, see Ellen Lutz, "Responses to Amnesties by the Inter-American System for the Protection of Human Rights," in *The Inter-American System of Human Rights,* ed. David John Harris and Stephen Livingstone (Oxford: Oxford University Press, 1998), 345–70.

15. Preamble to Republic of South Africa, Indemnity Act 35 of 1990.

16. "The Groote Schuur Minute," *South African Journal on Human Rights* 6, no. 3 (1990): 318–19 (setting forth "temporary immunity from prosecution of political offences" for ANC members as a means to the end of "peaceful political negotiations").

17. Section A(2)ii of Republic of South Africa, Government Notice R 2625, *Government Gazette* 12834, Regulation Gazette 4584, November 7, 1990.

18. Sections 1(1) and 2(1) of Republic of South Africa, Indemnity Act 35 of 1990.

19. Du Bois-Pedain, *Transitional Amnesty,* 24.

20. See Sections 3(1), 3(6), 4(6)b, 9, and 11(5) of Republic of South Africa, Government Notice R 2633, *Government Gazette* 12838, Regulation Gazette 4588, November 9, 1990.

21. Richard Abel, *Politics by Other Means: Law in the Struggle against Apartheid, 1980–1994* (New York: Routledge, 1995), 252; Lourens du Plessis, "Amnesty and Transition in South Africa; Legal Analysis," in *Dealing with the Past: Truth and Reconciliation in South Africa,* ed. Alex Boraine, Janet Levy, and Ronel Scheffer (Cape Town: IDASA, 1997), 110.

22. Chapter 2 of Republic of South Africa, Further Indemnity Act 151 of 1992.

23. Du Bois-Pedain, *Transitional Amnesty,* 41–43; Sarkin, *Carrots and Sticks,* 39–47.

24. On this point, see Lourens du Plessis, "Amnesty and Transition in South Africa; Legal Analysis," in *Dealing with the Past,* 108–16; Lourens du Plessis, "Observations on Amnesty or Indemnity for Acts Associated with Political Objectives in Light of South Africa's Transitional Constitution," *Tydskrif vir hedendaagse Romeins-Hollandse Reg,* vol. 57 (1994), 478.

25. See Sections 48(1) and (2) of Republic of South Africa, Promotion of National Unity and Reconciliation Act of 1995. Cf. du Plessis, "Amnesty and Transition in South Africa," 115 (outlining the argument according to which the Constitutional Court could have undone past indemnity acts).

26. Mallinder, "Indemnity, Amnesty, Pardon," 75–76.

27. Tutu, *No Future without Forgiveness,* 188–89.

28. As Jeremy Sarkin argues, "[T]he agreements between the ANC and the former government culminating in the Indemnity Acts of 1990 and 1992, gave indemnity to thousands of people and therefore kept them from applying for amnesty" (*Carrots and Sticks,* 5). Cf. Du Bois-Pedain, *Transitional Amnesty,* 40–43.

29. Not only was there arguably no need for the SADF to apply for amnesty (because many of their illegal actions were already legally protected by prior indemnities), but there was just as arguably even a need for the SADF *not* to apply for amnesty: on the Hobbesian logic accepted by so many commentaries on the South African transition, the allegiance of the SADF was indispensable for avoidance of civil war and a "peaceful transition." As John Storey put it in his forgotten but brilliant 1985 analysis of the South African conflict, the strategic goal of the apartheid government was to pursue reforms without also weakening its defense forces ("South African Perspectives: Workers' Revolution or Racial Civil War," *Inqaba ya basebenzi* 16–17 [January–June 1985]) (special supplement to issue 16–17). What Heinz Klug has argued about the question of "legal continuity" in transitional justice scholarship thus might also be said of the question of "military continuity" as well. As Tom Lodge points out, "[T]hroughout the duration of the TRC's operations, there were no doubts about the military's loyalty to the new government" (*Politics in South Africa*, 203). There is a sense in which the TRC did not investigate the SADF because, in political terms, it *could* not: the allegiance of the SADF was one of the indispensable institutional conditions for the very "peace" the TRC also pursued. Had the SADF's allegiance been in question, Tutu perhaps would not have been able to interpret military force as the sign par excellence of national reconciliation during the May 10 flyover salute to Mandela by the South African Air Force, that "these war machines that had for so long been raged against us were now *ours*—no longer just *theirs*—that this was indeed now *our* country in the profoundest possible way" (Tutu, *No Future without Forgiveness*, 7; emphasis in original.).

30. Published as *The Healing of a Nation?*, ed. Alex Boraine and Janet Levy (Cape Town: Justice in Transition, 1995).

31. This document proposed that members of the liberation movement "who have already received temporary indemnity should as a group be granted permanent indemnity, preferably in terms of the new statute rather than by proclamation in terms of the 1990 or 1992 Acts. If any statutory offences were committed by members of the security forces they too should be indemnified *en masse*." After emphasizing that "the statutory offences should be identified to avoid uncertainty or ambiguity," the document then went on to say that members of either should not be indemnified en masse for common-law offenses such as murder, attempted murder, or perjury. See Dullah Omar, "Amnesty Bill: Explanatory Memorandum" (n.d.), Records of the Legal Resources Centre, Johannesburg (AG 3006/1.30.2.1), Department of Historical Papers, Cullen Library, University of Witwatersrand, Johannesburg, 3.

32. *TRC Report*, vol. 1, chap. 7, ¶¶95–101. See also Tutu, *No Future without Forgiveness*, 187; Alex Boraine, *A Country Unmasked: Inside South Africa's Truth and Reconciliation Commission* (Oxford: Oxford University Press, 2000), 329–31.

33. On June 7, 1994, Omar issued a statement on "amnesty/indemnity," accompanied by a memo inviting individuals, organizations, religious bodies, and members of the public to submit comments and proposals about the topic by June 30, 1994. He conclud-

ed this memo by noting worries about the overlap between the new amnesty legislation and the existing indemnity legislation: "Whilst we are in the process of preparing legislation along the lines set out above, there exists great concern about the various applications for indemnity submitted under the existing Indemnity laws to the present government. Such applicants have an expectation that their applications will be processed and finalized in terms of the existing indemnity laws. I agree that these applications cannot await until a new law is passed. Hence consideration of all such applications under the existing Indemnity laws will be expedited. An Advisory Committee under the convenorship of Mr. Brian Currin, National Director of Lawyers for Human Rights will be set up immediately. Its task will be to scrutinize all such outstanding indemnity/amnesty applications which are still pending and to make appropriate recommendations to the State President. Those who qualify in terms of the two Indemnity laws will be released immediately. Those who do not qualify will together with the new applicants be given an opportunity to apply for amnesty through the new mechanisms which are being established in terms of the Constitution." See Dullah Omar, "Statement by Minister of Justice, Mr. Dullah Omar on Amnesty/Indemnity," June 7, 1994, Records of the Legal Resources Centre, Johannesburg (AG 3006/1.30.2.1), Department of Historical Papers, Cullen Library, University of Witwatersrand, Johannesburg, 4.

34. "Argentines Vote to Repeal Amnesty," *Washington Post*, August 13, 2003, A20; Larry Rohter, "Decades Later, Confronting a Bloody Past: Change of Climate in Latin America," *International Herald Tribune*, September 2, 2005, 2.

35. See, on this point, Naomi Roht-Arriaza, "The Role of International Actors in National Accountability Processes," in *The Politics of Memory: Transitional Justice in Democratizing Societies*, Ed. Carmen González Enríquez, Alexandra Barahona de Brito, Paloma Aguilar Fernández (Oxford: Oxford University Press, 2001), 40–65.

36. See "No Option but to Nullify Illegitimate Amnesty," *Negotiation News* 7 (1992): 12.

37. Jody Narandran Kollapen, "Accountability: The Debate in South Africa," *Journal of African Law* 37, no. 1 (Spring 1993), 4–9.

38. See, for example, the documents collected in *Amnesty: Forgiveness without Confession? Cover-up of Crime? Christians Need to Know!* (Western Province Council of Churches, 1992). See, in particular, Father Michael Lapsley, "Indemnity Bill and a General Amnesty," 5–9. On indemnity in Zimbabwe, see Richard Carver, "Zimbabwe: Drawing a Line through the Past," *Journal of African Law* 37, no. 1 (Spring 1993): 72–74.

39. Lodge, *Politics in South Africa*, 177.

40. To my knowledge, Antje du Bois-Pedain is alone in integrating into her analysis of the TRC a reading of the minister of justice's first draft of the bill that would become the PNR Act of 1995. See Du Bois-Pedain, *Transitional Amnesty*, 18–19.

41. Omar, "Amnesty/Indemnity," 2.

42. Omar, "Amnesty/Indemnity," 4.

43. Omar, "Amnesty/Indemnity," 3–4.

44. "The offences in respect of which amnesty may be applied for will be defined strictly within the framework of the constitutional provision on national unity and reconciliation" (Omar, "Amnesty/Indemnity," 3).

45. See, on this point, Lourens du Plessis, "Amnesty and Transition in South Africa; Legal Analysis," 109.

46. See, on this point, Lourens du Plessis, "Amnesty and Transition in South Africa; Legal Analysis," 112–14 (outlining the many ways in which existing indemnity legislation would not survive constitutional review).

47. Alexandre Kojève has put this point well: "[W]hen there is a genuine revolution, a given (positive) *Droit* [a system of law] dies in order to generate another, and one can say that every time that a *Droit* dies in order to generate another there is a genuine revolution. Revolution, therefore, is the *passage* from one *Droit* to another; it is very much an absence (which is a 'potentiality' [*puissance*]), a (creative) negation of *Droit*." See Alexandre Kojève, *Outline of a Phenomenology of Right*, trans. Bryan-Paul Frost and Robert Howse, ed. Bryan-Paul Frost (Boston: Rowman and Littlefield, 2000), 93 (emphasis in original).

48. Legal Resources Centre, Johannesburg, "Memorandum Prepared by the Legal Resources Centre, Johannesburg, in Response to the Statement by the Minister of Justice Mr. Dullah Omar on Amnesty/Indemnity Dated 7 June 1994," June 30, 1994, Records of the Legal Resources Centre, Johannesburg (AG 3006/1.30.2.1), Department of Historical Papers, Cullen Library, University of Witwatersrand, Johannesburg, 4.

49. Legal Resources Centre, Johannesburg, "Memorandum," 6.

50. Omar, "Amnesty Bill: Explanatory Memorandum," 1–5. For his part, Albie Sachs would not hesitate to describe this obligation using the language of indemnity. Speaking in February 1994, Sachs characterized the Negotiating Council's agreement over the new Constitution's "post-script" by arguing that "[a] balance was struck, and that was to say the issue would be left to the future parliament on the understanding that it would be committed in broad terms to granting an indemnity" (quoted in *Dealing with the Past*, ed. Boraine, Levy, and Scheffer, 145).

51. Omar, "Amnesty Bill: Explanatory Memorandum," 6–8.

52. "We cannot forgive on behalf of victims—nor do we have the moral right to do so. It is the victims themselves who must speak. Their voices need to be heard" (Omar, "Amnesty/Indemnity," 2).

53. Republic of South Africa, "Amnesty Bill No. . . . of 1994" (n.d.), Records of the Legal Resources Centre, Johannesburg (AG 3006/1.30.2.1), Department of Historical Papers, Cullen Library, University of Witwatersrand, Johannesburg, 1.

54. Republic of South Africa, "Amnesty Bill No. . . . of 1994," 4.

55. Republic of South Africa, "Amnesty Bill No. . . . of 1994," 4.

56. Republic of South Africa, "Amnesty Bill No. . . . of 1994," 4.

57. Republic of South Africa, "Amnesty Bill No. . . . of 1994," 6.

58. Republic of South Africa, "Amnesty Bill No. . . . of 1994," 7.

59. Republic of South Africa, "Amnesty Bill No. . . . of 1994," 8–9.

60. See, for example, Boraine and Levy, *Healing of a Nation?*, 5, 29, 134–35.

61. See, for example, Truth Commission Panel, "Working Document: Draft Legislative Framework for Proposed Bill to Set Up a Truth and Reconciliation Commission," July 1994 (on file with author), 5, 10, 20–28. See also Kader Asmal, Louise Asmal, and Ronald Suresh Roberts, *Reconciliation through Truth: A Reckoning of Apartheid's Criminal Governance*, 2nd ed. (New York: St. Martin's, 1997), 56–57.

62. Truth Commission Panel, "Working Document: Draft Legislative Framework," 26–27.

63. R. P. Rossouw, "Re: Promotion of National Unity and Reconciliation Bill, 1994," March 23, 1995, Document no. 1995-03-23 (on file with author).

64. Rossouw, "Re: Promotion of National Unity and Reconciliation Bill," 1.

65. Rossouw, "Re: Promotion of National Unity and Reconciliation Bill," 1.

66. Rossouw, "Re: Promotion of National Unity and Reconciliation Bill," 2–3 (emphasis in original).

67. Rossouw, "Re: Promotion of National Unity and Reconciliation Bill," 3–4 (emphasis in original).

68. Rossouw, "Re: Promotion of National Unity and Reconciliation Bill," 4–5 (emphasis in original).

69. See, for example, Republic of South Africa, *Debates of the National Assembly*, May 17, 1995, col. 1375; Republic of South Africa, *Debates of the Senate*, June 27, 1995, col. 2243.

70. See, on this point, Ziyad Motala, "The Promotion of National Unity and Reconciliation Act, the Constitution, and International Law," *Comparative and International Law Journal of Southern Africa* 28 (1995): 344–57; Ziyad Motala, "The Constitutional Court's Approach to International Law and Its Method of Interpretation in the 'Amnesty Decision': Intellectual Honesty or Political Expediency?," *South African Yearbook of International Law* 21 (1996): 35.

71. Kader Asmal, "International Law and the Liquidation of Apartheid," *Notes and Documents, United Nations Centre against Apartheid*, no. 43, Melville J. Herskovits Library of African Studies, Northwestern University (New York: United Nations, 1978), 9.

72. See, for example, Republic of South Africa, *Debates of the National Assembly*, May 17, 1995, col. 1390; Republic of South Africa, *Debates of the Senate*, June 27, 1995, cols. 2210, 2215.

73. Johnny de Lange, "The Historical Context, Legal Origins, and Philosophical Foundation of the South African Truth and Reconciliation Commission," in Villa-Vicencio and Verwoerd, *Looking Back, Reaching Forward*, 21. See also Lodge, *Politics in South Africa*, 191.

74. de Lange, "Historical Context, Legal Origins, and Philosophical Foundation," 19. On the "understated yet significant role" played by the concept of "legal continuity" in

South Africa's transition to democracy, see also Klug, *Constitution of South Africa*, 15–17.

75. Republic of South Africa, *Debates of the National Assembly*, May 17, 1995, col. 1384.

76. Republic of South Africa, *Debates of the National Assembly*, May 17, 1995, col. 1385.

77. While the preceding analysis tends to follow Tom Lodge's analysis, which suggests that the ANC was in favor of a general amnesty (Lodge, *Politics in South Africa*, 191–92), there is no clear consensus on this point. Cf., for example, Klug, *Constitution of South Africa*, 190; John Dugard, "Is the Truth and Reconciliation Process Compatible with International Law? The Unanswered Question," *South African Journal of Human Rights* 13 (1997): 258 (arguing that the National Party favored unconditional amnesty); Louise Mallinder, "Indemnity, Amnesty, Pardon, and Prosecution Guidelines in South Africa" (working paper no. 2, Beyond Legalism: Amnesties, Transition, and Conflict Transformation, Institution of Criminology and Criminal Justice, Queens University, Belfast, 2009), 134–35 (describing the NP's and the ANC's different paths toward amnesty).

78. These clauses were inserted into the act because of the equality clause of the 1996 Constitution, which prohibits different persons from being indemnified for the same crime on different grounds. See, on this point, Dullah Omar, "Justice Minister's Reply," in Boraine and Levy, *Healing of a Nation?*, 134–35.

79. Cf. Republic of South Africa, "Amnesty Bill No. . . . of 1994," 8–9; *TRC Report*, vol. 1, ¶¶74–75.

80. Dugard, "Truth and Reconciliation Process," 268.

81. AZAPO et al. v. President of the Republic of South Africa et al., 1996 (8) BCLR 1035 (¶33) (CC).

82. *AZAPO*, 1996 (8) BCLR 1042 (¶53) (CC) (stating, "[T]hat the discharges from civil liability are all incompatible with s 22 of the interim Constitution [Act 200 of 1993] is clear beyond question").

83. Indemnity was outlawed by the Interim Constitution as well as by the 1996 Constitution. See Section 34 (5) (b) of Republic of South Africa, Constitution of South Africa. Act 200 of 1993; Section 37 (5) (a) of Republic of South Africa, Constitution of South Africa, Act 108 of 1996.

84. *AZAPO*, 1996 (8) BCLR 1035 (¶¶34–35) (CC).

85. *AZAPO*, 1996 (8) BCLR 1027–28, 1036–37 (¶17, 36) (CC).

86. *AZAPO*, 1996 (8) BCLR 1032–33 (¶¶29–30) (CC). Even though, as Dugard notes, "Mahomed DP is correct in stating that 'there is no single or uniform international practice in relation to amnesty'" ("Truth and Reconciliation Process," 266), it is nevertheless telling that the Court was unable to cite a single concept of broad amnesty that did not derive from international law. This inability was even more pronounced in the Cape High Court's May 6, 1996, rejection of AZAPO's challenge to the constitu-

tionality of the amnesties dispensed by the TRC. See AZAPO et al v. TRC et al., 1996 (4) SALR 571H; 571–572D; 572F–573D; 575A–B (C).

87. But see John Dugard, "Reconciliation and Justice: The South African Experience," *Transnational Law and Contemporary Problems* 8 (1998): 305n139 (noting that "the Constitutional Court erred in its interpretation of art. 6(5) of Protocol II").

88. See Paul van Zyl, "Dilemmas of Transitional Justice: The Case of South Africa's Truth and Reconciliation Commission," *Journal of International Affairs* 52, no. 2 (1999): 651n8 (noting that "self-amnesties are generally viewed as illegal under international law"). See also Sarkin, "Trials and Tribulations," 627n59 (noting that the Centre for Applied Legal Studies at the University of the Witwatersrand "argued that the Constitution makes it clear that the amnesty to be granted applies to individuals only and not the state").

89. See Jeremy Sarkin, "The Trials and Tribulations of South Africa's Truth and Reconciliation Commission," *South African Journal of Human Rights* 12, no. 4 (1996): 627; see also Dugard, "Truth and Reconciliation Process," 264 (arguing that states are obliged "to try and extradite those alleged to have committed crimes against humanity" and that "under customary international law there is at least a prima facie case for an obligation to prosecute").

90. See, on this point, Daniel Herwitz, *Race and Reconciliation: Essays from the New South Africa* (Minneapolis: University of Minnesota Press, 2003), 28.

91. *AZAPO*, 1996 (8) BCLR 1035–36 (¶35) (CC).

92. *AZAPO*, 1996 (8) BCLR 1036–37 (¶36) (CC).

93. This is the case even with scholars who wish to recover indemnity as part of the prehistory of amnesty. See Eric Doxtader, "Easy to Forget or Never (Again) Hard to Remember? History, Memory, and the 'Publicity' of Amnesty," in Villa-Vicencio and Doxtader, *Provocations of Amnesty*, 131–38.

94. Sigmund Freud, *The Psychopathology of Everyday Life, vol. 6 of Standard Edition of the Complete Psychological Works of Sigmund Freud*, ed. James Strachey (London: Hogarth, 1961), 19–20.

95. See, for example, Teitel, *Transitional Justice*, 52–58; Jon Elster, *Closing the Books: Transitional Justice in Historical Perspective* (Cambridge: Cambridge University Press, 2004), 3–23; Barbara Cassin, "'Removing the Perpetuity of Hatred': On South Africa as a Model Example," *International Review of the Red Cross* 88, no. 862 (2006): 235–44.

96. H. R. Hahlo and Ellison Kahn, *The Union of South Africa: The Development of Its Laws and Constitution* (Cape Town: Juta, Ltd., 1960), 147n61.

97. Each of these indemnities was slightly different in scope. The purpose of Ordinance 10 of 1836 was "to indemnify the Governor of the Colony and all persons acting under his authority against certain acts done during the existence of Martial Law in certain parts of the Colony." The purpose of Ordinance 4 of 1847 was "to indemnify all Persons in regard to certain Acts done during the recent existence of Martial Law." The purpose of Ordinance 8 of 1853 was "to indemnify certain Persons in regard to Acts

done during the existence of Martial Law." See Cape of Good Hope, *Statutes of the Cape of Good Hope, 1652–1895*, vol. 1, *1652–1871*, ed. Hercules Tennant and Edgar Michael Jackson (Cape Town: Juta, 1895), 216, 419, 491. These ordinances are cited often in debates over indemnity. See Phillips v. Eyre, 1869 LR 4 QB 225, at 233; Phillips v. Eyre, 1870 LR 6 QB 1, at 18. See also *Debates of the Legislative Assembly of the Colony of Natal, Fourth Session of the Fourth Parliament, May 3 to August 9, 1906* (Pietermaritzburg: Davis and Sons, 1906), 433; Charles Mathew Clode, *The Military Forces of the Crown; Their Administration and Government*, vol. 2 (London: John Murray, 1869), 503–11. On Act 23 of 1878, see Cape of Good Hope, *Debates in the Legislative Council, in the Sixth Session of the Fifth Parliament of the Cape of Good Hope, Appointed to Meet 10th May, 1878, 41 Victoriae*, vol. 12, published by order of the Legislative Council (Cape Town: Saul Solomon, 1878), 244–45; Cape of Good Hope, *Debates in the House of Assembly, in the Third Session of the Tenth Parliament of the Cape of Good Hope, 20th July to 13th October, 1900* (Cape Town: Cape Times, 1900), 77.

98. Colony of Natal, Indemnity Act 14 of 1874.

99. See Section 61 ("Suppression of Riot by Persons Acting under Lawful Orders") of the Draft Penal Code, in Cape of Good Hope, *Report and Proceedings of the Government Commission on Native Laws and Customs* (Cape Town: W. A. Richards and Sons, 1883).

100. See Section 59 ("Suppression of Riot by Persons Acting under Lawful Orders") of Cape of Good Hope, Transkeian Territories Penal Code Act 24 of 1886: "Every one, whether subject to military or police law or not, acting in good faith in obedience to orders given by a justice of the peace for the suppression of a riot, is justified in obeying the orders so given, unless such orders are manifestly unlawful; and he is protected from criminal responsibility in using such force as he on reasonable and probable grounds believes to be necessary for carrying into effect such orders. It shall be a question of law whether any particular order is manifestly unlawful or not."

101. Cape of Good Hope, Indemnity and Special Tribunals Act 6 of 1900; Colony of Natal, Indemnity Act 15 of 1900; Colony of Natal, Indemnity Act 41 of 1901 (which extended Indemnity Act 15 of 1900); Colony of Natal, Indemnity Act 22 of 1902, Indemnity Act 30 of 1902 (which extended Indemnity Act 22 of 1902); Transvaal Colony, Indemnity and Peace Preservation Ordinance 38 of 1902; Orange River Colony, Martial Law Act 25 of 1902.

102. Martin Chanock, "Writing South African Legal History: A Prospectus," *Journal of African History* 30 (1989): 278.

103. Transvaal Colony, Indemnity and Peace Preservation Ordinance 38 of 1902, Indemnity (Burgher) Ordinance 22 of 1903; Colony of Natal, Indemnity Act 51 of 1906, Indemnity Act 5 of 1908.

104. Union of South Africa, Indemnity and Undesirables Special Deportation Act 1 of 1914, Indemnity and Special Tribunals Act 11 of 1915, Amnesty and Indemnity and Undesirables Deportation Act of 1914, Amendment Act 46 of 1919, and Indemnity and

Trial of Offenders Act 6 of 1922. One could also mention in this connection Republic of South Africa, Indemnity Act 13 of 1940, which was designed to protect from prosecution South African police officers who helped suppress the nationalist insurrection.

105. Union of South Africa, Proclamation 76 of 1920 (Protectorate of South-West Africa).

106. Republic of South Africa, Suggested Proclamation of an Indemnity Measure in Connection with the Bondelswartz Rebellion, Prime Minister Series, vol. 1/2/66, PM21/1A, National Archives, Pretoria.

107. On the Public Safety Act of 1953, see Hahlo and Kahn, *Union of South Africa,* 134. On the Defence Act of 1957, see Anthony Mathews, *Freedom, State Security, and the Rule of Law: Dilemmas of the Apartheid Society* (Cape Town: Juta, 1986), 193–94. On Proclamation 400, see Republic of South Africa, *Debates of the House of Assembly,* June 8, 1961, cols. 7629–30.

108. Indemnity Act of 1961 (Act 61 of 1961), Indemnity Act of 1977 (Act 13 of 1977), Indemnity Act of 1984 (Transkei) (Act 17 of 1984), Indemnity Act of 1985 (Ciskei) (Act 31 of 1985), Lebowa Indemnity Act of 1986 (Act 3 of 1986) (repealed in 1988), KwaNdebele Indemnity Act of 1986, Indemnity Act of 1990 (Decree 11 of 1990), Indemnity Amendment Decree of 1990 (Decree 36 of 1990), Indemnity Amendment Decree of 1991 (Decree 2 of 1991), Indemnity Second Amendment Decree of 1991 (Decree 21 of 1991), Indemnity Third Amendment Decree of 1991 (Decree 28 of 1991), Further Indemnity Act of 1992 (Act 151 of 1992), Special Indemnity Decree of 1993 (Decree 7 of 1993), and Indemnity Amendment Decree of 1993 (Decree No. 11 of 1993).

109. *TRC Report,* vol. 1, chap. 1, ¶1. In the emergency legislation of the late 1980s, as we shall see in chapter 3, indemnities were no longer *retrospective* but *prospective.* This temporal expansion of indemnity was not without precedent in South Africa. In the controversial Indemnity Acts of 1906 and 1914, the South African Parliament sought to convert indemnity from a retrospective to a prospective power. See Arthur Berriedale Keith, *Imperial Unity and the Dominions* (Oxford: Clarendon, 1916), 163.

110. Hahlo and Kahn, *Union of South Africa,* 145. See also Albie Sachs, *Justice in South Africa* (Berkeley: University of California Press, 1973), 237. See also Republic of South Africa, *Debates of the House of Assembly,* June 8, 1961, cols. 7550–51. Of course, this dynamic is not limited to South Africa. As Martin Chanock notes, "[T]hroughout the empire war, class struggle, racial rule, and ethnic division meant that the verbal formulae of the rule of law were highly qualified by statutory and emergency powers" (*The Making of South African Legal Culture, 1902–1936: Fear, Favor, and Prejudice* [Cambridge: Cambridge University Press, 2001], 470).

111. Cape of Good Hope, *Debates in the House of Assembly,* 76.

112. *Hansard Parliamentary Debates,* 5th ser., vol. 58 (1914), col. 373.

113. On June 9, 1961, F. C. Erasmus, minister of justice, argued, "The legal principle that a State can ask for indemnity is recognized, although there are very few examples in

the world. . . . That principle is recognized in Roman-Dutch law; and it is recognized in the common law of South Africa that a country can ask for indemnity under certain circumstances. That is the legal aspect. But by custom something has been added in South Africa which has also been done in England. In South Africa it has been done more pertinently [than in England], and that is what has been said here, namely, that only the Government and its agents will enjoy indemnity under our indemnity laws provided their actions were *bona fide*" (Republic of South Africa, *Debates of the House of Assembly*, June 9, 1961, col. 7680). In chapter 3, I consider whether the "addition" Erasmus here mentions isn't more of a "subtraction." For now, it is enough to note the nationalist self-consciousness with which the apartheid state's minister of justice, who here speaks at the high point of the apartheid state's parliamentary sovereignty, insists on the exceptional character of South African indemnity jurisprudence.

114. Chanock, *Making of South African Legal Culture*, 39; see also 517 (arguing that "for South African legal history we must acknowledge the powerful effects of the Diceyan paradigm"). As Dennis Davis, Matthew Chaskalson, and Johan de Waal argue, Dicey was, under apartheid, "the jurisprudential source of South African constitutional law," and "it was his concept of the rule of law which constituted the yardstick by which to test the democratic nature of the principles and content of South African public law." See "Democracy and Constitutionalism: The Role of Constitutional Interpretation," in *Rights and Constitutionalism: The New South African Legal Order*, ed. Dawid van Wyk, John Dugard, Bertus de Villiers, and Dennis Davis (Oxford: Clarendon, 1995), 1. See also Hahlo and Kahn, *Union of South Africa*, 146; Patric Mzolisi Mtshaulana, "The History and Role of the Constitutional Court of South Africa," in *The Post-Apartheid Constitutions: Perspectives on South Africa's Basic Law*, ed. P. Andrews and S. Ellman (Athens: Ohio University Press, 2001), 525.

115. According to many scholars and critics, it should be noted, one of the main problems of twentieth-century South African law was that there was not sufficient judicial review of parliamentary or executive sovereignty. In this connection, it should not be forgotten that indemnity acts were one of the ways in which parliament sidestepped judicial review. See, on this point, Chanock, *Making of South African Legal Culture*, 515.

116. Dicey, *Introduction*, 8th ed., 48, 228, 408–9. It hardly can come as a surprise, then, that Dicey and his student E. C. S. Wade would be quoted as authoritative sources in South African parliamentary debates over the meaning and limits of indemnity. For Mr. H. Miller's quotation of Dicey in opposition to the Indemnity Bill of 1961, see Republic of South Africa, *Debates of the House of Assembly*, June 7, 1961, col. 7548. Miller would also quote Dicey in opposition to the Indemnity Bill of 1977. See Republic of South Africa, *Debates of the House of Assembly*, January 31, 1977, col. 503. For the minister of justice's quotation of Wade and Phillips, see Republic of South Africa, *Debates of the House of Assembly*, June 9, 1961, col. 7680. For a similar quotation, see Mr. D. J. L. Nel, Republic of South Africa, *Debates of the House of Assembly*, February 1, 1977, col. 512.

117. G. W. F. Hegel, *Science of Logic*, trans. A. V. Miller (New York: Humanity Books, 1999), 126.

118. On June 9, 1961, South Africa's minister of justice F. C. Erasmus would argue, "In the circumstances there may be differences here and there, but if hon. Members will examine the wording of Act No. 1. Of 1914 and that of Act No. 7 of 1922, they will see that they were actually the basis which my Department used in drawing up this Bill—with just this difference that the two sides of the House have changed places" (Republic of South Africa, *Debates of the House of Assembly*, June 9, 1961, col. 7677).

119. Cf. Law Adviser's Report on Act 6 of 1922 (the Indemnity and Trial of Offenders Act), Minister of Justice Series, vol. 680, 1/47/22, National Archives, Pretoria, 8, 17 (tracing Act 11 of 1915 to the Indemnity Act 6 of 1900 [Cape Colony]), 3–4 (tracing Act 16 of 1922 to the Indemnity Act 11 of 1915); Law Adviser's Report on Act 11 of 1915 (the Indemnity and Special Tribunals Act of 1915), Governor General Series, vol. 337, 7/985, National Archives, Pretoria, 8, 17 (tracing Act 11 of 1915 to the Indemnity Act 6 of 1900 [Cape Colony]).

120. See "Cape Colony, Previous Declarations of Martial Law," in Martial Law Regulations (1900), High Commissioner Series, vol. 57, 155, National Archives, Pretoria (describing as a "good precedent" for martial law in 1900 the Martial Law Declarations of 1835, 1846, 1850, and 1877 and including a note referring to Ordinance 10 of 1836, "[t]o indemnify the Governor of the Colony, and all persons acting under his authority against certain acts done during the existence of Martial Law in certain parts of the Colony").

121. *TRC Report*, vol. 5, chap. 6, ¶101. Critics of *AZAPO et al.* have emphasized the way the Court's rulings violated not only international law but also South African law. In their 2002 coauthored text *Constitutional Law: Analysis and Cases* (Oxford: Oxford University Press, 2002), Ziyad Motala and Cyril Ramaphosa focus their criticism on the Constitutional Court's ruling on *trias politica*. Tacitly returning to the debates around *ultra vires* doctrine during the states of emergencies of the 1980s, Motala and Ramaphosa argue, "The Promotion of National Unity and Reconciliation Act took away the competence of the court in a particular category of disputes (very much like ouster clauses under the apartheid regime), and placed the adjudicative function in a number of executive appointees." They suggest, "The Court should have found that it is untenable and unconstitutional for executive appointees (as provided for in the Promotion of National Unity and Reconciliation Act), who clearly were not a part of the judicial branch of government, to carry out what is essentially an adjudicative function" (82). Given the apartheid regime's reliance on parliamentary sovereignty and unchecked executive power, Motala and Ramaphosa's opposition to the limitation of overarching judicial review cannot be rejected as a myopic insistence on the letter of the law at the expense of the spirit of the political transition as a whole. On the contrary, their concern cuts to the very substance of that political transition (see also van Zyl, "Dilemmas of Transitional Justice," 663, arguing that amnesty provisions "represent a fundamental subversion of the rule of law

and the institutions designed to uphold it"). Motala and Ramaphosa's critique of the "diminution of the Court's authority and denial of access to the Court" (83) is directed at the replication of one of the basic structures of apartheid governance itself, which Gunnar Theissen, in his analysis of the Court's ruling, rightly calls "the continuing legacy of parliamentary supremacy" ("Amnesty for Apartheid Crimes? The South African Truth and Reconciliation Commission and International Law" [LL.M. thesis, University of the Western Cape, 1998],14–15). Writing in 1997, John Dugard offered a similar observation on the point of international law. Though his argument is not unqualified on this point, we may infer, from his thoroughgoing critique of the Constitutional Court's deficient consideration of international law, that one of the lasting effects of *AZAPO et al.* will have been its repetition, with a difference, of the exceptionalism of South African law vis-à-vis international law (Dugard "Truth and Reconciliation Process," 262–66; cf. 267). Though now as its privileged example, rather than as its pariah, the Constitutional Court's ruling on amnesty leaves South African law immune from the intervention of international law. As Theissen puts it, "[I]t may sound strange—but on the turn of the new millennium—the best protection for apartheid criminals [from international law] is to be punished by their national courts" (90).

CHAPTER 2

1. See, on this point, Richard Cosgrove, *The Rule of Law: Albert Venn Dicey, Victorian Jurist* (Chapel Hill: University of North Carolina Press, 1980), 66.

2. Dicey, *Introduction*, 8th ed., 58.

3. Dicey, *Introduction*, 8th ed., 61.

4. John Dugard, *Human Rights and the South African Legal Order* (Princeton: Princeton University Press, 1978), 33. Dugard elsewhere argues, "In the early days of National Party rule every effort was made by the legislature to establish the principle that the South African Parliament is the uncommanded commander of society and, after initial obstruction from the Appeal Court, judicial acquiescence in this principle was secured. Thereafter the *volkswil* (the will of the Afrikaner people) expressed in Parliament became the supreme law of the land with the result that the National Party Government was able to enact a discriminatory and repressive body of law without fear of judicial disapproval" ("The Jurisprudential Foundations of *Apartheid* Legal Order," *Philosophical Forum* 18, nos. 2–3 [1986–87]: 115–16.).

5. See O. D. Schreiner, *The Contribution of English Law to South African Law; and the Rule of Law in South Africa* (Cape Town: Juta, 1967), 89, 91, 96, 100; Hahlo and Kahn, *Union of South Africa*, 133–46; Mathews, *Freedom, State Security, and the Rule of Law*, 15–16, 19–20; L. J. Boulle, *Constitutional Reform and Apartheid* (New York: St. Martin's, 1984), 4, 95–96; Patrick McAuslan and John McEldowney, "Legitimacy and the Constitution: The Dissonance between Theory and Practice," in *Law, Legitimacy, and the Constitution: Essays Marking the Centenary of Dicey's Law of the Constitution*, ed.

Patrick McAuslan and John McEldowney (London: Sweet and Maxwell, 1985), 11. See also *TRC Report*, vol. 5, chap. 5, ¶158 (d).

6. Dicey, *Lectures on the Relation between Law and Public Opinion*, 66–69.

7. Dugard, *Human Rights and the South African Legal Order*, 40–41; Sachs, *Justice in South Africa*, 261; Chanock, *Making of South African Legal Culture*, 517.

8. Chanock, "Writing South African Legal History," 269, 288.

9. The apartheid state's claim that it adhered to the principle of the rule of law was, of course, one of the main ways in which it sought to justify itself externally. In 1968, for example, the apartheid government's Department of Foreign Affairs published a pamphlet called *South Africa and the Rule of Law* to respond to allegations that "persons are detained and persecuted for their opposition to the South African Government and that South Africa is a 'police state' where the rule of law is continually being violated." Through a detailed exposition of South African law and an analysis of specific security provisions, the pamphlet strives to show that "[n]othing is further from the truth" (Republic of South Africa, *South Africa and the Rule of Law* [Pretoria: Government Printer, 1968], 5). Although, as Lewis Nkosi put it, this pamphlet was an "absurdity," it is also true that, as David Dyzenhaus has argued, "what made apartheid exceptional was that it was implemented and sustained through law." Indemnity, the power to legalize illegality, is a privileged point of departure for grasping this antinomy. Cf. Lewis Nkosi, *The Transplanted Heart: Essays on South Africa* (Benin City: Ethiope, 1975), 15; David Dyzenhaus, *Judging the Judges, Judging Ourselves: Truth, Reconciliation, and the Apartheid Legal Order* (Oxford: Hart, 1998), 149.

10. Chanock, "Writing South African Legal History," 288. See also Chanock, *Making of South African Legal Culture*, 513–14. It is true, of course, that Dicey criticizes the Bill of Rights and the Declaration of the Rights of Man (217), whereas South Africa's 1996 Constitution affirms versions of both. Yet not only is there no absolute difference between these traditions and Dicey's rule of law (such that Schreiner could argue that "an operative Bill of Rights seems to be the Rule of Law at its highest" [*Contribution of English Law*, 76–77]), but, as we shall see, the Bill of Rights and human rights traditions do not escape the paradoxes of sovereign power any more cleanly than does the Diceyan tradition.

11. For a reading of this type, see, for example, John McEldowney, "Dicey in Historical Perspective," in McAuslan and McEldowney, *Law, Legitimacy, and the Constitution*, 40.

12. On this point, see Schreiner, *Contribution of English Law*, 74.

13. H. W. Arndt, "The Origins of Dicey's Concept of 'The Rule of Law,'" *Australian Law Journal* 31 (1957): 121–23.

14. O. Hood Phillips, "Constitutional Conventions: Dicey's Predecessors," *Modern Law Review* 29, no. 2 (1966): 137–48.

15. Dicey, *Introduction*, 8th ed., 38.

16. William Blackstone, *Commentaries on the Laws of England*, vol. 1 (Chicago: University of Chicago Press, 1979), 160–61. See Dicey, *Introduction*, 39.

17. See, on this point, Wade, introduction to *Law of the Constitution*, by Alfred Venn Dicey, 9th ed. (New York: Macmillan, 1956), clxxxviii.

18. Dicey, *Introduction*, 8th ed., 22.

19. Dicey, *Introduction*, 8th ed., 23. To be clear, Dicey's distinction between laws and conventions is not the same thing as the distinction between written and unwritten law. Some statute law does not affect sovereign power at all, whereas some conventions—such as, to anticipate this book's argument, the tradition of indemnifying crimes committed in the name of the public good by ministers or public servants under conditions of crisis (see Dicey, *Introduction*, 418)—affect sovereign power in an extremely precise and substantial way, without, however, ever being written down anywhere. As such, Dicey argues, the jurist must examine what connections there are, if any, between the conventions of the constitution and the law of the constitution, or, put simply, what legal rules—rules recognized by the courts—are to be found in the various parts of the Constitution, whether written or unwritten (30).

20. Walter Bagehot, *The English Constitution* (Ithaca: Cornell University Press, 1966), 177–92; William Edward Hearn, *The Government of England: Its Structure and Its Development* (London: Longmans, Green, 1887), 131–36; Alpheus Todd, *Parliamentary Government in England: Its Origin, Development, and Practical Operation*, vol. 1 (London: Sampson Low, Marston, 1892), 3ff. This same collapse of theory into history determined the way the question of parliamentary sovereignty was posed in South Africa. Cf. E. C. S. Wade, introduction to *Law of the Constitution*, xl; E. C. S. Wade, "Appendix II: Parliament and the Courts: Opinion by Professor E. C. S. Wade Published by the Union Government," in *Parliamentary Sovereignty and the Commonwealth*, by Geoffrey Marshall (Oxford: Clarendon, 1957), 251. The latter was the contribution to *Harris et al. v. Dönges and Another* (1952 [1] TLR 1245) that Wade made at the request of the Union of South Africa.

21. Marshall, *Parliamentary Sovereignty*, 48. Cf. J. G. A. Pocock, *The Ancient Constitution and the Feudal Law: A Study of English Historical Thought in the Seventeenth Century* (Cambridge: Cambridge University Press, 1978), 312–13.

22. Dicey, *Introduction*, 8th ed., 67, 70, 179, 449, 463; Marshall, *Parliamentary Sovereignty*, 31.

23. Dicey, *Introduction*, 8th ed., 24–5.

24. Wade, introduction to *Law of the Constitution*, cxlvi.

25. Dicey, *Introduction*, 8th ed., 65.

26. Alpheus Todd, *Parliamentary Government in the British Colonies* (Boston: Little, Brown, and Co., 1880), 1–2. Cf. Dicey, *Introduction*, 8th ed., 24–25.

27. E. C. S. Wade and G. Godfrey Phillips, *Constitutional Law: An Outline of the Law and Practice of the Constitution, Including Central and Local Government and the Constitutional Relations of the British Commonwealth*, 6th ed. (London: Longman, 1960), 75, 80. See, for example, John Locke, *Two Treatises of Government and a Letter concerning Toleration* (New Haven: Yale University Press, 2003), 190–91 (§205).

28. Wade and Phillips, *Constitutional Law*, 41.

29. Todd, *Parliamentary Government in the British Colonies*, 2–3.

30. In Hahlo and Kahn's narration, "traces" of this maxim "survive to this day in English and American law in the doctrine of State immunity from Suit" (*The South African Legal System and Its Background* [Johannesburg: Juta, Ltd., 1968], 436.

31. Hearn, *Government of England*, 20.

32. Hearn, *Government of England*, 21–22.

33. Hearn, *Government of England*, 99.

34. Todd, *Parliamentary Government in the British Colonies*, 17–19, 22. See also Keith, *Imperial Unity*, 35, 85–86.

35. Dicey, *Introduction*, 8th ed., 24–25.

36. Todd, *Parliamentary Government in the British Colonies*, 17–19. As the Earl of Halsbury writes, "The Sovereign can do no wrong, and no legal proceedings of any kind can be brought against him. The only remedies for injuries caused by the Crown or the Government are, in cases of contract, a petition of right, and, in cases of tort, an action against or prosecution of the subordinate by whom the wrongful act was actually done" (*The Laws of England*, vol. 23 [London: Butterworth, 1912], 308).

37. Hobbes, *Elements of Law*, 172; Thomas Hobbes, *On the Citizen*, ed. Richard Tuck (Cambridge: Cambridge University Press, 1998), 143.

38. See, on this point, Hussain, *Jurisprudence of Emergency*, 69–72.

39. Dicey, *Introduction*, 8th ed., 217.

40. Dicey, *Introduction*, 8th ed., 218 (emphasis mine).

41. Dicey, *Introduction*, 8th ed., 218 (emphasis mine); see also 223.

42. Dicey, *Introduction*, 8th ed., 261.

43. Dicey, *Introduction*, 8th ed., 224.

44. Dicey, *Introduction*, 8th ed., 225.

45. Dicey, *Introduction*, 8th ed., 225–26.

46. Clinton Rossiter, *Constitutional Dictatorship: Crisis Government in the Modern Democracies* (New Brunswick, NJ: Transaction, 2002), 143–44.

47. Dicey, *Introduction*, 8th ed., 226–27.

48. Dicey, *Introduction*, 8th ed., 228.

49. Dicey, *Introduction*, 8th ed., 228.

50. Dicey, *Introduction*, 8th ed., 48.

51. Dicey, *Introduction*, 8th ed., 408.

52. Dicey, *Introduction*, 8th ed., 47; see also 228, 547. Dicey takes his meaning for the term *retrospective* from *Phillips v. Eyre* (1870), in which Justice Willes has recourse to the U.S. Supreme Court's distinction between "retrospective" laws and "*ex post facto*" laws in *Calder v. Bull* (1798): whereas retrospective laws (like pardons and oblivions) legalize illegal acts, *ex post facto* laws void and/or punish acts that were lawful when done. See Phillips v. Eyre, 1870 LR 6 QB 1, 1 at 25–27.

53. Dicey, *Introduction*, 8th ed., 48; see also 408. With this formulation, Dicey breaks

decisively with William Finlason, who argued in 1868 that indemnity does not necessarily presuppose illegality but only protects against the risk and vexation of prosecution. See William Finlason, *A Review of the Authorities as to the Repression of Riot or Rebellion, with Special Reference to Criminal or Civil Liability* (London: Stevens and Sons, 1868), 89, 141, 151, 166. Dicey also breaks with Pollock, who suggests that indemnity acts are little more than acts of prudence and grace. See Dicey, *Introduction*, 553–54. In *Regina v. Bekker and Naude* (1900), Judge Solomon will argue that Finlason's view on martial law is "practically exploded" and that Dicey's view is correct. See Regina v. Bekker and Naude, 1900 CTR 443, at 448. Judge de Villiers would quote this portion of Solomon's opinion approvingly and at length in *Krohn v. Minister of Defense* (1915). See Krohn v. Minister of Defence, 1915 AD 191, at 210–11.

54. Dicey, *Introduction*, 8th ed., 59, 38.

55. In their *Constitutional Law*, which was widely consulted by apartheid jurists and parliamentarians, Dicey's disciples E. C. S. Wade and G. Godfrey Phillips cite the example of indemnity legislation to illustrate the supremacy of parliament relative to the courts: "Parliament alone possesses the power to legalise past illegality. This power denies supremacy to the courts and has been used by an Executive which has a security majority to reverse inconvenient decisions of an impartial Judiciary" (43–44). In a more speculative sense (one that is not entirely within the framework of Dicey's text), we might explain the sovereignty expressed in the indemnity act by contrasting its legislation of illegality with an ordinary repeal. Whereas a repeal is a legislative act in which Parliament expresses its power "to make and unmake laws" by unmaking a single law, an indemnity act is a law that makes and unmakes law in one and the same gesture. Because the indemnity act has as its explicit object the legalization of illegality, it marks a moment at which law at once encounters its precise negative opposite and integrates that negative into itself. In no other sort of statute—not even the suspension act or martial law, which are both temporary measures—does Parliament so fully exercise its plenary powers. The indemnity act, in other words, names the threshold at which Dicey's account of the rule of law turns into its opposite. At the same time that it is, as we shall see, that convention that reconciles sovereignty to itself, that heals a split internal to sovereign power, it is also the theoretical and practical limit at which the rule of law affirms, blesses, and absolves its opposite, namely, the violation of the rule of law.

56. As Senator Wolmarans put it in parliamentary debates over indemnity in 1915, "[I]f it were known beforehand that Parliament would approve all illegal acts, then force became law" (Union of South Africa, *Debates of the Senate*, March 31, 1915, col. 87).

57. This, I should note in passing, was not lost on apartheid parliamentarians. Speaking in a 1961 debate over the Indemnity Bill of 1961, the National Party parliamentarian A. E. Erlank responded to liberal critics of the bill by observing, "[I]n the country from which they draw all their wisdom . . . there has been one axiom that has been in existence from beginning to end, and which still exists to-day, namely, 'The King can do no wrong.' . . . In other words, anything can happen, no matter how *male fide* it

may be, but if it is in the interests of the state, it is obviously indemnified" (Republic of South Africa, *Debates of the Senate*, June 15, 1961, col. 5335).

58. Dicey, *Introduction*, 8th ed., 413.

59. Dicey, *Introduction*, 8th ed., 419.

60. Dicey, *Introduction*, 8th ed., 418.

61. Dicey, *Introduction*, 8th ed., 230–31.

62. Dicey, *Introduction*, 8th ed., 70.

63. Dicey, *Introduction*, 8th ed., 72–73.

64. Dicey, *Introduction*, 8th ed., 74.

65. Alfred Venn Dicey, *Introduction to the Study of the Law of the Constitution*. 7th ed. (London: Macmillan, 1908), 72, 424–28, 479, 484. Dicey was perfectly aware of the danger that parliamentary sovereignty so construed could lend itself to racial despotism. In his 1898 lectures, he would mention Jamaican law and American slavery as examples of legislation being controlled by the sovereignty of opinion. See Dicey, *Lectures on the Relation between Law and Public Opinion*, 10–16, 305–6.

66. Dicey, *Introduction*, 8th ed., 424.

67. Ivor Jennings, "In Praise of Dicey: 1885–1935," *Public Administration* 13, no. 2 (1935): 123–34.

68. Dicey, *Introduction*, 8th ed., 426.

69. Dicey, *Introduction*, 8th ed., 426.

70. Dicey, *Introduction*, 8th ed., 425.

71. 35 Geo. 3 c. 13 ("An Act for indemnifying such Persons as have acted for the Service of the Publick, in advising or carrying into Execution two several Proclamations of the Lord Lieutenant and Council of this Kingdom, bearing Date the Twenty-fourth and Twenty-ninth Days of January, One thousand seven hundred and ninety-five respectively, and for continuing and giving effect to the said Proclamations"); 36 Geo 3 c. 6 ("An Act for indemnifying such Persons as have acted since the First Day of January, One thousand seven hundred and ninety-five, for the Preservation of the public Peace, and Suppression of the Insurrections prevailing in some Parts of this Kingdom"); 37 Geo. 3 c. 39 ("An Act for indemnifying such Persons as have acted since the First Day of January, One thousand seven hundred and ninety-seven, for the Preservation of the Public Peace, and Suppression of the Insurrections prevailing in some Parts of this Kingdom"); 38 Geo. 3 c. 19 ("An Act for Indemnifying such Persons as have acted since the Third Day of July, in the Year One thousand seven and ninety seven, for the Preservation of the Publick Peace, and Suppression of the Insurrections prevailing in some Parts of this Kingdom"); 39 Geo. 3 c. 3 ("An Act for indemnifying such Persons as have acted since the Sixth Day of October, One thousand seven hundred and ninety-eight, for the Preservation of the Public Peace, and Suppression of Insurrections prevailing in Several Parts of this Kingdom"); 40 Geo. 3 c. 89 ("An Act for indemnifying such Persons as have acted since the first Day of June, one thousand seven hundred ninety-nine, for the Preservation of the public Peace, and Suppression of the Insurrections prevailing in some Parts of this Kingdom, and to enable Sheriffs and

other Officers to make the Returns therein Specified"); and 41 Geo. 3 c. 66 ("An Act for Indemnifying such Persons as, since the first Day of February One thousand seven hundred and ninety three, have acted in the apprehending, imprisoning or detaining in Custody, in Great Britain, of Persons suspected of High Treason or Treasonable Practices").

72. *Hansard Parliamentary Debates*, 3rd ser., vol. 184 (1866), col. 1804.

73. *The Statutes at Large, Passed in the Parliaments Held in Ireland: From the Third Year of Edward the Second, A.D. 1310 to the Thirty-Eighth Year of George the Third, A.D. 1798, Inclusive*, vol. 13 (Dublin: George Grierson, 1798), 442–43, 790.

74. See, on this point, P. O'Higgins, "*Wright v. Fitzgerald* Revisited," *Modern Law Review* 25, no. 4 (1962): 413. See also Clode, *Military Forces*, 172–73; Finlason, *Review of the Authorities*, 153; Dicey, *Introduction*, 8th ed., 554.

75. On the indemnities of 1791–1803, see Dicey, *Introduction*, 8th ed., 231–33, 554.

76. William Lecky, *A History of England in the Eighteenth Century*, vol. 8 (Longmans, Green, 1890), 25; Thomas Bayly Howell, *State Trials*, vol. 27 (London: T. C. Hansard for Longman, Hurst, Rees, Orme, and Brown, 1816), col. 761.

77. The letter is reported to have read: "Sir, I am extremely sorry I cannot wait on you at the hour appointed, being unavoidably obliged to attend sir Lawrence Parsons, Yours, Baron de Clues" (Howell, *State Trials*, col. 770).

78. See Francis Plowden, *The History of Ireland from Its Invasion Under Henry II to Its Union with Great Britain*, vol. 2 (London: Booker et al., 1809), 545–47.

79. 38 Geo. 3 c. 19.

80. Lecky, *History of England*, 26.

81. Howell, *State Trials*, col. 765.

82. Howell, *State Trials*, col. 766.

83. O'Higgins, "*Wright v. Fitzgerald* Revisited," 418–19.

84. Howell, *State Trials*, col. 767. As one parliamentarian pointed out, the judges said nothing of the sort. See Howell, *State Trials*, col. 769.

85. Lecky, *History of England*, 30.

86. Howell, *State Trials*, cols. 816–17.

87. Howell, *State Trials*, col. 795.

88. Howell, *State Trials*, col. 799.

89. Howell, *State Trials*, col. 806.

90. *Phillips v. Eyre*, 1870 LR 6 QB 1, at 11. On the standard status of this claim within English legal history and theory, see O'Higgins, "*Wright v. Fitzgerald* Revisited," 413. O'Higgins, however, has flatly contradicted this common sense, arguing that "there are other Irish cases in which . . . actions were brought, some of them with success" (413).

91. Dicey, *Introduction*, 8th ed., 286–77.

92. Dicey, *Introduction*, 8th ed., 547–49.

93. Dicey, *Introduction*, 8th ed., 286, 300–302, 540, 543, 553.

94. Of course, the *salus publica* goes under various names. See Dicey, *Introduction*, 8th ed., 273, 275, 276, 539ff.

95. See, on this point, Raymond Ruiter, "The Maintenance of the Security of the State," in *The South African Constitution*, ed. Henry John May, 3rd ed. (Cape Town: Juta, 1955), 356.

96. Dicey, *Introduction*, 8th ed., 408–9.

97. See, on this point, George Frederickson, *White Supremacy: A Comparative Study in American and South African History* (Oxford: Oxford University Press, 1981), 14.

98. See Phillips v. Eyre, LR 6 QB 1 (1870), 1 at 18. Of these indemnities, only the New Zealand Parliament's Act 11 of 1866 would be refused the Royal Assent. These refusals of assent would recur frequently in debates over South Africa's indemnity acts. On the 1867/68 indemnity in New Zealand, see Arthur Berriedale Keith, *Responsible Government in the Dominions*, vol. 1 (Oxford: Clarendon, 1912), 162. Those that were modeled on the Irish Indemnity Act of 1798, such as the Indemnity Act of 1848 in Ceylon (Clode, *Military Forces*, 501), did, by contrast, receive Royal Assent.

99. Keith, *Responsible Government*, 270 (emphasis mine).

100. It is unclear to me to what Rossiter is here referring. To my knowledge, there were only two indemnity acts passed by the British Parliament in 1766, 6 Geo. 3 c. 7 and 6 Geo. 3 c. 51, and both indemnified persons who incurred penalties for violating the Stamp Act.

101. Rossiter, *Constitutional Dictatorship*, 139. Cf. Finlason, *Review of the Authorities*, 95 (but cf. 192). See also Hussain, *Jurisprudence of Emergency*, 108; Wade and Phillips, *Constitutional Law*, 376.

102. Rossiter, *Constitutional Dictatorship*, 141–42.

103. Wade and Phillips, *Constitutional Law*, 380–81.

104. *Hansard Parliamentary Debates*, 5th ser., vol. 128 (1920), col. 1796.

105. Finlason, *Review of the Authorities*, 97. We exclude from this claim the indemnity acts that were regularly passed in England between 1726 and 1867, on the grounds that these were connected not to martial law or to the jurisprudence of emergency but to questions of religious tolerance. See K. R. M. Short, "The English Indemnity Acts, 1762–1867," *Church History* 42, no. 3 (1973): 366–73.

106. Indeed, the peculiar verb form at the root of Dicey's most concise (and most repeated) formulation of the "action" of an indemnity act is absent from the Scottish or Irish indemnity acts of the eighteenth century (which confined themselves to negations of the negative, speaking only of preventing vexatious suits or rendering prosecutions null and void). Nowhere in these debates is the word *legalize* used to describe the legal effect of indemnity. There is a construction of this sort *only* in the indemnity act written by Governor Eyre (which concludes by stating that his acts "are hereby made and declared to be lawful, and are confirmed") and in the interpretation of that act by Justice Cockburn in his judgment in *Phillips v. Eyre* (1869), which characterized Eyre's crime as "an act originally wrongful, but legalized by an *ex post facto* law" and which Dicey cites at length (see Phillips v. Eyre, 1869 LR 4 QB 225, at 237, 241). The inner necessity for this theoretical choice is clear: it is better to have an indemnity act that (by Dicey's own ac-

count) is cruel, reckless, and inhumane but that unifies the empire than to have one that is invalid for its violation of the "common principles" of humanity but that places imperial unity in doubt. For a summary of the debates over the Scottish and Irish indemnity acts, see Lecky, *History of England*, 26–30.

107. Wade and Phillips, *Constitutional Law*, 10, 89.

108. Hart, *Concept of Law*, 111.

109. Wade and Phillips, *Constitutional Law*, 90.

110. See, in general, Section IV of the South Africa Act of 1909. See "The South Africa Act, 1909," *American Journal of International Law* 4, no. 1 (January 1910), 4–8.

111. On "opinion" as the sovereign power that is, in turn, the source of law, see Dicey, *Lectures on the Relation between Law and Public Opinion*, 10, 20, 26.

112. Dicey himself registered this state of affairs with vague regret, but certainly not with protest. In his final comprehensive introduction to *Law of the Constitution*, he concluded a discussion of the Boer War in South Africa by alluding to certain "events" that would make it difficult to grant equal citizenship to all imperial subjects (Dicey, *Introduction*, 8th ed., xxxvii).

113. Republic of South Africa, *Debates of the Senate*, June 15, 1961, cols. 5332–34.

114. Keith, *Responsible Government*, 270. For Dicey, by contrast, indemnity acts "almost invariably" supplement *Habeas Corpus* Suspension Acts. See Dicey, *Introduction*, 8th ed., 228.

115. Hahlo and Kahn, *Union of South Africa*, 146.

116. The KwaNdebele Indemnity Act of 1986, for example, indemnified "(a) the Government of KwaNdebele; or (b) any member of the Cabinet of KwaNdebele; or (c) any office or member of the KwaNdebele Police Force of seconded members to such a Force; or (d) any person employed in the public service of KwaNdebele; or (e) any person acting under the authority or by the direction or with the approval of any member, office or person mentioned in paragraph (b), (c), or (d)."

117. R. F. Alfred Hoernlé, *Race and Reason: Being Mainly a Selection of Contributions to the Race Problem in South Africa* (Johannesburg: Witwatersrand University Press, 1945), 77.

CHAPTER 3

1. Klug, *Constitution of South Africa*, 12.

2. Harold Wolpe, *Race, Class, and the Apartheid State* (London: James Currey, 1988), 66, 68. As Mandela would point out later, the general strike of 1961 carried far more significance than did the apartheid state's Republican conventions (Nelson Mandela, *The Struggle Is My Life* [London: Pathfinder, 1986], 119).

3. Wolpe, *Race, Class, and the Apartheid State*, 69.

4. "I think that to celebrate the inauguration of the republic and the turning over of a new page in the history of South Africa," argued Aaron Berman in 1961, "it would

have been both graceful and correct, and setting a new precedent, had the hon. the Minister not come with this Bill before the House. Mr. President, it would have tended to show the people of South Africa that this new era was not going to perpetuate the follies of the past, but that we were going to be broadminded, fair, and even generous to people whom we hurt. This Bill, Mr. President, should never have been placed before this House" (Republic of South Africa, *Debates of the Senate,* June 15, 1961, col. 5331).

5. Republic of South Africa, *Debates of the Senate,* June 15, 1961, col. 5328.

6. On the colonial status of the apartheid state, see Asmal, "International Law and the Liquidation of Apartheid," 21; Asmal, Asmal, and Roberts, *Reconciliation through Truth,* 182–83. On the "postcolonial" status of the United Nations, see Mazower, *No Enchanted Palace,* 199.

7. Dugard, *Human Rights and the South African Legal Order,* 110–11. See, more recently, Asmal, Asmal, and Roberts, *Reconciliation through Truth,* 55; Du Bois-Pedain, *Transitional Amnesty,* 29.

8. On Section 103*ter* in the Defence Act of 1957, see Mathews, *Freedom, State Security, and the Rule of Law,* 194; Kathleen Satchwell, "The Power to Defend: An Analysis of Various Aspects of the Defence Act," in *War and Society: The Militarisation of South Africa,* ed. Jacklyn Cock and Laurie Nathan (Cape Town: David Philip, 1989), 49–50. On its application in Namibia, see Tony Weaver, "The South African Defence Force in Namibia," in Cock and Nathan, *War and Society,* 94–95.

9. Hahlo and Kahn, *Union of South Africa,* 134.

10. There have been rare instances of indemnities being refused for having failed to satisfy certain criteria. For example, as opponents of the Natal Indemnity Act of 1906 pointed out in parliamentary debate, Royal Assent was refused in 1867 to the Indemnity Bill of 1866 in New Zealand, which was too widely drawn (see Keith, *Responsible Government in the Dominions,* 192). There is also the case of the Indemnity Bill of 1867 in Antigua, which was not retrospective but prospective and which the colonial secretary, Carnarvan, refused to recommend for Royal Assent on these grounds. See Finlason, *Commentaries upon Martial Law with Special Reference to Its Regulation and Restraint with an Introduction Containing Comments* (London: Stevens and Sons, 1867), 31–32. Finally, Keith reports Royal Assent being withheld from the Natal Indemnity Acts of 1906 and 1912 and from an indemnity act in Orange River as well (Keith, *Imperial Unity,* 149).

11. Hahlo and Kahn, *Union of South Africa,* 146.

12. For African populations, of course, this normalization of the exception had been in effect for a long time. As Z. K. Matthews wrote in 1934, citing Dicey, the authority to legislate by proclamation gave officers of Native Administration a discretionary power that was "consistent with the *droit administratif* of French law rather than with the rule of law which is so well established in England." See Z. K. Matthews, "Bantu Law and Western Civilization in South Africa: A Study in the Clash of Cultures," an essay presented to the Faculty of the Graduate School of Yale University in candidacy for the

degree of Master of Arts (May 1934), 33–34. See also, on this point, Kader Asmal, "International Law Aspects of the National Question in South Africa," in *The National Question in South Africa*, ed. Maria van Diepen (Atlantic Highlands, NJ: Zed Books, 1988), 127. We will return to the problem of the "normal emergency" at the end of section 8.3.

13. Krohn v. Minister of Defence, 1915 AD 191, at 197 (emphasis mine).

14. Mathews, *Freedom, State Security, and the Rule of Law*, 207n95. See also *Krohn*, 1915 AD 191, at 211.

15. See Colony of Natal, Indemnity Act 51 of 1906. On the controversy over this Act, see Keith, *Responsible Government in the Dominions*, 271–72; Chanock, *The Making of South African Legal Culture*, 134–35.

16. Max Weber, *The Protestant Ethic and the Spirit of Capitalism*, Trans. Talcott Parsons (New York: Routledge, 1992), 56–80.

17. On the amendments to the Defence Act, see Mathews, *Freedom, State Security, and the Rule of Law*, 199, 205; Kathleen Satchwell, "Indemnity Provided For in Emergency Regulations," in *Developments in Emergency Law*, ed. Nicholas Haysom and Clive Plasket (Johannesburg: Centre for Applied Legal Studies, 1989), 119; Asmal, Asmal, and Roberts, *Reconciliation through Truth*, 87; Du Bois-Pedain, *Transitional Amnesty*, 28–29; Kutz, *Amnestie*, 34–37.

18. Republic of South Africa, *Debates of the Senate*, June 15, 1961, cols. 5339–40, 5343. To the degree, however, that the precedents apply, opposition senators also noted, the National Party found itself contradicted by a historical irony: whereas the National Party had rejected the Indemnity Acts of 1914 and 1922 on the grounds that they unjustly absolved the South African Police of the massacre of Afrikaner workers, they were now using that same jurisprudence themselves. See Republic of South Africa, *Debates of the Senate*, June 15, 1961, cols. 5341, 5343, 5345.

19. "I think it is perfectly clear," argued Hyman Miller in 1961, "that all these Acts for which we have precedents in this country, and the Acts to which the hon. Minister referred [the 1920 Act], were passed in respect of incidents which took place either because of a war period or a set of circumstances which amounted to a protracted period of up-rising, terrorism and violence in this country." Republic of South Africa, *Debates of the House of Assembly*, June 7, 1961, col. 7543. See also Republic of South Africa, *Debates of the Senate*, June 15, 1961, cols. 5354–55. Of course, this argument worked the other way as well: whereas the South African Party had backed the Indemnity Acts of 1914 and 1922 when they were passed by the Smuts government, they were now hypocritically objecting to the same measures passed by the apartheid government.

20. Republic of South Africa, *Debates of the House of Assembly*, June 7, 1961, col. 7547.

21. In the Colony of Natal's Indemnity Act of 1874, we find an early example of the disjunction between indemnity and martial law that would become normalized under apartheid. See, on this point, United Kingdom, *Further Papers Relating to the Late Kafir*

Outbreak in Natal, Presented to Both Houses of Parliament by Command of Her Majesty (London: William Clowes and Sons, 1875), 2–4.

22. Republic of South Africa, *Debates of the House of Assembly*, June 7, 1961, col. 7547; cf. Republic of South Africa, *Debates of the Senate*, June 15, 1961, cols. 5326–27. National Party parliamentarian Dr. L. I. Coertze (Standerton) attempted to respond to these departures from precedent by raising the question of why there is martial law in the colonies but not in the metropole: "[I]n England itself they have never needed to declare martial law because they have practically never felt a war at home themselves.... Martial law was not declared because there was no need to do so and because there was never an emergency, even if there were strikes. That is the reason." Coertze went on to argue that there is no difference between a state of emergency and martial law, because both boil down to the question of self-defense or the law of necessity: "The fact of the matter is that it makes no difference whether or not there was martial law. The question is: Was there an emergency or not? If we had an emergency here in 1960, then the state was entitled to take emergency measures." In support of this claim, he quoted Judge Solomon's argument in the case of *Regina v. Bekker and Naude* (1900) that "at times of public danger," the maxim *salus respublicae suprema lex* justifies the state "to protect the republic against every action which threatens its security, its peace and its order and we are obliged to use all the means at our disposal in order to maintain that law and order." See Republic of South Africa, *Debates of the House of Assembly*, June 7, 1961, cols. 7550–52.

23. In *Rossouw v. Sachs*, the court would recognize that neither war nor state of emergency existed in South Africa at the time, but the court would nevertheless cite Cicero as grounds to justify the government's decision, on grounds of necessity, to deny Albie Sachs reading materials during his indefinite detention. See Rossouw v. Sachs, 1964 (2) SA 551 (A), at 563.

24. Republic of South Africa, *Debates of the House of Assembly*, January 31, 1977, col. 492.

25. Republic of South Africa, *Debates of the House of Assembly*, January 31, 1977, col. 500. The argument to novelty, of course, is itself a long-standing feature of the jurisprudence of emergency. In 1914, Jan Smuts would make much the same claim, proposing that the unprecedented scope of that year's indemnity act was necessitated by a threat (in this case syndicalism) that was entirely unanticipated by Roman-Dutch law. On this point, see Chanock, *The Making of South African Legal Culture*, 137–38.

26. Raymond Ruiter, "Maintenance of the Security of the State," 357.

27. Ruiter, "Maintenance of the Security of the State," 357.

28. Ruiter, "Maintenance of the Security of the State," 357.

29. Ruiter, "Maintenance of the Security of the State," 357–58.

30. Republic of South Africa, *Debates of the House of Assembly*, June 7, 1961, col. 7548.

31. In his sustained objection to the bill, John Cope argued, "[T]he state should be protected only from claims that were necessary, unavoidable and responsible in order to

preserve law and order. Those should be the three operative terms—'necessary, unavoidable, and responsible' acts. If they were so, then possibly there should be an Indemnity Bill, not simply when, as the Minister [of Justice] said, the acts were committed 'in good faith.' I hope the hon. Minister will withdraw those words. That is not good enough. The principle should be that the acts for which the Indemnity Bill is to be introduced were 'necessary, unavoidable and responsible" (Republic of South Africa, *Debates of the House of Assembly*, June 9, 1961, col. 7662).

32. Stanton v. Minister of Justice and Others, 1960 (3) SA 353, at 358.

33. Stanton, 1960 (3) SA 353, at 355.

34. Mawo v. Pepler, 1960 (4) SA 291.

35. Republic of South Africa, *Debates of the House of Assembly*, June 9, 1961, cols. 7661–63.

36. Republic of South Africa, *Debates of the House of Assembly*, June 9, 1961, col. 7681.

37. Republic of South Africa, *Debates of the House of Assembly*, January 31, 1977, col. 497. See, for example, Mr. Burrowes's objections to the clause of a 1799 indemnity bill that required juries who found for plaintiffs against defendants to show that the defendant had acted from malice (Howell, *State Trials*, cols. 791–93). In 1988, Basson and Viljoen would confirm this view, arguing that any "violating measures" undertaken by the state on the basis of the maxim *salus publica suprema lex* should be subject to judicial control and that it is "undesirable to restrict the court's control to *mala fide* violations only," which should, to the contrary, extend to "unlawful actions committed negligently." See Deon Basson and Hendrik Viljoen, *South African Constitutional Law* (Cape Town: Juta, 1988), 281n255.

38. Republic of South Africa, *Debates of the House of Assembly*, February 1, 1977, col. 564.

39. Hussain, *Jurisprudence of Emergency*, 108–17.

40. See, on this point, Republic of South Africa, *Debates of the House of Assembly*, June 7, 1961, cols. 7662–63.

41. Howell, *State Trials*, col. 799; Republic of South Africa, *Debates of the House of Assembly*, June 12, 1961, col. 7753. See also Mathews, *Freedom, State Security, and the Rule of Law*, 206. See also Satchwell, "Indemnity Provided For in Emergency Regulations," 119–20.

42. Mathews, *Freedom, State Security, and the Rule of Law*, 205.

43. Mathews, *Freedom, State Security, and the Rule of Law*, 206.

44. Mathews, *Freedom, State Security, and the Rule of Law*, 265.

45. Satchwell, "Indemnity Provided For in Emergency Regulations," 120–23.

46. Damane v. Minister of Police, 1979 (4) SA 400 (C).

47. Makhasa v. Minister of Law and Order, Lebowa Government, 1988 (3) SA 701 (A).

48. Matinkinca and Another v. Council of State, Republic of Ciskei, and Another, 1994 (4) SA 472 (Ck).

49. Abel, *Politics by Other Means*, 256–57.

50. As Mathews and Albino would put it in their 1966 criticism of *Rossouw v. Sachs* (1964), "One of the central weaknessnes of [this judgment] is that it fails to define with necessary legal precision the nature of an emergency which will disregard the rights of individuals. Unless 'emergency' is confined to open and widespread disorder and lawlessness, or to conditions of war, it is a term of no real meaning. Parliament has the power to enact a peace-time and permanent emergency; the courts need not do this for Parliament. If the Court had given effect to its own words 'in times of extreme emergency, such as war,' then the conclusion in *Rossouw v. Sachs* must have been different. Instead, the Court appears to have authorized the neglect of individual rights for as long as one can foresee" (A. S. Mathews and R. C. Albino, "The Permanence of the Temporary: An Examination of the 90- and 180-Day Detention Laws," *South African Law Journal* 16 [1996], 42). See also Dugard, *Human Rights and the South African Legal Order*, 112–23, esp. 121–22.

51. As Glen Moss wrote in 1986, after visiting and speaking with the residents of Fort Beaufort after Botha's declaration of the second state of emergency, "According to township residents interviewed, the pattern of abuses, beatings and shootings carried on as before, except that police now believed they were indemnified by emergency regulations." See Glen Moss, "Fort Beaufort under Emergency Rule," *Work in Progress* 40 (1986): 19.

52. By the *TRC Report*'s own account, the "culture of impunity" in apartheid South Africa originated in the Indemnity Act of 1961, which, according to the report, "began the process of placing the police above and beyond public scrutiny" (*TRC Report*, vol. 2, chap. 1, ¶42). A "convention" is, for Dicey, nothing other than a long-standing custom, a sedimented and inexplicit norm, a set of unspoken rules, or, in short, a "culture." In this respect, the notion of the "culture of impunity" is an excellent, if oblivious, translation of Dicey's concept of the "indemnification convention": the latter, exactly like the "culture of impunity" criticized by the TRC, designates a juridical situation in which state officials may act illegally, secure in the knowledge that if they honestly believe their illegal actions are necessary for the safety of the state, they will not be held liable for their actions under criminal or civil law. See Graeme Simpson, "A 'Culture of Impunity,'" *Star* (Johannesburg, South Africa), January 24, 1997.

53. See "Democracy and Constitutionalism: The Role of Constitutional Interpretation," in *Rights and Constitutionalism: The New South African Legal Order*, ed. Dawid van Wyk, John Dugard, Bertus de Villiers, and Dennis Davis (Oxford: Clarendon, 1995), 1.

54. Hobbes, *De Cive*, 158.

55. Michel Foucault, *Birth of Biopolitics: Lectures at the Collège de France, 1978–79*, ed. Michel Senellart, trans. Graham Burchell, (New York: Palgrave, 2008), 226ff.

56. Wolpe, *Race, Class, and the Apartheid State*, 49.

57. Republic of South Africa, *Debates of the House of Assembly*, February 1, 1977, col. 526.

58. Dugard, *Human Rights and the South African Legal Order*, 122.

59. Satchwell, "Indemnity Provided For in Emergency Regulations," 122–23.

60. On 1960 as a threshold in the criticism of apartheid in international law, see Asmal, "International Law and the Liquidation of Apartheid," 10, 22.

61. I set aside the question of whether the apartheid parliamentarians were indeed correct in their self-understanding of the unprecedented character of this juridical coupling or whether it is simply a reinvention, now under the rubric of indemnity jurisprudence, of the old practice of *lowbote*, or compensating those injured in a tumult. *Ex gratia* payments do not, of course, originate in 1961; they derive from long-standing practice within insurance law, where they designate payments that are not legally necessary but are made by insurance companies anyway for reasons of hardship, sympathy, or fair play.

62. Republic of South Africa, *Debates of the House of Assembly*, February 3, 1977, col. 682.

63. Republic of South Africa, *Debates of the House of Assembly*, June 9, 1961, col. 7666.

64. Republic of South Africa, *Debates of the House of Assembly*, January 31, 1977, col. 487; Republic of South Africa, *Debates of the House of Assembly*, February 1, 1977, col. 529.

65. Republic of South Africa, *Debates of the House of Assembly*, February 1, 1977, cols. 589–90.

66. Republic of South Africa, *Debates of the House of Assembly*, February 1, 1977, col. 541.

67. Republic of South Africa, *Debates of the House of Assembly*, February 1, 1977, cols. 510–11.

68. See, for example, Republic of South Africa, *Debates of the Senate*, June 15, 1961, cols. 5364–65, 5370; Republic of South Africa, *Debates of the House of Assembly*, June 9, 1961, col. 7542.

69. Republic of South Africa, *Debates of the Senate*, June 15, 1961, col. 5318.

70. Republic of South Africa, *Debates of the Senate*, June 15, 1961, col. 5333.

71. Republic of South Africa, *Debates of the House of Assembly*, June 9, 1961, col. 7666.

72. Republic of South Africa, *Debates of the House of Assembly*, February 1, 1977, col. 555.

73. Republic of South Africa, *Debates of the House of Assembly*, June 9, 1961, col. 7672–73; Republic of South Africa, *Debates of the Senate*, June 15, 1961, cols. 5333, 5362–63.

74. Republic of South Africa, *Debates of the House of Assembly*, January 31, 1977, col. 487; Republic of South Africa, *Debates of the House of Assembly*, February 1, 1977, cols. 529, 589–90.

75. Republic of Rhodesia, *Debates of the Senate*, September 18, 1975, col. 840.

76. Republic of South Africa, *Debates of the House of Assembly*, February 1, 1977, col. 524.

77. In their 1961 decision in the Adolf Eichmann trial, Judges Moshe Landau, Benjamin Halevi, and Yitzchak Raveh would cite Dicey to argue that "there is no justification to absolve the Accused from responsibility for the crimes he committed, although they were committed at the command of one of the state authorities. The personal responsibility of a government official for his acts is the basis of the rule of law, which we have adopted at the inspiration of the Common Law. It is thus explained by Dicey, *Law of the Constitution*." See *The Trial of Adolf Eichmann: Record of Proceedings in the District Court of Jerusalem*, vol. 5 (Jerusalem: Trust for the Publication of the Proceedings of the Eichmann Trial, in cooperation with the Israel State Archives and Yad Vashem, the Holocaust Martyrs' and Heroes' Remembrance Authority, 1992), 2195–96.

78. Mathews, *Freedom, State Security, and the Rule of Law*, 15ff. See also Schreiner, *Contribution of English Law*, 45. But cf. Sachs, *Justice in South Africa*, 239.

79. Mahmood Mamdani, *Citizen and Subject: Contemporary Africa and the Legacy of Late Colonialism* (Princeton: Princeton University Press, 1996), 16–18.

80. See, for example, Mamdani, *Citizen and Subject*, 24.

81. See Cape of Good Hope, *Report of a Commission Appointed by His Excellency the Governor to Inquire into and Report upon the Question of Colonial Defence*, Presented to Both Houses of Parliament by Command of His Excellency the Governor (Grahamstown, South Africa: Richards, Slater, 1877), 14.

82. Ashis Nandy, *The Intimate Enemy: Loss and Recovery of Self under Colonialism* (Delhi: Oxford University Press, 1983), 16. A single example will suffice here. In the late nineteenth century, during a period of war and colonial conquest (marked by, among other things, the Xhosa War of 1877–78, the Anglo-Zulu War of 1879, and the Transkeian Rebellion of 1880), two overlapping Commissions of Inquiry were created in the Eastern Cape. The first was formed in 1877 to study the question of "colonial defence" in the Eastern Cape. The question put to the commission was whether the existing police forces in the Eastern Cape would be able to resist an onslaught consisting of "a combination of the native tribes." The commission answered this question decisively in the negative: the colony's "puny" police force, they argued, "would go down before the first onset of the Kafir hordes, and the wave of barbarism would roll unchecked over the whole Eastern Districts." Against this danger, the commission not only called for the creation of a national defense force but also recommended improvements in the administration of native affairs, particularly in the area of land and law: "In the interests of peace the Commission recommends that the native locations within the Colony proper should be surveyed and titles given to deserving persons, so that people may feel that they have a personal interest in the land; that it does not belong to their chief, but is their own, dependent upon their good behaviour, and to be forfeited in case of rebellion. In the administration of native affairs, the great aim should be to break down the power of the chiefs; and few things in this direction are likely to be more effective than conferring upon the people a right in the land. Such a measure would be popular amongst the people themselves and would lead them to respect and confide in the Gov-

ernment." The commission went on to recommend "the compilation of Kafir Law for the guidance of magistrates places amongst the natives" (Cape of Good Hope, *Report of a Commission Appointed by His Excellency*, 18.). For this commission, improvements in the administration of native land and law derived their sense and importance from the military strategy in which they were but one among many tactics. In the nearly concurrent Commission of Inquiry on Native Laws and Customs (1881–83), meanwhile, an almost identical set of concerns emerged (pertaining, e.g., to land tenure and the power of chiefs), only within the more familiarly colonialist rubric of codifying and modifying hitherto "unwritten" African customary law into a less "barbaric" form (see Cape of Good Hope, *Reports and Proceedings, with Appendices, of the Government Commission on Native Laws and Customs*, Presented to Both Houses of Parliament by Command of His Excellency the Governor [Grahamstown, South Africa: Richards, Slater, 1883], 18). This thematic overlap and simultaneity between, on the one hand, the *military* project of colonial defense and, on the other hand, the *civilizing* project of native uplift is, needless to say, deeply symptomatic. It reveals that one and the same "Kafir" population was simultaneously the object of two governmentalities that were at once *incommensurable with one another* (because populations who were massacred by military means are no longer available to be "civilized" by means of colonial trusteeship) and *inseparable from one another* (not only because colonial trusteeship was itself a technique of destruction, albeit one aimed at customs rather than lives; but also because trusteeship was not able to implement its paternalistic project—to force "personal interest in the land" upon colonized populations as a means to the end of "breaking down the power of the chiefs"— without the constant potential for interventions by militaristic forces whose necessity it was obliged to disavow).

83. On this point, see the much later *Report of the Royal Commission on Police Powers and Procedure (1928–9)*, vol. 2, Presented to Both Houses of Parliament by Command of His Majesty (London: H. M. Stationery Office, 1929), 4.

84. Dicey, *Introduction*, 8th ed., 291–93.

85. See, on this point, Jeremy Bentham, *An Introduction to the Principles of Morals and Legislation* (New York: Hafner Publishing Co., 1948), 214–16. Cf. Finlason, *Review of the Authorities*, 176, 183–84. This distinction was supposed to hold even, especially, under conditions of martial law. See, on this point, A. W. Brian Simpson, *Human Rights and the End of Empire: Britain and the Genesis of the European Convention* (Oxford: Oxford University, 2001), 59–60.

86. Bentham is perfectly clear on the *quantitative* foundation for the otherwise *qualitative* distinction between crime and war: "Give force enough to robbery, and it swells into rebellion: give permanence enough to rebellion, and it settles into hostility" (*Introduction to the Principles of Morals and Legislation*, 217n 2). See also, for example, Jamaica Committee, *Facts and Documents Relating to the Alleged Rebellion in Jamaica, and the Measures of Repression; Including Notes on the Trial of Mr. Gordon* (London: Jamaica Committee, 1866), 74.

87. Bentham, *Introduction to the Principles of Morals and Legislation*, 217n2.

88. Understandably, therefore, the riot—understood as an incipient rebellion—would became the object of considerable juridical anxiety and concern in the late nineteenth century (when, time and again and particularly in Ireland, police forces alone were found insufficient for the purposes of quelling riots and, as undesirable as it may be, military forces were found to be necessary). See, for example, United Kingdom, *Report of the Commissioners of Inquiry into the Origin and Character of the Riots in Belfast in July and September, 1857*, Presented to Both Houses of Parliament by Command of Her Majesty (Dublin: Alex. Thom and Son, 1858), 5; United Kingdom, *Report of the Commissioners of Inquiry, 1869, into the Riots and Disturbances in the City of Londonderry*, Presented to Both Houses of Parliament by Command of Her Majesty (Dublin: Alexander Thom, 1869), 7; United Kingdom, *Report of the Committee Appointed to Inquire into the Circumstances Connected with the Disturbances at Featherstone on the 7th of September 1893*, Presented to Both Houses of Parliament by Command of Her Majesty (London: Eyre and Spottiswoode, 1893), 12.

89. This is true not only in English colonies. On the systematic confusion of police and military forces in French colonial administration, see Thomas Rid, "The Nineteenth Century Origins of Counterinsurgency Doctrine," *Journal of Strategic Studies* 33, no. 5 (2010): 727–58.

90. Finlason, *Review of the Authorities*, 121–22, 129; cf. Hussain, *Jurisprudence of Emergency*, 112–14; Kostal, *Jurisprudence of Power*, 228–45 (cf. 469–70, 481–82). In England, by contrast, martial law was usually limited to times of actual rebellion. It is declared at the moment civil authorities cannot repress a riot or rebellion in the absence of warlike measures, and it is lifted at the moment order is restored or actual conflict comes to an end. See Finlason, *Review of the Authorities*, 88–89, 49.

91. Kostal, *Jurisprudence of Power*, 434.

92. See John Brewer, *Black and Blue: Policing in South Africa* (Oxford: Oxford University Press, 1994), 17; M. E. Brogden, "The Origins of the South African Police—Institutional versus Structural Approaches," *Acta Juridica* 1 (1989): 2. See also Sachs, *Justice in South Africa*, 91; Chanock, "Writing South African Legal History," 278; Chanock, *Making of South African Legal Culture*, 45. This remains a problem in postapartheid South Africa. See Brewer, *Black and Blue*, 332–52; Pierre Olivier, "Our Policing Heritage: The Major Problems," in *Policing the Conflict in South Africa*, ed. M. L. Matthews, P. B. Heymann, and A. S. Matthews (Gainesville: University Press of Florida, 1993), 26; Jean and John Comaroff, "Criminal Obsessions, after Foucault: Postcoloniality, Policing, and the Metaphysics of Disorder," *Critical Inquiry* 30, no. 4 (Summer 2004), 800–824 (on the irony of calls for "more police" in postapartheid, post-totalitarian South Africa).

93. See, on this point, Union of South Africa, *Report of the Select Committee on the Union Defence Forces Bill*, Printed by Order of the House of Assembly, May 1921 (Cape Town: Cape Times, 1921), 4. See also Sachs, *Justice in South Africa*, 239; Chanock, *Making of South African Legal Culture*, 46; Annette Seegers, *The Military in the Making of*

Modern South Africa (New York: Tauris Academic Studies, 1996), 24. The tendency of the Natal Police Force to "govern through killing," in turn, must be understood with reference to the brutal suppression of the Bambatha Rebellion in 1906. On this, see Sean Redding, *Sorcery and Sovereignty: Taxation, Power, and Rebellion in South Africa, 1880–1963* (Athens, OH: Ohio University Press, 2006), 89–121.

94. Chanock, *Making of South African Legal Culture*, 514. See also Seegers, *Military in the Making of Modern South Africa*, 23.

95. Marian Lacey, "*Platskiet-politiek*: The Role of the Union Defence Force 1910–1924," in Cock and Nathan, *War and Society*, 28–39; Laurie Nathan, "Troops in the Townships, 1984–1987," in Cock and Nathan, *War and Society*, 67–78; Seegers, *Military in the Making of Modern South Africa*, 24–25.

96. D. D. T. Jabavu, "Bantu Grievances," in *Western Civilization and the Natives of South Africa: Studies in Culture Contact*, ed. Isaac Schapera (New York: Humanities Press, 1934), 297.

97. R. F. Alfred Hoernlé, *South African Native Policy and the Liberal Spirit* (Johannesburg: Witswatersrand University Press, 1945), 5.

98. Nkosi, *The Transplanted Heart*, 13, 17 (arguing that the apartheid state is "totalitarian" and that "[f]or the white minority in South Africa, the enemy is both external and internal").

99. Tutu, *No Future without Forgiveness*, 192. Cf. *TRC Report*, vol. 1, chap. 5, ¶104.

100. *TRC Report*, vol. 5, chap. 6, ¶¶85–86.

101. Perhaps already with the launch of *Umkhonto we Sizwe* (MK) in the early 1960s (a moment when, as Albie Sachs has put it, South Africa experienced the return of the colonial "frontier wars" of the nineteenth century) and certainly after the fall of Angola, Mozambique, and Rhodesia in the 1970s, everyday life in South African white supremacy proceeded with the force, planning, organization, paranoia, and intensity of a military occupation. See Sachs, *Justice in South Africa*, 229; Richard Leonard, *South Africa at War: White Power and the Crisis in Southern Africa* (Westport, CT: Lawrence, Hill, 1983), 98–130, 161–97; Philip Frankel, *Pretoria's Praetorians: Civil-Military Relations in South Africa* (Cambridge: Cambridge University Press, 1984), 29–70; Gavin Cawthra, *Brutal Force: The Apartheid War Machine* (London: International Defence and Aid Fund for Southern Africa, 1986), 42–110; Kenneth Grundy, *The Militarization of South African Politics* (Bloomington: Indiana University Press, 1986), esp. 58–87.

102. Achille Mbembe, "Necropolitics," trans. Libby Meintjes, *Public Culture* 15, no. 1 (Winter 2003): 24.

103. Republic of South Africa, *South Africa and the Rule of Law*, 45–46, 54 (arguing that the unprecedented reach of the Terrorism Act of 1967 responds to the commission of an unprecedented type of crime, the equivalent on land of piracy on the seas, which began with the commencement of guerrilla warfare within South Africa itself).

104. Thomas Hobbes, *Leviathan*, ed. Richard Tuck (Cambridge: Cambridge University Press, 1996), 88–89.

CHAPTER 4

1. Kader Asmal, "Victims, Survivors, and Citizens—Human Rights, Reparations, and Reconciliation" (inaugural lecture presented at Kader Asmal's installation as professor of human rights law, University of the Western Cape, Cape Town, May 25, 1992), 13.

2. Zalaquett, "Commissions of Truth and Reconciliation," in Boraine and Levy, *Healing of a Nation?*, 47–48.

3. *TRC Report*, vol. 5, chap. 6, ¶101.

4. See, for example, Republic of South Africa, *Debates of the House of Assembly*, January 31, 1977, cols. 504, 512.

5. Lodge, *Politics in South Africa*, 176.

6. Sigmund Freud, "'Wild' Psycho-Analysis," vol. 11 of the *Standard Edition of the Complete Psychological Works of Sigmund Freud*, ed. and trans. James Strachey (London: Hogarth, 1961): 219–28.

7. See *TRC Report*, vol. 5, chap. 6, ¶101; chap. 8, ¶72. This, of course, is consistent with Section 34(5) of South Africa's Interim Constitution, which "prohibits the creation of retrospective crimes as well as the indemnification of state organs or persons acting under state authority for unlawful actions undertaken during a state of emergency" (Deon Basson, *South Africa's Interim Constitution: Text and Notes* [Cape Town: Juta, 1994], 55).

8. As Jeremy Sarkin writes, "Most amnesty decisions really deal with two criteria only—that of 'full disclosure' and 'political objective.' With a few exceptions, all the other factors to be considered within the determination of these two broad criteria are hardly ever dealt with, or mentioned. In the decisions both criteria are usually either found, or determined not to be present. There is little analysis of the criteria and almost no application of the criteria to the facts. In fact, many of the decisions were short and often sketchy" (*Carrots and Sticks*, 247).

9. Republic of South Africa. Promotion of National Unity and Reconciliation Act of 1995.

10. Elizabeth Stewart, "The Proportionality Principle in Post-Apartheid South Africa," *Temple Political and Civil Rights Law Review* 113, no. 8 (Fall 1998): 124.

11. Stewart, "Proportionality Principle," 129–35.

12. See, on this point, Sections 20(1)(b) and 20(1)(c) of Act 34 of 1995 (Promotion of National Unity and Reconciliation Act). See also Marthinus Dawid Ras v. The Chairman of the Amnesty Committee of the Truth and Reconciliation Commission, Case No. 7285/00 (Cape of Good Hope Provincial Division).

13. "Report of the Working Group Established under Paragraph 1 of the Groote Schuur Minute," *South African Journal on Human Rights* 6, no. 3 (1990): 320. The working group also proposed that an adaptation of the Norgaard Principles be used in making the relevant decisions. These took into account aspects such as motive, context, the

nature of the political objective, the legal and factual nature of the offense (e.g., rape could never be considered a political offense), the object of the offense, and whether the act was committed in the execution of an order and with the approval of the organization concerned (*TRC Report*, vol. 1, chap. 4, ¶11).

14. Herman Ntchatcho, "Political Amnesty and Repatriation of Refugees in Nambia," *African Yearbook of International Law/Annuaire Africain de Droit International*, vol. 1, ed. Abdulqawi Yusuf (London: Martinus Nijhoff, 1993), 68.

15. Raylene Keightley, "Political Offences and Indemnity in South Africa," *South African Journal on Human Rights* 9, no. 3 (1993): 344.

16. For a review of this jurisprudence, see John Dugard, *International Law: A South African Perspective* (Cape Town: Juta, 1994), 135–40.

17. Keightley, "Political Offences," 345.

18. Cape of Good Hope, *Debates of the House of Assembly, in the Third Session of the Tenth Parliament of the Cape of Good Hope, 20th July to 13th October, 1900* (Cape Town: Cape Times, 1900), cols. 83–84.

19. Cape of Good Hope, *Debates of the House of Assembly, in the Third Session of the Tenth Parliament*, cols. 80–81.

20. Cape of Good Hope, *Debates of the House of Assembly, in the Third Session of the Tenth Parliament*, col. 80.

21. Walter Benjamin, "Critique of Violence," in *Reflections*, ed. Peter Demetz, trans. Edmund Jephcott (New York: Harcourt Brace Jovanovich, 1979), 283–84.

22. Anghie, *Imperialism, Sovereignty, and the Making of International Law*, 107–14.

23. Rid, "Nineteenth Century Origins of Counterinsurgency Doctrine," 754.

24. As Antje du Bois-Pedain has observed, the requirement of political offense in the PNR Act is "an amalgamation of many earlier provisions" (*Transitional Amnesty*, 29).

25. See Section 6.3 of the "Report of the Working Group Established under Paragraph 1 of the Groote Schuur Minute" (320).

26. Sarkin, *Carrots and Sticks*, 308.

27. Anurima Bhargava, "Defining Political Crimes: A Case Study of the South African Truth and Reconciliation Commission," *Columbia Law Review* 102, no. 5 (2002): 1329.

28. Du Bois-Pedain, *Transitional Amnesty*, 27–28.

29. Du Bois-Pedain, *Transitional Amnesty*, 29.

30. As Du Bois-Pedain puts it, "The Committee's preparedness to accept every strategy adopted by a political organization or institution during the conflict as political irrespective of the repulsiveness of that strategy in moral terms is the dominant feature of the Committee's decision practice" (*Transitional Amnesty*, 136).

31. Sarkin, *Carrots and Sticks*, 311 (see also 309–10). See, on the same point, Bhargava, "Defining Political Crimes," 1333.

32. Du Bois-Pedain, *Transitional Amnesty*, 133, 137.

33. Du Bois-Pedain, *Transitional Amnesty*, 140.

34. Du Bois-Pedain, *Transitional Amnesty*, 24.

35. Howell, *State Trials*, col. 799.

36. Republic of South Africa, *Debates of the House of Assembly*, June 12, 1961, col. 7753.

37. Mathews, *Freedom, State Security, and the Rule of Law*, 206.

38. Du Plessis, "Amnesty and Transition in South Africa," 111.

39. Stewart, "The Proportionality Principle," 117.

40. See, for example, Sarkin, *Carrots and Sticks*, 248, 292–93, 302, 334. In the earliest draft of the PNR Act, the question of the difference between "personal motives" and "political motives" in applications for "indemnity or amnesty" was already clarified with special emphasis on the language and principles of the bona fide test in indemnity jurisprudence: "The act claimed must not only have a political motive and object, but it must be capable of realizing that object, in the sense that, the means and the objectives must be in such a relationship that the idealistic motives connected with the objectives are strong enough. For instance, murder should not be indemnified unless it was the only means available of attaining the objective. In this regard one must also take into account the degree of political involvement of the applicant in the movement on behalf of which he acted, his personal commitment to and belief in the cause (on behalf of which he acted), and his personal conviction that the offence was justified or necessitated by the objectives and purposes of the ideological or political cause" (Truth Commission Panel, "Working Document, Draft Legislative Framework for Proposed Bill to Set Up a Truth and Reconciliation Commission," July 1994 [on file with author], 23).

41. Raylene Keightley argues that although the factor of personal motivation is recognized in the Norgaard Principles "as being a prerequisite for the classification of any offence as political, it is clear from the remaining five factors that a purely subjective approach [to the question of what constitutes a political crime] was not intended" ("Political Offences," 345).

42. Sarkin, *Carrots and Sticks*, 235.

43. Hart, *Concept of Law*, 92–94.

44. Du Bois-Pedain, *Transitional Amnesty*, 139.

45. Du Bois-Pedain, *Transitional Amnesty*, 139.

46. Sarkin, *Carrots and Sticks*, 250.

47. Sarkin, *Carrots and Sticks*, 274.

48. Du Bois-Pedain, *Transitional Amnesty*, 160. Gillian Slovo concurs: "Reading through some of the amnesty transcripts, it is difficult to avoid the conclusion that such was the pressure on the judges, and such their composition, that although they paid lip service to the full disclosure element of applications, some of them also began to feel that by applying for amnesty, and by admitting their general complicity, applicants had already shown enough good faith in the process to have earned themselves their prize. But all of this was, of course, inherent in the original compromise" ("Making History: South Africa's Truth and Reconciliation Commission," *openDemocracy*, December

5, 2002, accessed August 28, 2009, http://www.opendemocracy.net/democracy-africa_democracy/article_818.jsp).

49. Cape of Good Hope, *Debates of the House of Assembly, in the Third Session of the Tenth Parliament*, col. 84.

50. See, for example, Union of South Africa, *Debates of the Senate*, March 11, 1914, col. 102.

51. Du Bois-Pedain, *Transitional Amnesty*, 147.

52. Du Bois-Pedain, *Transitional Amnesty*, 149–50.

53. Du Bois-Pedain, *Transitional Amnesty*, 144.

54. Peter Parker and Joyce Mokhesi-Parker, *In the Shadow of Sharpeville: Apartheid and Criminal Justice* (New York: New York University Press, 1998), 78–79.

55. Joel Joffe, *The State vs. Nelson Mandela: The Trial That Changed South Africa* (Oxford: Oneworld, 2007), 30, 40, 106, 135, 137–38, 193, 200, 254. Bizos was part of the defense team in this trial.

56. Republic of South Africa, Criminal Procedure Act of 1977, Section 204(a)(iv).

57. Du Bois-Pedain, *Transitional Amnesty*, 145.

58. Republic of South Africa, Criminal Procedure Act of 1977, Section 204(a)(iii).

59. Parker and Mokhesi-Parker, *In the Shadow of Sharpeville*, 76.

60. Du Bois-Pedain, *Transitional Amnesty*, 146–7.

61. Republic of South Africa, "Amnesty Bill No. . . . of 1994" (on file with author), 1.

62. Warren Buford and Hugo van der Merwe, "Les réparations en Afrique australe," *Cahiers d'Études Africains* 44, nos. 173–74 (2004): 272; Tshepo Madlingozi, "Good Victim, Bad Victim: Apartheid's Beneficiaries, Victims, and the Struggle for Social Justice," in *Law, Memory, and the Legacy of Apartheid: Ten Years After AZAPO v President of South Africa*, ed. Wessel le Roux and Karin van Marle (Pretoria: Pretoria University Law Press, 2007), 122; Nthabiseng Mogale, "Ten Years of Democracy in South Africa: Revisiting the *AZAPO* decision," in le Roux and van Marle, *Law, Memory, and the Legacy of Apartheid*, 134.

63. For the TRC, reparation is "any form of compensation, *ex gratia* payment, restitution, rehabilitation or recognition" (Promotion of National Unity and Reconciliation Act of 1995, Section 1[1][xiv]).

64. *TRC Report*, vol. 5, chap. 5, ¶3.

65. This was a more general theme in apartheid jurisprudence. See Republic of South Africa, *South Africa and the Rule of Law*, 19 (arguing that "Bantu" who elect to use "Bantu courts" rather than "ordinary courts" have the advantage of "less expensive litigation").

66. See, for example, Republic of South Africa, *Debates of the Senate*, June 15, 1961, cols. 5318–19. For discussion of the fiscal necessity to use indemnity acts to prevent civil and criminal litigation, addressed in a speech by H. Miller, minister of justice, and a response by S. A. Pitman, see Republic of South Africa, *Debates of the House of Assembly*, January 31, 1977, cols. 479, 511–12; February 1, 1977, col. 547.

67. Republic of South Africa, *Debates of the House of Assembly*, February 1, 1977, cols. 511–12.

68. AZAPO et al. v. President of the Republic of South Africa et al., 1996 (8) BCLR 1037–38 (¶¶44–46) (CC). Or, as Claire Moon has put it, "amnesty, in effect, was cheap" (Moon, *Narrating Political Reconciliation: South Africa's Truth and Reconciliation Commission* [Lanham, MD: Lexington Books, 2008], 121).

69. Buford and van der Merwe, "Les réparations en Afrique australe," 276. The apartheid state left the postapartheid state with a triply debilitating inheritance. Not only did the postapartheid state—obscenely—face the prospect of liability for crimes committed against South African citizens on behalf of the apartheid state, but it also faced, and continues to face, the daunting task of reconstructing the social and political wasteland that the apartheid state left in its wake, all while inheriting the very debt that the apartheid state racked up from its military spending of the 1980s (spending, to be clear, that was aimed at eliminating the very existence of the same political organizations that now govern South Africa).

70. Elizabeth Stanley, "Evaluating the Truth and Reconciliation Commission," *Journal of Modern African Studies* 39, no. 3 (September 2001): 538; Buford and van der Merwe, "Les réparations en Afrique australe," 275.

71. Wilson, *Politics of Truth and Reconciliation in South Africa*, 23; Buford and van der Merwe, "Les réparations en Afrique australe," 268–69, 280; Madlingozi, "Good Victim, Bad Victim," 109.

72. Tutu, *No Future without Forgiveness*, 57–60, 221.

73. *TRC Report*, vol. 6, sec. 2, chap. 5, ¶¶8–14 (on the "Business Trust").

74. Madlingozi, "Good Victim, Bad Victim," 111–13. See also Tshepo Madlingozi, "On Transitional Justice Entrepreneurs and the Production of Victims," *Journal of Human Rights Practice* 2, no. 2 (2010), 220–21.

75. Tshepo Madlingozi, "Post-Apartheid Social Movements and the Quest for the Elusive 'New' South Africa," *Journal of Law and Society* 34, no. 1 (March 2007): 77–98; Patrick Bond, "'Can Reparations for Apartheid Profits Be Won in U.S. Courts?," *Africa Insight* 38, no. 2 (2008): 13–25.

76. Bond, "Can Reparations for Apartheid Profits Be Won in U.S. Courts?," 19.

77. Bond, "Can Reparations for Apartheid Profits Be Won in U.S. Courts?," 19.

78. Quoted in Bond, "Can Reparations for Apartheid Profits Be Won in U.S. Courts?," 17.

79. When Dicey explains the necessity and justice of an indemnity act, he argues, "The Parliament which destroys one of the main guarantees for individual freedom must hold, whether wisely or not, that a crisis has arisen when the rights of individuals must be postponed to considerations of state" (Dicey, *Introduction*, 8th ed., 230). This is the same argument that the Rhodesian Parliament would make to pass the Indemnity Act of 1975, which conferred on the president the power to halt legal proceedings "if it is in the national interest that the proceedings should be stopped" (Republic of Rhodesia,

Debates of the Senate, September 18, 1975, col. 831). It is also the argument we see in South Africa in the wake of the 1976 Soweto Uprising: "[I]n times of unrest, the civil and criminal courts are not entrusted with the right and the function to pass judgment in regard to any proceeding against the officials who have to maintain that peace" (Republic of South Africa, *Debates of the House of Assembly*, February 1, 1977, col. 579).

80. Garapon, "La justice comme reconnaissance," in Cassin, Cayla, and Salazar, *Vérité, Réconcilliation, Réparation*, 185–86. Some jurists have implicitly recognized just this. For a critique of the attempt to justify amnesty with reference to the concept of the "state of necessity," see Theissen, "Amnesty for Apartheid Crimes?," 87–89.

CHAPTER 5

1. Republic of South Africa, *Debates of the National Assembly*, May 17, 1995, col. 1427.

2. Kader Asmal, "Truth, Reconciliation, and Justice: The South African Experience in Perspective," *Modern Law Review* 63, no. 1 (2000): 1. See also Asmal, Asmal, and Roberts, *Reconciliation through Truth*, afterword, III–IV.

3. Du Bois-Pedain, *Transitional Amnesty*, 217.

4. *TRC Report*, vol. 1, chap. 6, ¶36.

5. Hugh McDowall Clokie and J. William Robinson, *Royal Commissions of Inquiry: The Significance of Investigations in British Politics* (New York: Octagon Books, 1969), 54–79.

6. *TRC Report*, vol. 5, chap. 6, ¶64.

7. *TRC Report*, vol. 1, chap. 13, addenda (containing a list of Commissions of Inquiry between 1960 and 1965).

8. Adam Ashforth, *The Politics of Official Discourse in Twentieth-Century South Africa* (Oxford: Clarendon, 1990), 2–4.

9. Michel Foucault, *The Archaeology of Knowledge*, trans. A. M. Sheridan Smith (New York: Pantheon, 1972), 15n2.

10. Ashforth, *Politics of Official Discourse*, 247–48. The Milner Commission, in turn, gave rise to the Natives' Land Act of 1913. See, on this point, Solomon Tshekisho Plaatje, *Native Life in South Africa, Before and Since the European War and the Boer Rebellion*, 3rd ed. (London: P.S. King & Son, 1917), 203. Plaatje is equally critical of the nearly concurrent "Lands Commission" of 1902, characterizing it as a "Segregation Commission" that was as absurd as it was destructive. See Plaatje, *Native Life in South Africa*, 357, 363.

11. The Natal Native Affairs Commission of 1847, for example, focused on the problem of "location," proposing measures for the control of native land by trustees, the control of the influx of refugees in and out of native locations, and the replacement of Native law with British law. See *Webb's Guide to the Official Records of the Colony of Natal*, ed. Jennifer Verbeek, Mary Nathanson, and Elaine Peel (Pietermaritzburg: University of Natal Press, 1984), 233.

12. Mamdani, *Citizen and Subject*, 93; Ivan Evans, *Bureaucracy and Race: Native Administration in South Africa* (Berkeley: University of California Press, 1997), 31–32, 48–49.

13. Brian Bunting, *The Rise of the South African Reich* (New York: Penguin Books, 1964), 229, 237.

14. John Allen, *Rabble-Rouser for Peace: The Authorized Biography of Desmond Tutu* (Boston: Simon and Schuster, 2006), 197–200.

15. One could equally discuss, among others, the 1914 Tuberculosis Commission (which declared the "Native Locations" a disgrace and proposed measures for their reform and refinement), the 1917 Beaumont Commission (created by the hated Native Land Act of 1913), the 1921 Asiatic Inquiry Commission (charged to consider the question of trading rights and landownership by Indians), the 1923 Godley Commission (which sought to normalize and regulate the living conditions of "urbanized" Africans), the 1923 Stallard Commission (on Transvaal local government, allowing natives within municipal areas only insofar as they meet the needs and wants of whites), the 1931 Native Economic Commission (which studied the effects of economic depression on populations in native reserves), the 1947 South African Penal Reform Commission (reaffirming, among other things, South Africa's commitment to capital punishment), the 1962–63 Odendaal Commission (recommending the forced removal of the Herero into arid regions of then South-West Africa), and the 1979 Riekert Commission (recommending new modes of "influx control" and new "pass law" practices and proposing to "repatriate" those who were "unlawfully employed" in South Africa).

16. One may apply to South Africa, in other words, Clokie and Robinson's observation that "[j]ust as there has been no Royal Commission of Inquiry into the Crown, so there has been no Royal Commission on Royal Commissions; but there has been an Inquiry by Commission into the exercise of some of the royal prerogatives . . . and there has been a departmental committee on Royal Commission procedure" (*Royal Commissions of Inquiry*, 141–42).

17. Oz Frankel, *States of Inquiry: Social Investigation and Print Culture in Nineteenth-Century Britain and the United States* (Baltimore: Johns Hopkins University Press, 2006), 141.

18. John Fortescue, *On the Laws and Governance of England*, ed. Shelley Lockwood (Cambridge: Cambridge University Press, 1997), 98. See also, generally, Luke Owen Pike, *Of the Reign of King Edward the Third, Years XIV and XV* (London: Her Majesty's Stationery Office, 1889), xxi–xlii; cf. W. S. Holdsworth, *A History of English Law*, vols. 3 and 4 (London: Methuen, 1903–24), 3:289–91.

19. Pike, *Of the Reign of King Edward the Third*, xxxiv. In 1360–61, for example, Parliament would pass a statute ordering that "all general Inquiries before this Time granted within any Seigniories, for the Mischiefs and Oppressions which have been done to the People by such Inquiries, shall cease utterly and be repealed." In 1368, meanwhile, Parliament would pass a statute ordering "[t]hat from henceforth in all Inquiries within the

Realm Commission shall be made to some of the Justices of the one bench or another" and no longer by "People not sufficient" who made their inquiries "in secret places." See United Kingdom, *The Statutes of the Realm*, vol. 1 (Buffalo, NY: William S. Hein, 1993), 365, 388.

20. Francis Bacon, *The Works of Francis Bacon*, ed. James Spedding, Robert Leslie Ellis, and Douglas Denon Heath, vol. 7 (London: Longman, 1859), 515. Similar criticisms were levied against a 1611 Commission of Inquiry (into abuses in the English navy) conducted by Robert Mansell and James Whitelocke, who were then promptly imprisoned by James I for their trouble. See A. P. McGowan, introduction to *The Jacobean Commission of Enquiry, 1608 and 1618*, Publications of the Navy Record Society, vol. 116 (London: William Clowes and Sons, 1971), xvi–xvii.

21. Frankel, *States of Inquiry*, 141.

22. Holdsworth, *History of English Law*, 4:69.

23. Holdsworth, *History of English Law*, 4:68. Like the standing committees of the privy council that were dedicated to recurring and regular administrative tasks of the nascent state (Home Office, War Office, Board of Trade, Board of Admiralty, Local Government Board), the commission was part of the general bureaucratization and governmentalization of the state that took place with the onset of the modern capitalism. Unlike committees, however, commissions had a specifically occasional structure: although some were permanent, most were formed in response to specific and usually novel events.

24. Foucault, *Security, Territory, Population*, 66, 75, 108–10.

25. Holdsworth, *History of English Law*, 4:61, 63, 67.

26. Frankel, *States of Inquiry*, 141.

27. See chapter 2, note 111.

28. "You have heard the Royal Warrant read and it explains in ancient form the status of the Commission as a Tribunal. All I wish to say in addition with regard to it is to emphasise the independence of a Royal Commission. It is not a departmental or other Committee answerable to any Department of the Government, or indeed to anyone except His Majesty the King, who appoints it." See United Kingdom, *Commission on Police Powers and Procedure*, 2.

29. On the way in which Commissions of Inquiry are apparatuses that operate with reference to the *persona*, see Herman Finer, *The Theory and Practice of Modern Government* (Ann Arbor: University of Michigan Press, 1949), 448.

30. Kostal, *Jurisprudence of Power*, 24, 40–55, 69–76.

31. Kostal, *Jurisprudence of Power*, 14–15, 20–21. As Kostal argues, "the *raison d'être* of the Jamaica Committee was to defend a liberal jurisprudence," not the desire for self-rule on the part of the colonized (473). Indeed, as Kostal points out, neither English radicals nor the English public were similarly outraged by other massacres during the same period.

32. Jamaica Committee, *Facts and Documents Relating to the Alleged Rebellion in Ja-*

maica, and the Measures of Repression; Including Notes on the Trial of Mr. Gordon, Jamaica Papers No. I (London: Jamaica Committee, 1866), 97.

33. United Kingdom, *Report of the Jamaica Royal Commission, Part I,* Presented to Both Houses of Parliament by Command of Her Majesty (London: Eyre and Spottis-woode, 1866), 3.

34. United Kingdom, *Report of the Jamaica Royal Commission, Part I,* 7.

35. Kostal, *Jurisprudence of Power,* 81, 119.

36. Kostal, *Jurisprudence of Power,* 79–80.

37. United Kingdom, *Report of the Jamaica Royal Commission, Part I,* 7.

38. United Kingdom, *Report of the Jamaica Royal Commission, Part I,* 8. It's worth noting that similar Commissions of Inquiry concurrently conducted in England or even Ireland did not similarly complain of excessive numbers of willing witnesses. One 1856 commission even complained about "a difficulty in obtaining evidence." "[W]ith one exception," these commissioners write, "no individual appeared to be prepared to make any statement or give any evidence before us with reference to the matters into which we had met to inquire." See United Kingdom, *Report of Her Majesty's Commissioners Appointed to Inquire into the Alleged Disturbance of the Public Peace in Hyde Park, on Sunday, July 1, 1855; and the Conduct of the Metropolitan Police in Connexion with the Same,* Presented to Both Houses of Parliament by Command of Her Majesty (London: Eyre and Spottiswoode, 1856), v.

39. Kostal, *Jurisprudence of Power,* 81.

40. Kostal, *Jurisprudence of Power,* 81.

41. United Kingdom, *Report of the Jamaica Royal Commission, Part I,* 8.

42. United Kingdom, *Report of the Jamaica Royal Commission, Part I,* 8. While in the field, the commissioners "determined also to investigate on the spot all the other alleged cases of a grave kind involving loss of life, or circumstances of a special hardship" (8).

43. United Kingdom, *Report of the Jamaica Royal Commission, Part I,* 8. This is a much different genre of complaint than, for example, the 1844 Commission of Inquiry investigating "recent acts of violence and outrage" in South Wales. The 1844 commission concluded its report by noting "the ignorance of the English language which pervades so large a portion of the country," but despite transcribing 468 pages of testimony, it did not call any of it into doubt (See United Kingdom, *Report of the Commissioners of Inquiry for South Wales,* Presented to Both Houses of Parliament by Command of Her Majesty [London: Clowes and Sons, 1844], 36; cf. Frankel, *States of Inquiry,* 15, 159–60). In this respect, the JRC was more like the preceding Commission of Inquiry into the Riots in Belfast. "The evidence runs to great length," wrote the authors of that commission's report (which, together with its supplements, numbered over seven hundred pages in length), "and necessarily, by reason of the nature of inquiries to be made in a public court, was often discursive, and sometimes, perhaps, not quite relevant; but we considered it the most prudent course, in discharging the duty which devolved upon us, to allow the parties before us a somewhat greater latitude in their evidence than to us

seemed necessary, *in order that we might not appear to prevent any parties who came before us from giving evidence which, it might afterwards be alleged, would have been material."* See United Kingdom, *Report of the Commissioners of Inquiry into the Origin and Character of the Riots in Belfast in July and September, 1857,* Presented to Both Houses of Parliament by Command of Her Majesty (Dublin: Alex. Thom and Son, 1858), 1 (emphasis mine).

44. Bentham, *An Introduction to The Principles of Morals and Legislation,* 310–11 (emphasis in original).

45. As Jennifer Pitts argues, Mill's involvement in the Jamaica Controversy stemmed from his desire "to preserve the rectitude of the colonial administration, to insulate it from the corruptions of the local white ruling class" (*A Turn to Empire: The Rise of Imperial Liberalism in Britain and France* [Princeton: Princeton University Press, 2005], 158; cf. Kostal, *Jurisprudence of Power,* 479–80, 482).

46. To the contrary, see Kostal, *Jurisprudence of Power,* 125. As Valentin Mudimbe points out in the context of a critique of colonial anthropology, the "cultural ethnocentrism" apparent in the behavior of this or that specific individual cannot be understood on its own terms but should be interpreted with reference to the "epistemological filiation" that precedes and authorizes it (*Invention of Africa,* 19).

47. Ashforth, *Politics of Official Discourse,* 1–2.

48. For an analogous practice in the United States, see Frankel, *States of Inquiry,* 4–5, 303.

49. United Kingdom, *Report of the Jamaica Royal Commission, Part I,* 40.

50. United Kingdom, *Report of the Jamaica Royal Commission, Part I,* 39.

51. For the Jamaica Committee's critique of, among other things, the concept "martial law," see Jamaica Committee, *Facts and Documents Relating to the Alleged Rebellion in Jamaica,* 68–83.

52. Gad Heuman, *"The Killing Time": The Morant Bay Rebellion in Jamaica* (Nashville: University of Tennessee Press, 1994), 171.

53. United Kingdom, *Report of the Jamaica Royal Commission, Part I,* 40.

54. *Hansard Parliamentary Debates,* 3rd ser., vol. 184 (1866), cols. 1763–64.

55. Edward Underhill, *The Tragedy of Morant Bay: A Narrative of the Disturbances in the Island of Jamaica in 1865* (London: Alexander and Shepheard, 1895), 191.

56. Uday Singh Mehta, *Liberalism and Empire: A Study in Nineteenth-Century British Liberal Thought* (Chicago: University of Chicago Press, 1999), 81.

57. *Hansard Parliamentary Debates,* 3rd ser., vol. 184 (1866), cols. 1798–1800.

58. Thomas Holt, *The Problem of Freedom: Race, Labor, and Politics in Jamaica and Britain, 1832–1938* (Baltimore: Johns Hopkins University Press, 1991), 306.

59. Pitts, *Turn to Empire,* 153, 158.

60. For Marx and Engels, the contradictoriness of a given Commission of Inquiry could not be understood solely with reference to the text of that commission's report but must instead be interpreted within the broader horizon of historical materialism in general, from world history interpreted as the history of class conflict. As such, Marx and

Engels do not assume that it is even possible for blue books to be internally consistent; rather, they are constitutively inconsistent, and their inconsistencies are symptoms and tactics of class conflict. On these grounds, it is not a surprise to Marx when Parliament chooses to ignore a commission's findings on, for example, child labor, for this inconsistency is expressive of a manifestly social and economic contradiction—a contradiction that is more fundamental than the mere "law of noncontradiction" and that cannot be solved with better or less contradictory logic. For Marx and Engels, Commissions of Inquiry are not only sources of distorted information; they are tactics for mitigating, deferring, and obscuring contradictions. It is therefore yet another sign of Marx's incomplete theorization of colonization that Marx did not interpret the Jamaica Affair in similar terms, reading it not as class conflict but as simple "turpitude." See, variously, Karl Marx, "Letter to Friedrich Engels, June 22, 1867," in *Marx/Engels Collected Work*, vol. 42 (New York: International Publishers, 1975), 383. See also Frankel, *States of Inquiry*, 10; Kostal, *Jurisprudence of Power*, 479.

61. Underhill, *Tragedy of Morant Bay*, 191.

62. *Hansard Parliamentary Debates*, 3rd ser., vol. 184 (1866), col. 1788. Adderley also claimed that Buxton's original resolution contained a reference to the fifth conclusion of the report. "Last night the hon. Gentleman was ready to ask the House to praise Governor Eyre for the skill, promptitude, and vigour, manifested by him in the early stages of the insurrection, and to-night he is ready to call the rebellion a mere trifle, and say there was a great deal of fear and very little danger. So much for the consistency of the hon. Member's views, and so much for the firmness of conviction at which he has arrived after a long study of the case" (*Hansard Parliamentary Debates*, 3rd ser., vol. 184 (1866), col. 1787).

63. *Hansard Parliamentary Debates*, 3rd ser., vol. 184 (1866), col. 1789.

64. *Hansard Parliamentary Debates*, 3rd ser., vol. 184 (1866), col. 1783.

65. Jamaica Committee, *The Blue Books, Jamaica Papers No. II* (London: Jamaica Committee, 1866), 51.

66. *Hansard Parliamentary Debates*, 3rd ser., vol. 184 (1866), col. 1820. Privately, of course, Cardwell had already written to Storks, the head of the commission, to say that he concurred with the commission's findings and to express his view that the report supported the government's position. See Underhill, *Tragedy of Morant Bay*, 186.

67. Holt, *Problem of Freedom*, 306–7.

68. Kostal, *Jurisprudence of Power*, 16.

69. Nicholas Capaldi, *John Stuart Mill: A Biography* (Cambridge: Cambridge University Press, 2004), 330.

70. Heuman, "*Killing Time*," 176–77.

71. Underhill, *Tragedy of Morant Bay*, 192. Underhill was a prominent humanitarian and supporter of prosecution who had a hand in spurring the uprising in the first place. See Kostal, *Jurisprudence of Power*, 6.

72. Underhill, *Tragedy of Morant Bay*, 192.

73. Kostal, *Jurisprudence of Power*, 82.

74. A similar strategy was used in 1836 by the Irish Poor Law Commission: to mitigate strife between the English and the Irish, the commission's final report did not attempt impartiality but simply set opposing points of view against one another in a carefully calibrated way. See Frankel, *States of Inquiry*, 157.

75. Hussain, *Jurisprudence of Emergency*, 113–16; Kostal, *Jurisprudence of Power*, 19, 21, 452, 478.

76. Arendt, *Origins*, 186.

77. In 1637, Charles I appointed a royal commission to inquire into the refusal by the governor of Barbados to accede to the centralization of authority under the king. The Commission of Inquiry traveled to Barbados and secured the submission of the governor, who returned to England as a prisoner. See George Louis Beer, *The Origins of the British Colonial System, 1578–1660* (New York: P. Smith, 1933), 332–33.

78. *Hansard Parliamentary Debates*, 3rd ser., vol. 242 (1878), col. 461. These investigations were not limited to Commissions of Inquiry but also took the form of Select Committees. As André du Toit has noted of the Select Committee on Aborigines established in London in 1834, "the Aborigines Committee may well be said to have been a kind of Truth Commission of its time, uncovering the political atrocities committed against the aborigines in South Africa, Australia and other parts of the British Empire." See André du Toit, "Experiments with Truth and Justice," 421.

79. On the intensification of the jurisprudence of emergency under conditions of decolonization, see Simpson, *Human Rights and the End of Empire*, 874–923.

80. Ann Laura Stoler, *Along the Archival Grain: Epistemic Anxieties and Colonial Common Sense* (Princeton: Princeton University Press, 2009), 142.

81. On the "cognitive problem" that martial law poses for jurisprudence, see Hussain, *Jurisprudence of Emergency*, 109, 113.

82. Frankel, *States of Inquiry*, 13, 162.

83. Kostal, *Jurisprudence of Power*, 120.

84. Sir Louis Blom-Cooper, "Public Inquiries," *Current Legal Problems* 46 (1993): 206.

85. Kostal, *Jurisprudence of Power*, 76.

86. Blom-Cooper, "Public Inquiries," 206.

87. This would present a special problem for South Africa's 1922 Martial Law Inquiry Judicial Commission, the appointment of which overlapped with incomplete government prosecutions of the main instigators of the 1922 Rand Riots. See Union of South Africa, *Report of the Martial Law Inquiry Judicial Commission*, Presented to Both Houses of Parliament by Command of His Royal Highness the Governor-General (Pretoria: Government Printing and Stationery Office, 1922), 1–2, 32. See also Blom-Cooper, "Public Inquiries," 217–20. It did not, however, present a problem for South Africa's 1941 Johannesburg Riots Commission, which was able to refer to a completed magistrate's inquest into the beating death of a soldier that occurred in the midst of the

riots. See Union of South Africa, *Report of the Commission Appointed to Enquire into the Riots Which Took Place in Johannesburg on 31st January 1941 and 1st February, 1941* (Cape Town: Cape Times, 1941), 7. Nor did it present a problem for the Zululand Commission, which openly stated that part of the function of their Commission of Inquiry was to aid the police. After stating the principle of the confidentiality of their hearings, the commissioners write, "[T]he Commission's terms of reference do not require it to report upon the criminal liability of the persons or parties involved. Many of the facts contained in the Report of this Commission will, no doubt, assist the police in their investigations, in the sense that they may provide pointers to fruitful avenues of inquiry" (Republic of South Africa, *Report of the Commission of Inquiry into the Violence Which Occurred on 29 October 1983 at the University of Zululand*, vol. 1, Appointed by the State President [Pretoria: Government Printer, 1985], 87).

88. Stoler, *Along the Archival Grain*, 141.

89. See, for example, Locke, *Two Treatises*, 164–65 (esp. §§143–44).

90. Finlason, *Review of the Authorities*, 153; O'Higgins, "Wright v. Fitzgerald Revisited," 421.

91. Dicey, *Introduction*, 8th ed., 232. For support of Dicey's view, see O'Higgins, "Wright v. Fitzgerald Revisited," 420–21.

92. See, on this point, Dicey, *Introduction*, 8th ed., 553–54.

93. Dicey, *Introduction*, 8th ed., 286–87.

94. "A proclamation of Martial Law in any district can only be justified on the principle of necessity. It is necessary for the purpose of suppressing rebellion; but when the rebellion has been suppressed, the necessity, and therefore the justification, for maintaining Martial Law no longer exists. The Parliamentary Commission which was sent to Jamaica after the suppression of the rebellion in that island made an exhaustive investigation into all the circumstances of the execution of Martial Law and reported that the declaration of Martial Law was justifiable, that the proceedings in the Island which justified it were rebellious and of deep design, and that the Commissioners fully approved the conduct of the Governor and Officers in the prompt measures which they took, *but that Martial Law was continued longer than was necessary*, because it was continued after the rebellion had been completely suppressed. I feel confident that any impartial investigation into the circumstances which led up to the proclamation of Martial Law in several of the districts of this Colony would justify such proclamation. We should take great care, therefore, that such an investigation, if it be made, should also find that it was not continued in force longer than necessary" (Richard Solomon, Memorandum, "Cape of Good Hope, Papers Relating to Martial Law in Certain Districts of the Colony, July 1900," CGR Series, 2/1/155, 29218, Cape Town Archives Repository, Cape Town, 17; emphasis in original).

95. On March 24, 1922, General Jan Smuts even insisted on this priority. Responding to General Hertzog's movement to append a Commission of Inquiry onto the Indemnity Bill of 1922, Smuts argued that if this amendment was passed, "they would

have a Commission of Inquiry, which would continue for months and months, and in the meantime it would be impossible for the House to pass the Indemnity Bill, and it would be impossible for the Government to withdraw martial law" (General Jan Smuts, Speech to Parliament, in *Debates of the House of Assembly of the Union of South Africa, as Reported in the Cape Times*, vol. 7, Second Session, Fourth Parliament, 17th February 1922 to 19th July, 1922 [Pretoria: State Library, 1969], 87).

96. See, on this point, Frankel, *States of Inquiry*, 13–19.

97. See, for example, Abel, *Politics by Other Means*, 256.

CHAPTER 6

1. Colony of Natal, *Proceedings and Report of the Commission Appointed to Inquire into the Past and Present State of the Kafirs in the District of Natal, and to Report upon Their Future Government, and to Suggest Such Arrangements as Will Tend to Secure the Peace and Welfare of the District, for the Information of His Honour Lieutenant-Governor Pine* (n.p., 1853), 3.

2. *Hansard Parliamentary Debates*, 3rd ser., vol. 242 (1878), cols. 461, 467.

3. Chanock, *Making of South African Legal Culture*, 257–58. The occasion for the failed 1878 commission (which was of unprecedented depth and scope) was the understanding that "measures should at once be taken to promote the civilization of the native tribes, and to facilitate their withdrawal from the savage state" (*Hansard Parliamentary Debates*, 3rd ser., vol. 242 [1878], col. 459). "Our first step," declared Sir Michael Hicks-Beach, "must be to ascertain what the Native law is, and the next step, I hope, will be carefully to amend that law in those particulars where it requires amendment, so as to introduce the benefits of civilization by degrees among a population who have hitherto been unaccustomed to them, and to introduce them in such a manner as to induce the Natives to work with us rather than against us" (*Hansard Parliamentary Debates*, 3rd ser., vol. 242 [1878], col. 470; see also cols. 451ff. [on polygamy], 459ff. [on liquor]). This was carried out by the 1883 Government Commission on Native Laws and Customs. This commission, which understood its task to be to propose gradual reforms to carry out the modification of "Kafir Law" initiated by Benjamin D'Urban in 1836, engaged in a systematic analysis of "Kafir jurisprudence," focusing particularly on issues of "Native Marriages and Ukulobola," "Native Marriages and Polygamy," "Land Tenure," and "Liquor Traffic." It concluded by "earnestly recommend[ing] to the Government the systematic organization of that branch of the public service which deals with the administration of Native affairs" (Cape of Good Hope, *Report and Proceedings of the Government Commission on Native Laws and Customs*, 53). Precisely this task would be the mandate of the South African Native Affairs Commission, which was appointed by the high commissioner "to enquire into and report on[:] (1) The status and condition of the Natives; the lines on which their natural advancement should proceed; their education, industrial training; and labor. (2) The tenure of land by Natives and the obligations to the State

which it entails. (3) Native law and administration. (4) The prohibition of the sale of liquor to Natives. (5) Native marriages. (6) The extent and effect of polygamy" (United Kingdom. *Report of the South African Native Affairs Commission, 1903–1905*. Presented to Both Houses of Parliament by Command of His Majesty [London: Printed for His Majesty's Stationery Office, by Darling & Son, 1905], 1).

4. Foucault, *Security, Territory, Population*, 165, 248.

5. Clokie and Robinson, *Royal Commissions of Inquiry*, 54–79; Frankel, *States of Inquiry*, 243–72.

6. Exemplary in this regard is Jan Smuts's 1917 claim that Commissions of Inquiry dealing with the "native question" would operate, in conjunction with the appendix of the South Africa Act of 1909, to enable the Union to govern natives on "entirely different lines" than whites. See Jan Smuts, "Problems in South Africa," *Journal of the Royal African Society* 16, no. 64 (1917): 279; see also Jan Smuts, "Native Policy in Africa," *Journal of the Royal African Society* 29, no. 115 (1930): 256, 263. From this follows the insufficiency of any criticism of the colonial Commission of Inquiry on the grounds of exclusion alone.

7. Timothy Keegan, *Colonial South Africa and the Origins of the Racial Order* (Charlottesville: University Press of Virginia, 1996), 143; Lalu, *Deaths of Hintsa*, 6.

8. These include the Witwatersrand Disturbances Commission (1913); the Indian Enquiry Commission (1914); the Judicial Commission of Inquiry into the Causes of and Circumstances Relating to the Recent Rebellion in South Africa (1916); the Rebellion Losses Commission (1916); the Commission of Inquiry into the Native Disturbances at Port Elizabeth on the 23rd October, 1920 (1921); the Bulhoek Native Disturbances Commission of Inquiry (1921); the Martial Law Inquiry Judicial Commission (1922); the Commission Appointed to Enquire into the Rebellion of the Bondelzwarts (1923); the Vereeniging Native Riots Commission of Enquiry (1938); the Commission to Enquire into the Riots Which Took Place in Johannesburg on 31st January, 1941, and 1st February, 1941 (1941); the Commission of Inquiry into Disturbances at African Educational Institutions (1946); the Commission of Enquiry into Riots in Durban (1949); the Commission to Inquire into the Acts of Violence by Natives on the Witwatersrand (1950); the Commission of Inquiry into Acts of Violence by Natives at Krugersdorp, Newlands, Randfontein, and Newclare (1950); the Commission of Enquiry into the Disturbances in the Witzieshoek Native Reserve (1951); the Commission Appointed by the City Council of Johannesburg to Enquire into the Causes and Circumstances of the Riots Which Took Place in the Vicinity of Dube Hostel in the South-Western Townships over the Week-end 14th–15th September, 1957 (1958); the Commission of Inquiry into Sharpeville, Evaton, and Vanderbijlpark Location Riots (1960); the Judicial Commission on Langa Location Riots (1961); the Commission Appointed to Inquire into the Events on 20–22 November 1962 at PAARL and the Causes Which Gave Rise Thereto (1963); the Commission of Inquiry into the Riots at Soweto and Elsewhere from 16 June 1976 to 28 February 1977 (1979); the Commission of Inquiry into the

Violence Which Occurred on 29 October 1983 at the University of Zululand (1985); the Commission of Inquiry into the Incident Which Occurred on 21 March 1985 at Uitenhage (1985); the Commission of Enquiry into the Incidents at Sebokeng, Boipatong, Lekoa, Sharpeville, and Evaton on 26 March 1990 (1990); the Commission of Enquiry into the 1986 Unrest and Alleged Mismanagement in KwaNdebele (1995); and the Commission of Inquiry into the Incidents That Led to the Violence in the Former Bophuthatswana on 11 March 1994, and the Deaths That Occurred as a Result Thereof (1998).

9. Mary Benson, *Nelson Mandela: The Man and the Movement* (New York: Norton, 1986), 49, 73.

10. I choose the word *tumult*, from the Roman Law concept *tumultus*, to indicate the juridical form underlying the otherwise wide range of riots, rebellions, disturbances, protests, and other incidents of "internal disturbance" or "internal disorder" that these commissions investigated. All of these commissions share the same basic set of problems or questions: Under what conditions did a certain quotient of the population begin to use coordinated or even only concerted violence against a constituted public authority? What is the legal status of the actions taken by those authorities to suppress that coordinated violence? It is important to note that the Tumult Commission, like the other juridical forms of the South African state, was shot through with racial anxieties. According to standard racial theories, whites engage in "strikes" in which the violence is governed by "rational self-interest," whereas blacks engage in "riots" in which the violence is irrational and unpredictable. In the Tumult Commissions, however, these distinctions break down: white strikes will turn into riots just as surely as black rioters will turn out to have been motivated by "rational self-interest." Here as elsewhere, in other words, the Commission of Inquiry in general is that administrative organ in which government reflects on and criticizes the limits of its own theories and practices.

11. On the way that the "native question" morphed into the problem of "race relations," see Ashforth, *Politics of Official Discourse*, 1–3.

12. On the way these tropes figured into the "Native Question" Commission, see Ashforth, *Politics of Official Discourse*, 247–54.

13. On sedition as a "poison," see Union of South Africa, *Report of the Commission Appointed to Enquire into the Rebellion of the Bondelzwarts*, Presented to Both Houses of Parliament (Cape Town: Cape Times, 1923), 28. On the way that "public disorders" are like "fevers" that "come to an end either by being overcome or by destroying their host, the State," see Union of South Africa, *Report of the Commission of Enquiry into Riots in Durban*, Issued by Authority (Cape Town: Cape Times, 1949), 6.

14. See, for example, United Kingdom, *Report of the South African Native Affairs Commission, 1903–1905*, 69.

15. Union of South Africa, *Report of the Commission Appointed to Enquire into the Riots Which Took Place in Johannesburg*, 10 (on precautions that could be taken by military authorities to prevent future disorders when soldiers are on leave). This conven-

tion pertained even when there was nothing to recommend. See Union of South Africa, *Report of the Witwatersrand Disturbances Commission* (Pretoria: Government Printer, 1913), 65 (arguing that "it appears to us that the method adopted by the military of silencing revolver fire does endanger the live [*sic*] of innocent persons and we sincerely hope that in the future some better method may be devised. We can suggest none, but we feel that there ought to be some more effective and less dangerous method"). It also pertained in the discourse of those who were not official commissioners. In a submission to the Wessels Commission, the bishop of Johannesburg (many of whose church members were residents of Sharpeville) clarified, "The purpose of these representations is not to dwell upon the horror of the killing and wounding, in time of peace, of 250 unarmed civilians by the South African Police. It is to assist the Commissioner in his task of ascertaining how the shooting took place and whether there was any justification for it, and thus to help ensure—in so far as that may be done by the ascertainment and publication of the truth—that such events will not occur again in South Africa" (Bishop of Johannesburg, *Submission on Behalf of the Bishop of Johannesburg to the Commission of Enquiry into the Occurrences at Sharpeville (and Other Places) on the 21st March, 1960*, vols. 1–2, Johannesburg, June 15, 1960, 1:1).

16. Polygamy, one of the main concerns of late nineteenth-century colonial missions of inquiry (e.g., the Native Laws and Customs Commission of 1882), was also a chief concern of the Natal Native Affairs Commission, which was set up to inquire into the causes of the 1906 Bambatha Rebellion and which recommended the legalization of polygamy as an acceptable alternative to the right to vote. Decisive here is the colonial supposition that the former administrative improvement, more than the latter political concession, could decrease the potential for the recurrence of native uprising. See Sachs, *Justice in South Africa*, 87.

17. The *form* of the Tumult Commission, as exemplified by the JRC, is to offer recommendations whose contradictoriness is a sign not of logical inconsistency but of the pursuit of equilibrium and balance within populations where passions of hatred and anger run high. As Deborah Posel has shown, a similar form was at work in the Sauer Commission of 1948, which, in her analysis, was "an internally contradictory and ambiguous document" that "straddled mutually exclusive sets of strategies" (Posel, "Meaning of Apartheid before 1948," 136–38). Our point is that this contradictoriness should be interpreted not as an incomplete expression of logical consistency, or as a simple violation of the law of noncontradiction, but rather as the complete expression of an administrative discourse whose aim was not pure logic but the maintenance of colonial hatred in an equilibrium more stable than unstable. For this purpose, "internal contradictoriness" is not a formal deficiency but a juridical form in and for itself, a form the Sauer Commission shares with Tumult Commissions more generally.

There is also significant overlap at the level of *content*. In 1914, the Indian Enquiry Commission investigating the violent suppression of a 1913 strike called by Gandhi concluded its investigation by ceding many of Gandhi's points about the "cause" of the

strike and offering fourteen recommendations that, in effect, remedied Gandhi's grievances about laws governing marriage, immigration, passes, thumb-printing, fees, and
documentation (Union of South Africa, *Report of the Indian Enquiry Commission* [Cape
Town, Cape Times, Government Printers, 1914], 37–38). In 1920, two out of three
commissioners tasked with looking into the "disturbances" at Port Elizabeth on October
23, in which vigilantes violently suppressed a gathering in support of the Industrial and
Commercial Workers Union, agreed that the union was justified in the demand that
had, in effect, led to the gathering, namely, a demand for a higher minimum wage (Union
of South Africa. *Report of the Commissioners Appointed to Enquire into the Causes of, and
Occurrences at, the Native Disturbances at Port Elizabeth on the 23rd October, 1920, and the
General Economic Conditions as They Effect the Native and Coloured Population*, Printed
by Direction of the Acting Prime Minster [Cape Town: Cape Times, 1921], 3). In 1923,
meanwhile, the Bondelzwart Rebellion Commission would recommend, as a response
to rebellion of the Bondelzwarts, "remedial legislation and improved administration,"
including gathering natives together into more geographically cohesive units, reestab-
lishing tribal forms of control (along the lines of the 1921 Native Reserves Commission), improvement of the degree and quality of native employment, improvement of
native education, reduction of the dog tax, boring for water, and improvement of stock;
the commission would also note with approval the appointment of a "Native Reserves
Commission" and express its hope that this commission would formulate a policy that
could help address the "Native problem" (Union of South Africa, *Report of the Commission Appointed to Enquire into the Rebellion of the Bondelzwarts*, 27–28, 33). Even as late
as 1951, the Witzieshoek Disturbances Commission would recommend, as remedies
to prevent future unrest and disturbances in the Witzieshoek Native Reserve, better
statistical record keeping, more permanent segregation between natives, better irrigation
schemes in Witzieshoek, more expert usage of agricultural land (up to and including
more efficient composting), extra pastures for cattle grazing, more accurate land survey-
ing, clearer communication between government and natives about cattle culling, development of electricity supply, and improved licensing practices between Europeans and
natives (Union of South Africa, *Report of the Commission of Enquiry into the Disturbances
in the Witzieshoek Native Reserve* [Parow: Cape Times, 1951], 30–35).

18. Union of South Africa, *Index to the Manuscript Annexures and Printed Papers of
the House of Assembly, Including Select Committee Reports and Bills; and Also to Principal
Motions and Resolutions and Commission Reports, 1910–1930*, Printed by Order of Mr.
Speaker (Cape Town: Cape Times, 1931), 267.

19. See, variously, Union of South Africa, *Index to the Manuscript Annexures and
Printed Papers of the House of Assembly, Including Select Committee Reports and Bills; and
Also to Principal Motions and Resolutions and Commission Reports, 1910–1920*, Printed by
Order of Mr. Speaker (Cape Town: Cape Times, 1921), 153–59; Union of South Africa,
Index . . . , 1910–1930, 267–76; Union of South Africa, *Index to the Manuscript Annexures
and Printed Papers of the House of Assembly, Including Select Committee Reports and Bills;*

and Also to Principal Motions and Resolutions and Commission Reports, 1931–1940, Printed by Order of Mr. Speaker (Cape Town: Cape Times, 1941), 119–23; Union of South Africa, *Index to the Manuscript Annexures and Printed Papers of the House of Assembly, Including Select Committee Reports and Bills; and Also to Principal Motions and Resolutions and Commission Reports, 1940-41–1950*, Printed by Order of Mr. Speaker (Cape Town: Cape Times, 1951), 115–21.

20. Cape of Good Hope, *Debates in the Legislative Council, in the Sixth Session of the Fifth Parliament of the Cape of Good Hope, Appointed to Meet 10th May, 1878*, 41 Victoriae, vol. 2, Published by Order of the Legislative Council (Cape Town: Saul Solomon, 1878), cols. 149–50 (emphasis mine).

21. On the notion that the native is a "sacred trust," see Union of South Africa, *Report of the Commission Appointed to Enquire into the Rebellion of the Bondelzwarts*, 33. On the ways in which numerous government inquiries preceded and enabled the formation of Indian policy in the United States, see Frankel, *States of Inquiry*, 241–301. For the metaphor of native labor as a resource akin to "water," see Sachs, *Justice in South Africa*, 103. For the metaphor of native labor as "human livestock," see Hoernlé, *South African Native Policy and the Liberal Spirit*, 133, 157.

22. Canada, *Summary of Proceedings, Imperial Conference, 1926*, Printed by Order of Parliament (Ottawa: F. A. Acland, 1926), 14.

23. More often than not, these are distinctions without a difference. Commissions of Inquiry would use their considerable discretionary power to define their procedures (as distinct from their mandates) in ways that render these distinctions irrelevant. In 1913, the Witwatersrand Disturbances Commission (which was a Royal Commission of Inquiry) would explicitly frame its inquiry according to the principles set forth by the Featherstone Commission, which was *not* a royal commission but a committee appointed under the auspices of the Home Secretary (55–56). In 1949, meanwhile, the Commission of Inquiry into Riots in Durban (which was not, technically, a Royal Commission of Inquiry but a commission appointed by the governor-general) would clarify, in response to the criticism that it afforded no rights of counsel to witnesses and no opportunity for counsel to cross-examine witnesses, that "British Royal Commissions of Inquiry provide a closer analogy to the present one than Tribunals of Inquiry set up under the provisions of the Tribunals of Inquiry (Evidence) Act, 1921 (11 Geo. 5. Ch. 7)" (Union of South Africa, *Report of the Commission of Enquiry into Riots in Durban*, 2. Judicial Commissions of Inquiry, meanwhile, would make use of the same historiography (remote and proximate causes) and same practices (collection, evaluation, and archivization of testimony) and would enable the same reading practices (exoneration, accusation, mourning) as Commissions of Inquiry appointed by the governor-general.

24. See Union of South Africa, *Report of the Witwatersrand Disturbances Commission*, 4–5, 46 (suggesting that although witnesses were heard under oath, some simply lied); Union of South Africa, *Report of the Martial Law Inquiry Judicial Commission*, 43, 44, 52 (describing inconsistent and possibly perjured testimony, even though witnesses

were heard under oath); Union of South Africa, *Report of the Commission of Enquiry into Riots in Durban*, 5, 8–9 (indicating exaggerated and perjured testimony). This, however, would become a refrain in South Africa. In 1916, for example, the Judicial Commission of Inquiry into the Causes and Circumstances Relating to the Recent Rebellion in South Africa would open their report by writing, "Your Commissioners regret . . . that owing to various causes, they experienced great difficulty in obtaining the necessary evidence to enable them to frame a full and satisfactory report upon the subject of their inquiry." See Union of South Africa, *Report of the Judicial Commission of Inquiry into the Causes of and Circumstances Relating to the Recent Rebellion in South Africa*, Presented to Both Houses of Parliament by Command of His Excellency the Governor-General (Cape Town: Cape Times, 1916), 1.

25. In 1913, the commissioners would find that "the firing of at least two of the soldiers was negligent and therefore the acts unjustifiable" (Union of South Africa, *Report of the Witwatersrand Disturbances Commission*, 64). In the 1914 report of the Indian Enquiry Commission, the commissioners would gently criticize police for opening fire on unarmed Gandhian satyagrahis on November 27, 1913: "The necessity for the general use of firearms on that occasion is not quite so clear. . . . It may be open to question whether that was absolutely necessary at the particular moment. At the same time it must be remembered that the Indians were very excited and violent" (Union of South Africa, *Report of the Indian Enquiry Commission*, 7). In 1920, "all the firing which took place after the mob broke away . . . was unnecessary, indiscriminate, and it was moreover brutal in its callousness, resulting in a terrible toll of killed and wounded without any sufficient reason or justification" (Union of South Africa. *Report of the Commissioners Appointed to Enquire into the Causes of, and Occurrences at, the Native Disturbances at Port Elizabeth on the 23rd October, 1920, and the General Economic Conditions as They Effect the Native and Coloured Population*, 9). In the 1923 report on the Rebellion of the Bondelzwarts, meanwhile, the commissioners criticize the military authorities for bombing natives without first giving them a warning ahead of time to enable the rebels to surrender and to enable women and children to leave (Union of South Africa, *Report of the Commission Appointed to Enquire into the Rebellion of the Bondelzwarts*, 24–25, 32). In 1941, a Commission of Inquiry found that "some of the South African Police, in carrying out the baton charges, used unnecessary violence in hitting on the head soldiers who were running away and soldiers who had already been struck down and were lying on the ground, and indiscriminately attacked persons, including women, who were obviously spectators" (Union of South Africa, *Report of the Commission Appointed to Enquire into the Riots Which Took Place in Johannesburg on 31st January 1941 and 1st February, 1941*, 10). As Naboth Mokgatle writes of the report of the Mineworkers Union Commission of Enquiry (1946), "When the Commission reported, the blame went to the people who deserved it: Hardy [the assistant manager of the City Council's Native Affairs Department], the police and the army" (*Autobiography of an Unknown South African* [Berkeley: University of California Press, 1971], 238).

26. *Hansard Parliamentary Debates*, 3rd ser., vol. 184 (1866), col. 1798.

27. See Union of South Africa, *Report of the Commission Appointed to Enquire into the Rebellion of the Bondelzwarts*, 26, 32.

28. After the 1946 Mineworkers Commission found fault with the police, Mokgatle writes, "[t]hat was all we heard of the Commission. The workers had lost their lives, Jan Christian Smuts was the ruler of South Africa, the second world war was raging, the children of those who lost their lives became orphans with no support" (*Autobiography of an Unknown South African*, 238). The Natives Representative Council, chaired by Z. K. Matthews, requested to make its own inquiry into the mineworkers strike, but the request was refused. See Benson, *Nelson Mandela*, 33.

29. Take, for example, the commission tasked with inquiring into the government suppression of the African Mineworkers Strike of 1920. This commission concluded that the inspector of police may have acted unwisely in not releasing Samuel Masabalala (president of the Natives Industrial and Commercial Union Association) from jail and that the fusillade directed by various civilians (mostly soldiers returned from war) at the backs of the fleeing mob may have been "unnecessary, indiscriminate . . . and brutal"; but it also found that the behavior of the natives in assembling "in defiance of law and order" in their attempt to release Masabalala "must be condemned in the strongest terms." In any case, it concluded that "the conduct of the [police] officers," up to and including the aforementioned inspector, "was most patient and exemplary in the face of the hostile and threatening conduct on the part of a certain section of the mob" (Union of South Africa, *Report of the Commissioners Appointed to Enquire into the Causes of, and Occurrences at, the Native Disturbances at Port Elizabeth*, 9). A similar "evenhandedness" is at work in the 1923 *Report of the Commission Appointed to Enquire into the Rebellion of the Bondelzwarts*, which was mandated to investigate the Union government's violent suppression of the uprising in South-West Africa in 1922 (involving, though not for the first time, the use of a military technology, the airplane, to punish and educate the natives, to "teach them a lesson" about the rule of law). In its 1923 discussion of the "remote" (as opposed to "immediate") causes of this rebellion, the commission was careful to narrate "both sides" of the story. On the one hand, "[t]he police reported that the Natives were insolent, lazy and thievish," while, on the other hand, "[t]he Natives regarded the police as provocative, unnecessarily severe, and harsh." Similarly, "the relationship between the Bondelzwarts and the European farmers [who employed them] became such that insolence and impertinence on the one hand, and severity and punishment on the other were not infrequent" (Union of South Africa, *Report of the Commission Appointed to Enquire into the Rebellion of the Bondelzwarts*, 6, 11, 24–25, 30, 32). This was not, however, the first time that airplanes were used to quell a riot in South Africa. See Union of South Africa, *Report of the Martial Law Inquiry Judicial Commission*, 14 (noting that "field artillery, machine guns, magazine rifles and aeroplanes" were used to quell the Rand Riots). The prohibition of bombardment from balloons and dirigibles in the Hague Peace Conference of 1899 was, of course, quickly undermined, beginning with the 1911 bombing of civilians

in Tripoli. See, generally, David Omissi, *Air Power and Colonial Control: The Royal Air Force, 1919–1939* (Manchester: Manchester University Press, 1990), 5–17; Nasser Hussain, "Air Power," in *Spatiality, Sovereignty, and Carl Schmitt: Geographies of the Nomos,* ed. Stephen Legg (New York: Routledge, 2011), 244–50.

30. Consider the use of the passive voice in the 1913 report of the Witwatersrand Disturbances Commission, which was mandated to investigate the government's violent suppression of a strike by white miners in July 1913. In their findings on the "proximate" (as opposed to "distant") cause of the disturbances, the commissioners argued that "terrorism" could spread in the mining districts because of "the insufficiency of the police and detective force"; because of "the fact that the minatory and inflammatory language on the part of the strikers and their leaders was allowed to pass unpunished"; because "the Industrial Disputes Act was treated as a dead letter"; because "actual open incitement of violence was not more firmly dealt with at the beginning of the trouble," because "the pickets of the strikers could assault men with impunity," because "no prosecution followed," and because "strikers and strike leaders were allowed to roam freely from mine to mine to induce men to strike" (Union of South Africa, *Report of the Witwatersrand Disturbances Commission,* 57; see also 14–15). The commission's use of the passive voice here accomplishes a very important task: it permits the commission to avoid placing blame for the disturbances on any single actor or agent, allowing it to suggest, instead, that the disturbances were caused *both* by the striking miners *and* by the authorities who did not suppress the disturbances promptly.

31. Union of South Africa, *Report of the Commission of Enquiry into Riots in Durban,* 6.

32. In 1893, the Featherstone Commission laid out the juridical conditions according to which soldiers could lawfully kill innocent bystanders and in which, as such, *no one* was to blame. The Featherstone Commission, as it was known, posed two questions: "Was what [the military] did necessary, and no more than was necessary, to put a stop to or prevent felonious crime? In so doing it did they exercise all ordinary skill and caution, so as to do no more harm than could be reasonably avoided? If these two conditions are made out, the fact that innocent people have suffered does not involve the troops in legal responsibility. A guilty ringleader who under such conditions is shot dead, dies by justifiable homicide. An innocent person killed under such conditions, where no negligence has occurred, dies by an accidental death. The legal reason is not that the innocent person has to thank himself for what has happened, for it is conceivable (though not often likely) that he may have been unconscious of any danger and innocent of all imprudence. *The reason is that the soldier who fired has done nothing except what was his strict legal duty"* (*Report of the Committee Appointed to Inquire into the Circumstances Connected with the Disturbances at Featherstone,* 11 (emphasis mine). See also Union of South Africa, *Report of the Witwatersrand Disturbances Commission,* 64 (arguing, "that sightseers or even innocent people were hurt whilst the soldiers were firing into the mob or endeavoring to silence the snipers does not involve the soldiers in any legal responsibility").

33. See, for example, *Report of the Commission on the Palestine Disturbances of August, 1929*, Presented by the Secretary of State for the Colonies to Parliament by Command of His Majesty, March 1930 (London: His Majesty's Stationery Office, 1930), 168.

34. For the narration of "tumults" in terms of tragedy, see, for example, Union of South Africa, *Report of the Martial Law Inquiry Judicial Commission*, 35 (on the "tragic and deplorable events" in which the "unavoidable" use of force by the military resulted in the deaths of several "innocent citizens"); Union of South Africa, *Report of the Commissioners Appointed to Enquire into the Causes of, and Occurrences at, the Native Disturbances at Port Elizabeth*, 8 (arguing that the inspector of police could have averted the "tragedy" in which a police fusillade killed numerous unnamed natives and one European); Union of South Africa, *Report of the Commission of Enquiry into Riots in Durban*, 5 (referring to riots between Indians and Natives as a "tragic explosion"); Bishop of Johannesburg, *Commission of Enquiry into the Occurrences at Sharpeville*, 2:192 (arguing that the "tragedy of Sharpeville" is that the police "disregarded both the letter and the spirit of their own Standing Orders and disobeyed the law of the land"); Republic of South Africa, *Report of the Commission Appointed to Investigate and Report on the Occurrences in the Districts of Vereeniging (Namely, at Sharpeville Location and Evaton) and Vanderbijlpark, Province of the Transvaal, on 21st March, 1960* (Pietermaritzburg: Government Relations Office, 1961), 3 (on the "tragic occurrences" of Sharpeville); and Republic of South Africa, *Report of the Commission of Inquiry into the Violence Which Occurred on 29 October 1983 at the University of Zululand*, 5, 82 (referring to the events that took place on October 29, 1983, as "tragic").

35. General Jan Smuts, speech to Parliament, in *Debates of the House of Assembly of the Union of South Africa, as Reported in the Cape Times*, vol. 8, Third Session, Fourth Parliament, 20th January 1923 to 25th June, 1923 (Pretoria: State Library, 1969), 328.

36. John Dugard, *The South West Africa/Namibia Dispute: Documents and Scholarly Writings on the Controversy between South Africa and the United Nations* (Berkeley: University of California Press, 1973), 72–74.

37. General Jan Smuts, speech to Parliament, *Debates of the House of Assembly of the Union of South Africa, as Reported in the Cape Times*, 8:329.

38. A. M. Davey, *The Bondelzwarts Affair: A Study of the Repercussions, 1922–1959* (Pretoria: Communications of the University of South Africa, 1961), 19–20.

39. Underhill, *Tragedy of Morant Bay*, 156.

40. Hobbes, *Leviathan*, 88.

41. Sachs, *Justice in South Africa*, 229.

42. The 1916 Judicial Commission of Inquiry into the 1915 Rand Riots is exemplary of this style of argumentation. The commissioners conclude that "the German South-West Africa Expedition, proposed by the Government and sanctioned by Parliament, was not an actual cause of the rebellion, but it was very unpopular with a considerable portion of the inhabitants in the country districts; and that these people were stirred

up by their leaders who were opposed to the Government policy into a condition of excitement and unrest which made for rebellion and facilitated the actual rising." See Union of South Africa, *Report of the Judicial Commission of Inquiry into the Causes of and Circumstances Relating to the Recent Rebellion in South Africa*, 101.

43. Union of South Africa, *Report of the Indian Enquiry Commission* (Cape Town, Cape Times, Government Printers, 1914), 1.

44. Union of South Africa, *Report of the Commission Appointed to Enquire into the Rebellion of the Bondelzwarts*, 4.

45. Union of South Africa, *Report of the Commission Appointed to Enquire into the Rebellion of the Bondelzwarts*, 24–25, 28.

46. Union of South Africa, *Report of the Commission of Enquiry into the Disturbances in the Witzieshoek Native Reserve*, 10.

47. Union of South Africa, *Report of the Commission of Enquiry into the Disturbances in the Witzieshoek Native Reserve*, 29. This emphasis on the "mutual and reciprocal necessity" between "black and white" is also apparent in the commissions of inquiry cited by the architects of apartheid itself. See, for example, Werner Eiselen, "The Meaning of Apartheid," *Journal of Race Relations* 15, no. 3 (1948), 75–76.

48. One sees this even in the Wessels Commission, which, even at the height of apartheid, is careful to include a paragraph acknowledging the sincerity of the grievances of the PAC protestors. See *Report of the Commission Appointed to Investigate and Report on the Occurrences in the Districts of Vereeniging*, 21.

49. *Hansard Parliamentary Debates*, 4th ser., vol. 20 (1894), col. 1292.

50. *Hansard Parliamentary Debates*, 3rd ser., vol. 242 (1878), col. 462. In 1951, "the appointment of a Commission of Enquiry was announced to the Natives and on that occasion the group under the leadership of Mopelinyana [the "disloyal" group] declared that they did not want anything to do with the Commission." After the arrival, fences burned, and a massive demonstration was called "which was without doubt intended to intimidate the Commission" (9).

51. See, in this regard, parliamentary debates over the 1914 indemnity in South Africa (*Hansard Parliamentary Debates*, 5th ser., vol. 58 [1914], col. 360).

52. As Victor Bruce Lords put it in 1890, "Commissions of Inquiry may be made the means of postponing a decision on troublesome subjects" (*Hansard Parliamentary Debates*, 3rd ser., vol. 252 [1880], col. 70).

53. In 1866, Edward Cardwell praised "the solemn decision of the Commissioners, arrived at after a most careful and anxious study of this painful subject. They were of opinion that the prompt repression of the disturbances was a measure of mercy, as well as a measure of justice—'A little fire is quickly trodden out Which, being suffered, rivers cannot quench'" (*Hansard Parliamentary Debates*, 3rd ser., vol. 184 [1866], col. 1820). The Witwatersrand Disturbances Commission reached a similar conclusion: "A riot must be quelled, and quelled at once, for the longer it is allowed to continue the greater the force required to subdue it and therefore the greater the likelihood of bloodshed. If the neces-

sity of the case is such that blood must be shed, then unpleasant as it is to say so, the more effective the force employed at the beginning the greater the eventual saving of life" (Union of South Africa, *Report of the Witwatersrand Disturbances Commission*, 60). So, too, did the Indian Enquiry Commission. Reporting on an incident where police used revolvers to shoot at Indian strikers who knocked four police officers to the ground, the commissioners argued that this "shows how necessary it was that the attack should have been repelled as promptly as possible. The only way in which this could have been done was by the use of revolvers, and regrettable as the loss of life was, we are clearly of opinion that the police were amply justified in firing when they did, and that, if they had not done so, in all probability the eventual loss of life would have been considerably greater than it actually was" (Union of South Africa, *Report of the Indian Enquiry Commission*, 6). In 1922, after describing the range of military weapons the government used to suppress the Rand Riots, including heavy bombing, the commissioners conceded that "it is no doubt true that the forces mobilized and sent to the scene of the disturbances proved to be greater than what was probably necessary to restore law and order. The Commission, however, is of opinion that this led to the saving of much bloodshed" (Union of South Africa, *Report of the Martial Law Inquiry Judicial Commission*, 14–15; see also 102 [noting that "the earnest and whole-hearted aim of the Government [was] promptly to suppress the rebellion and restore peace to the Union with the least possible shedding of blood"]). Merciless killing, inasmuch as it teaches the natives a lesson about law and thus also prevents future loss of life, here paradoxically qualifies as a form of mercy. See also, on this point, Kostal, *Jurisprudence of Power*, 471 (quoting a Victorian racist as saying that "it seems paradoxical to say so, but there may be mercy in a massacre").

54. Lalu, *Deaths of Hintsa*, 62; cf. Stoler, *Along the Archival Grain*, 142.

55. Jonathan Hyslop, "Gandhi, 1869–1915: The Transnational Emergence of a Public Figure," in *The Cambridge Companion to Gandhi*, ed. Judith M. Brown and Anthony Parel (Cambridge: Cambridge University Press, 2011), 47–48.

56. Various factions have stayed away from various commissions at various points in time. In 1913 and 1916, Afrikaner strikers stayed away from commissions (Union of South Africa, *Report of the Witwatersrand Disturbances Commission*, 4; Union of South Africa, *Report of the Judicial Commission of Inquiry into the Causes of and Circumstances Relating to the Recent Rebellion in South Africa*, 2, 103). In 1914, on Gandhi's recommendation, Indians would stay away (Union of South Africa, *Report of the Indian Enquiry Commission*, 2), and in 1949, the ANC, the South African Communist Party, and other liberation organizations would boycott the Durban Riot Commission (Union of South Africa. *Report of the Commission of Enquiry into Riots in Durban*, 1–2). In some cases (as in the 1914 Indian Commission), commissions had no power of subpoena to compel witnesses to come forward (3), but even where commissions were vested with this power, they often did not use it, on the assumption that an unwilling witness would not provide useful information (see, e.g., Union of South Africa, *Report of the Witwatersrand Disturbances Commission*, 42–45). See also Union of South Africa. *Report of the*

Commission of Enquiry into the Disturbances in the Witzieshoek Native Reserve (Parow: Cape Times, 1951), 2, 29. On the way in which Tumult Commissions were dominated by police testimony, see Union of South Africa, *Report of the Witwatersrand Disturbances Commission*, 4; Union of South Africa, *Report of the Indian Enquiry Commission*, 3; Union of South Africa, *Report of the Commissioners Appointed to Enquire into the Causes of, and Occurrences at, the Native Disturbances at Port Elizabeth*, 9; and Union of South Africa, *Report of the Commission of Enquiry into the Disturbances in the Witzieshoek Native Reserve*, 2.

57. Union of South Africa, *Report of the Indian Enquiry Commission*, 3–4; Union of South Africa, *Report of the Commission of Enquiry into Riots in Durban*, 5, 7–9. The latter also cleared the Durban Corporation of any and all allegations of "criminal neglect" (20).

58. Union of South Africa, *Report of the Indian Enquiry Commission*, 2.

59. Union of South Africa, *Report of the Indian Enquiry Commission*, 2.

60. See, for example, Union of South Africa, *Report of the Indian Enquiry Commission*, 11, 14.

61. Union of South Africa, *Report of the Indian Enquiry Commission*, 37–8.

62. Union of South Africa, *Report of the Commission of Enquiry into Riots in Durban*, 12.

63. Union of South Africa, *Report of the Commission of Enquiry into Riots in Durban*, 12.

64. Union of South Africa, *Report of the Commission of Enquiry into Riots in Durban*, 10.

65. Union of South Africa, *Report of the Commission of Enquiry into Riots in Durban*, 12.

66. Union of South Africa, *Report of the Commission of Enquiry into Riots in Durban*, 12–13.

67. Union of South Africa, *Report of the Commission of Enquiry into Riots in Durban*, 10, 13–19.

68. Union of South Africa, *Report of the Commission of Enquiry into Riots in Durban*, 11; Union of South Africa, *Report of the Commission of Enquiry into the Disturbances in the Witzieshoek Native Reserve*, 12–13; Republic of South Africa, *Report of the Commission of Inquiry into the Violence Which Occurred on 29 October 1983 at the University of Zululand*, 93–94.

69. See, for example, Union of South Africa, *Report of the Martial Law Inquiry Judicial Commission*, 32–34.

70. Union of South Africa, *Report of the Commission of Enquiry into Riots in Durban*, 10.

71. James Barber and John Barrett, *South Africa's Foreign Policy: The Search for Status and Security, 1945–1988* (Cambridge: Cambridge University Press, 1990), 25–28.

72. Mazower, *No Enchanted Palace*, 171–78.

73. This rationale for the creation of a Commission of Inquiry would persist in

South Africa. After the Sharpeville Massacre of 1961, for example, members of Parliament would argue that "good world publicity" was one of the reasons why the government should appoint a Commission of Inquiry (rather than a committee chaired by a government attorney) to investigate the actions of the police. See Republic of South Africa, *Debates of the House of Assembly*, June 9, 1961, cols. 7673–76.

74. *Hansard Parliamentary Debates*, 3rd ser., vol. 242 (1878), col. 467.

75. Union of South Africa, *Report of the Commission of Enquiry into Riots in Durban*, 21.

76. Union of South Africa, *Report of the Commission of Enquiry into Riots in Durban*, 13.

77. *The Compact Oxford English Dictionary, Second Edition* (Oxford: Clarendon Press, 1991), 2353.

78. Union of South Africa, *Report of the Commission of Enquiry into Riots in Durban*, 14. This, of course, is the standard justification for white supremacy within the discourse of demography. See Saul Dubow, *Scientific Racism in Modern South Africa* (Cambridge: Cambridge University Press, 1995), 66. On the "Grand Tradition" of Commissions of Inquiry, see Ashforth, *Official Discourse*, 8–9.

79. "Royal Commissions serve not only the informational function which led the nineteenth-century Benthamites to adopt them but also the other great Benthamite principle of government, namely, publicity" (Clokie and Robinson, *Royal Commissions of Inquiry*, 140).

80. The naming and the hearings of the commission, quite independently of its findings, functioned to solve the problem of "high emotions" until such passions were no longer relevant. See Herman Finer, *The Theory and Practice of Modern Government* (Ann Arbor: The University of Michigan Press, 1949), 447–48; Clokie and Robinson, *Royal Commissions of Inquiry*, 135.

81. "Recognizing that police massacres could not break the people's resistance," Govan Mbeki wrote of the aftermath of the 1960 Pondoland Massacre, "[T]he government announced that a Commission of Inquiry, composed of Bantu Administration officials, would be appointed to hear popular grievances." See Govan Mbeki, *South Africa: The Peasants' Revolt* (Baltimore: Penguin Books, 1964), 122.

82. Wolpe, *Race, Class, and the Apartheid State*, 68, 71; Saul Dubow, *The African National Congress* (Gloucestershire: Sutton, 2000), 62–64.

83. Writing in 1961, in the wake of Sharpeville, A. M. Davey argued that the Bondelzwarts Massacre, which, on its own terms, would have been just another colonial war, was the unacknowledged precursor for bad world public opinion over Sharpeville: "The Bondelzwarts affair was a domestic and an international issue. As a purely South African episode it might have been dismissed in the late 19th century as yet another 'Kaffir war' that aroused the customary echoes of approval and dissent in the local parliament and press. In the third decade of the 20th century, however, the expedition against an obscure Hottentot tribe in South West Africa was widely publicized in other countries

and resulted in a 'test-case' before an international forum." Davey then proceeded to ask whether the Bondelzwarts Massacre had not established the paradigm for the negative world public opinion formed about the apartheid state following the Sharpeville Massacre: "A substitution of 'National Party' for 'South African Party,' 'United Nations' for 'League of Nations' and 'Sharpeville' for 'Bondelzwarts' brings us to the fringe of current history. . . . Could it not be said that in 1922, rightly or wrongly, an unfavourable impression was created abroad that had lasting consequences? In many quarters the Union was thenceforth suspect as a ruler over non-white peoples; a climate was created in which lookers-on, especially the non-whites, would be on the alert for any signs of 'oppression.' The Bondelzwarts affair followed within a short space of the Bulhoek shooting and the bloody Rand revolt; the Union's critics at this time might have concluded, not unreasonably, that South Africans were tumultuous, ruthless and perhaps unfit to rule. In retrospect, it must be concluded that the Bondelzwarts affair was a grave setback for South Africa." See Davey, *Bondelzwarts Affair*, 5, 26–28.

84. Wolpe, *Race, Class, and the Apartheid State*, 67, 101.

85. Philip Frankel, *An Ordinary Atrocity: Sharpeville and Its Massacre* (Witwatersrand University Press, 2001), 187–88.

86. *Report of the Commission Appointed to Investigate and Report on the Occurrences in the Districts of Vereeniging*, 21.

87. Tom Lodge, *Sharpeville: A Massacre and Its Consequences* (Oxford: Oxford University Press, 2011), 329.

88. Lodge, *Sharpeville*, 328–29.

89. Lodge, *Sharpeville*, 328.

90. *Report of the Commission Appointed to Investigate and Report on the Occurrences in the Districts of Vereeniging*, 3.

91. Republic of South Africa, *Debates of the Senate*, June 15, 1961, col. 5341.

92. Frankel, *Ordinary Atrocity*, 199.

93. As the British international relations scholar Charles Manning wrote in 1964, "Individually the behavior of white men may in many instances be unforgivable. But collectively and officially the Europeans still reveal a sense of paternalistic concern which could all too easily be lost if the non-whites should be seen by the whites as potential political rivals, and therefore eventual rulers. No one who questions the sincerity of the white leadership to 'do the right thing' for the African can hope to understand the philosophy of apartheid; and it is presumably the fact that so many do seemingly doubt that sincerity which accounts for some of the incomprehension with which current policies are viewed" ("South Africa and the World: In Defense of Apartheid," *Foreign Affairs* 43, no. 1 (1964): 145.

94. Wolpe, *Race, Class, and the Apartheid State*, 74; Robert Price, *The Apartheid State in Crisis: Political Transformation of South Africa, 1975–1990* (Oxford: Oxford University Press, 1991), 59; Hein Marais, *South Africa: Limits to Change; The Political Economy of Transition* (Cape Town: University of Cape Town Press, 1998), 38–40.

95. The National Party would be criticized on this point in Parliament. See Republic of South Africa, *Debates of the House of Assembly*, February 1, 1977, cols. 571–72.

96. See, on this point, Aubrey Mokadi, *Narrative as Creative History: The 1976 Soweto Uprising as Depicted in Black South African Novels* (Johannesburg: Sedibeng, 2003), 50.

97. See, for example, Republic of South Africa, *Report of the Commission of Inquiry into the Riots at Soweto and Elsewhere from the 16th of June 1976 to the 28th of February*, vol. 1 (Pretoria: Government Printer, 1980), 395–97, 477.

98. Tutu, *No Future without Forgiveness*, 115.

99. Price, *Apartheid State in Crisis*, 60.

100. Price, *Apartheid State in Crisis*, 102. Price does not mention the Commission of Inquiry Relating to the Coloured Population Group (the "Theron Commission," named for its chair, Erika Theron, a sociologist at Stellenbosch University). In its report (which was tabled on June 18, 1976, the same day that the government announced the formation of the Cillié Commission), the Theron Commission recommended, among other things, that the Immorality Act and the Prohibition of Mixed Marriages Act be repealed, that all universities be opened to "Coloureds," and that job reservations for "Coloureds" be removed. The government's rejection of and silence on these recommendations was, at least according to Baruch Hirson, a factor in the spread of the Soweto Uprising to the Cape Province in August and September of 1976. See Baruch Hirson, *Year of Fire, Year of Ash: The Soweto Revolt, Roots of a Revolution?* (London: Zed Books, 1979), 224–26.

101. Price, *Apartheid State in Crisis*, 60.

102. Mokadi, *Narrative as Creative History*, 49; Helena Pohlandt-McCormick, *"I Saw a Nightmare": Doing Violence to Memory; The Soweto Uprising, June 16, 1976* (New York: Columbia University Press), accessed January 25, 2009, http://www.gutenberg-e.org/pohlandt-mccormick/.

103. Republic of South Africa, *Report of the Commission of Inquiry into the Riots at Soweto and Elsewhere*, 41–102, 103.

104. Republic of South Africa, *Report of the Commission of Inquiry into the Riots at Soweto and Elsewhere*, 587–604.

105. Republic of South Africa, *Report of the Commission of Inquiry into the Riots at Soweto and Elsewhere*, 604.

106. Republic of South Africa, *Report of the Commission of Inquiry into the Riots at Soweto and Elsewhere*, 617.

107. As remarkable as it is, this profound and intriguing disavowal is not, however, entirely unprecedented. In 1949, the Durban Riots Commission would concede that "tension" and "frustration" over inequalities between Indians and Africans would be at issue in the riots, but in a way that does not implicate the policies and laws that command and enforce those inequalities. The Cillié Commission simply radicalizes this disavowal, taking it to an extreme. A case in point is its argument about Bantu education: except for the fact that Bantu education gave rise to the riots, it had nothing to do with the riots.

108. Kostal, *Jurisprudence of Power*, 126.

109. Davey, *Bondelzwarts Affair*, 23.

110. Davey, *Bondelzwarts Affair*, 25.

CHAPTER 7

1. Van Zyl, "Dilemmas of Transitional Justice," 652–53.

2. See, for example, Martha Minow, *Between Vengeance and Forgiveness: Facing History after Genocide and Mass Violence* (Boston: Beacon, 1999), 57–61; Teitel, *Transitional Justice*, 82; Tutu, *No Future without Forgiveness*, 33.

3. Wessels argues that "it is . . . not the task of the Commission to report on the liability of persons for their acts and omissions. Findings of this sort fall in my view outside the scope of Your Excellency's instruction. This decision is, however, also supported by certain considerations of reasonableness. There were no litigating parties before the Commission and the course of proceedings was determined by the Commissioner. No person could legally lay claim to a proper opportunity to plead his own cause or to refute allegations against him. The members of the two groups most closely concerned with the tragic occurrences—namely, the South African Police and the Pan Africanist Congress—were not represented by legal practitioners. Where members of these two groups were called as witnesses this was done because they could give evidence about the occurrences and not to enable them to put a definite case or to make or refute allegations. The majority of the persons whose actions and omissions were discussed before the Commission participated in the proceedings neither as witnesses nor in any other capacity. In my view it would, therefore, have been extremely unreasonable to make findings of the above-mentioned nature" (Republic of South Africa, *Report of the Commission Appointed to Investigate and Report on the Occurrences in the Districts of Vereeniging*, 2).

4. See, on this point, Wilson, *Politics of Truth and Reconciliation in South Africa*, 34.

5. On the origins and limits of trauma studies, see John Mowitt, "Trauma Envy," *Cultural Critique* 46 (2000): 272–97; Christopher Colvin, "Trauma," in *New South African Keywords*, ed. Nick Shepherd and Steven Robins (Athens: Ohio University Press, 2008), 223–26. On traumatic suffering as an epistemological site for the theorization of "common humanity," see Didier Fassin and Richard Rechtman, *The Empire of Trauma: An Inquiry into the Condition of Victimhood*, trans. Rachel Gomme (Princeton: Princeton University Press, 2009), 39.

6. *TRC Report*, vol. 1, chap. 5, ¶¶40–42.

7. See, for example, *TRC Report*, vol. 1, chap. 2, ¶¶1, 13; *TRC Report*, vol. 5, chap. 8, ¶8; *TRC Report*, vol. 5, chap. 9, ¶385; Boraine, *A Country Unmasked*, 344.

8. As one of the nine arguments he advances for a Truth Commission, Asmal cites "the argument that comes from Gramsci," asking, "If the old order is dying and the new is not yet born, can there be reconciliation simply through an assertion that new structures

and new arrangements will be set in place? Is reconciliation between victim/survivor and the overlord possible on the basis of a Caliban and Prospero relationship, between master and servant?" ("Victims, Survivors, and Citizens," 11).

9. "The Road to South Africa Freedom: Programme of the South African Communist Party," *African Communist* 2, no. 2 (1963), 43–44.

10. Harold Wolpe, "The Theory of Internal Colonialism: The South African Case," in *Beyond the Sociology of Development*, ed. Ivar Oxall, Tony Barnett, and David Booth (London: Routledge, 1975), 229–51; Mamdani, *Citizen and Subject*, 28.

11. Wolpe, *Race, Class, and the Apartheid State*, 35.

12. Joe Slovo, "Has Socialism Failed?" *African Communist* 121, no. 2 (1990): 36–38.

13. Joe Slovo, "Beyond the Stereotype: The SACP in the Past, Present, and Future," *African Communist* 122, no. 2 (1991): 7–9.

14. Slovo, "Beyond the Stereotype," 9.

15. Martin Legassick, *Towards Socialist Democracy* (Pietermaritzburg: University of KwaZulu-Natal Press, 2007), 527–35.

16. Antonio Gramsci, *Selections from the Prison Notebooks*, ed. and trans. Q. Hoare and G. N. Smith (New York: International Publishers, 1971), 367.

17. Gramsci, *Prison Notebooks*, 418–19.

18. Gramsci, *Prison Notebooks*, 195, 246–47, 350.

19. On Gramsci and Croce, see Ernst Jouthe, *Catharsis et Transformation Sociale dans la Théorie Politique de Gramsci* (Québec: Presses de l'Université du Québec, 1990), 28–29, 34, 36–41. On ideas as material forces, cf. Gramsci, *Prison Notebooks*, 404.

20. Gramsci, *Prison Notebooks*, 366, 404.

21. Gramsci, *Prison Notebooks*, 195–96, 242.

22. Gramsci, *Prison Notebooks*, 247, 265–66, 268.

23. Antonio Gramsci, "Three Principles, Three Orders," in *History, Philosophy, and Culture in the Young Gramsci*, ed. Pedro Cavalcanti and Paul Piccone, trans. Pierluigi Molajoni et al. (New York: Telos, 1975), 75 (emphasis in original).

24. Gramsci, *Prison Notebooks*, 196.

25. Gramsci, *Prison Notebooks*, 263.

26. Asmal, "Victims, Survivors, and Citizens," 11.

27. Asmal, "Victims, Survivors, and Citizens," 9.

28. See Kader Asmal, "Human Rights, Reparations, and Reconciliation," Studies and Reports by the Ecumenical Foundation of Southern Africa (Institute for Theological and Interdisciplinary Research, University of Stellenbosch), October 24, 1991, 3. Others have made this point as well. See, for example, Heribert Adam and Kanya Adam, "The Politics of Memory in Divided Societies," in *After the TRC: Reflections on Truth and Reconciliation in South Africa*, ed. Wilmot James and Linda van de Vijver (Athens: Ohio University Press, 2001), 39.

29. Asmal, "Victims, Survivors, and Citizens,"16.

30. "[T]he catharsis argument . . . calls for an outlet of emotion, and through an act

of purgation allows for change without violent disruption" (Asmal, "Victims, Survivors, and Citizens," 12). Asmal would repeat the same argument three years later, in a speech before the National Assembly. As the fifth reason for a Truth Commission, he argued that "we must allow room for a cathartic release of emotion, but without the excesses of violent disruption." See Republic of South Africa, *Debates of the National Assembly*, May 17, 1995, col. 1381.

31. Asmal, Asmal, and Roberts, *Reconciliation through Truth*, 47–48 ("*sic*" in original).

32. Asmal, Asmal, and Roberts, *Reconciliation through Truth*, 46.

33. Asmal, Asmal, and Roberts, *Reconciliation through Truth*, 11.

34. The sense in which the TRC shared elements of revolutionary discourse is confirmed by its bitterest and most sympathetic critics alike. Cf. Dan Roodt, *Om Die Waarheidskommissie Te Vergeet* (Dainfern: Pro-Afrikaanse Aksiegroep, 2000), 38, 44–45, 124–26; Meister, *After Evil*, 20–49.

35. See, on this point, Hannah Arendt, *On Revolution* (New York: Penguin Books, 1991), 197; Hannah Arendt, *The Life of the Mind*, vol. 2 (New York: Harcourt Brace Jovanovich, 1978), 204–13. In a more properly Gramscian register, the nationalist narrations enabled by the TRC justified the route by which the nation achieved its "moment of arrival." See, on this point, Chatterjee, *Nationalist Thought and the Colonial World*, 51–52.

36. Frantz Fanon, "On National Culture," in *The Wretched of the Earth*, trans. Constance Farrington (New York: Grove Press, 1963), 239.

37. As Marx writes, "In order for the revolution of the people and the emancipation of a particular class of civil society to coincide, in order for one class to be regarded as the whole of society, all defects of society must, in reverse, be concentrated in another class, a particular class must be the class of universal offenses [*Anstoßes*], the incorporation of the universal barrier [*Schranke*], a particular social sphere must be regarded as the notorious crime [*notorische Verbrechen*] of the whole society, so that the liberation from this sphere can appear as universal self-liberation" (Karl Marx, "A Contribution to the Critique of Hegel's Philosophy of Right," in *Early Writings*, trans. Rodney Livingstone and Gregor Benton [New York: Vintage Books, 1975], 254; translation modified).

38. See, for example, the 1993 criticism of Kollapen, in "Accountability: The Debate in South Africa," 3.

39. *TRC Report*, vol. 1, chap. 5, ¶103.

40. *TRC Report*, vol. 1, chap. 1, ¶¶62, 19–20; *TRC Report*, vol. 1, chap. 4, ¶¶51–59 and appendix; *TRC Report*, vol. 5, chap. 5, ¶¶68–71, 101, chap. 9 (minority position submitted by Commissioner Wynand Malan), ¶¶18–20.

41. *TRC Report*, vol. 1, chap. 1, ¶¶19–20, 43, 59; *TRC Report*, vol. 5, chap. 5, ¶¶48–49, chap. 9 (minority position submitted by Commissioner Wynand Malano, ¶¶63–64.

42. Jacqueline Rose, "Apathy and Accountability: South Africa's Truth and Reconciliation Commission," *Raritan* 21, no. 4 (2002): 185–86.

43. *TRC Report*, vol. 1, chap. 1, ¶¶16, 43–46; *TRC Report*, vol. 5, chap. 4, ¶¶181–90; *TRC Report*, vol. 5, chap. 6, ¶101.

44. *TRC Report*, vol. 1, chap. 5, ¶108; *TRC Report*, vol. 5, chap. 6, ¶165.

45. Kader Asmal, Louise Asmal, Ronald Suresh Roberts, "When the Assassin Cries Foul: The Modern Just War Doctrine," in Villa-Vicencio and Verwoerd, *Looking Back, Reaching Forward*, 95; Asmal, Asmal, and Roberts, *Reconciliation through Truth*, 15 and afterword, XI–XII.

46. Asmal, "International Law and the Liquidation of Apartheid," 13.

47. See, on this point, Laura Moss, "'Nice Audible Crying': Editions, Testimonies, and *Country of My Skull*," *Research in African Literatures* 37, no. 4 (December 2006), 88; Taiwo Adetunji Osinubi, "Abusive Narratives: Antjie Krog, Rian Malan, and the Transmission of Violence," *Comparative Studies of South Asia, Africa, and the Middle East* 28, no. 1 (2008): 110. There are, needless to say, many other literary texts besides Krog's that take up the problematics of the TRC. See, for example, Louise Bethlehem, *Skin Tight: Apartheid Literary Culture and Its Aftermath* (Pretoria: University of South Africa Press, 2006); Joseph Slaughter, *Human Rights, Inc.: The World Novel, Narrative Form, and International Law* (New York: Fordham University Press, 2007), 141–52; Shane Graham, *South African Literature after the Truth Commission: Mapping Loss* (New York: Palgrave, 2009); Rosemary Jolly, *Cultured Violence: Narrative, Social Suffering, and Engendering Human Rights* (Liverpool: Liverpool University Press, 2010); Gready, *Era of Transitional Justice*, 58.

48. Carli Coetzee, "'They Never Wept, the Men of My Race': Antjie Krog's *Country of My Skull* and the White South African Signature," *Journal of Southern African Studies* 27, no. 4 (2001), 686–88; Moss, "'Nice Audible Crying,'" 87–88.

49. Mark Sanders, *Ambiguities of Witnessing: Law and Literature in the Time of a Truth Commission* (Stanford: Stanford University Press, 2007), 6, 21, 154.

50. See, for example, Antjie Krog, *Country of My Skull* (Johannesburg: Random House, 1998), 27–29, 50–55, 147–51, 177–90. For different criticisms of this same technique, see Ruden, "*Country of My Skull*," 170; Moss, "'Nice Audible Crying,'" 94.

51. Ruden, "*Country of My Skull*," 168–69; Moss, "'Nice Audible Crying,'" 86, 91–92.

52. Krog, *Country of My Skull*, 278.

53. See also, on this point, Moss, "'Nice Audible Crying,'" 92.

54. Krog, *Country of My Skull*, 196–97.

55. Krog, *Country of My Skull*, 170–71.

56. Krog, *Country of My Skull*, 171.

57. Moss, "Nice Audible Crying," 93.

58. Although the field of trauma studies has tended to universalize Freud's theory of trauma, not to mention desexualize it, Freud himself developed that theory with reference to a very specific experience: the symptoms of shell-shocked soldiers upon their return home from World War I. The imprints of this experience remain perceptible in the theory of trauma itself. Trauma theory emphasizes the phenomenon of *Nachträglich-*

keit, or "deferred action," and, later, post-traumatic stress syndrome. In this phenomenon, I experience my trauma for the first time only in its repetition—only when I belatedly become conscious of a violence that happened the first time too quickly for me to understand. Not only does this presuppose an experience of violence that, like a bomb, is punctual and quick, that happens too suddenly for me to consciously narrate; it also presupposes a distinction between war and peace, for *Nachträglichkeit* assumes that the trauma I experience in the space and time of war shall return in the symptoms I experience in the space and time of peace. See, on this point, Ruth Leys, *Trauma: A Genealogy* (Chicago: University of Chicago Press, 2000), 18–40, 83–199; Colvin, "Trauma," 229–31. These presuppositions certainly do allow trauma studies to make sense of the sort of individualized violence that the indemnification convention is predisposed to consider. But it is far from clear whether they are adequate either to the sort of confusion of peace and war that is characteristic of colonial administration or to the sort of state criminality that Asmal, Asmal, and Roberts, following Gramsci, want to put into question.

59. Colvin, "Trauma," 230. Already in 1991, Ramphele argued, "South Africa has become a huge industry in international development terms. The participants in this industry trade in the notion of 'victims of apartheid.' People's careers depend on their ability to play an advocacy role on behalf of the victims. The victim image is, however, ultimately disempowering. Whatever short-term gains are made out of this 'victimology,' disempowered people will need to be weaned from the resultant dependency. It also appears that too much dependence is placed by most political actors in South Africa on the goodwill of the international community to support transformation in South African social relations" (Mamphela Ramphele, "Empowerment and Symbols of Hope: Black Consciousness and Community Development," in *Bounds of Possibility: The Legacy of Steve Biko and Black Consciousness*, ed. N. Barney Pityana, M. Ramphele, M. Mpumiwana, and L. Wilson [Atlantic Highlands, NJ: Zed Press, 1992], 176). In the intervening decade, this dynamic has only intensified. On the relation between "victims" and "saviors" in the discourse of human rights, see Makau Mutua, "Savages, Victims, and Saviors: The Metaphor of Human Rights," *Harvard International Law Journal* 42 (Winter 2001): 227–42.

60. See, for example, Theodor Adorno, Else Frenkel-Brunswik, and Daniel J. Levinson, *The Authoritarian Personality* (New York: Norton, 1969), 448.

61. See Kenneth Burke, "The Thinking of the Body: Comments on the Imagery of Catharsis in Literature," *Psychoanalytic Review* 50 (Fall 1963): 375.

62. Achille Mbembe, *On the Postcolony* (Berkeley: University of California Press, 2001), 102–41, esp. 133.

63. Jane Taylor and William Kentridge, *Ubu and the Truth Commission* (Cape Town: University of Cape Town Press, 1998), 1. In the original *Ubu Roi*, the word *merdre* is a metonym for complicity in regicide: it is the password that Pa Ubu uses to order his coconspirator to comply with his order to murder the king of Poland. See Alfred Jarry, *Ubu Roi* (Paris: Gallimard, 2002), 29, 48.

64. On this point, see Cole, *Performing South Africa's Truth Commission*, 165.

65. Stephanie Marlin-Curiel, "Standard Bank National Arts Festival (Grahamstown, South Africa, 2–12 July 1998)," *Theatre Journal* 51, no. 1 (March 1999): 82.

66. Greig Coetzee, *Johnny Boskak Is Feeling Funny, and Other Plays* (Pietermaritzburg: University of KwaZulu-Natal Press, 2009).

67. Jacques Derrida, "Passions: An Oblique Offering," trans. David Wood, in *On the Name*, ed. Thomas Dutoit (Stanford: Stanford University Press, 1995), 28.

68. Greig Coetzee, *Past Imperfect* (n.p., n.d.) (on file with author; used with permission of Greig Coetzee).

CHAPTER 8

1. Asmal, Asmal, and Roberts, *Reconciliation through Truth*, 21; Albie Sachs, "His Name Was Henry," in James and van de Vijver, *After the TRC*, 96.

2. Desai, *We Are the Poors*, 70.

3. See, for example, Lodge, *Politics in South Africa*, 231, 235; Kiss, "Moral Ambition," 81, 86–87; Boraine, *A Country Unmasked*, 425–26; Drucilla Cornell and Kenneth Michael Panfilio, *Symbolic Forms for a New Humanity: Cultural and Racial Reconfigurations of Critical Theory* (Bronx, NY: Fordham University Press, 2010), 164–65.

4. State v. Makwanyane and Mchunu, 1995 (3) SA 237 (CC).

5. Wilson, *Politics of Truth and Reconciliation*, 9; Claire Moon, *Narrating Political Reconciliation: South Africa's Truth and Reconciliation Commission* (Lanham, MD: Lexington Books, 2008), 42, 140.

6. Chakrabarty, *Provincializing Europe*, 17.

7. Sanders, *Ambiguities of Witnessing*, 24.

8. Wilson, *Politics of Truth and Reconciliation*, 9–10; Eleni Coundouriotis, "The Dignity of the 'Unfittest': Victims' Stories in South Africa," *Human Rights Quarterly* 28, no. 4 (November 2006): 866–67; Moon, *Narrating Political Reconciliation*, 36, 118. For a response to this critique, see Bronwyn Leebaw, *Judging State-Sponsored Violence, Imagining Political Change* (New York: Cambridge University Press, 2011), 130–37.

9. Tutu, *No Future without Forgiveness*, 35; Krog, *Country of My Skull*, 263; Michael Battle, *Ubuntu: I in You and You in Me* (New York: Seabury Books, 2009), 3.

10. Sanders, *Ambiguities of Witnessing*, 16ff.

11. Mudimbe, *Invention of Africa*, 161. On the centrality of linguistics for modern racial theories, see also Roberto Esposito, *Third Person: Politics of Life and Philosophy of the Impersonal*, trans. Zakiya Hanafi (Malden, MA: Polity Press, 2012), 36–53.

12. That discipline contributed just as much as biological racism, if not more, to the apartheid state's theorization and implementation of its "Bantustan" system. Writing in 1968, for example, the apartheid state's Department of Foreign Affairs would argue, "The Bantu (African) peoples of South Africa viz. the Xhosa, Zulu, Sotho, Tsana, Tsonga, Ndebele and Venda do not form a single nation. They are distinctively different nations although they are referred to collectively as the 'Bantu peoples.' The term *Bantu*,

which is much in usage in South Africa, does not have a racial connotation like the word 'negro' or 'black.' It derives from a word-stem meaning people [i.e., -ntu] and occurs in various forms in all the languages of the large Bantu language family. A Bantu nation is, therefore, a nation speaking a language belonging to one family of languages, much in the same way as the Dutch can be referred to as a nation speaking in an Indo-Germanic language. However, each Bantu nation has its own language and a Zulu cannot understand a Sotho any better than a German can understand an Englishmen" (Republic of South Africa, *South Africa and the Rule of Law*, 18). On the way that comparative philology contributed to the genesis of the theory and practice of apartheid, see Dubow, *Scientific Racism in Modern South Africa*, 74–82, esp. 81; Jean-Pierre Chrétien, "Les bantous, de la philologie allemande à l'authenticité Africaine: Un mythe racial contemporain," *Vingtième Siècle: Revue d'histoire* 8 (1985): 43–66, esp. 61. The inner connection between ethnophilosophy and apartheid would lead Frantz Fanon, in his 1952 criticism of Placide Tempels's 1945 book *La philosophie bantoue*, to sharply juxtapose Tempels's ontological account of "Bantu philosophy" to a long description of the administrative despotism in the South African Bantustans. As Fanon put it, "There is nothing ontological about segregation" (*Black Skin, White Masks*, trans. Charles Lam Markmann [New York: Grove, 1967], 186).

13. Mudimbe, *Invention of Africa*, x–xi, 186, and esp. 37 (on Paulin Hountondji's argument for the need for African philosophers to "weaken" or "impoverish" [*appauvrir*] the received concept of "Africa").

14. Sanders, *Ambiguities of Witnessing*, 96.

15. Lodge, *Politics in South Africa*, 231.

16. On the translation of the Zulu *umuntu* by "person," see John W. Appleyard, *The Kafir Language: Comprising a Sketch of Its History; Which Includes a General Classification of South African Dialects, Ethnological and Geographical; Remarks upon Its Nature; and a Grammar* (Graham's Town: Godlonton and White, 1850), 44; Lewis Grout, *The Isizulu: A Grammar of the Zulu Language* (Natal: May and Davis, 1859), 79; John William Colenso, *First Steps in Zulu: An Abridgement of the Elementary Grammar of the Zulu-Kafir Language* (Ekukanyeni, 1859), 4; *The Encyclopedia of Missions: Descriptive, Historical, Biographical, Statistical*, ed. Edwin Munsell Bliss, vol. 1 (New York: Funk and Wagnalls, 1891), 120–21; F. Mayr, *Zulu Simplified: Being a New, Practical, and Easy Method of Learning the Zulu Language* (Pietermaritzburg: Davis and Sons, 1899), 9.

17. Jean-Pierre Vernant, *Mortals and Immortals: Collected Essays*, ed. Froma Zeitlin (Princeton: Princeton University Press, 1991), 30, 142.

18. John Donne, *The Complete English Poems*, ed. Albert James Smith (New York: Penguin Books, 1971), 314–15. On the theological concept of the person, see Battle, *Ubuntu*, 5.

19. Hobbes, *Leviathan*, 111–15, 120.

20. See, on this point, Robert Bernasconi, "Persons and Masks: The *Phenomenology of Spirit* and Its Laws," in *Hegel and Legal Theory*, ed. Drucilla Cornell, Michel Rosenfeld, and David Carlson (New York: Routledge, 1991), 78–93; Susan Buck-Morss, *Hegel*,

Haiti, and Universal History (Pittsburgh: University of Pittsburgh Press, 2009), 52n90, 55–56. See, more generally, Timothy Campbell and Adam Sitze, "Introduction," *Law, Culture, and the Humanities* 8, no. 1 (February 2012): 6–16.

21. Mahmood Mamdani, *Define and Rule: Native as Political Identity* (Cambridge, MA: Harvard University Press, 2012), 74–84.

22. According to William Blackstone, the "rights of the person" comprise one of four great divisions of English common law. See William Blackstone, *Commentaries on the Laws of England*, vol. 1 (Chicago: University of Chicago Press, 1979), 118.

23. John Locke, *Two Treatises of Government; and a Letter Concerning Toleration* (New Haven: Yale University Press, 2003), 122–32 (§§52–76).

24. J. S. Mill, *'On Liberty' and Other Writings* (Cambridge: Cambridge University Press, 1989), 13–14. See also Mehta, *Liberalism and Empire*, 98–103; Anghie, *Imperialism, Sovereignty, and the Making of International Law*, 32–99. Here, it is also worth returning to the 1877 Commission of Inquiry into "colonial defence" we discussed in section 3.4 above. From this Commission it is clear that the concept of "person" operated as part of an apparatus of colonial control. To give "deserving persons" titles to land, so as to produce a feeling of a "personal interest in the land," was for this Commission a means to the end of achieving the "great aim" of the administration of native affairs: "to break down the power of the chiefs." See Cape of Good Hope, *Report of a Commission Appointed by His Excellency the Governor To Inquire Into and Report upon the Question of Colonial Defence*, 18.

25. See, on this point, Mbembe, *On the Postcolony*, 26–29, 134n8, 235–43.

26. Anghie, *Imperialism, Sovereignty, and the Making of International Law*, 65–99.

27. Anghie, *Imperialism, Sovereignty, and the Making of International Law*, 172–78.

28. Slaughter, *Human Rights, Inc.*, 56.

29. Slaughter, *Human Rights, Inc.*, 149.

30. Slaughter, *Human Rights, Inc.*, 3.

31. Slaughter, *Human Rights, Inc.*, 17, 58.

32. Slaughter, *Human Rights, Inc.*, 82–83.

33. Slaughter, *Human Rights, Inc.*, 93.

34. Esposito, *Third Person*, 64–87. See also Roberto Esposito, *"Dispositif* of the Person," trans. Timothy Campbell, *Law, Culture, and the Humanities* 8, no. 1 (February 2012): 17–30. On the "slave," see Aristotle, *Nicomachean Ethics*, 1161a30–1161b10; Aristotle, *Politics*, 1253b28–1254a17.

35. On "identity," see John Locke, *An Essay concerning Human Understanding* (Oxford: Oxford University Press, 2008), 208–19. On "dignity" and "respect," see Immanuel Kant, "The Metaphysics of Morals," in *Practical Philosophy*, trans. and ed. Mary Gregor (Cambridge: Cambridge University Press, 1996), 557–58. On "rights" and "obligation," see Hans Kelsen, *Pure Theory of Law*, trans. Max Knight (Berkeley: University of California Press, 1967), 172.

36. See, on this point, Joan Dayan, "Poe, Persons, and Property," *American Literary History* 1, no. 3 (Autumn 1999): 405–25.

37. Hahlo, "Law of Persons and Family Relations (Excluding the Law of Husband and Wife)," in *The Union of South Africa*, 345, cf. 41–42.

38. Hahlo, "Law of Persons and Family Relations," in *The Union of South Africa*, 345.

39. Hahlo, "Law of Persons and Family Relations," in *The Union of South Africa*, 346.

40. Hahlo, "Law of Persons and Family Relations," in *The Union of South Africa*, 346.

41. See also, on this point, Matthews, "Bantu Law and Western Civilization in South Africa," 214–15.

42. See, for example, Kojève, *Outline of a Phenomenology of Right*, 52–66.

43. See especially Pius Langa's concurring opinion in *State v. Makwanyane*, 1995 (3) SA, 224, 260 (CC).

44. In his rebuke of what he understood to be Cesare Beccaria's objection to the death penalty, Kant argues that Beccaria could confuse capital punishment with suicide writ large only because Beccaria did not observe any distinction between the *homo noumenon* (the "moral personality" who is the locus of "pure reason within me") and the *homo phoenomenon* (the "sensuous being" who is the locus of my desire to preserve myself in my "animal being"). When I consent to suffer the penalty of death at the hands of the sovereign, in Kant's view, it is not that I "desire" my own death in a suicidal manner. It is that "I" am the locus of two distinct beings, a *person* (the *homo noumenon*) and a *living being* (the *homo phoenomenon*), and that the *person* within me (i.e., the nameless force of pure reason, which "desires" nothing other than universality and necessity itself) dictates a perfectly consistent set of penal laws to which I then subject my own *living being*. (And I do so quite independently of whether those laws happen to result in my pleasure or in my pain, for as Kant will write in *The Critique of Practical Reason*, "the majesty of duty has nothing to do with the enjoyment of life.") Because the social contract is grounded not in the *conditional* duty of self-preservation but in the *unconditional* duty of adherence to the moral law, there is no contradiction at all when I (the *homo noumenon*) "will" the sovereign person (who is nothing other than the personification of the laws that "pure reason within me" has dictated) to kill my living being (in other words, to end my existence as *homo phoenomenon*).

Nothing could be further from suicide. Whereas the death penalty is that act by which my *homo noumenon* wills the killing of my *homo phoenomenon* in accordance with pure reason, suicide is the crime in which my *homo phoenomenon* murders my *homo noumenon* for merely contingent and empirical reasons (e.g., to take the famous example from Kant's *Groundwork*, a desire to release my animal being from an experience of intolerable suffering). Suicide is a violation of my unconditional duty: when my living being ends its own existence, it destroys its capacity to host pure reason and to bear a moral personality. In contrast to capital punishment, which is not murder because it is willed by pure reason, suicide is therefore a crime (because it is not willed by pure reason: pure reason, understood as the manifestation of the law of noncontradiction, indeed cannot will its own annihilation). "To annihilate the subject of morality in one's own person," Kant will therefore write, "is to root out the existence of morality from the world," and this can never be willed by morality itself. Whereas suicide is a violation of my human rights—of the "humanity in my own person"—the death penalty "honors" those rights. If a person is, as Kant will say, "a subject whose actions can be imputed to him," then the death penalty is an apparatus for treating the criminal like a person: it imputes to the criminal a faculty for pure reason, a capacity for freedom and autonomy in the strict and purely human sense, and therefore, on this same basis—out of respect for the criminal *as a person*, out of respect for what the pure reason *personified "in"* the criminal will have willed, and independently of what this or that empirical criminal will have desired—it executes the criminal. See Kant, *Practical Philosophy*, 53, 73–74, 80, 211, 476, 547.

45. Antije Krog has argued that the authors of South Africa's Constitution turned to the concept of *ubuntu* because they could not find in Latin phrases and Roman-Dutch concepts a word to describe a vision for a postapartheid society ("Choice for Amnesty," 117). This, however, underestimates the degree to which "legal continuity" was the overriding principle of the South African negotiated settlement. Daniel Herwitz, by contrast, has suggested that *ubuntu* be thought in and through its comparison with the lexicon of modern political philosophy, above all in its comparison with concepts of community, justice, decency, and humanity (*Race and Reconciliation*, xxvi). The argument that follows pursues the latter more than the former.

46. Hart, "The Ascription of Responsibility and Rights," 175.

47. Chanock, *Making of South African Legal Culture*, 33–35. All advocates are required to take two courses in Roman law as a part of their studies for their LLB degree, the minimum academic qualification for practicing as an advocate (South Africa Department of Foreign Affairs, *South Africa and the Rule of Law*, 25–26.) The apartheid state's Department of Foreign Affairs maintained, "The South African legal system is the modern outcome of a continuous process of development from ancient Roman Law" (Republic of South Africa, *South Africa and the Rule of Law*, 7; cf. 7–8 [emphasizing that Roman law has survived not in a pure form but in its cross-referencing first with Dutch customary law (Grotius in particular) and then, much later, with English common law]). There is a long-standing desire on the part of the school of South African historical jurisprudence to purify law in South Africa of all but its Roman roots. See, on this point, Dugard, *Human Rights and the South African Legal Order*, 9, 396–97.

48. Thus, in the aftermath of the Soweto Uprising, the event that sent apartheid into the crisis from which it would never recover, we witness the National Party arguing, "What we are faced with today is based on a principle that dates from the time of the Romans, namely, that the security of the State is the primary right. This rule was not laid down by the National Party; it dates from Roman times" (Republic of South Africa, *Debates of the House of Assembly*, February 1, 1977, col. 579). References of this sort were not at all uncommon in South African law. Cicero's maxim grounded the Public Safety Act of 1953, which permitted declarations of states of emergency in South Africa in 1960 and 1985 and again from 1986 to 1990. It also grounded some of the worst state security laws passed in South Africa, such as the Unlawful Organisations Act of 1960,

the General Amendment Act of 1962, and the Internal Security Amendment Act of 1976. Apartheid's apologists turned to Cicero to explain why apartheid judges could argue both that the republic respects the rule of law and that it breaks the rule of law. In 1966, Hahlo and Maisels could argue, "The Government of the Republic freely admits that much of its legislation falls short of the precepts of the rule of law but justifies it by the doctrine of *salus rei publicae*" (see, on this point, H. R. Hahlo and I. A. Maisels, "The Rule of Law in South Africa," *Virginia Law Review* 52, no. 1 [1966]: 27).

49. Krog, *Country of My Skull*, 110. This is certainly the case for the quasi-communitarian translation of *ubuntu*, but it is even the case for the translations of *ubuntu* that are closer to human rights discourse as explicated by Slaughter. Interpreters of *ubuntu* who gloss the concept by arguing that "no human is an island" are, after all, very much in line with the emphasis in the *Bildungsroman* on the prior community through which the person alone can realize itself. The same is true where *ubuntu* is defined as the notion that "the identity of the self is understood to be formed interdependently through community" (Battle, *Ubuntu*, 3).

50. Mudimbe, *Invention of Africa*, 146–47.

51. As Aristotle writes in book 1 of the *Politics*, "The polity is by nature clearly prior to the family and to the individual, since the whole is of necessity prior to the part; for example, if the whole body be destroyed, there will be no foot or hand, except homonymously, as we might speak of a stone hand; for when destroyed the hand will be no better than that" (1253a19–30).

52. Republic of Zimbabwe, *Debates of the House of Assembly*, January 21, 1981, col. 1307–8. Although it is made in postindependence Zimbabwe, this claim is identical in substance to a claim in the context of a debate over indemnity in Rhodesia in 1975. Quoting the chief justice of South Africa, Senator Strong argues that "everything must give way to the need for communal protection; all acts and measures coming within the purview of this principle are absolutely protected" (Republic of Rhodesia, *Debates of the Senate*, September 18, 1975, col. 839).

53. See, for example, Hans Morgenthau, "The Evil of Politics and the Ethics of Evil," *Ethics: An International Journal of Social, Political, and Legal Philosophy* 61, no. 1 (October 1945): 4–5. See also Hahlo and Kahn, *South African Legal System*, 438.

54. In *Behemoth*, for example, Hobbes writes that "the pretence of the Long Parliament's rebellion was *salus populi*," while Locke would later cite the same maxim to specify the conditions under which a legislature or prince has breached the "trust" conferred on it by the people, such that the people then reacquire the right to form an entirely new legislature. See Thomas Hobbes, *Behemoth, or The Long Parliament*, ed. Ferdinand Tönnies (Chicago: University of Chicago Press, 1990), 180; Locke, *Two Treatises*, 170–71, 197 (§§158, 222).

55. Quite prior to its career as the justification for the declaration of states of emergency and other sovereign exceptions that set aside the rule of law, in fact, the maxim of *salus populi* even served as the norm *governing* sovereign exceptions. Thus Hobbes calls

Cicero's maxim "the law over them that have the sovereign power," and Locke, writing in the context of the prince's prerogative, argues that it is "so just and fundamental a rule, that he, who sincerely follows it, cannot dangerously err." Even Jean Bodin, who hardly can be classified as a political liberal, calls Cicero's maxim "the principle to which there is no exception." See Hobbes, *Elements of Law*, 172 (see also Hobbes, *Dialogue*, 61, 63, 152–53); Locke, *Two Treatises*, 170 (§158); Jean Bodin, *The Six Books of the Commonwealth*, trans. M. J. Tooley (Oxford: Basil Blackwell, 1955), 471.

56. On *salus publica* as the regulative ideal for the pardon power, see Lucius Annaeus Seneca, "De Clementia," in *Seneca: Moral Essays*, trans. J. Basore (Cambridge: Harvard University Press, 1970), 413, 421–23; and Niccolò Machiavelli, *The Prince*, trans. A. Codevilla (New Haven: Yale University Press, 1997), 61.

57. Foucault, *Security, Territory, Population*, 109.

58. Foucault, *Security, Territory, Population*, 256.

59. Foucault, *Security, Territory, Population*, 124, 136, 151. See also Michel Foucault, "'Omnes et Singulatim': Toward a Critique of Political Reason," in *Power*, vol. 3 of *The Essential Works of Michel Foucault, 1954–1984*, ed. James D. Faubion, trans. Robert Hurley et al. (New York: New Press, 2000), 307.

60. Foucault, *Security, Territory, Population*, 167; Foucault, "'Omnes et Singulatim,'" 307–9; Michel Foucault, "The Subject and Power," in *Power*, 333.

61. Foucault, "'Omnes et Singulatim,'" 307; cf. Michel Foucault, *The Hermeneutics of the Subject: Lectures at the Collège de France 1981–82*, trans. Graham Burchell, ed. Frédéric Gros, François Ewald, and Allesandro Fontana (New York: Palgrave, 2005), 184.

62. Foucault, *Security, Territory, Population*, 126, 166–69, 192. See also Foucault, "'Omnes et Singulatim,'" 302; Foucault, "Subject and Power," 333; Michel Foucault, "Security, Territory, and Population" and "Technologies of the Self," in *Ethics: Subjectivity and Truth*, vol. 1 of *The Essential Works of Michel Foucault, 1954–1984*, ed. Paul Rabinow, trans. Robert Hurley et al. (New York: New Press, 1997), 67–68, 242.

63. Foucault, *Security, Territory, Population*, 129, 169–70.

64. Foucault, *Security, Territory, Population*, 174–77, 183, 195–96.

65. Foucault, *Security, Territory, Population*, 165, 234–37.

66. Foucault, "Subject and Power," 334.

67. Foucault, *Security, Territory, Population*, 229, 231.

68. Foucault, "Subject and Power," 334; Foucault, "Technologies of the Self," 215.

69. Foucault, *Security, Territory, Population*, 273.

70. Foucault, "Subject and Power," 334; Foucault, "Security, Territory, and Population," 67.

71. Michel Foucault, *"Society Must Be Defended": Lectures at the Collège de France, 1975–76*, ed. Mauro Bertani and Allesandro Fontana, trans. David Macey (New York: Picador, 2003), 242–43; Foucault, *History of Sexuality*, 139; Foucault, "Subject and Power," 334.

72. Foucault, *Security, Territory, Population*, 261.

73. Foucault, *Security, Territory, Population*, 126. See also Foucault, "Security, Territory, and Population," 67–68; "Technologies of the Self," 242; "'*Omnes et Singulatim*,'" 315, 317.

74. Thus Hobbes will argue that the end for which the commonwealth is instituted is "the Peace, and Security of the people"—or, as Locke put it, the formation of a political society is to be directed "to no other end but the peace, safety, and public good of the people." See Hobbes, *Leviathan*, 131; Locke, *Two Treatises*, 157 (§131).

75. Foucault, *Birth of Biopolitics*, 110.

76. Foucault, *Birth of Biopolitics*, 320.

77. Foucault, *Birth of Biopolitics*, 28.

78. Slaughter, *Human Rights, Inc.*, 21.

79. Foucault, *Birth of Biopolitics*, 63–64, 226.

80. Although Hayek holds up nineteenth-century British liberalism as the explicit paradigm for the liberalism he opposes to the despotic administrative excesses of totalitarianism, he oddly understands that same liberalism outside of the horizon of its own self-understanding: Hayek is completely silent on the way in which nineteenth-century British liberalism affirmed despotic state administration as an intrinsic and necessary element of its imperial and colonial project—as if one could return to the former without also returning to the latter. Arendt, by contrast, will argue that the colony is the very origin of the bureaucratic rule so radicalized by the totalitarian regimes; and not only Arendt but also Foucault will argue that the colony is also the origin for the genocidal racism exemplified in Europe by Nazism. The presupposition—systematic within neoliberalism—that nineteenth-century liberalism is the antidote to twentieth-century European totalitarianism is thus questionable at best. See Arendt, *Origins*, 185–221; Foucault, "*Society Must Be Defended*," 257.

81. François Venter, "Salus reipublicae suprema lex," *Tydskrif vir hedendaagse Romeins-Hollandse Reg* 40 (1977): 233, 243.

82. V. G. Hiemstra and H. L. Gonin, *Engels-Afrikaanse Regswoordeboek* (Kaapstad: Juta, 1963), 123.

83. J. L. Pretorius, "Aanhouding sonder verhoor in die noodtoestand" [Arrest without hearing in the state of emergency], *Woord en Daad*, February 1987, 14.

84. Pretorius, "Aanhouding sonder verhoor in die noodtoestand," 14.

85. Pretorius, "Aanhouding sonder verhoor in die noodtoestand," 15.

86. Basson and Viljoen, *South African Constitutional Law*, 268.

87. Basson and Viljoen, *South African Constitutional Law*, 218.

88. Basson and Viljoen, *South African Constitutional Law*, 12–13.

89. Basson and Viljoen, *South African Constitutional Law*, 268.

90. Basson and Viljoen, *South African Constitutional Law*, 246.

91. Basson and Viljoen, *South African Constitutional Law*, 246 (emphasis in original).

92. On aura and Latin quotations, see Peter Goodrich, "Distrust Quotations in Latin," *Critical Inquiry* 29, no. 2 (Winter 2003): 193–215.

93. Reinhart Koselleck, "A Response to Comments on the *Geschichtliche Grundbegriffe*," in *The Meaning of Historical Terms and Concepts: New Studies on Begriffsgeschichte*, ed. Hartmut Lehmann and Melvin Richter (Washington, DC: German Historical Institute, 1996), 64.

94. Already in 1975, Lewis Nkosi diagnosed the recuperative quality of this sort of anxiety, arguing that jurists who trace South Africa's political repression to the disappearance of traditions of Roman-Dutch law are simply lending respectability and camouflage to a regime with a legal process that is "phoney" (*Transplanted Heart*, 16).

95. Gerhard Erasmus, "Limitation and Suspension," in van Wyk et al., *Rights and Constitutionalism*, 658–59.

96. Erasmus, "Limitation and Suspension," 630, 651.

97. Basson and Viljoen, *South African Constitutional Law*, 246.

98. Taken together, Sections 33, 34, and 8 render defunct and inapplicable the doctrines of martial law and the prerogative powers that dominated the apartheid state: on the basis of these Sections, Cicero's maxims cannot function as a valid premise for juridical reasoning in South Africa, not even as "implied provisions." See David van Wyk, "Introduction to the South African Constitution," in van Wyk et al., *Rights and Constitutionalism*, 163; Gerhard Erasmus, "Limitation and Suspension," 651, 659.

99. Erasmus, "Limitation and Suspension," 634, 643.

100. *State v. Makwanyane*, 1995 (3) SA 131 (CC).

101. Pumla Gobodo-Madikizela, *A Human Being Died That Night: A South African Story of Forgiveness* (Boston: Houghton Mifflin Harcourt, 2003), 139.

102. Locke, *Two Treatises*, 104, 107, 177 (§§11, 16, 171–72).

103. See note 44.

104. Wulf Sachs, "Racism: The Solution," *Democrat* (Johannesburg), January 20, 1944, 15–16.

105. Dubow, *African National Congress*, 29.

106. Quoted in Boraine, *A Country Unmasked*, 362 (emphasis mine).

107. As Dubow writes of Lembede, "With puritanical distaste, he disdained the cosmopolitan and sophisticated existence of black Johannesburg as evidence of moral degeneracy and cultural confusion, seeking the basis of black identity instead in an immanent 'African spirit' rooted in the soil and history of the continent. The mix of cultural and racial essentialism which suffuses Lembede's thought led him to proclaim Africa as a 'blackman's country.' He was inclined to reject political cooperation with white and Indian radicals and, notwithstanding a clear intellectual debt to various brands of European romantic nationalism, he denounced all foreign ideologies—communism in particular—as a threat to indigenous self-assertion" (*African National Congress*, 29).

108. We may punctuate this with a concrete example of the way the "*ntu* vision of the human being," translated into quasi-communitarian terms, lends itself to the excesses of postcolonial authoritarianism. This becomes clearest from an article on the "*ntu* vision of the human being" written by the philosopher Tshiamalenga Ntumba in 1973, at the

height of Mobuto Seke Seso's 1971–76 "authenticity campaign" in Zaire. This campaign, which took place during the same years that Mobuto fought alongside the apartheid state in Angola, combined authoritarian presidentialism (Seke Seso quickly normalized the *regime d'exception* he declared in 1965) and censorship (directed particularly at Belgian Catholics) as a means to the end of producing "mental decolonization" and "cultural disalienation," on the one hand, and Zairianization of the economy, on the other hand. Teaching in the Faculté de Théologie Catholoque de l'Université Nationale du Zaire, which had been a Catholic institution called Lovanium University until its nationalization in 1971, Ntumba wrote under conditions that do not allow us to rule out the threat of persecution as a factor in his argumentation.

There are, however, very few suggestions to this effect in his text. The purpose of Ntumba's article was to outline the "linguistic and anthropological philosophy" of *ntu* and, in so doing, to defend the "traditional philosophy of man" from the critiques of philosophers like Paulin Hountondji. According to Ntumba, the very grammar of *ntu* is the basis of a "radical community": inasmuch as human beings (*muntu*) and things ("*cintu*") all share a similar root (*ntu*), they partake in the same essence. The *ntu* vision of humanity involves a "radical communion between all classes of *ntu*, a philosophy in which one *ntu* partakes of the essence of all other *ntu*. The *ntu* vision of human being is, in short, that the human being is essentially a "being-through-relations" and that the modality of this being's relationships is not "to have" but "being-with." As Ntumba sums up this vision, "Among human beings, every human being is a 'human being-with-me' (*muntu Nanyi*), a 'child-of-our-family,' a brother (*muanetu*), a 'being-coming to-God-through-Others' (*muntu-wa-Bende-wa-Mvidi-Yukulu*). The stranger who comes from other horizons is not a stranger; he is a guest (*muenyi*)."

In Ntumba's own view, Seke Seso's "philosophy of authenticity" is nothing other than another name for this "anthropological philosophy": "To the extent that 'authenticity' defines itself as a will 'to be one's self,' it's based on the traditional philosophy of man." Ntumba's "traditional man," like Seke Seso's "authentic man," puts "society before the individual, the public good before private or personal interest, the political over the religious." The watchword of Ntumba's "traditional man," like Seke Seso's "Manifeste de la N'Sele," was "*servir et non se servir.*" See Tshiamalenga Ntumba, "La vision *ntu* de l'homme: Essai de philosophie linguistique et anthropologique," *Cahiers des religions africaines* 7, no. 14 (July 1973): 176–99; Crawford Young and Thomas Turner, *The Rise and Decline of the Zairian State* (Madison: University of Wisconsin Press, 1985), 54, 56, 68.

109. Tutu, *No Future without Forgiveness*, 34–35; see also 154.

110. Tutu, *No Future without Forgiveness*, 10.

111. Tutu, *No Future without Forgiveness*, 36, 213.

112. See L. Reed, "'Socialist' Mugabe Detains Fourteen Socialists," *Inqaba ya basebenzi: Journal of the Marxist Workers' Tendency of the African National Congress* 16–17 (January–June 1985), 8–14.

113. Keith Kyle, *The Politics of the Independence of Kenya* (New York: Palgrave, 1999), 198.

114. The full title of the 1972 law (chapter 44 of the Laws of Kenya) is "Act of Parliament to Restrict the Taking of Legal Proceedings in Respect of Certain Acts and Matters Done in Certain Areas between the 25th December 1963 and 1st December 1967." Section 3 of the act states, "No proceeding or claim to compensation or injury shall be instituted or entertained by any Court or by any authority or tribunal established by or under any Law for or on account of or in respect of Act, matter or thing done within or in respect of the prescribed area, after the 25th December 1963 and before 1st December 1967 . . . [i]f it was done in good faith or done in execution of duty in the Public interest by a Public Officer or member of the armed forces." Section 2 of the act defines the areas affected by the act. In 2010, following a decadelong debate and the formation of Kenya's Truth, Justice, and Reconciliation Commission in 2008, the Kenyan Parliament repealed the 1972 Indemnity Act (even if, in 2011, President Kibaki would refuse his assent) and approved a new constitution with provisions banning indemnity. See Section 58 (7) of the Republic of Kenya, Constitution of the Republic of Kenya, 2010.

115. See, for example, Republic of Kenya, *Debates of the House of Assembly*, March 19, 1970, cols. 1601–2. This repeated similar language from independence. See David Anderson, *Histories of the Hanged: The Dirty War in Kenya and the End of Empire* (New York: Norton, 2005), 329–30.

116. Wade and Phillips, *Constitutional Law*, 573.

117. In the Zimbabwe of 1980 and the Kenya of 1970, as in the South Africa of 1994, *ubuntu* coincides with the same sort of emergency jurisprudence one finds in postcolonial India and Pakistan—regimes that make no claim to *ubuntu* but that do share with Kenya, South Africa, and Zimbabwe the English jurisprudence of emergency (Hussain, *Jurisprudence of Emergency*, 1–2, 102–3, 137–40). The converse holds as well: in postcolonial Zaire, which did not inherit English jurisprudence, an especially communitarian iteration of *umuntu* was pressed into the service of Sese Seko's authoritarian presidentialism (cf. note 108 earlier in the present chapter).

118. See, on these points, Desai, *We Are the Poors*, 10ff.

119. Desai, *We Are the Poors*, 72.

120. Desai, *We Are the Poors*, 12–13.

121. Richard Rive, *Emergency Continued* (London: Readers International, 1990), 8. As Anthony Mathews put it, "There is something decidedly artificial about discussing emergency legislation and the rule of law in South Africa. 'Ordinary' and permanent legislation has already brought about a ninety-percent destruction of the rule of law and put the country into a permanent state of emergency" (*Freedom, State Security, and the Rule of Law*, 265).

122. Desai, writing with Richard Pithouse, argues that "life in neo-liberal South Africa remains, for the poor, a permanent state of emergency." See Ashwin Desai and Rich-

340 / NOTES TO PAGES 249-54

ard Pithouse, "'But We Were Thousands': Dispossession, Resistance, Repossession, and Repression in Mandela Park," *Journal of Asian and African Studies* 39, no. 4 (2004): 260.

EPILOGUE

1. G. W. F. Hegel, *The Philosophy of Right*, trans. T. M. Knox (Oxford: Oxford University Press, 1967), 13, translation modified.

2. Kader Asmal, "Truth, Reconciliation and Justice: The South African Experience in Perspective," *Modern Law Review* 63, no. 1 (2000), 23 (arguing that the "[t]he global discourse of transitional justice . . . has been conceptually simplistic to date").

3. Emmanuel Chukwudi Eze, "Transition and the Reasons of Memory," *South Atlantic Quarterly* 103, no. 4 (Fall 2004): 758. On the "limit" at work in the TRC, see also Nicholas Dawes, "Constituting Nationality: South Africa in the Fold of the 'Interim,'" *Jouvert: A Journal of Postcolonial Studies* 1, no. 2 (1997), ¶2, accessed December 5, 2012, http://english.chass.ncsu.edu/jouvert/v1i2/DAWES.HTM.

4. Klug, *Constitution of South Africa*, 6. Cf. Abel, *Politics by Other Means*, 17.

5. Dicey, *Introduction*, 8th ed., 228.

6. On the depoliticizing effects of the "technicism" of transitional justice, see Neocosmos, "Transition, Human Rights, and Violence," 362–63, 366–67.

7. Boraine, *A Country Unmasked*, 278.

8. See Chanock, *Making of South African Legal Culture*, 513.

9. Klug, *Constitution of South Africa*, 15–17, 41–43. For examples of analyses of the TRC that trace its practices to precedents in colonial and apartheid jurisprudence, see Sanders, *Ambiguities of Witnessing*, 59–75, 153–54 (on the reiteration of customary law in testimony given before the TRC); Cole, *Performing South Africa's Truth Commission*, 28–62 (on the TRC's counterintuitive precedents in the "show trials" of the 1950s and 1960s).

10. See Mandela, *Struggle Is My Life*, 184–89; Sachs, *Justice in South Africa*, 157–58.

11. Lodge, *Politics in South Africa*, 176.

12. For an example of this dynamic, one could review Lourens du Plessis's fine 1994 article on the question of "indemnity and amnesty." In this overlooked text, du Plessis enumerated the many ways in which existing indemnity acts would not survive constitutional review and explained how existing indemnity jurisprudence could not serve as a guide for the application of the "amnesty" set forth in the postscript of the 1993 Interim Constitution. After an unusually detailed explanation of these points, du Plessis then argued that it would be wise "for the government of national unity, and especially the legislature, to deal with the issue of amnesty or indemnity before the matter is taken to court and to do so in the spirit of the broadly phrased value statements embodied in the postscript to the Constitution. The objectives thus spelt out allow for legislation calling into existence a 'commission of truth and reconciliation,' like the one that was established in Chile." See du Plessis, "Observations on Amnesty or Indemnity for Acts

Associated with Political Objectives in Light of South Africa's Transitional Constitution," *Tydskrif vir hedendaagse Romeins-Hollandse Reg* 57 (1994): 473–81, 479. For du Plessis, the creation of a "commission of truth and reconciliation" on the Chilean model was not an attempt to chart a "middle way" between the "victor's justice" of Nuremberg, on the one hand, and Argentinian amnesty, on the other. It was part of an attempt to think the application of "amnesty" as something other than, something more and different than, a simple repetition of "indemnity." For du Plessis, that is to say, the turn *to* Latin America was part of a turn *away from* indemnity jurisprudence, from a jurisprudence that was as unusable *for* South Africa's transition as it was central *to* that transition. Transitional justice, by contrast, tends to study South Africa's turn to Latin America in a one-dimensional manner, as though it were unrelated to and uncompelled by the need to turn away from indemnity jurisprudence.

13. On "paradigms" as "exemplars," see Thomas Kuhn, "Postscript—1969," in *The Structure of Scientific Revolutions*, 3rd ed. (Chicago: University of Chicago Press, 1996), 174–210. On the TRC as a paradigm for transitional justice, see Boraine, *A Country Unmasked*, 379–422; Robert Rotberg, "Truth Commissions and the Provision of Truth, Justice, and Reconciliation," in Rotberg and Thompson, *Truth v. Justice: The Morality of Truth Commissions*, 19–20; Heribert Adam and Kogila Moodley, *Seeking Mandela: Peacemaking Between Israelis and Palestinians* (Philadelphia: Temple University Press, 2005), 124; Chapman and van der Merwe, "Introduction: Assessing the South African Transitional Justice Model," 8, 12, 16 17; Fiona Ross, "Truth and Reconciliation," in Shepherd and Robins, *New South African Keywords*, 235; Moon, *Narrating Political Reconciliation*, 4; Cole, *Performing South Africa's Truth Commission*, 124.

14. Hayner lists Argentina; Chile 1; El Salvador; Germany; Haiti; South Korea; Ghana; Sierra Leone; Chile 2; Greensboro, North Carolina, United States; Paraguay; Indonesia and Timor-Leste; South Korea; Liberia; Ecuador 2; Mauritius; Solomon Islands; Togo; Canada; and Kenya. See Hayner, *Unspeakable Truths*. Her five "strongest" Truth Commissions are South Africa, Guatemala, Peru, East Timor, and Morocco.

15. Eqbal Ahmad, "The Neofascist State: Notes on the Pathology of Power in the Third World," in Bengelsdorf, Cerullo, and Chandrani, *Selected Writings of Eqbal Ahmad*, 144, 149. Jean and John Comaroff, meanwhile, suggest that contemporary anxieties over and fascinations with law in the postcolonial world are the counterpoint to other elements distinctive to many postcolonial societies, such as "the rise of the felonious state, private indirect government, and endemic cultures of illegality" ("Law and Disorder in the Postcolony: An Introduction," in *Law and Disorder in the Postcolony*, ed. Jean Comaroff and John Comaroff [Chicago: University of Chicago Press, 2006], 26).

16. The exception to the rule here is Asmal, Asmal, and Roberts's *Reconciliation through Truth*, which raises questions of how the TRC can and should deal with the specifically colonial status of the apartheid state (see, e.g., 8, 182–89, IX). This emphasis, which was part of the official policy of the ANC (in the form of the theory of "internal colonialism") since 1969, has been a part of Asmal's theorization of apartheid within the

framework of international law for decades (see, e.g., Asmal, "International Law Aspects of the National Question in South Africa," 128–31). As Asmal shows in these early documents, colonialism was consistently at issue in many of the UN General Assembly's formal resolutions on apartheid, particularly in the late 1970s, when a fresh wave of newly decolonized states joined the United Nations. Given this consistency, it would seem reasonable to suppose that the critique of colonialism is an essential part of any systematic critique of apartheid within human rights discourse. It is therefore all the more startling to find no critique of colonialism whatsoever in leading North American studies of the TRC within transitional justice (e.g., Ruti Teitel's *Transitional Justice*). Like Asmal, the scholars behind these studies rely on human rights discourse to wrestle with the dilemma of how best to hold to account murderers and torturers in the apartheid state's police force and security bureaucracy (see Asmal, "International Law and the Liquidation of Apartheid," 14). Unlike Asmal, however, these scholars seem to suppose it possible to criticize apartheid within the horizon of human rights discourse without also speaking of colonialism. Given Asmal's leading role in the creation of the TRC, it is difficult to underestimate the significance of this almost complete erasure, within transitional justice's study of the TRC, of Asmal's treatment of colonialism as a central theoretical concern for any international legal account of apartheid.

17. See, on this point, Bogumil Jewsiewicki, "African Historical Studies: Academic Knowledge as 'Usable Past' and Radical Scholarship," *African Studies Review* 32, no. 3 (December 1989): 8–9; Paulin Hountondji, "Recapturing," in *The Surreptitious Speech: Présence Africaine and the Politics of Otherness, 1947–1987*, ed. V. Y. Mudimbe (Chicago: University of Chicago Press, 1992), 240; Chatterjee, *Nationalist Thought and the Colonial World*, 3–4.

18. On March 10, 2003, to take a late example, the U.S. National Security Council proposed to President George W. Bush and his war cabinet that members of Saddam Hussain's Baath Party "be subjected to a South Africa–style 'truth and reconciliation process'" (see Rajiv Chandrasekaran, *Imperial Life in the Emerald City: Inside Iraq's Green Zone* [New York: Vintage Books, 2006], 79). Although this proposal was not implemented, President Bush is reported to have approved of it (see Ross, "Truth and Reconciliation," 235), and the transitional justice language of "national reconciliation" would remain a decisive part of the lexicon of the U.S. occupation of Iraq (see, in particular, United States Institute of Peace, *The Iraq Study Group Report*, by James A. Baker III and Lee H. Hamilton, cochairs, December 6, 2006, 43, 46–48 [recommending that Iraq produce a "far-reaching amnesty agreement," pursue a "national reconciliation dialogue," and achieve "reconciliation efforts" by May 2007]).

19. Tutu, *No Future without Forgiveness*, 219.

20. Jonathan Tepperman, "Truth and Consequences," *Foreign Affairs* 81, no. 2 (2002), 128. See also, on this point, Moon, *Narrating Political Reconciliation*, 2–5.

21. Samuel Huntington, *The Third Wave: Democratization in the Late Twentieth Century* (Norman: University of Oklahoma Press, 1992), 231.

Bibliography

CASES

AZAPO et al v. TRC et al., 1996 (4) SALR 562 (C)

AZAPO et al. v. President of the Republic of South Africa et al., 1996 (8) BCLR 1035 (CC).

Calder v. Bull, 3 US 386 (1798).

Damane v. Minister of Police, 1979 (4) SA 400 (C).

Harris et al. v. Dönges and Another, 1952 (1) TLR 1245.

Howell, Thomas Bayly. *State Trials.* Vol. 27. London, 1816.

Krohn v. Minister of Defence, 1915 AD 191.

Makhasa v. Minister of Law and Order, Lebowa Government, 1988 (3) SA 701 (A).

Marthinus Dawid Ras v. The Chairman of the Amnesty Committee of the Truth and Reconciliation Commission, Case No. 7285/00 (Cape of Good Hope Provincial Division).

Matinkinca and Another v. Council of State, Republic of Ciskei, and Another, 1994 (4) SA 472 (Ck).

Mawo v. Pepler, 1960 (4) SA 291.

Phillips v. Eyre, 1869 LR 4 QB 225.

Phillips v. Eyre, 1870 LR 6 QB 1.

Regina v. Bekker and Naude, 1900 CTR 443.

Rossouw v. Sachs, 1964 (2) SA 551 (A).

Stanton v. Minister of Justice and Others, 1960 (3) SA 353.

State v. Makwanyane and Mchunu, 1995 (3) SA 224.

The Trial of Adolf Eichmann: Record of Proceedings in the District Court of Jerusalem. Vol. 5. Jerusalem: Trust for the Publication of the Proceedings of the Eichmann Trial, in cooperation with the Israel State Archives and Yad Vashem, the Holocaust Martyrs' and Heroes' Remembrance Authority, 1992.

GOVERNMENT DOCUMENTS

Canada. *Summary of Proceedings, Imperial Conference, 1926.* Printed by Order of Parliament. Ottawa: F. A. Acland, 1926.

Cape of Good Hope. *Statutes of the Cape of Good Hope, 1652–1895.* Vol. 1, *1652–1871.* Ed. Hercules Tennant and Edgar Michael Jackson. Published by Authority of the Supreme Court of the Cape of Good Hope. Cape Town: Juta, 1895.

Cape of Good Hope. *Debates in the Legislative Council, in the Sixth Session of the Fifth Parliament of the Cape of Good Hope, Appointed to Meet 10th May, 1878.* 41 Victoriae, vol. 12. Published by Order of the Legislative Council. Cape Town: Saul Solomon, 1878.

Cape of Good Hope. *Debates in the House of Assembly, in the Third Session of the Tenth Parliament of the Cape of Good Hope, 20th July to 13th October, 1900.* Cape Town: Cape Times, 1900.

Cape of Good Hope, "Cape Colony, Previous Declarations of Martial Law," in *Martial Law Regulations* (1900), High Commissioner Series, vol. 57, 155, National Archives, Pretoria.

Cape of Good Hope. Indemnity and Special Tribunals Act 6 of 1900.

Cape of Good Hope. *Report and Proceedings of the Government Commission on Native Laws and Customs.* Cape Town: W. A. Richards and Sons, 1883.

Cape of Good Hope. *Reports and Proceedings, with Appendices, of the Government Commission on Native Laws and Customs.* Presented to Both Houses of Parliament by Command of His Excellency the Governor. Grahamstown, South Africa: Richards, Slater, 1883.

Cape of Good Hope. *Report of a Commission Appointed by His Excellency the Governor to Inquire into and Report upon the Question of Colonial Defence.* Presented to Both Houses of Parliament by Command of His Excellency the Governor. Grahamstown, South Africa: Richards, Slater, 1877.

Cape of Good Hope. Transkeian Territories Penal Code Act 24 of 1886.

Colony of Natal. *Debates of the Legislative Assembly of the Colony of Natal, Fourth Session of the Fourth Parliament, May 3 to August 9, 1906.* Pietermaritzburg: Davis and Sons, 1906.

Colony of Natal. *Proceedings and Report of the Commission Appointed to Inquire into the Past and Present State of the Kafirs in the District of Natal, and to Report upon Their Future Government, and to Suggest Such Arrangements as Will Tend to Secure the Peace and Welfare of the District, for the Information of His Honour Lieutenant-Governor Pine.* N.p., 1853.

Colony of Natal. Indemnity Act 14 of 1874.

Colony of Natal. Indemnity Act 15 of 1900.

Colony of Natal, Indemnity Act 41 of 1901.

Colony of Natal. Indemnity Act 22 of 1902.

Colony of Natal. Indemnity Act 30 of 1902.

Colony of Natal. Indemnity Act 51 of 1906.

Colony of Natal. Indemnity Act 5 of 1908.

Hansard Parliamentary Debates. 3rd ser., vol. 184 (1866).

Hansard Parliamentary Debates. 3rd ser., vol. 242 (1878).

Hansard Parliamentary Debates. 3rd ser., vol. 252 (1880).

Hansard Parliamentary Debates. 4th ser., vol. 20 (1894).

Hansard Parliamentary Debates. 5th ser., vol. 58 (1914).

Hansard Parliamentary Debates. 5th ser., vol. 128 (1920).

Ireland. *The Statutes at Large, Passed in the Parliaments Held in Ireland: From the Third Year of Edward the Second, A.D. 1310 to the Thirty-Eighth Year of George the Third, A.D. 1798, Inclusive.* Vol. 18. Dublin: George Grierson, 1798.

Orange River Colony. Martial Law Act 25 of 1902.

Republic of Kenya. "Act of Parliament to Restrict the Taking of Legal Proceedings in Respect of Certain Acts and Matters Done in Certain Areas between the 25th December 1963 and 1st December 1967." Chapter 44 of the Laws of Kenya.

Republic of Kenya. *Debates of the House of Assembly.* March 19, 1970.

Republic of Kenya. Constitution of the Republic of Kenya. 2010.

Republic of Rhodesia. *Debates of the Senate.* September 18, 1975.

Republic of South Africa. Amnesty Bill No. . . . of 1994. On file with author.

Republic of South Africa. Constitution of South Africa. Act 200 of 1993.

Republic of South Africa, Constitution of South Africa, Act 108 of 1996.

Republic of South Africa. *Debates of the House of Assembly.* June 7, 1961.

Republic of South Africa. *Debates of the House of Assembly.* June 8, 1961.

Republic of South Africa. *Debates of the House of Assembly.* June 9, 1961.

Republic of South Africa. *Debates of the House of Assembly.* June 12, 1961.

Republic of South Africa. *Debates of the Senate.* June 15, 1961.

Republic of South Africa. *Debates of the House of Assembly.* January 31, 1977.

Republic of South Africa. *Debates of the House of Assembly.* February 1, 1977.

Republic of South Africa. *Debates of the House of Assembly.* February 3, 1977.

Republic of South Africa. Criminal Procedure Act of 1977, Section 204.

Republic of South Africa. *Debates of the National Assembly.* May 17, 1995.

Republic of South Africa. *Debates of the Senate.* June 27, 1995.

Republic of South Africa. Government Notice R 2625. *Government Gazette* 12834. Regulation Gazette 4584. November 7, 1990.

Republic of South Africa. Government Notice R 2633. *Government Gazette* 12838. Regulation Gazette 4588. November 9, 1990.

Republic of South Africa. Indemnity Act 13 of 1940.

Republic of South Africa. Indemnity Act 61 of 1961.

Republic of South Africa. Indemnity Act 13 of 1977.

Republic of South Africa (Transkei). Indemnity Act 17 of 1984.

Republic of South Africa (Ciskei). Indemnity Act 31 of 1985.

Republic of South Africa, Lebowa Indemnity Act 3 of 1986.

Republic of South Africa. KwaNdebele Act of 1986.

Republic of South Africa. Indemnity Act 11 of 1990.

Republic of South Africa. Indemnity Act 35 of 1990.

Republic of South Africa. Indemnity Act 41 of 1991.

Republic of South Africa. Indemnity Amendment Decree 36 of 1990.

Republic of South Africa. Indemnity Amendment Decree 2 of 1991.

Republic of South Africa. Indemnity Second Amendment Decree 21 of 1991.

Republic of South Africa. Indemnity Amendment Third Decree 28 of 1991.

Republic of South Africa. Further Indemnity Act 151 of 1992.

Republic of South Africa. Special Indemnity Decree 7 of 1993.

Republic of South Africa. Indemnity Amendment Decree 11 of 1993.

Republic of South Africa. Promotion of National Unity and Reconciliation Act of 1995.

Republic of South Africa. *Report of the Commission Appointed to Investigate and Report on the Occurrences in the Districts of Vereeniging (Namely, at Sharpeville Location and Evaton) and Vanderbijlpark, Province of the Transvaal, on 21st March, 1960.* Pietermaritzburg: Government Relations Office, 1961.

Republic of South Africa. *Report of the Commission of Inquiry into the Riots of Soweto and Elsewhere from the 16th of June 1976 to the 28th of February.* Vol. 1. Pretoria: Government Printer, 1980.

Republic of South Africa. *Report of the Commission of Inquiry into the Violence Which Occurred on 29 October 1983 at the University of Zululand.* Volume 1. Appointed by the State President. Pretoria: Government Printer, 1985.

Republic of South Africa. *South Africa and the Rule of Law.* Pretoria: Government Printer, 1968.

Republic of South Africa. Suggested Proclamation of an Indemnity Measure in Connection with the Bondelswartz Rebellion. Prime Minister Series, vol. 1/2/66, PM21/1A. National Archives, Pretoria.

Republic of South Africa. Special Indemnity Decree 7 of 1993.

Republic of Zimbabwe. *Debates of the House of Assembly.* January 21, 1981.

Transvaal Colony. Indemnity and Peace Preservation Ordinance 38 of 1902.

Transvaal Colony. Ordinance 30 of 1902.

Transvaal Colony. Indemnity (Burgher) Ordinance 22 of 1903.

Truth and Reconciliation Commission of South Africa. *Truth and Reconciliation Commission of South Africa Report.* 7 vols. Vols. 1–5, London: Macmillan Reference, 1999. Vols. 1–7, Cape Town: Juta.

Truth Commission Panel. "Working Document: Draft Legislative Framework for Proposed Bill to Set Up a Truth and Reconciliation Commission." South Africa, July 1994. On file with author.

Union of South Africa. Amendment Act 46 of 1919.

Union of South Africa. Amnesty and Indemnity and Undesirables Deportation Act of 1914.

Union of South Africa. *Debates of the Senate.* March 11, 1914.

Union of South Africa. *Debates of the Senate.* March 31, 1915.

Union of South Africa. Indemnity and Undesirables Special Deportation Act 1 of 1914.

Union of South Africa. Law Adviser's Report on Act 11 of 1915 (the Indemnity and

Special Tribunals Act of 1915). Governor General Series, vol. 337, 7/985. National Archives, Pretoria.

Union of South Africa. Indemnity and Special Tribunals Act 11 of 1915.

Union of South Africa. Law Adviser's Report on Act 6 of 1922 (the Indemnity and Trial of Offenders Act). Minister of Justice Series, vol. 680, 1/47/22. National Archives, Pretoria.

Union of South Africa. Indemnity and Trial of Offenders Act 6 of 1922.

Union of South Africa. *Index to the Manuscript Annexures and Printed Papers of the House of Assembly, Including Select Committee Reports and Bills; and Also to Principal Motions and Resolutions and Commission Reports, 1910–1920.* Printed by Order of Mr. Speaker. Cape Town: Cape Times, 1921.

Union of South Africa. *Index to the Manuscript Annexures and Printed Papers of the House of Assembly, Including Select Committee Reports and Bills; and Also to Principal Motions and Resolutions and Commission Reports, 1920–1930.* Printed by Order of Mr. Speaker. Cape Town: Cape Times, 1931.

Union of South Africa. *Index to the Manuscript Annexures and Printed Papers of the House of Assembly, Including Select Committee Reports and Bills; and Also to Principal Motions and Resolutions and Commission Reports, 1931–1940.* Printed by Order of Mr. Speaker. Cape Town: Cape Times, 1941.

Union of South Africa. *Index to the Manuscript Annexures and Printed Papers of the House of Assembly, Including Select Committee Reports and Bills; and Also to Principal Motions and Resolutions and Commission Reports, 1940–41–1950.* Printed by Order of Mr. Speaker. Cape Town: Cape Times, 1951.

Union of South Africa. Proclamation 76 of 1920 (Protectorate of South-West Africa).

Union of South Africa. *Report of the Witwatersrand Disturbances Commission.* Pretoria: Government Printer, 1913.

Union of South Africa. *Report of the Indian Enquiry Commission.* Cape Town, Cape Times, Government Printers, 1914.

Union of South Africa. *Report on the Outbreak of the Rebellion and the Policy of the Government with Regard to Its Suppression.* Pretoria: Government Printer and Stationary Office, 1915.

Union of South Africa. *Report of the Commissioners Appointed to Enquire into the Causes of, and Occurrences at, the Native Disturbances at Port Elizabeth on the 23rd October, 1920, and the General Economic Conditions as They Effect the Native and Coloured Population.* Printed by Direction of the Acting Prime Minster. Cape Town: Cape Times, 1921.

Union of South Africa. *Report of the Select Committee on the Union Defence Forces Bill.* Printed by Order of the House of Assembly, May 1921. Cape Town: Cape Times, 1921.

Union of South Africa. *Report of the Commission Appointed to Enquire into the Rebellion of the Bondelzwarts.* Presented to Both Houses of Parliament. Cape Town: Cape Times, 1923.

Union of South Africa. *Report of the Commission Appointed to Enquire into the Riots Which Took Place in Johannesburg on 31st January 1941 and 1st February, 1941.* Cape Town: Cape Times, 1941.

Union of South Africa. *Report of the Commission of Enquiry into Riots in Durban.* Issued by Authority. Cape Town: Cape Times, 1949.

Union of South Africa. *Report of the Commission of Enquiry into the Disturbances in the Witzieshoek Native Reserve.* Parow: Cape Times, 1951.

Union of South Africa. *Report of the Judicial Commission of Inquiry into the Causes of and Circumstances Relating to the Recent Rebellion in South Africa.* Presented to Both Houses of Parliament by Command of His Excellency the Governor-General. Cape Town: Cape Times, 1916.

Union of South Africa. *Report of the Martial Law Inquiry Judicial Commission.* Presented to Both Houses of Parliament by Command of His Royal Highness the Governor-General. Pretoria: Government Printing and Stationery Office, 1922.

United Kingdom. 35 Geo. 3 c. 13. "An Act for indemnifying such Persons as have acted for the Service of the Publick, in advising or carrying into Execution two several Proclamations of the Lord Lieutenant and Council of this Kingdom, bearing Date the Twenty-fourth and Twenty-ninth Days of January, One thousand seven hundred and ninety-five respectively, and for continuing and giving effect to the said Proclamations."

United Kingdom. 36 Geo. 3 c. 6. "An Act for indemnifying such Persons as have acted since the First Day of January, One thousand seven hundred and ninety-five, for the Preservation of the public Peace, and Suppression of the Insurrections prevailing in some Parts of this Kingdom."

United Kingdom. 37 Geo. 3 c. 39. "An Act for indemnifying such Persons as have acted since the First Day of January, One thousand seven hundred and ninety-seven, for the Preservation of the Public Peace, and Suppression of the Insurrections prevailing in some Parts of this Kingdom."

United Kingdom. 38 Geo. 3 c. 19. "An Act for Indemnifying such Persons as have acted since the Third Day of July, in the Year One thousand seven and ninety seven, for the Preservation of the Publick Peace, and Suppression of the Insurrections prevailing in some Parts of this Kingdom."

United Kingdom. 39 Geo. 3 c. 3. "An Act for indemnifying such Persons as have acted since the Sixth Day of October, One thousand seven hundred and ninety-eight, for the Preservation of the Public Peace, and Suppression of Insurrections prevailing in Several Parts of this Kingdom."

United Kingdom. 40 Geo. 3 c. 89. "An Act for indemnifying such Persons as have acted since the first Day of June, one thousand seven hundred ninety-nine, for the Preservation of the public Peace, and Suppression of the Insurrections prevailing in some Parts of this Kingdom, and to enable Sheriffs and other Officers to make the Returns therein Specified."

United Kingdom. 41 Geo. 3 c. 66. "An Act for Indemnifying such Persons as, since the first Day of February One thousand seven hundred and ninety three, have acted in the apprehending, imprisoning or detaining in Custody, in Great Britain, of Persons suspected of High Treason or Treasonable Practices."

United Kingdom. *Report of Her Majesty's Commissioners Appointed to Inquire into the Alleged Disturbance of the Public Peace in Hyde Park, on Sunday, July 1, 1855; and the Conduct of the Metropolitan Police in Connexion with the Same.* Presented to Both Houses of Parliament by Command of Her Majesty. London: Eyre and Spottiswoode, 1856.

United Kingdom. *Report of the Commission on the Palestine Disturbances of August, 1929.* Presented by the Secretary of State for the Colonies to Parliament by Command of His Majesty, March 1930. London: His Majesty's Stationery Office, 1930.

United Kingdom. *Report of the Commissioners of Inquiry, 1869, into the Riots and Disturbances in the City of Londonderry.* Presented to Both Houses of Parliament by Command of Her Majesty. Dublin: Alexander Thom, 1869.

United Kingdom. *Report of the Commissioners of Inquiry for South Wales.* Presented to Both Houses of Parliament by Command of Her Majesty. London: Clowes and Sons, 1844.

United Kingdom. *Report of the Commissioners of Inquiry into the Origin and Character of the Riots in Belfast in July and September, 1857.* Presented to Both Houses of Parliament by Command of Her Majesty. Dublin: Alex. Thom and Son, 1858.

United Kingdom. *Report of the Committee Appointed to Inquire into the Circumstances Connected with the Disturbances at Featherstone on the 7th of September 1893.* Presented to Both Houses of Parliament by Command of Her Majesty. London: Eyre and Spottiswoode, 1893.

United Kingdom. *Report of the Jamaica Royal Commission, Part I.* Presented to Both Houses of Parliament By Command of Her Majesty. London: Eyre and Spottiswoode, 1866.

United Kingdom. *Further Papers Relating to the Late Kafir Outbreak in Natal.* Presented to Both Houses of Parliament by Command of Her Majesty. London: William Clowes and Sons, 1875.

United Kingdom. *Report of the South African Native Affairs Commission, 1903–1905.* Presented to Both Houses of Parliament by Command of His Majesty. London: Printed for His Majesty's Stationery Office, by Darling & Son, 1905.

United Kingdom. *Report of the Royal Commission on Police Powers and Procedure (1928–9).* Vol. 2. Presented to Both Houses of Parliament by Command of His Majesty. London: His Majesty's Stationery Office, 1929.

United Kingdom. *The Statutes of the Realm.* Vol. 1. Buffalo, NY: William S. Hein, 1993.

United States Institute of Peace. *The Iraq Study Group Report,* by James A. Baker III and Lee H. Hamilton, cochairs, December 6, 2006.

BOOKS AND ARTICLES

Abel, Richard. *Politics by Other Means: Law in the Struggle against Apartheid, 1980–1994.* New York: Routledge, 1995.

Adam, Heribert, and Kanya Adam. "The Politics of Memory in Divided Societies." In James and van de Vijver, *After the TRC*, 32–50.

Adam, Heribert, and Kogila Moodley. *Seeking Mandela: Peacemaking Between Israelis and Palestinians*. Philadelphia: Temple University Press, 2005.

Adorno, Theodor, Else Frenkel-Brunswik, and Daniel J. Levinson. *The Authoritarian Personality*. New York: Norton, 1969.

Ahmad, Eqbal. *The Selected Writings of Eqbal Ahmad*. Ed. Carollee Bengelsdorf, Margaret Cerullo, and Yogesh Chandrani. New York: Columbia University Press, 2006.

Allen, John. *Rabble-Rouser for Peace: The Authorized Biography of Desmond Tutu*. Boston: Simon and Schuster, 2006.

Anderson, David. *Histories of the Hanged: The Dirty War in Kenya and the End of Empire*. New York: Norton, 2005.

Anghie, Antony. *Imperialism, Sovereignty, and the Making of International Law*. New York: Cambridge University Press, 2005.

Appleyard, John W. *The Kafir Language: Comprising a Sketch of Its History; Which Includes a General Classification of South African Dialects, Ethnological and Geographical; Remarks upon Its Nature; and a Grammar*. Graham's Town: Godlonton and White, 1850.

Arendt, Hannah. *Origins of Totalitarianism*. New York: Harcourt Brace Jovanovich, 1976.

Arendt, Hannah. *The Life of the Mind*. Vol. 2. New York: Harcourt Brace Jovanovich, 1978.

Arendt, Hannah. *On Revolution*. New York: Penguin Books, 1991.

"Argentines Vote to Repeal Amnesty." *Washington Post*, August 13, 2003, A20.

Aristotle. *The Complete Works of Aristotle*. Trans. B. Jowett. Ed. Jonathan Barnes. Princeton: Princeton University Press, 1984.

Arndt, H. W. "The Origins of Dicey's Concept of 'The Rule of Law.'" *Australian Law Journal* 31 (1957): 117–23.

Ashforth, Adam. *The Politics of Official Discourse in Twentieth-Century South Africa*. Oxford: Clarendon, 1990.

Asmal, Kader. "Human Rights, Reparations, and Reconciliation." Studies and Reports by the Ecumenical Foundation of Southern Africa (Institute for Theological and Interdisciplinary Research, University of Stellenbosch), October 24, 1991.

Asmal, Kader. "International Law and the Liquidation of Apartheid." *Notes and Documents, United Nations Centre against Apartheid*, no. 43, Melville J. Herskovits Library of African Studies, Northwestern University (New York: United Nations, 1978), 1–24.

Asmal, Kader. "International Law Aspects of the National Question in South Africa." In *The National Question in South Africa*, ed. Maria van Diepen, 125–41. Atlantic Highlands, NJ: Zed Books, 1988.

Asmal, Kader. "Truth, Reconciliation, and Justice: The South African Experience in Perspective." *Modern Law Review* 63, no. 1 (2000): 1–24.

Asmal, Kader. "Victims, Survivors, and Citizens—Human Rights, Reparations, and Reconciliation." Inaugural lecture presented at Kader Asmal's installation as professor of human rights law, University of the Western Cape, Cape Town, May 25, 1992.

Asmal, Kader, Louise Asmal, and Ronald Suresh Roberts. *Reconciliation through Truth: A Reckoning of Apartheid's Criminal Governance.* 2nd ed. New York: St. Martin's, 1997.

Asmal, Kader, Louise Asmal, and Ronald Suresh Roberts. "When the Assassin Cries Foul: The Modern Just War Doctrine." In Villa-Vicencio and Verwoerd, *Looking Back, Reaching Forward,* 86–98.

Bacon, Francis. *The Works of Francis Bacon.* Ed. James Spedding, Robert Leslie Ellis, and Douglas Denon Heath. Vol. 7. London: Longman, 1859.

Badiou, Alain. *The Rebirth of History.* Trans. Gregory Elliot. London: Verso Books, 2012.

Bagehot, Walter. *The English Constitution.* Ithaca: Cornell University Press, 1966.

Barber, James, and John Barrett. *South Africa's Foreign Policy: The Search for Status and Security, 1945–1988.* Cambridge: Cambridge University Press, 1990.

Basson, Deon. *South Africa's Interim Constitution: Text and Notes.* Cape Town: Juta, 1994.

Basson, Deon, and Hendrik Viljoen. *South African Constitutional Law.* Cape Town: Juta, 1988.

Battle, Michael. *Ubuntu: I in You and You in Me.* New York: Seabury Books, 2009.

Beer, George Louis. *The Origins of the British Colonial System, 1578–1660.* New York: P. Smith, 1933.

Benjamin, Walter. "Critique of Violence." In *Reflections,* ed. Peter Demetz, trans. Edmund Jephcott, 277–300. New York: Harcourt Brace Jovanovich, 1979.

Benson, Mary. *Nelson Mandela: The Man and the Movement.* New York: Norton, 1986.

Bentham, Jeremy. *An Introduction to the Principles of Morals and Legislation.* New York: Hafner Publishing Co., 1948.

Bernasconi, Robert. "Persons and Masks: The *Phenomenology of Spirit* and Its Laws." In *Hegel and Legal Theory,* ed. Drucilla Cornell, Michel Rosenfeld, and David Carlson, 78–93. New York: Routledge, 1991.

Bethlehem, Louise. *Skin Tight: Apartheid Literary Culture and Its Aftermath.* Pretoria: University of South Africa Press, 2006.

Bhargava, Anurima. "Defining Political Crimes: A Case Study of the South African Truth and Reconciliation Commission." *Columbia Law Review* 102, no. 5 (2002): 1304–39.

Bishop of Johannesburg. *Submission on Behalf of the Bishop of Johannesburg to the Commission of Enquiry into the Occurrences at Sharpeville (and Other Places) on the 21st March, 1960.* Vols. 1–2. Johannesburg, June 15, 1960.

Blackstone, William. *Commentaries on the Laws of England.* Vol. 1. Chicago: University of Chicago Press, 1979.

Blom-Cooper, Sir Louis. "Public Inquiries." *Current Legal Problems* 46 (1993): 204–20.

Bodin, Jean. *The Six Books of the Commonwealth*. Trans. M. J. Tooley. Oxford: Basil Blackwell, 1955.

Bond, Patrick. "Can Reparations for Apartheid Profits Be Won in U.S. Courts?" *Africa Insight* 38, no. 2 (2008): 13–25.

Boraine, Alex. *A Country Unmasked: Inside South Africa's Truth and Reconciliation Commission*. Oxford: Oxford University Press, 2000.

Boraine, Alex. "Truth and Reconciliation in South Africa: The Third Way." In Rotberg and Thompson, *Truth v. Justice*, 141–57.

Boraine, Alex, and Janet Levy, eds. *The Healing of a Nation?* Cape Town: Justice in Transition, 1995.

Boraine, Alex, Janet Levy, and Ronel Scheffer, eds. *Dealing with the Past: Truth and Reconciliation in South Africa*. Cape Town: IDASA, 1997.

Boulle, L. J. *Constitutional Reform and Apartheid*. New York: St. Martin's, 1984.

Brewer, John. *Black and Blue: Policing in South Africa*. Oxford: Oxford University Press, 1994.

Brogden, M. E. "The Origins of the South African Police—Institutional versus Structural Approaches." *Acta Juridica* 1 (1989): 4–19.

Buck-Morss, Susan. *Hegel, Haiti, and Universal History*. Pittsburgh: University of Pittsburgh Press, 2009.

Buford, Warren, and Hugo van der Merwe. "Les réparations en Afrique australe." *Cahiers d'Études Africains* 44, nos. 173–74 (2004): 263–322.

Bunting, Brian. *The Rise of the South African Reich*. New York: Penguin Books, 1964.

Burke, Kenneth. "The Thinking of the Body: Comments on the Imagery of Catharsis in Literature." *Psychoanalytic Review* 50 (Fall 1963): 375–418.

Call, Charles. "Is Transitional Justice Really Just?" *Brown Journal of World Affairs* 11, no. 2 (Summer/Fall 2004): 101–13.

Capaldi, Nicholas. *John Stuart Mill: A Biography*. Cambridge: Cambridge University Press, 2004.

Carver, Richard. "Zimbabwe: Drawing a Line through the Past." *Journal of African Law* 37, no. 1 (Spring 1993): 69–81.

Cassin, Barbara. "Amnistie et pardon: Pour une ligne de partage entre éthique et politique." In Cassin, Cayla, and Salazar, *Vérité, Réconcilliation, Réparation*, 37–57.

Cassin, Barbara. "'Removing the Perpetuity of Hatred': On South Africa as a Model Example." *International Review of the Red Cross* 88, no. 862 (2006): 235–44.

Cassin, Barbara, Olivier Cayla, and Philippe-Joseph Salazar, eds. *Vérité, Réconcilliation, Réparation*. Paris: Seuil, 2004.

Cawthra, Gavin. *Brutal Force: The Apartheid War Machine*. London: International Defence and Aid Fund for Southern Africa, 1986.

Chakrabarty, Dipesh. *Provincializing Europe: Postcolonial Thought and Historical Difference*. Princeton: Princeton University Press, 2000.

Chandrasekaran, Rajiv. *Imperial Life in the Emerald City: Inside Iraq's Green Zone*. New York: Vintage Books, 2006.

Chanock, Martin. *The Making of South African Legal Culture, 1902–1936: Fear, Favor, and Prejudice*. Cambridge: Cambridge University Press, 2001.

Chanock, Martin. "Writing South African Legal History: A Prospectus." *Journal of African History* 30 (1989): 265–88.

Chapman, Audrey, and Hugo van der Merwe. "Introduction: Assessing the South African Transitional Justice Model." In Chapman and van der Merwe, *Truth and Reconciliation in South Africa*, 12–17.

Chapman, Audrey, and Hugo van der Merwe. *Truth and Reconciliation in South Africa: Did the TRC Deliver?* Philadelphia: University of Pennsylvania Press, 2008.

Chatterjee, Partha. *Nationalist Thought and the Colonial World: A Derivative Discourse?* Minneapolis: University of Minnesota Press, 1993.

Chrétien, Jean-Pierre. "Les bantous, de la philologie allemande à l'authenticité Africaine: Un mythe racial contemporain." *Vingtième Siècle: Revue d'histoire* 8 (1985): 43–66.

Clode, Charles Matthew. *The Military Forces of the Crown: Their Administration and Government*. Vol. 2. London: John Murray, 1869.

Clokie, Hugh McDowall, and J. William Robinson. *Royal Commissions of Inquiry: The Significance of Investigations in British Politics*. New York: Octagon Books, 1969.

Cock, Jacklyn, and Laurie Nathan, eds. *War and Society: The Militarisation of South Africa*. Cape Town: David Philip, 1989.

Coetzee, Carli. "'They Never Wept, the Men of My Race': Antjie Krog's *Country of My Skull* and the White South African Signature." *Journal of Southern African Studies* 27, no. 4 (2001): 685–96.

Coetzee, Greig. *Johnny Boskak Is Feeling Funny, and Other Plays*. Pietermaritzburg: University of KwaZulu-Natal Press, 2009.

Coetzee, Greig. *Past Imperfect*. N.p., n.d. On file with author.

Cole, Catherine *Performing South Africa's Truth Commission: Stages of Transition*. Bloomington: Indiana University Press, 2010.

Colenso, John William. *First Steps in Zulu: An Abridgement of the Elementary Grammar of the Zulu-Kafir Language*. Ekukanyeni, 1859.

Colvin, Christopher. "Trauma." In Shepherd and Robins, *New South African Keywords*, 223–34.

Comaroff, Jean, and John Comaroff. "Criminal Obsessions, after Foucault: Postcoloniality, Policing, and the Metaphysics of Disorder." *Critical Inquiry* 30, no. 4 (Summer 2004): 800–824.

Comaroff, Jean, and John Comaroff. "Law and Disorder in the Postcolony: An Introduction." In *Law and Disorder in the Postcolony*, ed. Jean Comaroff and John Comaroff, 1–56. Chicago: University of Chicago Press, 2006.

Cornell, Drucilla, and Kenneth Michael Panfilio. *Symbolic Forms for a New Humanity: Cultural and Racial Reconfigurations of Critical Theory*. Bronx, NY: Fordham University Press, 2010.

Cosgrove, Richard. *The Rule of Law: Albert Venn Dicey, Victorian Jurist*. Chapel Hill: University of North Carolina Press, 1980.

Coundouriotis, Eleni. "The Dignity of the 'Unfittest': Victims' Stories in South Africa." *Human Rights Quarterly* 28, no. 4 (November 2006): 842–67.

Davey, A. M. *The Bondelzwarts Affair: A Study of the Repercussions, 1922–1959.* Pretoria: Communications of the University of South Africa, 1961.

Davis, Dennis, Matthew Chaskalson, and Johan de Waal. "Democracy and Constitutionalism: The Role of Constitutional Interpretation." In van Wyk et al., *Rights and Constitutionalism*, 1–130.

Dawes, Nicholas. "Constituting Nationality: South Africa in the Fold of the 'Interim.'" *Jouvert: A Journal of Postcolonial Studies* 1, no. 2 (1997). Accessed September 1, 2011. http://english.chass.ncsu.edu/jouvert/v1i2/DAWES.HTM.

Dayan, Joan. "Poe, Persons, and Property." *American Literary History* 1, no. 3 (Autumn 1999): 405–25.

de Lange, Johnny. "The Historical Context, Legal Origins, and Philosophical Foundation of the South African Truth and Reconciliation Commission." In Villa-Vicencio and Verwoerd, *Looking Back, Reaching Forward*, 14–31.

Derrida, Jacques. "Passions: An Oblique Offering." Trans. David Wood. In *On the Name*, ed. Thomas Dutoit, 3–35. Stanford: Stanford University Press, 1995.

Desai, Ashwin. *We Are the Poors: Community Struggles in Post-Apartheid South Africa.* New York: Monthly Review Press, 2002.

Desai, Ashwin, and Richard Pithouse. "'But We Were Thousands': Dispossession, Resistance, Repossession, and Repression in Mandela Park." *Journal of Asian and African Studies* 39, no. 4 (2004): 239–69.

Dicey, Alfred Venn. *Introduction to the Study of the Law of the Constitution.* 7th ed. London: Macmillan, 1908.

Dicey, Alfred Venn. *Introduction to the Study of the Law of the Constitution.* 8th ed. London: Macmillan, 1924.

Dicey, Alfred Venn. *Lectures on the Relation between Law and Public Opinion in England during the Nineteenth Century.* New Brunswick, NJ: Transaction, 1981.

Donne, John. *The Complete English Poems.* Ed. Albert James Smith. New York: Penguin Books, 1971.

Douglas, Lawrence. *The Memory of Judgment: Making Law and History in the Trials of the Holocaust.* New Haven: Yale University Press, 2001.

Doxtader, Eric. "Easy to Forget or Never (Again) Hard to Remember? History, Memory, and the 'Publicity' of Amnesty." In Villa-Vicencio and Doxtader, *Provocations of Amnesty*, 121–55.

Doxtader, Eric. "La reconciliation avant la reconciliation: La 'précédence' sud-africaine." In Cassin, Cayla, and Salazar, *Vérité, Réconcilliation, Réparation*, 243–59.

du Bois-Pedain, Antje. *Transitional Amnesty in South Africa.* Cambridge: Cambridge University Press, 2007.

Dubow, Saul. *The African National Congress.* Gloucestershire: Sutton, 2000.

Dubow, Saul. *Scientific Racism in Modern South Africa.* Cambridge: Cambridge University Press, 1995.

Dugard, John. *Human Rights and the South African Legal Order.* Princeton: Princeton University Press, 1978.

Dugard, John. *International Law: A South African Perspective.* Cape Town: Juta, 1994.

Dugard, John. "Is the Truth and Reconciliation Process Compatible with International Law? An Unanswered Question." *South African Journal on Human Rights* 13 (1997): 258–63.

Dugard, John. "The Jurisprudential Foundations of *Apartheid* Legal Order." *Philosophical Forum* 18, nos. 2–3 (1986–87): 115–16.

Dugard, John. "Reconciliation and Justice: The South African Experience." *Transnational Law and Contemporary Problems* 8 (1998): 277–311.

Dugard, John. *The South West Africa/Namibia Dispute: Documents and Scholarly Writings on the Controversy between South Africa and the United Nations.* Berkeley: University of California Press, 1973.

du Plessis, Lourens. "Amnesty and Transition in South Africa; Legal Analysis." In Boraine, Levy, and Scheffer, *Dealing with the Past,* 108–16.

du Plessis, Lourens. "Observations on Amnesty or Indemnity for Acts Associated with Political Objectives in Light of South Africa's Transitional Constitution." *Tydskrif vir hedendaagse Romeins-Hollandse Reg* 57 (1994): 473–81.

du Toit, André. "The Task for Civil Society." In Boraine, Levy, and Scheffer, *Dealing with the Past,* 94–98.

du Toit, André. "Experiments with Truth and Justice in South Africa: Stockenström, Gandhi, and the TRC." *Journal of Southern African Studies* 31, no. 2 (2005): 419–48.

Dyzenhaus, David. *Judging the Judges, Judging Ourselves: Truth, Reconciliation, and the Apartheid Legal Order.* Oxford: Hart. 1998.

Dyzenhaus, David. "The Pasts and Futures of the Rule of Law in South Africa." In *After Apartheid: Reinventing South Africa?,* ed. Ian Shapiro and Kahreen Tebeau, 251–59. Charlottesville: University of Virginia Press, 2011.

Earl of Halsbury. *The Laws of England.* Vol. 23. London: Butterworth, 1912.

Eiselen, Werner. "The Meaning of Apartheid." *Race Relations Journal* 15, no. 3 (1948): 69–86.

Elster, Jon. *Closing the Books: Transitional Justice in Historical Perspective.* Cambridge: Cambridge University Press, 2004.

The Encyclopedia of Missions: Descriptive, Historical, Biographical, Statistical. Ed. Edwin Munsell Bliss. Vol. 1. New York: Funk and Wagnalls, 1891.

Erasmus, Gerhard. "Limitation and Suspension." In van Wyk et al., *Rights and Constitutionalism,* 629–63.

Esposito, Roberto. "*Dispositif* of the Person." Trans. Timothy Campbell. *Law, Culture, and the Humanities* 8, no. 1 (February 2012): 17–30.

Esposito, Roberto. *Third Person: Politics of Life and Philosophy of the Impersonal.* Trans. Zakiya Hanafi (Malden, MA: Polity Press, 2012).

Evans, Ivan. *Bureaucracy and Race: Native Administration in South Africa.* Berkeley: University of California Press, 1997.

Eze, Emmanuel Chukwudi. "Transition and the Reasons of Memory." *South Atlantic Quarterly* 103, no. 4 (Fall 2004): 755–69.

Fanon, Frantz. *Black Skin, White Masks*. Trans. Charles Lam Markmann. New York: Grove, 1967.

Fanon, Frantz. "On National Culture." In *The Wretched of the Earth*, trans. Constance Farrington, 206–48. New York: Grove, 1963.

Fassin, Didier, and Richard Rechtman. *The Empire of Trauma: An Inquiry into the Condition of Victimhood*. Trans. Rachel Gomme. Princeton: Princeton University Press, 2009.

Finer, Herman. *The Theory and Practice of Modern Government*. Ann Arbor: University of Michigan Press, 1949.

Finlason, William. *Commentaries upon Martial Law with Special Reference to Its Regulation and Restraint with an Introduction Containing Comments*. London: Stevens and Sons, 1867.

Finlason, William. *A Review of the Authorities as to the Repression of Riot or Rebellion, with Special Reference to Criminal or Civil Liability*. London: Stevens and Sons, 1868.

Fortescue, John. *On the Laws and Governance of England*. Ed. Shelley Lockwood. Cambridge: Cambridge University Press, 1997.

Foucault, Michel. *The Archaeology of Knowledge*. Trans. A. M. Sheridan Smith. New York: Pantheon Books, 1972.

Foucault, Michel. "Nietzsche, Genealogy, History." In *Aesthetics, Method, and Epistemology*, vol. 2 of *The Essential Works of Michel Foucault, 1954–1984*, ed. James D. Faubion, trans. Robert Hurley et al., 369–92. New York: New Press, 1998.

Foucault, Michel. "Truth and Juridical Forms." In *Power*, vol. 3 of *The Essential Works of Michel Foucault, 1954–1984*, ed. James D. Faubion, trans. Robert Hurley et al., 6–89. New York: New Press, 2000.

Foucault, Michel. *The History of Sexuality. Vol. 1, An Introduction*. Trans. Robert Hurley. New York: Vintage Books, 1990.

Foucault, Michel. "Society Must Be Defended." In *Ethics: Subjectivity and Truth*, vol. 1 of *The Essential Works of Michel Foucault, 1954–1984*, ed. Paul Rabinow, trans. Robert Hurley et al., 59–67. New York: New Press, 1997.

Foucault, Michel. *"Society Must Be Defended": Lectures at the Collège de France, 1975–76*. Ed. Mauro Bertani and Allesandro Fontana. Trans. David Macey. New York: Picador, 2003.

Foucault, Michel. "Security, Territory, and Population." In *Ethics: Subjectivity and Truth*, vol. 1 of *The Essential Works of Michel Foucault, 1954–1984*, ed. Paul Rabinow, trans. Robert Hurley et al., 67–72. New York: New Press, 1997.

Foucault, Michel. *Security, Territory, Population: Lectures at the Collège de France, 1977–78*. Trans. Graham Burchell. New York: Macmillan, 2009.

Foucault, Michel. "'Omnes et Singulatim': Toward a Critique of Political Reason." In *Power*, vol. 3 of *The Essential Works of Michel Foucault, 1954–1984*, ed. James D. Faubion, trans. Robert Hurley et al., 326–48. New York: New Press, 2000.

Foucault, Michel. *Birth of Biopolitics: Lectures at the Collège de France, 1978–79*. Ed. Michel Senellart. Trans. Graham Burchell. New York: Palgrave, 2008.

Foucault, Michel. "The Subject and Power." In *Power*, vol. 3 of *The Essential Works of Michel Foucault, 1954–1984*, ed. James D. Faubion, trans. Robert Hurley et al., 326–48. New York: New Press, 2000.

Foucault, Michel. "Technologies of the Self." In *Ethics: Subjectivity and Truth*, vol. 1 of *The Essential Works of Michel Foucault, 1954–1984*, ed. Paul Rabinow, trans. Robert Hurley et al., 223–52. New York: New Press, 1997.

Foucault, Michel. *The Hermeneutics of the Subject: Lectures at the Collège de France, 1981–82*. Trans. Graham Burchell. Ed. Frédéric Gros, François Ewald, and Allesandro Fontana. New York: Palgrave, 2005.

Frankel, Oz. *States of Inquiry: Social Investigation and Print Culture in Nineteenth-Century Britain and the United States*. Baltimore: Johns Hopkins University Press, 2006.

Frankel, Philip. *An Ordinary Atrocity: Sharpeville and Its Massacre*. Johannesburg: Witwatersrand University Press, 2001.

Frankel, Philip. *Pretoria's Praetorians: Civil-Military Relations in South Africa*. Cambridge: Cambridge University Press, 1984.

Frederickson, George. *White Supremacy: A Comparative Study in American and South African History*. Oxford: Oxford University Press, 1981.

Frei, Norbert. *Adenauer's Germany and the Nazi Past: The Politics of Amnesty and Integration*. Trans. Joel Golb. New York: Columbia University Press, 2002.

Freud, Sigmund. *The Psychopathology of Everyday Life*. Vol. 6 of the *Standard Edition of the Complete Psychological Works of Sigmund Freud*. Ed. James Strachey. London: Hogarth, 1961.

Freud, Sigmund. "'Wild' Psycho-Analysis." In Vol. 11 of the *Standard Edition of the Complete Psychological Works of Sigmund Freud*, ed. and trans. James Strachey, 219–28. London: Hogarth, 1961.

Garapon, Antoine. "La justice comme reconnaissance." In Cassin, Cayla, and Salazar, *Vérité, Réconcilliation, Réparation*, 181–203.

Gobodo-Madikizela, Pumla. *A Human Being Died That Night: A South African Story of Forgiveness*. Boston: Houghton Mifflin Harcourt, 2003.

Goodrich, Peter. "Distrust Quotations in Latin." *Critical Inquiry* 29, no. 2 (Winter 2003): 193–215.

Graham, Shane. *South African Literature after the Truth Commission: Mapping Loss* (New York: Palgrave, 2009).

Gramsci, Antonio. *Selections from the Prison Notebooks*. Ed. and trans. Q. Hoare and G. N. Smith. New York: International Publishers, 1971.

Gramsci, Antonio. "Three Principles, Three Orders." In *History, Philosophy, and Culture in the Young Gramsci*, ed. Pedro Cavalcanti and Paul Piccone, trans. Pierluigi Molajoni et al., 70–74. New York: Telos, 1975.

Gready, Paul. *The Era of Transitional Justice: The Aftermath of the Truth and Reconciliation Commission in South Africa and Beyond*. New York: Routledge, 2011.

"The Groote Schuur Minute." *South African Journal on Human Rights* 6, no. 3 (1990): 318–19.

Grout, Lewis. *The Isizulu: A Grammar of the Zulu Language*. Natal: May and Davis, 1859.

Grundy, Kenneth. *The Militarization of South African Politics*. Bloomington: Indiana University Press, 1986.

Gumede, William Mervin. *Thabo Mbeki and the Battle for the Soul of the ANC*. London: Zed Books, 2005.

Hahlo, H. R., and Ellison Kahn. *The South African Legal System and Its Background*. Johannesburg: Juta, 1968.

Hahlo, H. R., and Ellison Kahn. *The Union of South Africa: The Development of Its Laws and Constitution*. Cape Town: Juta, 1960.

Hahlo, H. R., and I. A. Maisels. "The Rule of Law in South Africa." *Virginia Law Review* 52, no. 1 (1966): 1–31.

Hart, H. L. A. "The Ascription of Responsibility and Rights." *Proceedings of the Aristotelian Society* 49 (1949): 171–94.

Hart, H. L. A. *The Concept of Law*. 2nd ed. Oxford: Oxford University Press, 1994.

Hayner, Priscilla. "Same Species, Different Animal: How South Africa Compares to Truth Commissions Worldwide." In Villa-Vicencio and Verwoerd, *Looking Back, Reaching Forward*, 32–41.

Hayner, Priscilla. *Unspeakable Truths: Facing the Challenge of Truth Commissions*. New York: Routledge, 2002.

Hearn, William Edward. *The Government of England: Its Structure and Its Development*. London: Longmans, Green, 1887.

Hegel, G. W. F. *The Philosophy of Right*. Trans. T. M. Knox. Oxford: Oxford University Press, 1967.

Hegel, G. W. F. *Science of Logic*. Trans. A. V. Miller. New York: Humanity Books, 1999.

Herwitz, Daniel. *Race and Reconciliation: Essays from the New South Africa*. Minneapolis: University of Minnesota Press, 2003.

Heuman, Gad. *The Killing Time: The Morant Bay Rebellion in Jamaica*. Nashville: University of Tennessee Press, 1994.

Hiemstra, V. G., and H. L. Gonin. *Engels-Afrikaanse Regswoordeboek*. Kaapstad: Juta, 1963.

Hirson, Baruch. *Year of Fire, Year of Ash: The Soweto Revolt, Roots of a Revolution?* London: Zed Books, 1979.

Hobbes, Thomas. *The Elements of Law, Natural and Politic*. Ed. J. C. A. Gaskin. Oxford: Oxford University Press, 1994.

Hobbes, Thomas. *On the Citizen*. Ed. Richard Tuck. Cambridge: Cambridge University Press, 1998.

Hobbes, Thomas. *Leviathan*. Ed. Richard Tuck. Cambridge: Cambridge University Press, 1996.

Hobbes, Thomas. *Behemoth, or The Long Parliament.* Ed. Ferdinand Tönnies. Chicago: University of Chicago Press, 1990.

Hobbes, Thomas. *A Dialogue between a Philosopher and a Student of the Common Laws of England.* Chicago: University of Chicago Press, 1971.

Hoernlé, R. F. Alfred. *Race and Reason: Being Mainly a Selection of Contributions to the Race Problem in South Africa.* Johannesburg: Witswatersrand University Press, 1945.

Hoernlé, R. F. Alfred. *South African Native Policy and the Liberal Spirit.* Johannesburg: Witswatersrand University Press, 1945.

Holdsworth, W. S. *A History of English Law.* Vols. 3 and 4. London: Methuen, 1903–24.

Holt, Thomas. *The Problem of Freedom: Race, Labor, and Politics in Jamaica and Britain, 1832–1938.* Baltimore: Johns Hopkins University Press, 1991.

Hountondji, Paulin. "Recapturing." In *The Surreptitious Speech: Présence Africaine and the Politics of Otherness, 1947–1987,* ed. V. Y. Mudimbe, 238–48. Chicago: University of Chicago Press, 1992.

Huntington, Samuel. *The Third Wave: Democratization in the Late Twentieth Century.* Norman: University of Oklahoma Press, 1992.

Hussain, Nasser. "Air Power." In *Spatiality, Sovereignty, and Carl Schmitt: Geographies of the Nomos,* ed. Stephen Legg, 244–50. New York: Routledge, 2011.

Hussain, Nasser. *The Jurisprudence of Emergency: Colonialism and the Rule of Law.* Ann Arbor: University of Michigan Press, 2003.

Hyslop, Jonathan. "Gandhi, 1869–1915: The Transnational Emergence of a Public Figure." In *The Cambridge Companion to Gandhi,* ed. Judith M. Brown and Anthony Parel, 30–50. Cambridge: Cambridge University Press, 2011.

An Intermediate Greek-English Lexicon, Founded upon the Seventh Edition of Liddel and Scott's Greek-English Lexicon. Oxford: Clarendon, 1987.

Jabavu, D. D. T. "Bantu Grievances." In *Western Civilization and the Natives of South Africa: Studies in Culture Contact,* ed. Isaac Schapera, 285–99. New York: Humanities Press, 1934.

Jamaica Committee. *Facts and Documents Relating to the Alleged Rebellion in Jamaica, and the Measures of Repression; Including Notes on the Trial of Mr. Gordon.* Jamaica Papers No. I. London: Jamaica Committee, 1866.

Jamaica Committee. *The Blue Books. Jamaica Papers.* No. II. London: Jamaica Committee, 1866.

James, Wilmot, and Linda van de Vijver, eds. *After the TRC: Reflections on Truth and Reconciliation in South Africa.* Athens: Ohio University Press, 2001.

Jarry, Alfred. *Ubu Roi.* Paris: Gallimard, 2002.

Jennings, Ivor. "In Praise of Dicey: 1885–1935." *Public Administration* 13, no. 2 (1935): 123–34.

Jewsiewicki, Bogumil. "African Historical Studies: Academic Knowledge as 'Usable Past' and Radical Scholarship." *African Studies Review* 32, no. 3 (December 1989): 1–76.

Joffe, Joel. *The State vs. Nelson Mandela: The Trial That Changed South Africa.* Oxford: Oneworld, 2007.

Jolly, Rosemary. *Cultured Violence: Narrative, Social Suffering, and Engendering Human Rights* (Liverpool: Liverpool University Press, 2010).

Jouthe, Ernst. *Catharsis et Transformation Sociale dans la Théorie Politique de Gramsci.* Québec: Presses de l'Université du Québec, 1990.

Judt, Tony. *Postwar: A History of Europe since 1945.* New York: Penguin Books, 2005.

Kant, Immanuel. *Practical Philosophy.* Trans. and ed. Mary Gregor. Cambridge: Cambridge University Press, 1996.

Keegan, Timothy. *Colonial South Africa and the Origins of the Racial Order.* Charlottesville: University Press of Virginia, 1996.

Keightley, Raylene. "Political Offences and Indemnity in South Africa." *South African Journal on Human Rights* 9, no. 3 (1993): 334–57.

Keith, Arthur Berriedale. *Imperial Unity and the Dominions.* Oxford: Clarendon, 1916.

Keith, Arthur Berriedale. *Responsible Government in the Dominions.* Vol. 1. Oxford: Clarendon, 1912.

Kelsen, Hans. *Pure Theory of Law.* Trans. Max Knight. Berkeley: University of California Press, 1967.

Kiss, Elizabeth. "Moral Ambition within and beyond Political Constraints: Reflections on Restorative Justice." In Rotberg and Thompson, *Truth v. Justice,* 68–98.

Klug, Heinz. *The Constitution of South Africa: A Contextual Analysis.* Oxford: Hart, 2010.

Kojéve, Alexandre. *Outline of a Phenomenology of Right.* Trans. Bryan-Paul Frost and Robert Howse. Ed. Bryan-Paul Frost. Boston: Rowman and Littlefield, 2000.

Kollapen, Jody Narandran. "Accountability: The Debate in South Africa." *Journal of African Law* 37, no. 1 (Spring 1993): 1–9.

Koselleck, Reinhart. "A Response to Comments on the *Geschichtliche Grundbegriffe.*" In *The Meaning of Historical Terms and Concepts: New Studies on Begriffsgeschichte,* ed. Hartmut Lehmann and Melvin Richter. Washington, DC: German Historical Institute, 1996.

Kostal, R. W. *A Jurisprudence of Power: Victorian Empire and the Rule of Law.* Oxford: Oxford University Press, 2005.

Krog, Antjie. "The Choice for Amnesty: Did Political Necessity Trump Moral Duty?" In Villa-Vicencio and Doxtader, *Provocations of Amnesty,* 115–20.

Krog, Antjie. *Country of My Skull.* Johannesburg: Random House, 1998.

Kuhn, Thomas. *The Structure of Scientific Revolutions.* 3rd ed. Chicago: University of Chicago Press, 1996.

Kutz, Florian. *Amnestie für politische Straftäter in Südafrika Von der Sharpeville-Amnestie bis zu den Verfahren der Wahrheits- und Versöhnungskommission.* Berlin: Berlin Verlag Arno Spitz, 2001.

Kyle, Keith. *The Politics of the Independence of Kenya.* New York: Palgrave, 1998.

Lacey, Marian. "*Platskiet-politiek*: The Role of the Union Defence Force, 1910–1924." In Cock and Nathan, *War and Society*, 28–39.

Lalu, Premesh. *The Deaths of Hintsa: Postapartheid South Africa and the Shape of Recurring Pasts*. Cape Town: Human Sciences Research Council, 2009.

Lapsley, Father Michael. "Indemnity Bill and a General Amnesty." In Western Province Council of Churches, *Amnesty: Forgiveness without Confession?*

Lecky, William. *A History of England in the Eighteenth Century*. Vol. 8. Longmans, Green, 1890.

Leebaw, Bronwyn. "The Irreconcilable Goals of Transitional Justice." *Human Rights Quarterly* 30, no. 1 (February 2008): 95–118.

Leebaw, Bronwyn. *Judging State-Sponsored Violence, Imagining Political Change*. New York: Cambridge University Press, 2011.

Legal Resources Centre, Johannesburg. "Memorandum Prepared by the Legal Resources Centre, Johannesburg, in Response to the Statement by the Minister of Justice Mr. Dullah Omar on Amnesty/Indemnity Dated 7 June 1994." June 30, 1994. Records of the Legal Resources Centre, Johannesburg (AG 3006/1.30.2.1). Department of Historical Papers. Cullen Library, University of Witwatersrand, Johannesburg.

Legassick, Martin. *Towards Socialist Democracy*. Pietermaritzburg: University of KwaZulu-Natal Press, 2007.

Leman-Langlois, Stéphane. "Constructing a Common Language: The Function of Nuremberg in the Problematization of Postapartheid Justice." *Law and Social Inquiry* 27, no. 1 (2002): 79–100.

Lenta, Patrick. "In Defence of *AZAPO* and Restorative Justice." In le Roux and van Marl, *Law, Memory, and the Legacy of Apartheid*, 152–58.

Leonard, Richard. *South Africa at War: White Power and the Crisis in Southern Africa*. Westport, CT: Lawrence, Hill, 1983.

le Roux, Wessel, and Karin van Marl. *Law, Memory, and the Legacy of Apartheid: Ten Years after AZAPO v President of South Africa*. Pretoria: Pretoria University Law Press, 2007.

Leys, Ruth. *Trauma: A Genealogy*. Chicago: University of Chicago Press, 2000.

Locke, John. *An Essay concerning Human Understanding*. Oxford: Oxford University Press, 2008.

Locke, John. *Two Treatises of Government and a Letter concerning Toleration*. New Haven: Yale University Press, 2003.

Lodge, Tom. *Politics in South Africa: From Mandela to Mbeki*. Bloomington: Indiana University Press, 2003.

Lodge, Tom. *Sharpeville: A Massacre and Its Consequences*. Oxford: Oxford University, 2011.

Loraux, Nicole. *The Divided City: On Memory and Forgetting in Ancient Athens*. Trans. Corinne Pache with Jeff Fort. New York: Zone Books, 2002.

Lutz, Ellen. "Responses to Amnesties by the Inter-American System for the Protection of Human Rights." In *The Inter-American System of Human Rights*, ed. David John Harris and Stephen Livingstone. Oxford: Oxford University Press, 1998.

Machiavelli, Niccolò. *The Prince*. Trans. A. Codevilla. New Haven: Yale University Press, 1997.

Madlingozi, Tshepo. "Good Victim, Bad Victim: Apartheid's Beneficiaries, Victims, and the Struggle for Social Justice." In le Roux and van Marl, *Law, Memory, and the Legacy of Apartheid*, 107–26.

Madlingozi, Tshepo. "Post-Apartheid Social Movements and the Quest for the Elusive 'New' South Africa." *Journal of Law and Society* 34, no. 1 (March 2007): 77–98.

Madlingozi, Tshepo. "On Transitional Justice Entrepreneurs and the Production of Victims." *Journal of Human Rights Practice* 2, no. 2 (2010): 208–28.

Mallinder, Louise. "Indemnity, Amnesty, Pardon, and Prosecution Guidelines in South Africa." Working paper no. 2, Beyond Legalism: Amnesties, Transition, and Conflict Transformation. Institution of Criminology and Criminal Justice, Queens University, Belfast, 2009.

Mamdani, Mahmood. *Citizen and Subject: Contemporary Africa and the Legacy of Late Colonialism*. Princeton: Princeton University Press, 1996.

Mamdani, Mahmood. *Define and Rule: Native as Political Identity*. Cambridge, MA: Harvard University Press, 2012.

Mandela, Nelson. *The Struggle Is My Life*. London: Pathfinder, 1986.

Manning, Charles. "South Africa and the World: In Defense of Apartheid." *Foreign Affairs* 43, no. 1 (1964): 135–49.

Marais, Hein. *South Africa: Limits to Change; The Political Economy of Transition*. Cape Town: University of Cape Town Press, 1998.

Marlin-Curiel, Stephanie. "Standard Bank National Arts Festival (Grahamstown, South Africa, 2–12 July 1998)." *Theatre Journal* 51, no. 1 (March 1999): 80–82.

Marshall, Geoffrey. *Parliamentary Sovereignty and the Commonwealth*. Oxford: Clarendon, 1957.

Marx, Karl. "A Contribution to the Critique of Hegel's Philosophy of Right." In *Early Writings*, trans. Rodney Livingstone and Gregor Benton, 243–58. New York: Vintage Books, 1975.

Marx, Karl. "Letter to Friedrich Engels, June 22, 1867." In *Marx/Engels Collected Work*, vol. 42: 383. New York: International Publishers, 1975.

Mathews, A. S., and R. C. Albino. "The Permanence of the Temporary: An Examination of the 90- and 180-Day Detention Laws." *South African Law Journal* 16 (1996): 16–43.

Mathews, Anthony. *Freedom, State Security, and the Rule of Law: Dilemmas of the Apartheid Society*. Cape Town: Juta, 1986.

Matthews, Zachariah Keodirelang. "Bantu Law and Western Civilization in South Africa: A Study in the Clash of Cultures." An essay presented to the Faculty of the Graduate School of Yale University in candidacy for the degree of Master of Arts (May 1934).

Mayr, F. *Zulu Simplified: Being a New, Practical, and Easy Method of Learning the Zulu Language*. Pietermaritzburg: Davis and Sons, 1899.

Mazower, Mark. *No Enchanted Palace: The End of Empire and the Ideological Origins of the United Nations*. Princeton: Princeton University Press, 2009.

Mbeki, Govan. *South Africa: The Peasants' Revolt*. Baltimore: Penguin Books, 1964.

Mbembe, Achille. "Necropolitics." Trans. Libby Meintjes. *Public Culture* 15, no. 1 (Winter 2003): 11–40.

Mbembe, Achille. *On the Postcolony*. Berkeley: University of California Press, 2001.

McAuslan, Patrick, and John McEldowney. "Legitimacy and the Constitution: The Dissonance between Theory and Practice." In *Law, Legitimacy, and the Constitution: Essays Marking the Centenary of Dicey's Law of the Constitution*, ed. Patrick McAuslan and John McEldowney, 1–38. London: Sweet and Maxwell, 1985.

McEldowney, John. "Dicey in Historical Perspective." In *Law, Legitimacy, and the Constitution: Essays Marking the Centenary of Dicey's Law of the Constitution*, ed. Patrick McAuslan and John McEldowney, 39–61. London: Sweet and Maxwell, 1985.

McGowan, A. P. Introduction to *The Jacobean Commission of Enquiry, 1608 and 1618*. Publications of the Navy Record Society, vol. 116, xiii–xxvii. London: William Clowes and Sons, 1971.

Mehta, Uday Singh. *Liberalism and Empire: A Study in Nineteenth-Century British Liberal Thought*. Chicago: University of Chicago Press, 1999.

Meister, Robert. *After Evil: A Politics of Human Rights*. New York: Columbia University Press, 2011.

Mill, J. S. *'On Liberty' and Other Writings*. Cambridge: Cambridge University Press, 1989.

Milner, Alfred. Minute No. 184, "Cape of Good Hope, Papers Relating to Martial Law in Certain Districts of the Colony, July 1900." CGR Series, 2/1/155, 29218. Cape Town Archives Repository, Cape Town.

Minow, Martha. *Between Vengeance and Forgiveness: Facing History after Genocide and Mass Violence*. Boston: Beacon, 1999.

Mogale, Nthabiseng. "Ten Years of Democracy in South Africa: Revisiting the *AZAPO* decision." In le Roux and van Marl, *Law, Memory, and the Legacy of Apartheid*, 127–48.

Mokadi, Aubrey. *Narrative as Creative History: The 1976 Soweto Uprising as Depicted in Black South African Novels*. Johannesburg: Sedibeng, 2003.

Mokgatle, Naboth. *Autobiography of an Unknown South African*. Berkeley: University of California Press, 1971.

Moon, Claire. *Narrating Political Reconciliation: South Africa's Truth and Reconciliation Commission*. Lanham, MD: Lexington Books, 2008.

Morgenthau, Hans. "The Evil of Politics and the Ethics of Evil." *Ethics: An International Journal of Social, Political, and Legal Philosophy* 61, no. 1 (October 1945): 1–18.

Moss, Glen. "Fort Beaufort under Emergency Rule." *Work in Progress* 40 (1986): 18–25.

Moss, Laura. "'Nice Audible Crying': Editions, Testimonies, and *Country of My Skull*." *Research in African Literatures* 37, no. 4 (December 2006): 85–104.

Motala, Ziyad. "The Promotion of National Unity and Reconciliation Act, the Constitution, and International Law." *Comparative and International Law Journal of Southern Africa* 28 (1995): 338–62.

Motala, Ziyad. "The Constitutional Court's Approach to International Law and Its Method of Interpretation in the 'Amnesty Decision': Intellectual Honesty or Political Expediency?" *South African Yearbook of International Law* 21 (1996): 29–59.

Motala, Ziyad, and Cyril Ramaphosa. *Constitutional Law: Analysis and Cases.* Oxford: Oxford University Press, 2002.

Mowitt, John. "Trauma Envy." *Cultural Critique* 46 (2000): 272–97.

Mtshaulana, Patric Mzolisi. "The History and Role of the Constitutional Court of South Africa." In *The Post-Apartheid Constitutions: Perspectives on South Africa's Basic Law,* ed. P. Andrews and S. Ellman, 525–55. Athens: Ohio University Press, 2001.

Mudimbe, V. Y. *The Invention of Africa: Gnosis, Philosophy, and the Order of Knowledge.* Bloomington: Indiana University Press, 1988.

Mutua, Makau. "Savages, Victims, and Saviors: The Metaphor of Human Rights." *Harvard International Law Journal* 42, no. 1 (Winter 2001): 201–42.

Nagy, Rosemary. "Transitional Justice as a Global Project: Critical Reflections," *Third World Quarterly* 29, no. 2 (2008): 275–89.

Nandy, Ashis. *The Intimate Enemy: Loss and Recovery of Self under Colonialism.* Delhi: Oxford University Press, 1983.

Nathan, Laurie. "Troops in the Townships, 1984–1987." In Cock and Nathan, *War and Society,* 67–89.

Neocosmos, Michael. "Transition, Human Rights, and Violence: Rethinking a Liberal Political Relationship in the African Neo-Colony." *Interface: a journal for and about social movements* 3, no. 2 (November 2011): 359–99.

Nkosi, Lewis. *The Transplanted Heart: Essays on South Africa.* Benin City: Ethiope, 1975.

"No Option but to Nullify Illegitimate Amnesty." *Negotiation News* 7 (1992): 12.

Ntchatcho, Herman. "Political Amnesty and Repatriation of Refugees in Namibia." In *African Yearbook of International Law/Annuaire Africain de Droit International,* vol. 1, ed. Abdulqawi Yusuf, 61–80. London: Martinus Nijhoff, 1993.

Ntumba, Tshiamalenga. "La vision *ntu* de l'homme: Essai de philosophie linguistique et Anthropologique." *Cahiers des religions africaines* 7, no. 14 (July 1973): 176–99.

O'Higgins, P. "*Wright v. Fitzgerald* Revisited." *Modern Law Review* 25, no. 4 (1962): 413–22.

Olivier, Pierre. "Our Policing Heritage: The Major Problems." In *Policing the Conflict in South Africa,* ed. M. L. Matthews, P. B. Heymann, and A. S. Matthews, 21–32. Gainesville: University Press of Florida, 1993.

Omar, Dullah. "Amnesty Bill: Explanatory Memorandum." N.d. Records of the Legal Resources Centre, Johannesburg (AG 3006/1.30.3.1). Department of Historical Papers, Cullen Library, University of Witwatersrand, Johannesburg.

Omar, Dullah. "Justice Minister's Reply." In Boraine and Levy, *Healing of a Nation?*, 130–36.

Omar, Dullah. "Statement by Minister of Justice, Mr. Dullah Omar on Amnesty/Indemnity." June 7, 1994. Records of the Legal Resources Centre, Johannesburg (AG 3006/1.30.2.1). Department of Historical Papers, Cullen Library, University of Witwatersrand, Johannesburg.

Omissi, David. *Air Power and Colonial Control: The Royal Air Force, 1919–1939*. Manchester: Manchester University Press, 1990.

Orr, Wendy. "Reparation Delayed Is Healing Retarded." In Villa-Vicencio and Verwoerd, *Looking Back, Reaching Forward*, 239–49.

Osinubi, Taiwo Adetunji. "Abusive Narratives: Antjie Krog, Rian Malan, and the Transmission of Violence." *Comparative Studies of South Asia, Africa, and the Middle East* 28, no. 1 (2008): 109–23.

Parker, Peter. "The Politics of Indemnities, Truth Telling, and Reconciliation in South Africa." *Human Rights Law Journal* 17 (1996): 1–13.

Parker, Peter, and Joyce Mokhesi-Parker. *In the Shadow of Sharpeville: Apartheid and Criminal Justice*. New York: New York University Press, 1998.

Phillips, O. Hood. "Constitutional Conventions: Dicey's Predecessors." *Modern Law Review* 29, no. 2 (1966): 137–48.

Pike, Luke Owen. *Of the Reign of King Edward the Third, Years XIV and XV*. London: Her Majesty's Stationery Office, 1889.

Pitts, Jennifer. *A Turn to Empire: The Rise of Imperial Liberalism in Britain and France*. Princeton: Princeton University Press, 2005.

Plaatje, Solomon Tshekisho. *Native Life in South Africa, Before and Since the European War and the Boer Rebellion*. 3rd ed. London: P.S. King & Son, 1917.

Plato. *Laws*. Trans. Thomas Pangle. Chicago: University of Chicago Press, 1988.

Plowden, Francis. *The History of Ireland from Its Invasion under Henry II to Its Union with Great Britain*. Vol. 2. London: Booker et al., 1809.

Pocock, J. G. A. *The Ancient Constitution and the Feudal Law: A Study of English Historical Thought in the Seventeenth Century*. Cambridge: Cambridge University Press, 1978.

Pohlandt-McCormick, Helena. *"I Saw a Nightmare": Doing Violence to Memory; The Soweto Uprising, June 16, 1976*. New York: Columbia University Press. Accessed January 25, 2009. http://www.gutenberg-e.org/pohlandt-mccormick/.

Posel, Deborah. "The Meaning of Apartheid before 1948: Conflicting Interests and Forces within the Afrikaner Nationalist Alliance." *Journal of Southern African Studies* 14, no. 1 (1987): 123–39.

Posel, Deborah. "The TRC Report: What Kind of Truth? What Kind of History?" In Posel and Simpson, *Commissioning the Past*, 147–72.

Posel, Deborah, and Graeme Simpson, eds. *Commissioning the Past: Understanding South Africa's Truth and Reconciliation Commission*. Johannesburg: Witwatersrand University Press, 2002.

Pretorius, J. L. "Aanhouding sonder verhoor in die noodtoestand." *Woord en Daad*, February 1987, 13–15.

Price, Robert. *The Apartheid State in Crisis: Political Transformation of South Africa, 1975–1990.* Oxford: Oxford University Press, 1991.

Ramphele, Mamphela. "Empowerment and Symbols of Hope: Black Consciousness and Community Development." In *Bounds of Possibility: The Legacy of Steve Biko and Black Consciousness,* ed. N. Barney Pityana, M. Ramphele, M. Mpumiwana, and L. Wilson, 154–78. Atlantic Highlands, NJ: Zed Press, 1992.

Redding, Sean. *Sorcery and Sovereignty: Taxation, Power, and Rebellion in South Africa, 1880–1963.* Athens, OH: Ohio University Press, 2006.

Reed, L. "'Socialist' Mugabe Detains Fourteen Socialists." *Inqaba ya basebenzi: Journal of the Marxist Workers' Tendency of the African National Congress* 16–17 (January–June 1985): 8–14.

"Report of the Working Group Established under Paragraph 1 of the Groote Schuur Minute." *South African Journal on Human Rights* 6, no. 3 (1990): 319–24.

Rid, Thomas. "The Nineteenth Century Origins of Counterinsurgency Doctrine." *Journal of Strategic Studies* 33, no. 5 (2010): 727–58.

Rive, Richard. *Emergency Continued.* London: Readers International, 1990.

"The Road to South Africa Freedom: Programme of the South African Communist Party." *African Communist* 2, no. 2 (1963): 24–70.

Roht-Arriaza, Naomi. "The Role of International Actors in National Accountability Processes." In *The Politics of Memory: Transitional Justice in Democratizing Societies,* ed. Carmen González Enríquez, Alexandra Barahona de Brito, and Paloma Aguilar Fernández, 40–64. Oxford: Oxford University Press, 2001.

Rohter, Larry. "Decades Later, Confronting a Bloody Past: Change of Climate in Latin America." *International Herald Tribune,* September 2, 2005, 2.

Roodt, Dan. *Om Die Waarheidskommissie Te Vergeet.* Dainfern: Pro-Afrikaanse Aksiegroep, 2000.

Rose, Jacqueline. "Apathy and Accountability: South Africa's Truth and Reconciliation Commission." *Raritan* 21, no. 4 (2002): 175–95.

Ross, Fiona. "Truth and Reconciliation." In Shepherd and Robins, *New South African Keywords,* 235–46.

Rossiter, Clinton. *Constitutional Dictatorship: Crisis Government in the Modern Democracies.* New Brunswick, NJ: Transaction, 2002.

Rossouw, R. P. "Re: Promotion of National Unity and Reconciliation Bill, 1994." March 23, 1995. Document no. 1995-03-23. On file with author.

Rotberg, Robert, and Dennis Thompson, eds. *Truth v. Justice: The Morality of Truth Commissions.* Princeton: Princeton University Press, 2000.

Ruden, Sarah. "*Country of My Skull:* Guilt and Sorrow and the Limits of Forgiveness in the New South Africa." *ARIEL: A Review of International English Literature* 30, no. 1 (January 1999): 165–85.

Ruiter, Raymond. "The Maintenance of the Security of the State." In *The South African Constitution,* ed. Henry John May, 343–53. 3rd ed. Cape Town: Juta, 1955.

Sachs, Albie. "His Name Was Henry." In James and van de Vijver, *After the TRC*, 94–100.

Sachs, Albie. *Justice in South Africa*. Berkeley: University of California Press, 1973.

Sachs, Wulf. "Racism: The Solution." *Democrat* (Johannesburg), January 20, 1944.

Sanders, Mark. *Ambiguities of Witnessing: Law and Literature in the Time of a Truth Commission*. Stanford: Stanford University Press, 2007.

Sarkin, Jeremy. *Carrots and Sticks: The TRC and the South African Amnesty Process*. Antwerp: Intersentia, 2004.

Sarkin, Jeremy. "The Trials and Tribulations of South Africa's Truth and Reconciliation Commission." *South African Journal of Human Rights* 12, no. 4 (1996): 617–40.

Satchwell, Kathleen. "Indemnity Provided For in Emergency Regulations." In *Developments in Emergency Law*, ed. Nicholas Haysom and Clive Plasket, 117–23. Johannesburg: Centre for Applied Legal Studies, 1989.

Satchwell, Kathleen. "The Power to Defend: An Analysis of Various Aspects of the Defence Act." In Cock and Nathan, *War and Society*, 40–66.

Schreiner, O. D. *The Contribution of English Law to South African Law; and the Rule of Law in South Africa*. Cape Town: Juta, 1967.

Seegers, Annette. *The Military in the Making of Modern South Africa*. New York: Tauris Academic Studies, 1996.

Seneca, Lucius Annaeus. "De Clementia," in *Seneca: Moral Essays*. Trans. J. Basore. Cambridge: Harvard University Press, 1970.

Shepherd, Nick, and Steven Robins, eds. *New South African Keywords*. Athens: Ohio University Press, 2008.

Short, K. R. M. "The English Indemnity Acts, 1762–1867." *Church History* 42, no. 3 (1973): 366–76.

Simpson, A. W. Brian. *Human Rights and the End of Empire: Britain and the Genesis of the European Convention*. Oxford: Oxford University, 2001.

Simpson, Graeme. "A 'Culture of Impunity.'" *Star* (Johannesburg, South Africa), January 24, 1997.

Slaughter, Joseph. *Human Rights, Inc.: The World Novel, Narrative Form, and International Law*. New York: Fordham University Press, 2007.

Slovo, Gillian. "Making History: South Africa's Truth and Reconciliation Commission." *openDemocracy*, December 5, 2002. Accessed August 28, 2009. http://www.open democracy.net/democracy-africa_democracy/article_818.jsp.

Slovo, Joe. "Beyond the Stereotype: The SACP in the Past, Present, and Future." *African Communist* 122, no. 2 (1991): 7–9.

Slovo, Joe. "Has Socialism Failed?" *African Communist* 121, no. 2 (1990): 36–38.

Smuts, Jan. "Native Policy in Africa." *Journal of the Royal African Society* 29, no. 115 (1930): 248–68.

Smuts, Jan. "Problems in South Africa." *Journal of the Royal African Society* 16, no. 64 (1919): 273–82.

Smuts, Jan. Speech to Parliament. In *Debates of the House of Assembly of the Union of South Africa, as Reported in the Cape Times*, vol. 7, *Second Session, Fourth Parliament, 17th February 1922 to 19th July, 1922*. Pretoria: State Library, 1969.

Smuts, Jan. Speech to Parliament. In *Debates of the House of Assembly of the Union of South Africa, as Reported in the Cape Times*, vol. 8, *Third Session, Fourth Parliament, 20th January 1923 to 25th June, 1923*. Pretoria: State Library, 1969.

Solomon, Richard. Memorandum, "Cape of Good Hope, Papers Relating to Martial Law in Certain Districts of the Colony, July 1900." CGR Series, 2/1/155, 29218. Cape Town Archives Repository, Cape Town.

Sooka, Yasmin. "Prosecutions." In Villa-Vicencio and du Toit, *Truth and Reconciliation in South Africa*, 17–22.

"The South Africa Act, 1909." *American Journal of International Law* 4, no. 1 (January 1910): 4–8.

Stanley, Elizabeth. "Evaluating the Truth and Reconciliation Commission." *Journal of Modern African Studies* 39, no. 3 (September 2001): 525–46.

Stewart, Elizabeth. "The Proportionality Principle in Post-Apartheid South Africa." *Temple Political and Civil Rights Law Review* 113, no. 8 (Fall 1998): 113–24.

Stoler, Anne Laura. *Along the Archival Grain: Epistemic Anxieties and Colonial Common Sense*. Princeton: Princeton University Press, 2009.

Storey, John. "South African Perspectives: Workers' Revolution or Racial Civil War." *Inqaba ya basebenzi: Journal of the Marxist Workers' Tendency of the African National Congress* 16–17 (January–June 1985) (special supplement to issue 16–17).

Taylor, Jane, and William Kentridge. *Ubu and the Truth Commission*. Cape Town: University of Cape Town Press, 1998.

Teitel, Ruti. *Transitional Justice*. Oxford: Oxford University Press, 2002.

Tepperman, Jonathan. "Truth and Consequences." *Foreign Affairs* 81, no. 2 (2002): 129–45.

Theissen, Gunnar. "Amnesty for Apartheid Crimes? The South African Truth and Reconciliation Commission and International Law." LL.M. thesis, University of the Western Cape, 1998.

Todd, Alpheus. *Parliamentary Government in England: Its Origin, Development, and Practical Operation*. Vol. 1. London: Sampson Low, Marston, 1892.

Todd, Alpheus. *Parliamentary Government in the British Colonies*. Boston: Little, Brown, 1880.

Truths Drawn in Jest: Commentary on the TRC through Cartoons, ed. Wilhelm Verwoerd and Mahlubi Mabizela (Cape Town: David Philip, 2000).

Tutu, Desmond. *No Future without Forgiveness*. London: Rider Books, 1999.

Underhill, Edward. *The Tragedy of Morant Bay: A Narrative of the Disturbances in the Island of Jamaica in 1865*. London: Alexander and Shepheard, 1895.

van Wyk, Dawid. "Introduction to the South African Constitution." In van Wyk et al., *Rights and Constitutionalism*, 131–70.

van Wyk, Dawid, John Dugard, Bertus de Villiers, and Dennis Davis, eds. *Rights and Constitutionalism: The New South African Legal Order*. Oxford: Clarendon, 1995.

van Zyl, Paul. "Dilemmas of Transitional Justice: The Case of South Africa's Truth and Reconciliation Commission." *Journal of International Affairs* 52, no. 2 (1999): 647–67.

Venter, François. "Salus reipublicae suprema lex." *Tydskrif vir hedendaagse Romeins-Hollandse Reg* 40 (1977): 233–52.

Vernant, Jean-Pierre. *Mortals and Immortals: Collected Essays.* Ed. Froma Zeitlin. Princeton: Princeton University Press, 1991.

Verwoerd, William. "Towards the Recognition of Our Past Injustices." In Villa-Vicencio and Verwoerd, *Looking Back, Reaching Forward*, 155–65.

Villa-Vicencio, Charles, and Eric Doxtader, eds. *The Provocations of Amnesty: Memory, Justice, and Impunity.* Trenton, NJ: Africa World Press, 2003.

Villa-Vicencio, Charles, and Fanie du Toit, eds. *Truth and Reconciliation in South Africa: Ten Years On.* Claremont, South Africa: David Philip, 2006.

Villa-Vicencio, Charles, and Wilhelm Verwoerd, eds. *Looking Back, Reaching Forward: Reflections on the Truth and Reconciliation Commission of South Africa.* Cape Town: University of Cape Town Press, 2000.

Wade, E. C. S. "Appendix II: Parliament and the Courts: Opinion by Professor E. C. S. Wade Published by the Union Government." In *Parliamentary Sovereignty and the Commonwealth*, by Geoffrey Marshall, 251–59. Oxford: Clarendon, 1957.

Wade, E. C. S. Introduction to *Law of the Constitution*, by Alfred Venn Dicey, xxvii–clvi. 9th ed. New York: Macmillan, 1956.

Wade, E. C. S., and G. Godfrey Phillips. *Constitutional Law: An Outline of the Law and Practice of the Constitution, Including Central and Local Government and the Constitutional Relations of the British Commonwealth.* 6th ed. London: Longman, 1960.

Weaver, Tony. "The South African Defence Force in Namibia." In Cock and Nathan, *War and Society*, 90–102.

Weber, Max. *The Protestant Ethic and the Spirit of Capitalism.* Trans. Talcott Parsons. New York: Routledge, 1992.

Webb's Guide to the Official Records of the Colony of Natal. Ed. Jennifer Verbeek, Mary Nathanson, and Elaine Peel. Pietermaritzburg: University of Natal Press, 1984.

Western Province Council of Churches. *Amnesty: Forgiveness without Confession? Cover-up of Crime? Christians Need to Know!* Western Province Council of Churches, 1992.

Wilson, Richard. *The Politics of Truth and Reconciliation in South Africa: Legitimizing the Post-Apartheid State.* Cambridge: Cambridge University Press, 2001.

Wolpe, Harold. *Race, Class, and the Apartheid State.* London: James Currey, 1988.

Wolpe, Harold. "The Theory of Internal Colonialism: The South African Case." In *Beyond the Sociology of Development*, ed. Ivar Oxall, Tony Barnett, and David Booth, 229–51. London: Routledge, 1975.

Young, Crawford, and Thomas Turner. *The Rise and Decline of the Zairian State.* Madison: University of Wisconsin Press, 1985.

Zalaquett, José. "Commissions of Truth and Reconciliation: Chile." In Boraine and Levy, *Healing of a Nation?*, 44–55.

Index

P7 of < cólinder
              merop wd